The Family of Mary Pitt

Janelle Cust

2nd Edition

First published in 2009

© Copyright Janelle Cust 2018

Except as permitted under the Act, no part of this publication may be reproduced, stored in a retrieval system or communicated in any form or by any means without prior permission of the publisher.

ISBN 978-0-6481075-3-8

Published by

www.minipublishing.com.au

ACKNOWLEDGEMENTS

I am most grateful for help received in compiling *The Family of Mary Pitt*. Colin Sale drew the maps. Salli Chmura shared her information on the family headed by Thomas Matcham Pitt. Margaret Betts supplied advice on the history, topography and current use of the grants of Mary Pitt and Thomas Matcham Pitt. The Maple-Browns explained the Springfield sale arrangements and made a special effort to provide an image of Mary Deane Faithfull. Ted Baker assisted me with his knowledge of the Wilshire family. Also Yvonne Bullock, Jeanette Dixon, Graham Searle, Sam Sellin and John Matcham Pitt gave or offered help. Special thanks go to Margaret Killin for her many suggestions and practical support.

Front/Back Cover & Title Page: *Sydney, New South Wales, S.View, 1824* by unknown artist. Source: Dixson Library, State Library of New South Wales.

THE FAMILIES OF MARY PITT'S CHILDREN

Susannah Pitt=William Faithfull						
William Pitt Faithfull =Mary Deane	Robert Faithfull	Alice Faithfull =Andrew Gibson				George Faithfull
Lucy Pitt=John Wood						
George Pitt Wood =Eliz Markwell	Sophia Wood =Samuel Pinder Henry					
Thomas Matcham Pitt=Elizabeth Laycock						
George Matcham Pitt =Julia Johnson	Mary Matcham Pitt =Thos W E B Laycock	Robert Pitt =Sarah John		William Henry Pitt		
Eliza Pitt =Austin Forrest Willshire						
Jemima Pitt=Austin Forrest=Robert Jenkins						
Eliza Forrest	Robert Pitt Jenkins =M Louisa Plunkett	William Warren Jenkins =Matilda Pitt Wilshire				
Esther Pitt=James Wilshire						
Louisa Wilshire =Philip Elliot	William Pitt Wilshire =C Maria Robertson	James Robert Wilshire =Elizabeth Thompson		Austin Forrest Wilshire =Eliza Pitt		
Eliz M Wilshire	Esther Wilshire =Henry R Whittell	Sarah Thompson Matilda Pitt Wilshire =Wm Warren Jenkins		Thomas MP Wilshire		
John J Wilshire	Amelia J Wilshire	Joseph Wood Wilshire =Anne Osborne		=Helen Eliza Faithfull		

CONTENTS

Acknowledgements iii
The Families of Mary Pitt's Children iv
Illustrations vii
Conversion Table xi
Abbreviations xiii
Introduction xv

1 Bound for the New South Wales 1
2 Pacific Islands Odyssey 9
3 Settling at the Hawkesbury 21
4 Sealing in the Southern Ocean 45
5 Contributions to Macquarie's Reforms 57
6 The Grandchildren Marry 99
7 Squatting and Its Perils 137
8 The Grandchildren's Generation Centre Stage 173
9 Untimely Deaths 221
10 The Great-Grandchildren Take Over 265

Birth, Marriage and Death Charts 307
Name Index 361

ILLUSTRATIONS

Figure 1. Robert Pitt
Pencil drawing by William Pitt Wilshire from a portrait brought to Sydney by Robert's widow and lost at sea in the *Royal Charter* in 1859
Mitchell Library, State Library of New South Wales
.... xviii

Figure 2. George Matcham
Portrait by Gilbert Stuart
Illustrated London News, 10 October 1931, p573....xix

Figure 3. Grants and Purchases of the Pitt Family near Richmond Hill.
Map drawn by Colin Sale..6

Figure 4. Pacific Ocean locations of the Woods and Henrys.
Map drawn by Colin Sale..10

Figure 5. Society Islands and Tuamotu Archipelago locations of the Woods and Henrys
Map drawn by Colin Sale..10

Figure 6. Margaret Catchpole (1762-1819)
Sketch by unknown artist
Dixson Collection, State Library of New South Wales
....22

Figure 7. James Wilshire
Spurway, John, T., ed., *Australian Biographical and Genealogical Record*, Series 1, 1788-1841, A.B.G.R. and Society of Australian Genealogists, Sydney, 1992, p478..28

Figure 8. Church of St. Philip. Built of hewn stone and named after the colony's first governor, the church was

	erected in present Lang Park between 1800 and 1809. Watercolour 1809 by John William Lewin Mitchell Library, State Library of New South Wale .35
Figure 9.	Southern Pacific and Southern Oceans locations of John Wood 1809-1812 Map drawn by Colin Sale..46
Figure 10.	Brig *Perseverance* Sketch by unknown artist Royal Military College of Australia Archives...........47
Figure 11.	Lachlan Macquarie Portrait in oils c1805 by John Opie Mitchell Library, State Library of New South Wales 58
Figure 12.	Elizabeth Henrietta Macquarie Watercolour miniature on ivory 1819 by Richard, the Elder Tasmania Museum and Art Gallery.......................59
Figure 13.	Robert Jenkins Courtesy of his granddaughters Matilda J and Elinor M Warren Jenkins Mitchell Library, State Library of New South Wales 69
Figure 14.	Andrew Gibson Charles MacAlister, *Old Pioneering Days in the Sunny South*, Chas. MacAlister Book Publication Committee, Goulburn, 1907, opp. p8......................116
Figure 15.	George Matcham Pitt Oil on canvas by unknown artist Elders Ltd., Collection...148
Figure 16.	Julia Johnson Pitt Oil on canvas by unknown artist Elders Ltd., Collection...149
Figure 17.	Tiranna Homestead Hardy Wilson, *Old Colonial Architecture in New South Wales and Tasmania*, Sydney, 1924, Plate XLIX 163
Figure 18.	An approximation of the George Street Complex of James Wilshire in September 1840

Figure 19. William Faithfull
Charles F.Maxwell, *Australian Men of Mark 1788-1888*, vol 1, McCarron, Bird and Co., Melbourne, 1889, opp. p376 183

Figure 20. William Pitt Faithfull
Charles F.Maxwell, *Australian Men of Mark 1788-1888*, vol 1, McCarron, Bird and Co., Melbourne, 1889, opp. p378 189

Figure 21. Mary Deane Faithfull
Portrait 1846 by Joseph Backler
Courtesy of the Maple-Brown Family, Goulburn ... 190

Figure 22. James Robert Wilshire
Courtesy Australasian Pioneers Club
Mitchell Library, State Library of New South Wales
.... 204

Figure 23. Austin Forrest Wilshire
Spurway, John,T., ed., *Australian Biographical and Genealogical Record*, Series 1, 1788-1841, A.B.G.R and Society of Australian Genealogists, Sydney, 1992, p478 205

Figure 24. Eliza Pitt Wilshire
Spurway, John,T., ed., *Australian Biographical and Genealogical Record*, Series 1, 1788-1841, A.B.G.R and Society of Australian Genealogists, Sydney, 1992, p336 205

Figure 25. An approximation of the Darling Harbour Complex of the Wilshires in November 1847
Bk 15, No 681 Department of Lands 207

Figure 26. Samuel Henry
Mitchell Library, State Library of New South Wales
.... 227

Figure 27. Plan of Wilshire Place
Bk 61, No 984, Department of Lands 231

Figure 28. Springfield House

Bk 15, Nos 376,620,916; Bk 121, No 582, Department of Lands 176

Figure 29. *Australian Town and Country Journal* 24 January 1874, p140 246

Figure 29. *Royal Charter*
Graphite Sketch by unknown artist,
National Maritime Museum, Greenwich, London .. 251

Figure 30. Route of the *Royal Charter* 25-26th October 1859
Map drawn by Colin Sale.
Alexander Mc Kee, The Golden Wreck, Hodder and Stoughton, Kent, England, 1988, p42 251

Figure 31. Matilda Pitt Wilshire Jenkins
Wollongong City Library and Illawarra Historical Society 254

Figure 32. William Warren Jenkins
Wollongong City Library and Illawarra Historical Society 255

Figure 33. Berkeley House
Australian Town and Country Journal, 18 October 1879, p745 256

Figure 34. William Pitt Wilshire
Presented by grandson Claude Wilshire & great-grandsons Mervyn and Esmond Wilshire.
Mitchell Library, State Library of New South Wales 286

Figure 35. Camp of "Blanket", by William Pitt Wilshire
Oil on canvas c1886 by William Pitt Wilshire.
Mitchell Library, State Library of New South Wales 287

Figure 36. Bronte House, 2008
Photographed 22nd December 2008 by Margaret Betts 294

CONVERSION TABLE

IMPERIAL		METRIC
Currency		
1d	1 penny	0.8 cents
1s (12d)	1 shilling	10 cents
£1 (20s)	1 pound	$2.00
£1 1s (21s)	1 guinea	$2.10
Weight		
1lb	1 pound	0.45 kilograms
1 bushel	~ 60 pounds wheat ~ 47 pounds barley ~ 40 pounds oats	27 kilograms 21 kilograms 18 kilograms
1 ton	2240 pounds	1000 kilograms
Length		
1 inch		2.54 centimetres
12 inches	1 foot	30.5 centimetres
3 feet	1 yard	0.914 metres
1760 yards	1 mile	1.61 kilometres
Area		
1 perch		0.0025 hectare
1 rood	40 perches	0.1 hectare
1 acre	4 roods	0.405 hectare
1 square mile	640 acres	2.59 sq. kilometres
Volume		
1 gallon		4.55 litres
52 gallons	1 hogshead	236.5 litres

ABBREVIATIONS

ADB	*Australian Dictionary of Biography* 1788-1850, vols 1-2, Melbourne University Press, Carlton, Victoria 1966-7; 1851-1890, vols 3-6, Melbourne University Press, Carlton, Victoria, 1976
Aus	*Australian*
CCJ	New South Wales Court of Civil Jurisdiction
SCCJ	New South Wales Supreme Court of Civil Jurisdiction
BT	Bonwick Transcripts. Transcribed from Bigge, J.T. *Report of the Commissioner of Inquiry into the State of the Colony of New South Wales,* Facsim edn., Libraries Board of South Australia, 1966, First pub London, 1822
DL	Department of Lands, Prince Albert Road, Sydney
GC	Governor's Court of New South Wales
GG	New South Wales Government Gazette
HRA	Historical Records of Australia
HRNSW	Historical Records of New South Wales
HRV	Historical Records of Victoria
LA, V&P	NSW Legislative Assembly, Votes and Proceedings
JRAHS	*Journal of the Royal Australian History Society*
NSW JA Rg	New South Wales Judge-Advocate's Office, *Register of Assignments and Other Legal Documents*
ML	Mitchell Library, State Library of New South Wales
ML MSS	Mitchell Library, Manuscript Collection, State Library of New South Wales
SAG	Society of Australian Genealogists
SG	*Sydney Gazette*
SMH	*Sydney Morning Herald*
SRNSW	State Records of New South Wales

INTRODUCTION

The Family of Mary Pitt describes events in the lives of Mary Pitt, five of her children, her grandchildren and, to a lesser extent, her great-grandchildren.

Mary, née Matcham of Child Okeford, married Robert Pitt of Belchalwell on 27th December 1770 at Child Okeford in County Dorset. (Figure 1) Robert died in 1787 leaving Mary and her seven children "not in good circumstances". Sons George and William migrated to the United States while Mary, Susannah, Lucy, Thomas, Jemima and Hesther settled in the penal colony of New South Wales.[1] Mary received help from her first cousin, George Matcham (c1754-1833), who worked in the civil service of the East India Company.[2] (Figure 2) George Matcham had married Catherine Nelson, sister of Admiral Lord Horatio Nelson, Britain's greatest naval leader, a connection also benefiting the Pitts.

The origins of Mary Matcham and Robert Pitt are the focus of Barbara Lamble's book, *The Pitts of Dorset and Richmond NSW, an account of research in Dorset, London, Bristol and Sydney.* The Matchams lived in Dorset from at least the sixteenth century. Lamble believed Mary's father was Thomas Matcham (christened

1704) but she did not discover her mother or birthplace. To account for Mary Matcham's early years, Lamble relied on information provided by Mary's grandson, George Matcham Pitt. Mary "came originally from Ireland", the country of her birth, perhaps. After Mary's father died, her mother remarried and migrated to the United States of America. Mary "crossed over to England and lived with two maiden aunts until death carried them away at 81 and 83". Lamble thought the aunts were Mary and Hester Matcham. The Pitts resided in Dorset from the late seventeenth century. They were yeoman, able to read and write, and responsible members of the community. Robert Pitt was christened on 9th October 1734 in Sturminster Newton, the second son of William Pitt and Rose Belbin who married in the village on 6th September 1730.[3]

In researching and writing the story of the Pitts, I faced three problems common to family historians. Several unsubstantiated claims about the Pitts circulate. One example is the assertion that on their arrival the Pitts stayed at Government House as guests of Governor King.[4] I have excluded unconfirmed and unlikely statements. The men dominate the story. With a few exceptions men bought and sold property, wrote to the Colonial Secretary, signed petitions, worked on committees, administered the law as magistrates, and governed the colony as politicians. There was no solution to this problem. The reader may struggle to grasp where individuals fit in the family. I have provided a chart of the families of Mary Pitt's five children at the end of the book. And I have stated an individual's full name each time he or she enters the story.

Introduction

Note: The endnotes include references for births, baptisms, marriages, deaths and burials. The Birth, Marriage and Death Charts record this information except for baptisms and burials. Before civil registration in 1856, ministers conducted baptisms and burials, noting births and deaths on the relevant records. Early death records omit the cause of death.

1   Lamble, Barbara, *The Pitts of Dorset and Richmond NSW, an account of research in Dorset, London, Bristol and Sydney*, 1990, p7
2   *Illustrated London News*, 10 October 1931, p573
3   Lamble, 1990, opp pp3, 7, 8, 20
4   Hardy, Bobbie, *Early Hawkesbury Settlers*, Kangaroo Press, Kenthurst, 1985, p 182

Figure 1. Robert Pitt

Figure 2. George Matcham

1
BOUND FOR THE NEW SOUTH WALES

Mary Pitt decided to settle with her children Susannah, Lucy, Thomas, Jemima and Hester, in the relatively new and distant penal colony of New South Wales. She achieved this goal with help from George Matcham, his brother-in-law Admiral Horatio Nelson and Nelson's father, the Reverend Edmund Nelson. Their efforts are obvious in this chapter which tracks the Pitts from Dorset in England to Richmond Hill in New South Wales.

In a letter dated 1st January 1801, Horatio Nelson asked George Matcham to send Mr Davidson information on each member of the Pitt Family bound for New South Wales:

> *Long ago Mr King has been asked the questions about your friend's journey to Botany Bay. Mr King says they shall be sent free of cost and desires that their names, ages and descriptions be sent. Mr Davidson has kindly undertaken to arrange between you and Mr King (Governor) therefore please send him the necessary answers to the questions.*[1]

By mid April 1801 the *Canada*, *Minorca* and *Nile* had anchored in Portsmouth to prepare the ships. Authorities at Whitehall expressed concern for the welfare of free settlers making the trip to New South Wales, "wives and families in very indigent circumstances . . . are utterly unable to provide themselves with the necessary cloathing (sic) for the voyage". The agent for Naval Transports at Portsmouth, Captain Patton, received instructions to:

> *provide forthwith for each respective family that shall be found, upon strict observation, to stand in need of such cloathing (sic), some small articles to the value, upon average, of five pounds for each family, to be delivered to them upon their arrival at Portsmouth.*[2]

From Bath on 1st May 1801, George Matcham wrote to Mary, attaching a letter Horatio's father had written to Governor King:

> *The Rev Mr Nelson, father of Lord Horatio Nelson, has written a letter to Governor King on your behalf. I now enclose it with another of my own. Mr Nelson's letter will be of great consequence to You so pray put a handsome wafer upon it when you have read it. Write me how you and all the rest are. Have as much patience as possible till the voyage is over and then comforts will crowd upon you.*[3]

A week later, Samuel Gambier, an official in the British Naval Office, informed George Matcham the Pitts should set out for Portsmouth:

> *I have the pleasure to acquaint you that I have arranged everything for the embarkation of your good people agreeably to my wishes. To save time which runs short with me at present I enclose Commissioner Georges letter to me on the subject which pray return to me. Your friends will therefore proceed to Portsmouth conformably to what I at first wrote to you and on their arrival there make Application to Captain Patton ... If you think it necessary I will get a letter to him for them to*

deliver by way of identifying their persons. Let me therefore know how I am in future to direct to you as you say you are going to Dorsetshire to marshall (sic) your adventurers.[4]

By 29th May 1801 the Pitts were in Portsmouth. Naval Lieutenant Robert Braithwaite, recently returned to England after seven years in the Colony, called on Mary at the request of an acquaintance. On learning Mary was the cousin of George Matcham, Braithwaite alerted George to the poor treatment of settlers in New South Wales:

On their arrival they have been put on the Store with a ration of Provisions Women having less than the men and Children of a certain age having less than the women. They have been continued on the store for Eighteen Months and allowed two Servants for a family for the same time. When that is expired then servants are taken from them and theirselves discharged from being any longer an incumbrance on the Government - if after the aforementioned expiration of eighteen months they can maintain any number of Convicts - they are allowed to ... have the benefit of their labor but must either find them the Government Rations or pay the Government Twenty Pounds.[5]

Braithwaite sent Governor King "contrary directions to the proceeding" in treating Mrs Pitt.

In all likelihood the "acquaintance" was a member of the Rose family. Thomas Rose (1749-1833) and Mary Rose, née Topp, (c1756- 1827), of Blandford, just south of Sturminster Newton, were among the first free settlers to arrive in the colony on the *Bellona* in 1792.[6] The Rose family received a letter, dated March 1798, from family members in Dorset which mentioned the death of William Pitt in February. William was the younger brother of Robert Pitt.[7]

The Pitts boarded the *Canada* on 30th May 1801. The next day a distressed Mary wrote to George Matcham. Neither Braithwaite's comments on the colony nor their first day on the *Canada* were reassuring.

> *My situation here is very bad; and the shocking account of the wicked country, I dread I have brought up my children with fear and care. God knows my heart. I would rather fall into the hands of the merciful creator; or to suffer any poverty by his grace to sustain me, rather than fall into the hands of wicked people. A gentleman who came from N.S.W informs me that the whole land is full of a corrupted and wicked people. If (it) please God my children and I should live, I hope they will find a friend in the Governor, according to your good intentions. I cannot expect to live long. I am in a little hole here among all sorts of people - I can scarce see to write. God Almighty be my guide, and send me a place of rest; and his blessing attend you, and yours for ever ...*[8]

Mary, in a better frame of mind, composed a letter to George Matcham on 11th June. She had received George's letter of 1st May.

> *We are all well, and I believe the ship will sail soon. We have on board a hundred and six convicts-soldiers-and nearly forty passengers are here, and expected; so that we have only just room to creep out of our nests. The Captain told me he had parted his cabin. His lady is with him and intends going on the voyage. At first the ship's crew were continually passing by to the stores, and the surgeon's room close to us; which I complained of to Captain Patten as being a very unfit place for women. Since then there are some alterations.*[9]

Finally, on 21st June 1801 the 403 ton newly built *Canada* sailed from Portsmouth with Captain William Wilkinson at the helm.[10] The ship carried about 101 male convicts, 16 military personnel, three of their women and three of their children, and 29 free passengers, including the six Pitts. At Portsmouth, the captains and surgeons of the *Canada*, *Minorca* and *Nile* had received detailed instructions designed to safeguard the health and welfare of the passengers. The ship's diary was to note "strict adherence" to the "obligations", including fumigating, ventilating, scrubing, sweeping, scraping and airing, as well as a proper diet, pure water and appropriate medicines, and hospital procedures.[11]

After almost six uncomfortable months, the *Canada* arrived in Sydney Cove on 14th December 1801. The attention to health and welfare paid dividends since the passengers were "all in good health". In the colony there were fewer than 6,000 people, nearly a third of them convicts.[12] The Pitts and other free passengers on the *Canada* were sent to Parramatta where, on 26th December, they received their first supplies of Government Stores. Lucy Pitt relied on the stores for 29 days.[13]

During the voyage a romance developed between Lucy and John Wood, third mate in the *Canada*'s crew of 32. John got his discharge from the East India Company before the couple married by special licence on 11th January 1802 at St John's Parramatta.[14] Samuel Marsden conducted the wedding in the simple wooden church on the corner of present-day George and Marsden Streets.[15] Jemima and Thomas were the witnesses. John, aged about 27 or 28, was from Deptford, a dockyard area on the Thames River downstream from London where Captain James Cook's *Endeavour* and the First Fleet's *Sirius* and *Supply* were fitted out.[16] Since John Wood was such a common name, it was not possible to identify his baptism and parents.

In March 1802, Governor King granted Mary Pitt about 100 acres at Mulgrave Place, an early name for the Hawkesbury district.[17] (Figure 3) The land was close to Richmond Hill, which Governor Phillip named after the third Duke of Richmond, Charles Lennox, who served with Prime Minister William Pitt.[18] The family probably followed the rough dirt road from Parramatta to Green Hills (later Windsor), then the tracks to sparsely settled Richmond Hill. When settlers reported arms in their possession in April 1802, Thomas Matcham Pitt and John Wood were at the Hawkesbury, Thomas with two guns and John with a sword. Presumably the women were with them.[19]

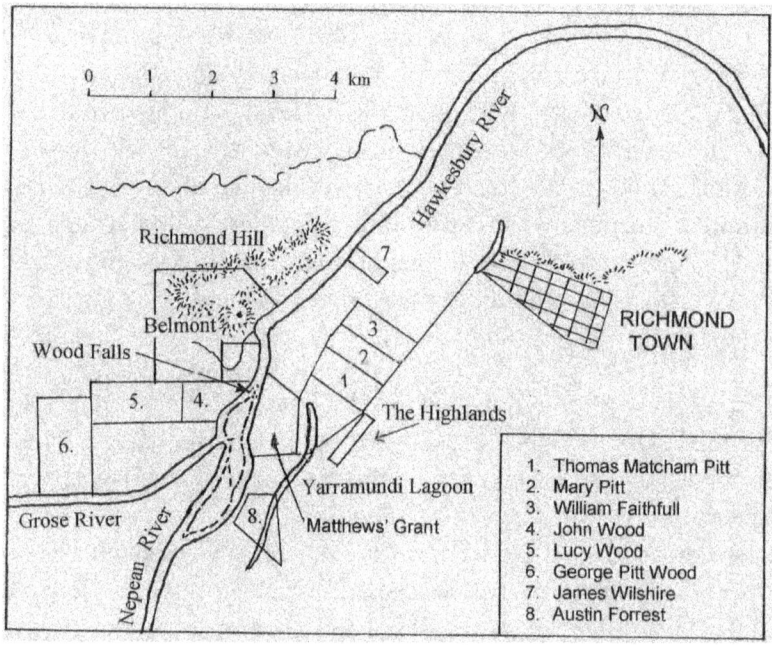

Figure 3. Grants and Purchases of the Pitt Family near Richmond Hill.

1	Letter of 1 January 1801, Lord Nelson to George Matcham, Fearn, Marie A.J., Family of Pitt, ML D80, Item 7
2	HRNSW 4, pp346-7
3	Letter of 1 May 1801, George Matcham to Mary Pitt, Fearn, ML D80, Item 7

4	Letter of 7 May 1801, Samuel Gambier to George Matcham, Fearn, ML D80, Item 7
5	Letter of 29 May 1801, Robert Braithwaite to George Matcham, ML Ab 114
6	HRA 1, pp366-7
7	Letter of March 1798, Thomas Topp to Thomas Rose, ML Doc 409
8	Letter of 31 May 1801, Mary Pitt to George Matcham, ML Am 166
9	Letter of 11 June 1801, Mary Pitt to George Matcham, ML Am 166
10	Indents of Convict Ships 1801-1804, SRNSW, 4/4004, COD 138, p33
11	HRA 1, 3, pp379, 380, 452; HRNSW 4, pp399-402, 646
12	Clark, C.M.H., *Select Documents in Australian History 1788-1850*, Angus and Robertson, Sydney, 1950, pp405-6
13	King Papers Vol 1, MLA1976, p108, CY 904
14	East India Company Logs 16 May 1801 - 25 Mar 1805, *Canada*, ML AJCP M1623
15	Pollon Frances, *The Cradle City of Australia*, The Council of the City of Parramatta, 1983, p121
16	Nicholson, I. H., *Gazetteer of Sydney Shipping 1788-1840*, Roebuck, Sydney, 1981, p48
17	Grants and Leases of Land, Bk 3c, No 88, DL; County Cumberland, Parish Ham Common, 1927, Map No 24, L/F, DL
18	HRA 1, 1, pp29, 155, 48
19	Particulars of Arms in Possession, SRNSW 4/1719, Reel 6041, p94

2
PACIFIC ISLANDS ODYSSEY

At the beginning of June 1802 John Wood signed on as first mate of the *Margaret*. Built of British oak at the Isle of Wight in 1799, the brig weighed 121 tons and measured 73 feet by 20 feet. The ship had a square stem, two masts, square tucked sails, one and a half decks, a quarterdeck, and 10 mounted guns.[1] John Buyers captained the ship and John Turnbull managed the cargo. John Wood ensured the crew carried out the captain's orders and commanded the ship in the captain's absence. Lucy joined John on the long and eventful trip to O'Tahiti and other Pacific Ocean islands and atolls.[2] (See Figures 4 & 5 for locations visited)

In 1798 Turnbull and Buyers sold goods in New South Wales and visited China where they noted the profitable fur trade with the north-west coast of America. On returning to London, the pair persuaded two merchants to join them in buying the *Margaret*. After getting a licence from the East India Company, Turnbull and Buyers left in July 1800 and arrived at Port Jackson in January 1801. Buyers sailed south, leaving a gang of men to seal on King Island. Incidentally, the sealers were still on the island in December 1802. Turnbull remained in the colony to sell the goods. Governor King bought 2,200 gallons of spirits for the civil and military officers

9

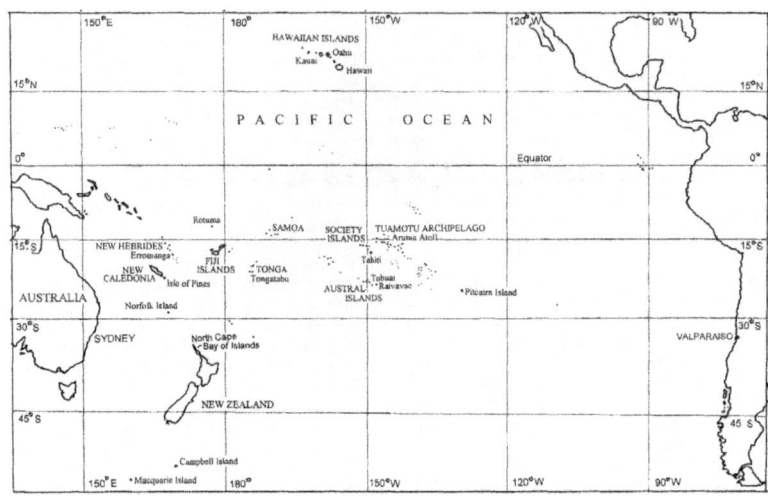

Figure 4. Pacific Ocean locations of the Woods and Henrys.

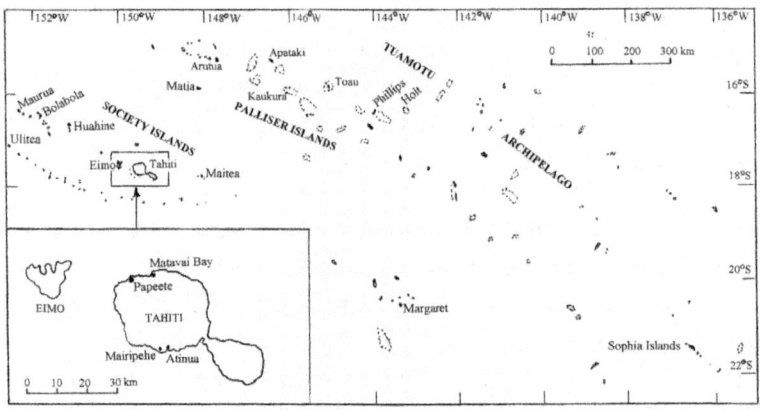

Figure 5. Society Islands and Tuamotu Archipelago locations of the Woods and Henrys

and publicans but with several ships in the harbour and little money in circulation, Turnbull was unable to sell the remaining cargo. The two made other plans. In March 1801 Buyers sailed the *Margaret* to north-west America for fur. In August Turnbull left on a whaler for Norfolk Island to trade and collect earnings from a sale. The American project having failed, Buyers returned to Port Jackson in February 1802. Turnbull heard the bad news on Norfolk Island.[3]

With much of the colony's pork imported from Great Britain at a pricey 1s a lb, Governor King sought alternate sources of the meat. A majority of the 6000 population received government rations at a yearly cost of £16 7s 6d a person, and of this sum £10 8s 0d was spent on pork. Buyers learned Tahiti was a good source of pigs when he called at the island in January 1802 on his return from America. These circumstances encouraged the Englishmen to embark on the Tahitian pork trade. They share with the English owners of the *Nautilus* the distinction of being the first private enterprise based in the colony to engage in foreign trade. On 5th June 1802, port authorities at Sydney Cove cleared the *Margaret* to sail with about 28 men, mostly convicts, and Lucy Wood, apparently the only woman.[4]

The *Margaret* called at Norfolk Island to collect John Turnbull who had organized dry food for the trip. He used Indian meal (corn) to make pleasant tasting biscuits but as the corn did not keep well, he took 50 bushels of dried corn-cobs and two pairs of millstones to grind the cobs into meal for porridge and a pudding. Turnbull employed off-duty soldiers to catch fish, which salted down filled two hogsheads. He traded for potatoes and melted hog's lard. Fresh fruits and vegetables were available at islands along the way. The *Margaret* left Norfolk Island on 9th August 1802, reaching Maitea Island by 23rd September, the prevailing winds requiring an easterly approach to Tahiti. At sunset three natives arrived in a canoe. The natives offered the visitors breadfruit, coconuts and bananas, and they sang and danced. The *Margaret* sailed during the night, anchoring the next morning off Matavai Bay in "beautiful and picturesque" O'Tahiti.[5] H.M.S. *Porpoise* and the colonial brig *Norfolk* were already there, the former to collect hogs, the latter driven ashore "in a violent gale of wind" eight months previously.[6] Members of the London Missionary Society, who arrived in O'Tahiti in 1797 to preach Christianity, fortified their house with guns from the wrecked *Norfolk*.[7] Buyers, Turnbull and the Woods met Captain Scott of the *Porpoise*, Captain House of the *Norfolk*, the missionaries, and landscape painter John Lewin, a passenger on the *Norfolk* sent by the colonial authorities. The new arrivals heard about the tribal wars and the shortage of pigs.

Although ships had stopped at Tahiti for at least 25 years to barter for tropical fruits, breadfruit, coconuts, fowls and hogs, residents "assembled in great numbers on the reefs ... along the shore" to see the *Margaret*.[8] Various members of the Royal Family, including King Otoo (later King Pomare II), approached the crew. Otoo's father, King Pomare I, at least six feet four inches tall, boarded the ship and touched noses with Turnbull. Otto's mother, Edeah or Ideah, separated from Pomare, arrived in her canoe. Other members of the royal family visited the *Margaret*, hoping to receive gifts, chiefly firearms, and often dined on-board. Though curious about all the objects on the *Margaret*, above all the dark skin and short woolly hair of two men fascinated the Tahitians. One of the Negroes "struck up a tune on the violin" and a Spaniard "performed the fandango". Pomare supplied the party with hogs, breadfruit, coconuts and bananas, repeating "the same civility at different times".[9] With fresh supplies scarce owing to the tribal wars, his help averted difficulty at times. The locals continually interrupted the visitors to request repair of their tools. Being dependent on the Tahitians' goodwill; the *Margaret*'s blacksmith set up a forge.

Lucy gave birth to George Pitt Wood during the trip or after reaching Tahiti. Obviously the missionaries baptized George since he practised their Wesleyan religion. Lucy giving her son the middle name Pitt was a custom adopted by her sisters.

Turnbull and his workers spent about a month getting fewer-than-expected hogs, before the *Margaret* left for the Sandwich (Hawaiian) Islands to obtain salt. Bearing in mind the distance to Hawaii, Lucy and infant George probably stayed with the Henry and Eyre missionary families in their new house at Matavai Bay. The *Margaret* called at Huahine to check the supply of pigs. Again the sailors met members of the Royal family, the sailors singing to the violin, the natives responding with "a grand dance".[10] Huahine was not promising. A resident, who deserted the *Margaret* on her return from America, advised them to call at Ulitea.

On arrival at Ulitea in November 1802, the King and his chiefs welcomed the people on the *Margaret*. The Tahitians made many requests, including sleeping on-board, to which Turnbull mostly agreed. An Englishman called Pulpit and his Tahitian "wife" asked to leave on the *Margaret*. Pulpit had escaped the "savage murderers" on Huahine with the help of his "wife"; however he felt threatened on Ulitea.[11] Four men deserted the night before the *Margaret*'s departure. Turnbull spent all day in "fruitless negotiation" with the island chiefs for the return of men, only to find the chiefs involved in their disappearance.[12] Keeping the men was difficult with the needs of life plentiful and women readily available. At 10.30 pm, hours before their departure, Buyers woke Turnbull. Cut away from its moorings and towed on shore, the ship "lay with her broadside against a reef of coral rocks".[13] Buyers moved the ship away from the reef, annoying the natives who intended pillaging the vessel. Hostilities continued, the natives attacking the *Margaret*, stones and firearms severely damaging the ship. The situation became critical, the people on the *Margaret* in fear of being whipped or roasted. The humane practice of firing over the heads of the natives had lost its deterrent effect so Turnbull fired a 3lb shot across the bow of an advancing canoe. He explained, "whatever might have been our indignation at their treachery, we considered it as giving us no further right to punish, than what was indispensably necessary for our defence".[14] Late in the night, on perhaps the third day of the conflict, a wind change enabled the crew to set sail and move the *Margaret*, unnoticed, out of the reach of the natives. Owing to poor weather the ship anchored until daylight. Turnbull thought about recovering two lost anchors until John Wood delivered a message from the ship's men to the quarterdeck; leave immediately in case the wind threw them "into the hands of this treacherous and savage people".[15] The *Margaret* left, passing Bolabola reputed to have the fiercest warriors, stopping at Maurua, the smallest and most leeward of the Society Islands.

The crew stressed the dangers in crossing the equator to torment the six Tahitians on-board, "their terror furnished an inexhaustible fund of amusement to our mischievous sailors."[16] However, the Neptune ceremony impressed the Tahitians. "Scanty winds" delayed their arrival at the Hawaiian Islands until 17th December 1802. The islands visited, Whahoo (Oahu), Attowaie (Kauai), Onehow (Niihau) and Owhyhee (Hawaii), were not promising; the salt, yams and hogs scarcer and dearer than expected. Commerce with Americans and Europeans had inflated prices although Hawaiian objects were superior to those produced by the Tahitians. Before leaving, Turnbull, fearing his men would desert if employed, paid the natives an "unreasonable charge" for a supply of water. The ship's carpenter and two Tahitians had already abandoned ship. Another likely to abscond, the second mate, a most useful person, wanted to take a Sandwich Island woman with him, a practice usually disallowed. John Wood "intimated that unless they complied with the mate's wish, he would leave us at the first opportunity".[17] Before sailing, the people of the *Margaret* stood on the eastern shore to take advantage of a land breeze, and "a very full view of some eruptions from volcanoes in the centre of the island of Owhyhee".[18] The *Margaret* left on 21st January 1803.

On watch about 11.30 pm on 5th March 1803, John Wood heard "the surf beating upon the beach". He went down to the cabin to tell the captain land was near.[19] The *Margaret* was in the Tuamotu Archipelago. The crew sighted several islands and visited others, naming Margaret Island (Nukutipipi) on 6th March, and Phillip's Island (Makemo) and neighbouring Holt's Island (Taenga) on 10th March. A native, probably a chief or warrior, appeared wearing pearl shells around his neck, the first sighting by Europeans of pearl shell in the Eastern Pacific.[20] Turnbull exchanged a looking-glass for a pearl necklace on 13th. The ship stopped at Matia Island, then Maitea Island. At Maitea, for 20 hogs, Turnbull bartered hatchets, scissors, knives, paper and looking-glasses. The *Margaret* reached Tahiti on 21st March 1803, the trip for salt taking about six months.

During the absence of the *Margaret*, the *Nautilius* had taken many of the hogs so the Englishmen devised a new plan. Captain Buyers would sail "to some of the islands lying to windward" for live hogs.[21] Turnbull would stay behind with two or three of the men to salt pigs; a skill learned on Norfolk Island from Lieutenant Governor Major Joseph Foveaux. Once Pomare gave Turnbull permission to trade in all parts of the island, the experienced Peter the Swede Hagerstein rounded up every European on the island, including deserters. Turnbull converted his "common dwellinghouse" into a "mansion" with many "divisions".[22] He set aside half the house for himself and the other half for "our people, four in number".[23] Presumably, John and Lucy were two of "our people".

In early April 1803, John and Lucy Wood, infant George and 16 others boarded the *Margaret*, expecting the trip to last no longer than three weeks.[24] Getting windward took a fortnight as "contrary winds and lee-currents" buffeted the *Margaret*.[25] Buyers began to trade for pearls on the 16th April. A day later the ship lay wrecked on a "low reef of rocks and sand-banks in the vicinity of a cluster of islands called the Pallisers" in the Tuamotu Archipelago.[26] The difficulty of finding a way through the extensive coral reefs accounted for the Archipelago's other names, Labyrinth and Dangerous. The group was marooned on a sandbank:, about 40 yards wide and four feet above sea level, near the uncharted Arutua Atoll, roughly 200 miles from Tahiti.[27] Each person was rationed to two wineglasses of freshwater a day, the only other water available, brackish water taken from some depth in the sandbank. During the night natives stole their small boat, muskets and ammunition, though they saved the stores within their reach.

The men began making a boat from the deck of the *Margaret*. When nearly finished, "the natives of the neighbouring islands began to collect in vast numbers and annoy them exceedingly; their situation truly dismal".[28] The boat failed to clear the circular reef. Using the boat's planks and nails, they built a flat-bottomed vessel resembling a large chest or square tub.[29] Natives continued to worry them, "not a day passed without some skirmish with these savages".[30] Following five weeks on the atoll, the group set off in the makeshift craft; their only possessions a few muskets, a small quantity of powder, a bag of bread and 10 gallons of brackish water. After clearing the reef with difficulty, "the savages rushed on board, and tore open and took away every thing portable".[31]

Following five days on "this most miserable of craft", the "nearly exhausted" group arrived at Tahiti on 27th May 1803.[32] They reached the most leeward part of the island with difficulty, after Buyers found Matavai Bay impossible to enter. A relieved Turnbull welcomed them after an absence of two months. Lucy and young George were "in a very reduced state".[33] Dr Elder, the missionaries' surgeon, "saved" the most severely injured man whose bowels "hung out". He was one of two men speared on sentry duty. The survivors were "too fatigued and worn out" to attend the chapel. Instead, the Reverend John Jefferson, "with that anxious piety which distinguishes him", preached a special service in Turnbull's house.[34] Pomare "no sooner heard of their arrival ... than he hastened to their assistance. He conducted them to his mansion, roasted a hog and bread-fruit, and spared nothing to alleviate their sufferings".[35] Jefferson believed the residence of the missionaries at Matavai was "instrumental in saving their lives".[36]

The *Margaret* lost, the men from New South Wales and the Tahitians refused to work for Turnbull. The prospects bleak for the two Englishmen; the few objects saved from the *Margaret* less valuable now the Tahitians had a good supply. Turnbull decided Eimo (Moorea) might be a better place to trade. Fewer ships had called at the island and he heard it had more hogs. The trip to the island was rough. While sleeping on Eimo someone stole Turnbull's treasure chest and two pistols which he recovered by using all of his shrewdness. The nine-day trip was unsuccessful, the people of Eimo wanting scarce items such as muskets and powder for their hogs.

Turnbull wrote, "of the whole of our former crew, the cook, the mate, the captain and myself, were alone united in a common cause, that of returning to our native country".[37] Most of the men enjoyed the lazy Tahitian lifestyle and did not intend returning to the colony, Jefferson labelling them, "mostly very abandoned characters".[38] Three months passed and those planning to return "almost ceased to hope" for a passage to Sydney Cove. Then, on the afternoon of 27th August, they heard a cry, "Te pahia, te pahia", a ship, a ship.[39] It was the brig *Dart*, a sealer 14 months out of London and, much to their delight, headed for Port Jackson.[40]

With the little property left divided between all their shipmates, Buyers, Turnbull, the Woods and three or four others, negotiated a passage on the *Dart*. As they were about to sail on 3rd September 1803, Pomare I approached the *Dart* in a canoe, when a violent pain gripped him. The paddle dropped from his hand and he fell face down. He died soon after the canoe reached the shore. Out of respect for the King, "a steady friend and powerful protector of the missionaries", the *Dart*, carrying 1000 sealskins as well as

Turnbull's pork, salt and other goods, did not leave until 4th.[41] A day was spent at Eoa in the Friendly Islands (Tonga), the natives bartering for axes and scissors, Turnbull for clubs, paddles, and spears. Turnbull also stocked up on coconuts, breadfruit, bananas and sugar cane. The *Dart* called at Norfolk Island to collect a sick Foveaux. On 30th September 1803 the ship reached Port Jackson.[42] Lucy's stamina was extraordinary during nearly 16 months.

John Turnbull remarked that, compared to Sydney in January 1801, "the appearance of the whole town (was) much changed for the better". New buildings included a gaol, church, hospital and bridge, all built of stone, "quarried on the very spot, almost, of their foundation".[43] Fire destroyed the previous wooden gaol and church. Turnbull and Buyers left on the *Calcutta* in March 1804.

Note:

The main reference for this chapter is: Turnbull, John, *A Voyage Round the World in the Years 1800, 1801, 1802, 1803, 1804*, Richard Phillips, London, 1805, 2nd ed., A. Maxwell, Bell Yard, Temple Bar, London, 1813. Only quotations from the book are referenced.

1. Board of Trade, UK, *Transcripts and Transactions*, Public Record Office, London 107/13, p137f
2. SG 2 October 1803, plb,c,2b
3. Statham, Pamela, *Of Officers and Men in NSW 1788-1800*, Working Papers in Economic History, No 101, Australian National University, Canberra, 1988, pp21, 24; HRA 1, 3, pp 129,131,637,639, 763, 763 (Note 20), 771-2 (Note 64); Logs, Diaries and Journals of Exploration, SRNSW; SZ 994, Fiche 3272, p6; HRNSW 4, pp302, 669, 793, 794
4. HRA 1, 3, pp430-2; Clark, C.M.H. *Select Documents in Australian History 1788-1850*, Angus and Robertson, Sydney 1962, p405; Rowland Hassall Papers, MLA859, p61; Maude, H. E., The Tahitian Pork Trade: 1800-1830, *Journal de la Societies des Oceanistes*, Vol xv, No 15, December 1959; HRNSW, 4, p794
5. Turnbull, 1813, ch 11, p130
6. Turnbull, 1813, ch 11, p130
7. HRA 1, 3, p727-8, 783 (Note 130)
8. Turnbull, 1813, ch 11, p129
9. Turnbull, 1813, ch 11, p142

10	Turnbull, 1813, ch 12, pl58
11	Turnbull, 1813, ch 13, p164
12	Turnbull, 1813, ch 13, pl 72
13	Turnbull, 1813, ch 13, p173
14	Turnbull, 1813, ch 14, p183
15	Turnbull, 1813, ch 14, pl86
16	Turnbull, 1813, ch 16, p195
17	Turnbull, 1813, ch 22, p265
18	Turnbull, 1813, ch 21, p244
19	Turnbull, 1813, ch 21, p245
20	Maude, 1959, pp63-4
21	Turnbull, 1813, ch 23, p269
22	Turnbull, 1813, ch 23, p270
23	Turnbull, 1813, ch 23, p271
24	SG 2 October 1803, plc; London Missionary Society, Letter of John Jefferson, 29 August 1803, ML FM4/345
25	Turnbull, 1813, ch 26, p301
26	Turnbull, 1813, ch 26, p302
27	Jefferson, 1803; T; Nicholson, 1981, pl2
28	Turnbull, 1813, ch 26, pp302-3
29	SG 2 Oct 1803, plc
30	Turnbull, 1813, ch 26, p303
31	Turnbull, 1813, ch 26, p305
32	Turnbull, 1813, ch 26, p305
33	SG 2 Oct 1803, plc
34	Turnbull, 1813, ch 26, p301
35	Turnbull, 1813, ch 26, p300
36	Jefferson, 1803
37	Turnbull, 1813, ch 29, p323
38	Jefferson, 1803
39	Turnbull, 1813, ch 29, p323
40	HRA 1, 3, pp525,527
41	London Missionary Society, *Narrative of the Mission at O'Taheiti and Other Islands in the South Seas*, London, 1818, p7
42	SG 2 October 1803, plb,c, p2b
43	Turnbull, 1813, ch 37, p408

3
SETTLING AT THE HAWKESBURY

The typical home of an early Hawkesbury settler was a simple hut-like construction with wattle and daub walls and a thatched roof.[1] Farming the fertile soil was the chief means of making a living. However, the periodic floods depositing the rich soil, threatened the livelihood of the farmers. The floods also imperilled the colony's food supply for the Hawkesbury was the granary of the colony.[2] Because they lost their hunting and food-gathering lands, the Aborigines raided farmhouses and crops. Luckily, the tribe at Richmond Hill offered settlers friendship and help.[3]

The muster in mid 1802 shows Mary Pitt with 130 acres, seven cleared and planted with wheat and maize, two sheep, four goats and 10 hogs. She had eight bushels of maize stored. Thomas bought the extra 30 acres beside the east bank of the Hawkesbury near Greenhills.[4] Two servants helped Thomas.[5] In September Governor King granted Thomas 100 acres bordering Mary's land.[6] (Figure 3) The grants consisted of some high ground for the home and vegetables, but most was flood-prone river flats for crops and stock.[7] On 1st January 1803, 29 settlers of Richmond Hill thanked Governor Philip Gidley King "for the manifold blessings we freely enjoy from your determined, just, and salutary blessings".[8]

Figure 6. Margaret Catchpole (1762-1819)

The Remarkable Margaret Catchpole

Born in Suffolk on 2nd March 1762 to Elizabeth Catchpole and a farm labourer, Margaret Catchpole spent her early life on farms worked by her father. As a young woman, Margaret was employed by several families with the time spent as undercook and undernurse for Mrs John Cobbold, wife of an Ipswich brewer, especially rewarding. The Cobbolds accepted her as a member of their family and taught her to read and write. Margaret saved the lives of the Cobbold children on three occasions. In mid 1795 she left the Cobbolds who apparently disapproved of her lover, William Laud, a sailor turned smuggler. Gravely ill for some months and unemployed, on the night of 23rd May 1797 Margaret stole John Cobbold's horse valued at £30. She rode 70 miles to London in 10 hours, reputedly to help Laud who was hiding in London to avoid arrest for an unpaid fine. Margaret was caught and sentenced to death at the Summer Suffolk Summer Assizes; the sentence commuted to transportation for seven years. Imprisoned in Newgate Gaol, Margaret moved to Ipswich Gaol, where Laud was confined for smuggling. Before Laud left gaol, the couple planned to meet outside the goal, go to his sister on the Suffolk coast, and flee on a smuggling ship to Holland and there marry. On 25th March 1800, Margaret used a clothes line to scale a 22-foot goal wall. The two reached the coast where William was shot dead and Margaret captured. In Suffolk in July 1800, Margaret again received a death sentence, the sentence converted to transportation for life (21 years). She arrived in the *Nile* in December 1801. For 18 months Margaret cooked for Commissary John Palmer in Sydney. By 1804 she was overseer for the Rouse family at Richmond Hill and afterwards kept a small store in Richmond. Margaret's letters, which "reveal ... a warm, loving, intelligent woman of great integrity", include the statement, "Mrs Pitt is very fond of me". Margaret received a pardon in January 1814 and died on 13th May 1819, after catching an infection from an ill employee of the Pitts. The Reverend Fulton buried her in Richmond Cemetery. George Burnett Barton, who married a grand-daughter of Esther and James Wilshire, wrote Margaret's story.[9]

The family's supplies from Government stores ended in July 1803.[10]

Soon after reaching the colony in late September 1803, John Wood found further work on the 31 ton schooner *Endeavour* owned by Kahle and Company.[11] The captain was to deliver nine convicts to the new settlement of Van Diemen's Land before heading for the sealing grounds in Bass Strait. On 20th October the *Endeavour* sailed out of Sydney Cove. Off Botany Bay a thunderstorm produced "extremely vivid" lightning, the "flashes of unusually long continuance." The lightning temporarily blinded mate Higgins. John Wood was struck in the loins and, his injury "so severe", the *Endeavour* returned to Sydney Cove for medical aid.[12]

Margaret Catchpole delivered the second child of Lucy and John Wood, Sophia Wood, on 11th May 1804. (Figure 6) In her simple English, Margaret wrote of "spending time with Mr and Mrs Wood" and of going "to nurs Mrs Wood".[13] Since Sophia was the last child of the Woods, John's injury probably restricted the size of his family. In April John sold the government two breeding sows and two hogs, possibly pigs from the Society Islands.[14] In July Governor King granted John about 100 acres at the junction of the Hawkesbury River and the mountain-fed Grose River where the soil was "extremely rich", but the land low and subject to flood.[15] At the side of the grant, the Hawkesbury becomes the Nepean, the two names resulting from the separate discovery of the river's lower and upper reaches.[16] Governor Arthur Phillip (1788-1792) named the river after Evan Nepean and Lord Hawkesbury, members of William Pitt's administration in the years 1788-1801. The Grose took its name from Major Francis Grose acting governor of the colony from 1792-1794.[17] The river falls alongside the Woods acres are named "Wood Falls".[18] (Figure 3)

Mary Pitt's eldest daughter, Susannah Pitt, married William Faithfull at St John's, Parramatta, on 21st November 1804. The Reverend Samuel Marsden officiated in the new church he opened in April 1803 in Quaker Street (Church Street). Thomas and Hester witnessed the ceremony.[19] William signed the marriage register with a cross, his inability to write no barrier to a successful life. Most likely he was the William Faithfull baptised on 14th December 1774 at St Thomas in Winchester, Hampshire, the child of William Faithfull and Ann Dibsdale who married there the previous year.[20] In March 1791, William enlisted to escape his stepfather and seek adventure abroad.[21] Expecting to fight in the Spanish Wars but assigned to the New South Wales Corps, William arrived in the *Pitt* under Major Francis Grose and Captain Joseph Foveaux in February 1792.[22]

William Faithfull participated in an incident of some notoriety in October 1795. William, Foveaux's servant, was at his master's place in the barracks when several pigs wandered into the yard. Next door neighbour, Quartermaster Thomas Laycock, and William rounded up the pigs.[23] Laycock ordered William to shoot a pig as an example to those letting their pigs freely roam. William shot a pregnant sow owned by settler John Boston, with whom Laycock had previously clashed. After hearing the fate of his pig, Boston hurried to the scene to find "the damned rascal that shot my sow". Boston's use of the term, "rascal", "a man without genitals", enraged Laycock.[24] He urged William to "thresh" Boston "as long as he could stand". Using his loaded gun William struck Boston on the back of his head. William also received a blow on the forehead, which bled profusely. Boston sought damages of £500 from Laycock, William and two other soldiers who took part in the event. The whole colony keenly watched the case heard over seven days in December in the Court of Civil Jurisdiction, before First Fleet naval officers David Collins and George Johnston, and First Fleet surgeon William Balmain. In the final sitting, Boston asked the judges to "dismiss Mr Faithfull from the Action, he was a poor subordinate agent, from him the plaintiff would scorn to receive compensation". The assault was proved and damages of 20s awarded against both William and Laycock.[25] The next

January, William appealed the decision in the Superior Court of Civil Jurisdiction presided over by Governor John Hunter. William justified his action on two grounds. One, Boston was the first assailant. If other soldiers present at the incident had given evidence in the original case, their testimony would have confirmed he was not the aggressor. Two, the Government Orders of July 1793 sanctioned shooting stray pigs. Hunter pointed out the orders did not apply to pigs on private property. The Governor, who thought the penalty lenient, confirmed the original verdict.[26]

In 1798 William Faithfull was promoted to corporal in Foveaux's company, his monthly salary averaging about £1 16s. However, he resigned on 29th October 1799.[27] Governor Hunter granted William two adjacent grants of 25 acres at Petersham Hill in 1799 and 1800.[28] (George Pitt Wood (1871-1941), grandson of George Pitt Wood, bequeathed part of William's 1800 grant, now in Charlotte Street Ashfield, to the Presbyterian Church as a home for aged women.[29] Pittwood is now a nursing home.) William lived on his grants and worked the nearby 100 acres of Foveaux. On his retirement, William also owned 60 acres, part of 125 acres, at Richmond downstream from the Pitts, where again Foveaux had property.[30] In 1801 Foveaux rewarded William with a flock of sheep, a two-volume set of bibles and a gold pocket watch.[31] Robert Campbell also leased William 99 acres, which William returned with £70 in July 1803.[32]

In the mid 1802 muster, William Faithfull owned 118 acres, 18 planted with maize, two horses, two sheep, three goats and 35 pigs. He had set aside 20 bushels of wheat and 80 of maize.[33] In July 1804, in the Civil Court of Jurisdiction, George Crossley, a solicitor, brought an action of "trespass" and "ejectment" to "dispossess" William Faithfull, James Baker and William Baker, Hawkesbury storekeeper, of the 125 acres at Richmond. Baker, who held the title to the land, defended alone and won the case.[34] Crossley appealed but lost.[35] William took Baker to court, either to get the title for his

60 acres, or the money he paid the storekeeper for the farm as well as the expenses incurred in clearing 15 acres and planting six with wheat.[36] After marrying, William made £92 10s on selling Baker his "excellent farm" with two houses, a barn fronting the river and every convenience.[37]

Susannah and William Faithfull settled next to Mary Pitt on 100 acres owned by First Fleet marine Thomas Spencer.[38] (Figure 3) While working on the property in January 1805, William suffered "a shocking accident". He fell on a pitchfork projecting from a stack of hay or com, "the prigs entering the lower part of the belly and passing upwards through his right side". Although his recovery was doubtful, he regained his health in the following months.[39] About June, friend James Morris, who had a house in Sydney where William often stayed, sued William in the Civil Court of Jurisdiction for "propagating a report prejudicial to his character". Morris alleged during his "dangerous illness", William circulated the rumour that on his death the plaintiff planned to claim £200 or more from his estate. William denied the rumour originated with him. The court accepted William's testimony. The judge stated Morris's character was "too well established to sustain injury from such an attack". Each paid his court costs.[40]

Mary Pitt's youngest daughter, Esther, wed James Wilshire at St Philips Church in Sydney on 12th February 1805. Reverend Samuel Marsden conducted the marriage, witnessed by Thomas and Jemima. Baptised in Aylesbury, Buckinghamshire, on 9th August 1771, James was the son of William Wilshire and Martha Wilshire, formerly Thompson. (Figure 7) He arrived in the colony in November 1800 after seven months aboard the *Royal Admiral*.[41] On the ship James kept a diary which, in the words of a librarian, "reflects the experiences and views of an intelligent observer". The diary revealed that during the trip the convicts "behaved menacingly enough" for the free passengers to form four-hourly watches.[42] On 20th December 1799 James was appointed a clerk

Figure 7. James Wilshire

in the Commissariat built near today's ferry terminal at Circular Quay.⁴³ John Palmer, a naval officer in the First Fleet and head of the Commissariat, recommended the position to James. Palmer was on leave in England before James left for the colony.⁴⁴

With no treasury or private bank in the colony, the biggest trading institution was the Commissariat. Nearly everyone dealt with the Government Stores at Sydney Cove, Parramatta, and Green Hills. Farmers sold their meat and grain in return for store receipts. Convicts, military and civil officers, and new settlers received food and clothes. Any colonist could obtain the local and imported goods by purchase, barter or credit.⁴⁵ Despite the heavy workload, one commissary, two deputies, three storekeepers and six clerks staffed the three stores.⁴⁶ Clerk James Wilshire was responsible for quarterly exchange of store receipts for goods or British Treasury bills, the latter readily exchanged for sterling.⁴⁷ Sterling and treasury bills were legal tender for the scarce, highly priced goods imported by the ships' captains, merchants and military officers. Most deals in the colony involved paper money, not only store receipts but also promissory or currency notes, simple signed documents containing a written promise by an individual to pay a stated sum to the bearer or a specified person. Workers, though, were often paid in spirits, depriving them of income to buy necessities.⁴⁸

Commissary John Palmer and James were bondsmen for James Stewart, captain of the *Anne*, in July 1801. Bonds set out the conditions binding the captain, for example, forbidding some sea routes and passage to convicts and debtors. Port authorities exacted hefty fines if a captain did not adhere to the conditions.⁴⁹ In December 1801, William Page entered James's home at Brickfield Hill and with "force and arms" stole a pistol and clothes belonging to James Gilders. Brickfield Hill was named after the brickworks set up in 1788 and the hilly terrain.⁵⁰ James had bought 2 acres west of Brickfield Hill granted to the colony's first clergyman, Richard Johnson. He sold the land in November 1802 for £50.⁵¹ When

James informed authorities of the gun in his possession in April 1802, he had already moved to the most desirable part of Chapel Row (Castlereagh Street).[52] Built of weatherboard, shingled and glazed, the house had two spacious rooms, a loft, detached kitchen, storerooms and a garden.[53] James sold the house to William Stewart for £100 in 1804. Although James advertised for payment in "storeable wheat or good bills", mariner Stewart arranged to pay half the cost in elephant seal oil within eight months.[54] In December 1803, Sir Henry Browne Hayes paid James £210 14s 6d for unidentified services. Hayes, an eccentric rascal formerly of Cork, received a death sentence for kidnapping an heiress he intended to marry.[55]

In 1803 James Wilshire got a grant, set up a tannery and received a promotion in the Commissariat. Governor King awarded James a 14-year lease of nearly an acre on the east side of later-named George Street at its junction with later-made Liverpool Street, in Brickfield Hill.[56] James started the tannery on finding colonists "put to enormous Expenses in procuring leather for shoes", imported leather costing 9s to 12s a lb. He also found the bark of several trees and bushes "possessed the tanning Properties". Before long, he was producing leather "equal to English Manufactures".[57] At Lane Cove James paid £40 for 245 acres granted to five settlers.[58] Problems beset the leased farm. Fire destroyed crops and trespassers felled trees. About 200 natives tied up workers and took all their bedding and "necessaries". The intruders scattered after James and his helpers arrived at the farm the next day.[59] Appointed Acting Deputy Commissary in March 1804, James held the position until August 1806.[60] Esther settled with James at Brickfield Hill which was "thought a Sabbath-day's journey" from the town.[61]

At Green Hills on 11th August 1805 the Reverend Samuel Marsden conducted divine service in the spacious new, but unfinished, two-storey brick building which served as a church and school.[62] At this service Marsden baptised Sophia Wood, one of more than

40 children, many born in the 1790s, including a three-year-old native boy adopted by Thomas Rickerby.[63] With the Hawkesbury parish not formed until 1810, Marsden recorded the baptisms in the register of St John's, Parramatta.[64]

A flood in the Hawkesbury district in March 1806 caused much destruction with lives lost, houses flooded, grain ruined and livestock destroyed.[65] The flood covered the low-lying farm of the Woods and the river flats of the Pitts and Faithfulls.[66] The loss of grain placed the colony in peril. On 24th March, Governor King asked Austin Forrest, captain and part owner of the *Sydney*, and later husband of Jemima Pitt, to alter his trip to England. Would he take the *Sydney* to Calcutta and return with 400 tons of wheat or rice? Austin assured the Governor, "the Ship *Sydney* is at Your disposal".[67] James Wilshire was bondsman for the *Sydney* when it left on 14th April 1806. On the way to Calcutta, the *Sydney* was wrecked off the Coast of New Guinea. Fortunately all survived.[68] James also had a financial stake in the Richmond, a small colonial vessel employed on the Hawkesbury. Owner Robert Rushworth failed to repay James. He could not sell the schooner, so he gave James 32 Church (York) Street in February 1806. The next year James sold Church Street for £73 10s. In December 1807, James paid £30 5s for a cart, goods and a house, its location not identified.[69]

William Bligh of Bounty fame replaced Philip King as Governor of the colony in August 1806. The Hawkesbury settlers welcomed Bligh with an address identifying their concerns: the distress caused by the flood; the reduced price of produce; the lack of freedom of trade; and the problems with paper money. Thomas Matcham Pitt was an author, presenter and signatory of the address. William Faithfull signed the address. Again in January and February 1807, and January 1808, the Hawkesbury people presented petitions in appreciation of Bligh introducing reforms such as increasing the price of wheat and banning spirits as payment for grain, food, clothes or labour. Thomas Matcham Pitt, William Faithfull and John Wood signed the petitions.[70]

Before King's administration ended, he ordered musters of the colonists and their land and stock.[71] The Pitts of Richmond assembled at the Hawkesbury, the women and children at Green Hills on 13th August 1806, the men "above Green Hills" on the 20th. John Wood owned 110 acres; the extra 10 acres bought from Matthew's subdivided grant.[72] (Figure 3) John, still injured, rented his land to free-by-servitude William Chapman. John's land supported a quarter acre of potatoes, four acres of maize, 15 acres of wheat, a goat, three sheep and seven hogs. Five bushels of maize were stored. John and Lucy had a garden and orchard. Thomas Pitt, owner of 130 acres, lived on the 200 acres at Richmond. Jemima kept house for her brother. Apparently Mary was in Sydney; the muster lists her as the wife of Mr Wilshire! Three convicts helped Thomas cultivate one acre of barley and 20 each of wheat and maize and take care of a horse, 25 sheep, and 52 hogs. He had reserved 20 bushels wheat and 20 of maize. Incidentally, in the month of the muster Thomas gave James Badgery a six-month loan of £13 9s.[73] On Thomas Spencer's 100 acre farm William Faithfull had planted 10 acres of both wheat and maize and raised two horses, two cows, 31 sheep and 20 pigs. Fifteen bushels of wheat were set aside. Three convicts worked for William. The muster lists Susannnah with a child even though it was 11th October 1806 before Margaret Catchpole delivered firstborn, William Pitt Faithfull.[74] There was no sign of William's christening.

Civil and military officers completed separate returns of their holdings by 12th August. James employed a manager and two convicts to run his farm at Lane Cove. They grew wheat, maize and barley on 145 of James's 245 acres and looked after a horse, cow, ox and 12 goats. Six bushels of wheat were in storage.[75] The official muster contains an item relevant to James. The Wood's lessee, William Chapman, rented John Ryan's 50 acres, which

James bought for £27 2s about 1809. (Figure 3) At the same time, James paid £28 for a bull named Captain Fear![76] On 13th March 1806, Esther had given birth to their first child who they named Louisa Wilshire at her baptism at St Philips on 8th June.

At Green Hills in October 1807 Thomas Matcham Pitt received an offer of £150 for his mare. Soon after Thomas accepted "a note" for £157 10s offered by Thomas Biggers. The issuer, William Gore, could not honour the note so Thomas sued Biggers for fraud in the Civil Court of Jurisdiction. Witness James Wilshire said Thomas brought the promissory note to Sydney and gave it to Gore, who expressed surprise. He had told Biggers not to present the note until January. Later, on seeing Biggers near the Orphan House, Thomas and James tried to return the note. Following much deliberation, the court found Thomas accepted the note without signing it and awarded the case to Biggers.[77] The misfortune of Thomas highlighted the unsatisfactory nature of paper currency. Also in the Court of Civil Jurisdiction, Thomas issued a writ in July 1808 for the arrest of storekeeper Andrew Thompson for £50. Further details of the case were unavailable.[78]

Meanwhile, the colony was chaotic in the early evening of 26th January 1808, a significant date in the colonial calendar. The commanding officer of the Corps, Lieutenant Colonel George Johnston, arrested Governor William Bligh, declared martial law, and assumed control of the colony. To his enemies, officers of the New South Wales Corps and most businesspeople, Bligh was a "selfseeking tyrant". To his supporters, nearly all the Hawkesbury settlers, he was a reformer devoted to public welfare. The truth probably lies between the two extremes. The Rum Rebellion had complex causes, but little to do with conflict over the trade in spirits which gave the uprising its name in the 1850s. Johnston placed the government of the colony in the hands of "the military and a few malcontents".[79] Thomas Matcham Pitt and James Wilshire played parts in the rebellion.

George Crossley, London solicitor, ex-convict, and close ally of Bligh, "heard Mr Pitt say that Badgery had told him Mr Macarthur had expressed in his presence certain words relative to the Government of this colony". It appears Crossley passed Macarthur's alleged words to the Governor. At the Hawkesbury, Bligh's supporters, magistrates John Palmer and Dr Thomas Arndell, questioned James Badgery, Thomas Pitt, Thomas Hobby and Crossley on the veracity of Crossley's claim. When examined after the coup on 26th January, Palmer stated the evidence differed of Badgery, Pitt and Hobby, while Dr Arndell claimed Crossley's information "false and illfounded". At his resumed trial for sedition on 2nd February 1808, Macarthur "assured his favourite court mode as prosecutor" as he cross-examined Palmer, "Did not Mr Pitt contradict the Charges of Crossley, and in y'r presence call Crossley a perjured old Villain"? Palmer replied, "He did, until Crossley was put upon his oath, when Pitt acknowledged in part the charges".[80]

James Wilshire signed the address of 1st January 1808 in support of Bligh. On 26th January James signed Johnston's letter which called on the Governor to resign and submit to arrest. After the arrest of Bligh, James signed a petition backing Johnston's removal of the Governor. The signatures on the third petition may have been collected by coercion.[81] George Johnston ordered A.F. Kemp, William Minchin, William Lawson and Garnham Blaxcell to question officers of the Commissariat, the four putting three questions to James on the 26th. When had Bligh received the last return of expenditure for the grains and other supplies in James's charge? James said he received the return three weeks or a month ago. Had Commissary Palmer taken wheat, flour and maize from the stores at various times and used the grains for "his own private purposes as a baker"? James recalled Palmer owed 100 bushels of wheat, about 2000 pounds of flour and 100 bushels of maize. Was Palmer in the habit of submitting maize in place of wheat? James understood Palmer returned two quantities of maize for one quantity wheat and thus "made good the wheat for which he then stood indebted".[82] (John Palmer was honest by the standards of the day, however, in March 1809 the rebels charged him with distributing Bligh's proclamation announcing New South Wales Corps in a mutinous state. Palmer was fined and spent three months in gaol.[83]) In February 1808 Bligh named James a witness at the trial of Colonel George Johnston in England but, though listed, he did not sail to England in April.[84] It would please Esther to have James at home, for while the witnesses were away she gave birth to her second and third children. William Pitt Wilshire was born on 15th October 1807 and baptised at St Philips on 22nd December 1807. James Robert Wilshire was born on 29th July 1809 and baptised on 29th December 1809 at the newly completed church of St Philips. (Figure 8)

Appointed Acting Deputy Commissary on 2nd September 1808, James Wilshire was "to have charge of Government Stores during the suspension of Mr James Williamson, Acting Commissary".

Figure 8. Church of St. Philip. Built of hewn stone and named after the colony's first governor, the church was erected in present Lang Park between 1800 and 1809.

After Williamson's arrest for alleged embezzlement, James replaced him as Acting Commissary on 9th November.[85] Thinking he was off to England, James let Thomas Rushton his malt house, malt kiln, brew house and a small house. The brewer agreed to pay James £105 for twelve months; the first of the quarterly payments due on 23rd May 1808. The deal required Rushton to repair the brewery.[86] In August a fire damaged the kiln in which the malt dried, Rushton using logs instead of charcoal. Rushton fixed the kiln, but James would not recompense him for the repairs. The brewer refused to pay the rent for February 1809. In the Court of Civil Jurisdiction, James sought damages of £105 from Rushton who had "carelessly or wantonly allowed the kiln to catch fire". James won the quarterly rental for February 1809.[87] In the Appeals Court before the Governor, Rushton unsuccessfully challenged the decision.[88] Rushton failed in another bid to prosecute James for £64 in the Court of Civil Jurisdiction in January 1811.[89] James successfully sued several other colonists in the civil court, their debts ranging from about £1 to £250.[90]

During the rebel administration in 1808-9, interim Governor, Lieutenant Colonel Joseph Foveaux, granted adjacent land in the district of Liberty Plains to Jemima Pitt, William Faithfull, and James Wilshire. Foveaux granted the land "in consequence of a strong recommendation" for Jemima and wives Susannah and Hester "from the late illustrious and lamented Admiral Lord Viscount Nelson to His Excellency Governor King". Because he served Foveaux, William received the most generous grant of 1000 acres, while James got 570 acres and Jemima 500 acres, the farms known as Faithfull's, Wilshire's and Jemima's.[91] Using the names of today's suburbs and street, the grants of James and Jemima covered much of Strathfield and Homebush, respectively, whereas William's grant extended from Croydon to Burwood and south of Liverpool Road.[92] Lieutenant Colonel William Paterson, interim Governor after Foveaux, granted Thomas Matcham Pitt 300 acres bounded by South and Badgery's Creeks. Thomas intended calling his land Nelson and Bronte Farms.⁹³ Pitt Street in Badgery's Creek traverses the grant of Thomas. The absent landlords experienced problems. In a joint notice William and James cautioned trespassers, for instance, those removing timber.⁹⁴ Also William's blind mare strayed while minded by Mr Edward Powell. William offered a reward of 20s and expenses for delivering the mare to Mr Wilshire, or to Mr Powell whose property bordered Parramatta Road near today's West Concord.⁹⁵ News at William's home was more agreeable; a new son born to Susannah on 2nd July 1808. He was christened Robert Faithfull at Windsor on 18th April 1810.⁹⁶

The Pitt Family coped with an accident and floods in 1809. In April, William Faithfull and Mr and Mrs Badgery stopped at an accident to Mrs Mason, wife of William Mason of Green Hills, who was "taking an excursion to Richmond for benefit of her health" with her daughter and Mr Kahle. She was thrown from her chaise after it struck a stump and her horse took fright. William and the Badgerys assisted Mrs Mason, but she did not survive.⁹⁷ In late May the Hawkesbury flooded. In early August "another inundation of the Hawkesbury more extensively destructive than any former one" took place. The water rose 10 feet higher than the flood of 1806 resulting in extensive destruction of wheat and cattle.⁹⁸ The floods inundated the Woods' farm and the riverflats of the Faithfull and Pitt farms. The river took the life of George Rouse, infant son of Richard Rouse in September. At the inquest into his death in Richmond, Thomas and William Faithfull were jurists and Thomas foreman of the jury.⁹⁹

In these early years, the Pitt Family experienced mixed fortunes. Lucy and John Wood and baby George were marooned for five weeks on a coral atoll in the Tuamotu Archipelago. John Wood and William Faithfull suffered serious accidents, John at sea and William on the farm at Richmond. The Hawkesbury floods of 1806 and 1809 affected the livelihoods of the Pitts. The rebellion of 1808 divided the colony. Hopefully, the happy events prevailed. Lucy,

Susannah, and Esther married and produced seven grandchildren. Family members received land grants at the Hawkesbury, Brickfield Hill, Liberty Plains and Badgery's Creek. Cheap convict labour was available to work the land.

1   HRNSW 5, p294
2   Fletcher, Brian H., "The Hawkesbury Settlers and the Rum Rebellion", JRAHS, Vol 54, Pt 3, pp217-237
3   SG 17 June 1804, p2c, 3a; SG 1 July 1804, p2b,c; SG 12 May 1805, p3a,b,c; "Robert Campbell of the Wharf", JRAHS, Nov 24, 1936.
4   Registers of Copies of Wills 1800-1901, SAG Will 1/112; Bowd, D.G *Hawkesbury Journey*, Library of Australian History, 1986. See map inside front cover for Daniel Barnett's land
5   Baxter, Carol J., ed. *Musters and Lists, New South Wales and Norfolk Island, 1800-1802*, Australian Biological and Genealogical Record and Society of Australian Genealogists, Sydney, 1988, pp 72, 83
6   Grants and Leases of Land, Bk 3, No 99, DL; Bk 73, No 433, DL
7   Emails 28, 31(10.57 am) March 2006, Margaret Betts to Janelle Cust, re topography of Bronte
8   HRA 1, 4, p503
9   Barton, G. B., The True Story of Margaret Catchpole, Cornstalk Publishing Co., Sydney, 1924; Indents of Convict Ships 1801-1804, SRNSW 4/4004, COD 13 8, p46; *NSW Governors Despatches*, ML All 92, p823; ADB 1, Catchpole; Margaret Catchpole Papers 1797-1811, Letter of 8 October 1806, ML MSS 618; Mutch Index, Catchpole
10 King Papers, Vol 1, ML A1976, p108
11 HRA 1, 4, p515
12 SG 23 October 1803, p2b, 3a; 30 October 1803, 2b
13 Margaret Catchpole Papers, 1797-1811, Letter of 8 October 1806, ML MSS 618
14 HRA, 1, 4, p625
15 Grants and Leases of Land, Bk 3c, Pg 139, DL; HRNSW 6, p350
16 15 HRNSW, 2, p500
17 HRA 1, 1, pp155, 746; Bowd, D.G., *Macquarie Country*, Library of Australian History, Sydney, re.ed., 1982, p3
18 County of Cook, Parish Kurrajong, 9th ed., Map No 25, DL
19 SG 17 April 1803,p3a
20 International Genealogical Index, Baptism ofWilliam Faithful; Marriage of William Faithfull/Ann Dibsdale
21 Maxwell, Charles F., *Australian Men of Mark 1788-1888*, Vol 1, Mc Carron, Bird and Co., Melbourne, 1889, pp376-7

3 Settling at the Hawkesbury

22 Statham, Pamela ed., *A Colonial Regiment, New Sources Relating to the New South Wales Corps 1789-1810*, Australian National University, Canberra, 1992,pp278,281,287
23 Maxwell, 1889, p376; HRNSW 5, following p837, Grimes 1800 map. See for locations ofFoveaux and Laycock
24 Whitaker, Anne-Maree, *Joseph Foveaux: Power and Patronage in Early New South Wales*, Sydney, 2000, p209
25 HRA 1, 1, pp604-43
26 CCJ, Case Papers, SRNSW 2/8132, ppl-38
27 War Office, Muster Rolls and Pay Lists, ML WO 12/9899, Reels 412,423, 3906; Statham, 1992, p278
28 Grants of Land, Bk 2, Pg 293, DL; Grants and Leases of Land, Bk 3c, Pg 17, DL
29 Coupe, S. and R., *Speed the Plough, Ashfield 1788-1988*, The Council of the Municipality of Ashfield, 1988, p23; Letter of6 May 1981, Town Clerk of Ashfield to G.M. Cust; Vol 2825, Fol 70, DL
30 BT, Box 88, p36. See map at Ref 34
31 http://www.nma.gov.au/collections/ Search "Faithfull"
32 NSW JA Rg., Bk 1, Pg 74, No 350, MLA3609
33 Musters 1800-1802, pp5, 75
34 CCJ, Proceedings, June-September 1804, ML CY1098, pp36-49; SG 26 August 1804, p2a,b; Map of Ham Common, SRNSW Map 2976, H.220. See Endeavour Fann of 125 acres
35 CCJ, Court of Appeals, Case Papers, SRNSW 2/8134, pp 1-134
36 CCJ, Rough Minutes and Proceedings and Related Case Papers, SRNSW 2/8148, p501
37 SG 20 October 1805, p2c; SG 15 December 1805, plb; NSW JA Rg., MLA3609, Bk 1, Pg 113, No 649
38 Baxter, Carol J. ed., *Musters of New South Wales and Norfolk Island, 1805-1806*, Australian Biological and Genealogical Record and Society of Australian Genealogists, Sydney, 1989, p39
39 SG 13 January 1805, p2a
40 SG 9 June 1805, p2c, 3a
41 BT, Biographies, MLA200, CY 679, Vol 4, Pg 1810
42 Wilshire James, Journal ... kept on board the Royal Admiral. .. from England to New South Wales 5 May-16 August 1800, MLMSS 1296
43 Memorial 1821, SRNSW Fiche 3040, 4/1827, No 51; HRA I, 3, p53; Thomas, Bryan, Map of Early Sydney 1803-1810, SRNSW 1/5477
44 See Ref 41; Parsons, T.G., "Colonial Commissaries", in R.T., Appleyard and C.B., Schedvin eds., *Australian Financiers*, Globe Press, Melbourne 1988, ch 1, p17
45 Parsons, in Appleyard and C.B., Schedvin eds., Melbourne 1988, ch 1, ppll-14
46 HRA I, 3, p419
47 *Government and General Orders* 3 April 1801-22 January 1802, SRNSW

SZ988, Reel 6037, pp24, 37
48   HRNSW 6, pp249-50
49   Hainsworth, D. R., *The Sydney Traders, Simeon Lord and His Contemporaries 1788-1821*, Melbourne University Press, Melbourne, 1981, ch 12, pl 91; Special Bundles, SRNSW 4/1093.1, Reel 6020, ppl75-8
50   NSW Court of Criminal Jurisdiction, Indictments and Informations, 1796-1808, 5/1145, pl83, Reel 2392; Emerson, Arthur, *Historical Dictionary of Sydney*, The Scarecrow Press, London, 2001, p5 1
51   NSW JA Rg., Bk 1, Pg 46, No 208, MLA3609
52   Particular of arms in Possession, SRNSW 4/1719, Reel 6041, p86
53   SG 19 February 1804, plc
54   NSW JA Rg., Bk 1, Pg 82, No 417, ML A3609
55   NSW JA Rg., Bk 1, Pg 77, No 367, ML A3609; JRAHS, 1917, Vol 3, Part 11, pp507-8
56   Grants and Leases of Land, Bk 3c, Pg 110, DL; HRNSW, 6, opp p366; HRNSW, 7, p429 & footnote
57   Main Series of Letters Received 1818, SRNSW 4/1741, Reel 6047, p43
58   NSW JA Rg., Bkl, Pg 83, No 429; Pg 103, No 570; Pg 119, Nos 692, 693; Pg 134, Nos 1048, 1049 ML A3609
59   SG 23 Oct 1803, p3c; 2 September 1804, p2b; 5 May 1804, le; 11 November 1804, p2a
60   HRA 1, 5, pp 158,449, 774; Jenkins, Matilda, Career of James Wilshire, ML Aw94/1
61   SG 13 May 1826, p2c
62   HRA 1, 5, ppl 1, 46, 91
63   SG 12 August 1804, pla; 11 August 1805, p2a
64   Sophia Wood, NSWV 1804 1477 IA
65   SG 30 March 1806, ppl, 2, 3a; HRA, 1, 5, pp704-5; HRA, 1, 5, pp759-60
66   Letters Received Relating to Land, SRNSW 2/8010, Reel 1200, LW 3 June 1835; Email 28 March 2006, Margaret Betts to Janelle Cust
67   HRA, 1, 5, pp709-10
68   HRA 1, 6, pp 128, 712; CCJ, *Case Papers*, SRNSW 2/8134, pp281-370; SG 15 February 1807, p2a, b
69   NSW JA Rg., Bk 1, Pg 142, No 1098, ML A3609; Bk 8, Pg 145, No 1121; Pg 156, No 1186; Pg 147, ML A3617
70   Joseph Banks Papers, Correspondence Received by Joseph Banks from Bligh, 1805-1811, ML Series 40.109, CY 3007/484-7; Series 40.115 CY 3007/501-4; Series 40,116, CY 3007 /505-6; Series 40.092, CY 3007/401-5
71   Baxter, Carol J. ed, *Musters of New South Wales and Norfolk Island 1805-1806,* ABGR & Society of Australian Genealogists, Sydney, 1989, ppxii, 39, 42, 83, 86, 108, 114, 123 (AO772) 136-7, 138-9 (BO580) 140-1, 142, 160, 172, 181,244, 339. See index of family names for servants
72   Registers of Copies of Wills 1800-1901, SAG Will 1/2771

3 Settling at the Hawkesbury

73 NSW JA Rg., Bk 4, Pg 15, No 1465, ML A3610
74 Margaret Catchpole Papers 1797-1811, Letter of 8 October 1806, ML MSS 618
75 HRA 1, 5, pp606-7, 774-5
76 Musters 1805-1806. See Chapman p23 (A0772), pp138-9 (BO580); NSW JA Rg., ML A3610, Bk 3, Pg 5, Nos 34, 35
77 CCJ, Rough Minutes of Proceedings and Related Case Papers 4 July 1806-26 December 1809, SRNSW 2/8149, pp545-7; SG 14 August 1808, p2a,b
78 CCJ, Minutes of Proceedings, SRNSW 5/1102, July 1808
79 Fitzgerald, Ross, and Heam, Mark, *Bligh, Macarthur and the Rum Rebellion*, Kangaroo Press, Kenthurst, 1988 ch 5, ch 6, pp107-8 See Ref 2, pp217-37
80 HRA 6, pp280-1, 288, 337-8, 342
81 Joseph Banks Papers, Series 40,116 CY 3007 /505-6; HRNSW 6, opp p434 & opp p454
82 HRA I, 6, pp208, 214, 353-4
83 Parsons, 1988, ch I, pp 14, 16, 17; HRA 1, 7, pl30
84 HRA 1, 6, pp254, 260
85 HRNSW 6, p728; HRA 1, 6, pp653, 698
86 NSW JA Rg., Bk 2, Pg 11, No 22, ML A3610; SG 16 April 1809, p2b
87 Appeals from the decisions of the Court of Civil Jurisdiction, SRNSW SZ993, Reel 6037, p67
88 CCJ, Court of Appeals, Case Papers 1807-10, SRNSW xl984, pp183-212
89 CCJ, Minutes of Proceedings, SRNSW 5/1105, No 14
90 CCJ, Minutes of Proceedings, SRNSW 5/1102. See Addy, Medcalf, Foster, Dowling, etc.
91 Copies of Letters Sent by Lt Governor Foveaux to Governor Bligh 28 Jul 1808, SRNSW SZ760, Reel 6001, pl36b; Grants and Leases of Land, Bk 3c, Pgs 235, 236, 237, DL
92 HRA 1, 6, p703; SG 28 May 1814, p2d; Letters Relating to Land, SRNSW, 2/7892-93, Reel 1146, JJ Nov 1830; County of Cumberland, 1925, NSW Department of Lands, SRNSW
93 Grants and Leases of Land, Bk 4d, Pg 117, DL; County Cumberland, Parish Bringelly, Map 7, large; portion 31, DL
94 SG 26 September 1812, plc
95 SG 5 February 1809, p2a
96 Browning, Yvonne, *St Peters Richmond, The Early People and Burials 1791-1855*, Browning, Kurrajong, 1990, pl 7. The information in the Mutch Index on the location of Robert Faithfull's baptism is confusing; however according to Browning, the first baptisms at Richmond occurred on the 22 April 1810.
97 SG 16 April 1809, p2a

98   HRA I, 7, pp162, 174; SG 4 June 1809, p2a; 6 August 1809, p2a,b; HRNSW 7, p218
99   Special Bundles and Other Records, 1805-1823, Coroner's Inquests, SRNSW 4/1819, Reel 6021, pp611-12

4
SEALING IN THE SOUTHERN OCEAN

Sealers lived a harsh and dangerous life. Some were drowned, some were murdered by Maories, scurvy ate in to others. Many were marooned for months, even years, on islands bare of vegetation and often swept by spray. They waited out their sojourn destitute of articles which even the poor of Sydney would have considered necessitites.[1]

In February 1809, before the floods, Lucy Wood, Thomas Matcham Pitt and James Wilshire sold wheat to the government stores at Green Hills.[2] John Wood had joined the crew of the *Active*, a brig of 120 tons built about 1808 in Calcutta for Campbell, Clark and Company. Robert Campbell set up a branch of the firm in the colony in 1800.[3] The damaged *Active* returned from sealing in late July. The vessel had experienced:

many heavy gales, and sustained much damage from her being driven on shore at Western Point, which unfortunate event took place on 11th June; previous to which Captain Bader had procured about 1800 skins, many of which were lost.[4]

It was the earliest report of a boat stranded in Western Port Bay.[5] John did not wait for repairs to the Active.[6] (See Figure 9 for locations visited by the Active)

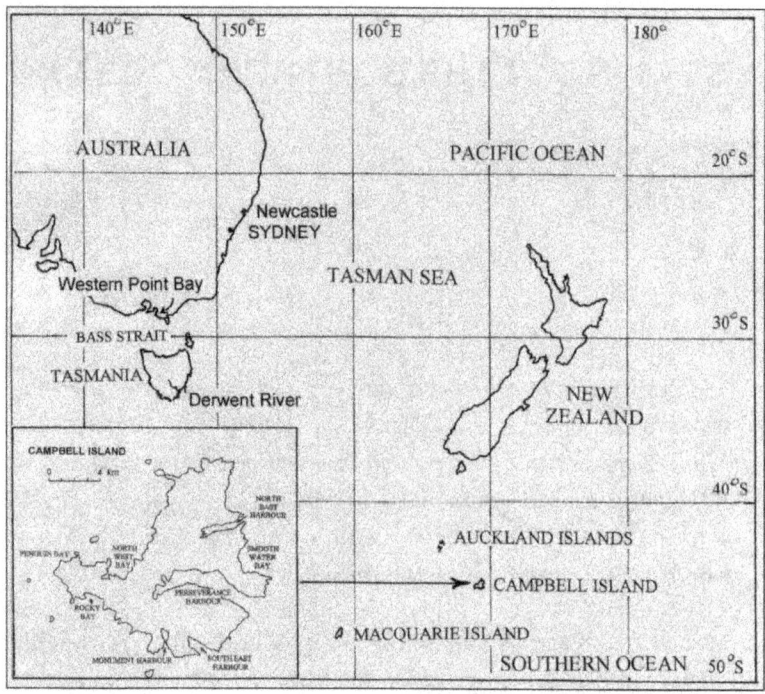

Figure 9. Southern Pacific and Southern Oceans locations of John Wood 1809-1812

On 30th September 1809 in Campbell's Cove on the western side of today's Circular Quay, John Wood signed on as second mate of the *Perseverance*, a brig of 136 tons built in the Sydney shipyards of Robert Campbell in 1807. (Figure 10) The Articles of Agreement bound the men in the service of Campbell for 18 months. During the period covered by the agreement, Charles Hook, part owner in Campbell's Company, managed the company while Campbell was a witness for Bligh at Johnston's court-martial in England.

Campbell agreed to pay £20 a ton of right whale oil or elephant seal oil, 6s for a salted skin of the fur seal and 3s for a salted skin of the hair seal. -(The skin of the fur seal and oil of the elephant seal and black whale were almost the only goods exported from the colony.) The men received a predetermined part of the whole gang's profits, John's share 1/40th, the 1st mate's 1/30th, the others between 1/80th and 1/100th. If either party breached the articles of agreement the penalty was £100.[7] The weekly rations, "minimal and an invitation to scurvy", included 7lbs of pork, 8lbs of bread or flour, and 11lbs of sugar.[8] The *Perseverance* sailed on 23rd October 1809 and with the sealing grounds in Bass Strait exhausted, Captain Frederick Hasselburg headed for the islands off the coast of New Zealand.[9] The crew of about 25 were "one of the most experienced sealing gangs ever to sail out of Port Jackson".[10]

Figure 10. Brig *Perseverance*

By the end of November 1809 the men were sealing at the Auckland Islands south of New Zealand. (See Figure 9 for locations visited by the *Perseverance*.) At the close of the year they left the Aucklands having made two crew changes. One change was important to John Wood: Miles Holding of the King George replaced first mate of the *Perseverance*, Phillip Goodenough. On 4th January 1810, about 280 miles from the southern coast of New Zealand, Hasselburg discovered an island which he charted and called Campbell for his employer. Roughly 20 miles long and five miles wide, the island had two relatively safe harbours, the southernmost and best of these named "Perseverance". Hasselburg left superviser John Wood and a gang of six men on the island. Their gruesome task involved seizing seals along the rocky coast, clubbing them to death, skinning them and boiling down their carcasses for oil.[11]

The *Perseverance* returned to Sydney Cove at the end of April 1810. It was 25th June before the ship sailed with instructions to "proceed direct for Campbell Island" to collect the oil and relieve John's party.[12] On 11th July 1810 Hasselburg sighted the "last vestige of land to be found in the vast expanse of the Southern Ocean to the south of Australia". He named the island "Macquarie" in honour of the colony's new Governor. Finding sea elephants teeming on the island, the captain decided to leave Miles Holding in charge of seven men with supplies intended for the men on the Campbell Island. On 18th July Hasselburg left Macquarie Island to get more men and supplies, the *Perseverance* docking at Port Jackson on 17th August. Three weeks later the ship sailed with a new gang of 15 men, under Articles dated 1st September 1810.[13] The captain was to leave the new gang on Macquarie Island:

> *thence proceed to Campbells (sic) Island to relieve the Gang you left there taking on board whatever oil they may have procured, with which you will return direct to Port Jackson, where if you can arrive before the Hunter is ready for Sea it will be of infinite advantage to the Concern, and you will upon no account suffer*

any new Discovery you may make in your Rout (sic) to induce you to deviate from the above instructions.[14]

On 2nd October 1810 the *Perseverance* reached Macquarie Island where the new gang worked alongside the gang that signed the articles dated 30th September. Hasselburgh sailed to Campbell Island on 17th.[15]

For about ten months John Wood and his gang endured isolation, deprivation and subantarctic conditions. The island was lashed by frequent "violent... salt-laden winds" and chilled by a mean yearly temperature of seven degrees Celsius. Their rations exhausted, the men existed on nesting sea birds for three or four months. Catching fish was too dangerous. Not surprisingly, "some friction" occurred between John Wood and Martin Bryant. Bryant was charged with mutinous conduct. John described the incident:

I was second officer on board the Brig Perseverance, Martin Bryant was Cooper. After sailing from this port, myself, the prisoner and some others were landed at Campbell Island for the purpose of procuring oil on the 4th of January 1810. I was overseer of the gang ... After some time all my provisions were expended and we provided for ourselves as well as we could in killing birds. I went upon some ground to kill birds and the prisoner sent a New Zealand boy to tell me if I did not get off that ground he would make me. We had afterwards a dispute about this boy in the hut, and he knocked me down. I struck him again in my defence. I never entered this transaction in my life. I did not report this transaction on my return to Mr Hook or make any complaint respecting it. It arose out of a private quarrel, nor was it attended with any detriment to my owners on the voyage.

The Bench acquitted Bryant probably on two grounds, the effect of the appalling conditions on the men and the plaintiff considering the dispute a private matter.[16]

Three people who arrived at Campbell Island in the *Perseverance* lost their lives. On Sunday 4th November 1810 Captain Hasselburg sailed the jollyboat about five miles to inspect oil casks. With him were Elizabeth Farr, his young female companion from Norfolk Island, the ship's carpenter James Bloodworth, 12-year old George Allwright, seaman Richard Jackson and a native New Zealand boy. On their way back a sudden gust of wind sunk the boat nearly two miles from the shore. Three drowned, Captain Hasselburg, Elizabeth Farr and George Allwright; Hasselburg's survival hindered by the thick "flushing boat coat" and "strong high water-boots" he wore to combat the cold. The three survivors "hailed the *Perseverance*" and the brig's second boat picked them up.[17] Robert Murray, sent to relieve John Wood, took command of the *Perseverance*. On 20th November 1810 the ship left Campbell Island with John's gang, plus 47 tons and 147 gallons of oil. They reached Port Jackson on 8th January 1811.[18] Four days later Campbell and Company advertised sea elephant oil in quantities of not less than 20 gallons. The *Hunter* had left for Calcutta in November 1810.[19]

With no one available to captain the *Perseverance* to Macquarie Island, Charles Hook sent Robert Murray to collect coal and cedar wood at the Coal River (Newcastle). John Wood was on the *Perseverance* when it left about 19th February 1811.[20] At the Coal River about 1st March, the *Perseverance* beached in the harbour on the sand spit known as Middle Ground, "where she lay for three days and nights broadside ... in a very perilous position". The commander of the penal settlement, Captain Purcell, mobilised the local boats and employed convicts to remove the ballast and float the vessel. Bearing little damage, the *Perseverance*, carrying 90 tons of coal and 12,000 feet of cedar, arrived at Port Jackson on 22nd March.[21] A seaman, who refused to keep watch at Newcastle, was sentenced to hard labour for 30 days in a gaol gang, his youth accounting for the light sentence.[22]

Once the Articles of Agreement expired on 30th March 1811, Miles Holding was asked to dismiss John Wood but he refused saying John needed alternate employment first. On 9th June 1811 the *Perseverance* left for Macquarie Island, with John second officer under Captain James Gordon and first officer Robert Murray. As a leak forced the *Perseverance* to stop for repairs at the Derwent River, they did not reach Macquarie Island until 25th or 26th September. The men loaded 35,740 of the 56,974 skins, jointly collected by the gangs landed by Hasselburg in July and October of 1810, before bad weather forced them to leave the island. The *Perseverance* arrived at Port Jackson on 31st October 1811. [23]

Campbell's company failed to settle the accounts of the men who signed the Articles of 30th September 1809. On 15th January 1812, John Wood, carpenter James Bloodworth, boatswain Jeremiah Harrigan and ten others took Robert Campbell's Company to the Court of Civil Jurisdiction presided over by judge-advocate, Gregory Blaxland. For John and all the men, the most contentious issue, the items making up their lay. John argued his 1/40th lay included:

> *a share of a quantity of Oil, Seal Skins & other substances or matters procured and brought to this port at different times by the Perseverance and the Mary and Sally (the Elizabeth and Mary?) ... by the articles ... bearing (the) date 30th Sept. 1809 in force for eighteen months.*

John presented three more claims: recovery of wages for his employment beyond the agreed 18 months; compensation for the lack of supplies on Campbell Island (usually remunerated at 10s a week); and £100 for his employer's breach of the Articles. In all, he sought £1250 sterling, £500 for services as a mariner and sealer, and £750 for damages. Defendant George Crossley, Campbell's solicitor, conceded John had a right to 1/40th share of 34,062 seal skins (Macquarie Island), 47 tons and 147 gallons of elephant oil (Campbell Island), 33 spars (Bay ofIslands), and £350 (Coal River, Newcastle). According to Crossley, for two years' work as a mariner and sealer, John had already received £358.19s.7d in approved bills, an overpayment of £50 or £60.[24]

To support his main claim John Wood relied on the testimony of Antony Keams. The seaman signed the first articles, sailed with the first gang, then landed on Macquarie Island with the second gang on 2nd October 1810. Keams stated at Macquarie Island Hasselburg said the two gangs from the *Perseverance* "were to be considered as one party, one gang ... he had the owners (sic) instructions to that affect". As well, Keams "heard Captain James Gordon ... say when he arrived (on 31st December 1810) that they were to be considered as one gang". Called by John to give evidence, Gordon disagreed, "The gang I carried down did not join with the gangs previously left there in the services of Mr Campbell. I did not take any provisions in the *Elizabeth and Mary* for these gangs". In answering a question put by John, Gordon said, "I have offered Wood the Plaintiff a lay upon the division of the skins procured by the two gangs, and upon the oil and other things". Miles Holding told the court, "I never sailed under two articles. I have never known it". Nevertheless, he criticised the shortage of provisions, saying the deficiency affected the number of skins collected. Merchants Henry Kahle, James Underwood and Simeon Lord backed Crossley on the separate payment of multiple gangs. On 17th January 1812 Alexander Riley delivered the verdict for John, £16 19s 9½d for damages and £2 4s 1 0d for costs.[25]

> *The New South Wales Court of Civil Jurisdiction may not have been insensitive to the injustices suffered by sealers. Suits against sealing masters seem to have received a sympathetic hearing and damages were awarded against their employers.*

However, it is usually difficult to establish which points they the sealers gained and which they lost, since they received only a portion of the damages they sort.[26]

In the months following the court case John Wood lost his life. Much later when trying to wind up John's estate, Lucy wrote:

John Wood took his departure from the Colony of NSW in prosecution of a voyage some time previous to the year 1811. That your petitioner has had various accounts from persons arriving in the Colony who were acquainted with the said John Wood and was in or about the year 1812 informed of his death.[27]

Hoping to discover more about John's death, the author examined the *Sydney Gazette* for movements of colonial vessels and accidents to seamen. The *Perseverance* sailed for Macquarie Island on 23rd February 1812 with further trips to the south on 4th July and 5th September, but it is unlikely John worked again for Campbell.[28] Other ships left in February, the *Boyd* for Norfolk Island, the *Concord* for Macquarie Island and England, and the *Mary and Sally* for Macquarie and Campbell Islands. The only accident reported in the relevant months involved the loss of five men from the *Mary and Sally* owned by widow, Sarah Wills.[29]

On 15th February 1812 the *Mary and Sally* set sail for Macquarie Island and Campbell Island. The ship reached Macquarie Island, via the Derwent River, on 20th March. Six men were left on Campbell Island.[30] Captain William Stewart of the *Cumberland* found the cooper of the gang, Henry Neale, exhausted on Campbell Island. Neale told Stewart, "he had been left two months entirely alone, the whole of his companions having gone in a boat on some excursion from which they returned no more". Stewart passed the news to Joseph Murrell, captain of the *Elizabeth and Mary*, in Twofold Bay. Murrell arrived at Sydney Cove by 27th June with "the melancholy information". This mostly undated sequence of events suggests the five lost their lives in April or early May.[31] The *Cumberland* brought Henry Neale, to Port Jackson on 3rd July. The *Mary and Sally* arrived with a cargo of black whale oil on 17th September 1812.[32] On 4th October 1812 Lucy organized a service to commemorate John's death.[33]

1	Hainsworth, D, R., *The Sydney Traders, Simeon Lord and His Contemporaries 1788-1821*, Cassell Australia, Melbourne, 1972, ch 9, pp146-7
2	Vouchers and Weekly Returns of the Government Storekeeper, Nov 1808-Nov 1810, SRNSW 9/2673, Reel 6040, pp5, 7, 14, 33, 61
3	John Wood NSW Vol 7, No 80; SG 29 February 1812, plc; HRA 1, 2 p548; HRA 1, 4, p668
4	SG 30 July 1809, plc
5	Woodley, Arthur E., *Western Port Wrecks and Maritime Mishaps*, Brown, Prior Anderson, Pty, Ltd., Burwood, Victoria, 1992, pl
6	SG 12 November 1809, p2c
7	Cumpston, J.S., *Macquarie Island,* ANARE Scientific Reports, Government Printing office, Canberra, 1968, ch 1, pp1-2
8	CCJ, Minutes of Proceedings 1788-1814, 6 January 1812-24 April 1812, SRNSW 5/1107, Pt 12, p13; Hainsworth, D.R., *The Sydney Traders, Simeon Lord and His Contemporaries 1788-1821*, Cassell Australia, Melbourne, 1972, ch 9, p144
9	CCJ, Minutes of Proceedings 1788-1814, 6 January 1812-24April 1812, SRNSW 5/1107, Pt 12, pl0; Kerr, Ian, *Campbell Island: A History*, AH. and AW. Reed, Wellington, 1976, ch 2, p7
10	Cumpston, 1968, ch 1, p3
11	Kerr, 1976, chs 1, pp1-3; ch 2, pp 7-9, 12; SG 5 January 1811, p3a,b
12	Cumpston, 1968, chl, p4; The Hook Letter Book, ML MSS Set 109, FM 3/64, p6, Letter of 19 June 1810
13	Cumpston, 1968, chl, ppl, 5, 6
14	The Hook Letter Book, ML MSSSet 109, FM 3/64, p14; Cumpston, 1968, chl, p4
15	Cumpston, 1968, chl, pp6,7
16	Kerr, 1976, ch 1, pp 2-4, ch 2, pp12-3, Appendix A, p152
17	SG 12 January 1811, p2a,b,c
18	Cumpton, 1968, p8; CCJ, SRNSW 5/1107, Pt 12, pl0
19	SG 24 November 1810, p2b
20	The Hook Letter Book. ML MSS Set 109, FM 3/64, p32, Letter of 19 February 1811 to Robert Murray; CCJ, SR NSW 5/1107, Pt 12, pll

4 Sealing in the Southern Ocean

21 Letters Received-Newcastle 1804-1812, SRNSW 4/1804, Reel 2185, p64
22 SG 13 April 1811, p2a
23 SG 18 May 1811, p2c; SG 7 September 1811, p2a; 2 November 1811, p2b; SG 2 November 1811, p2b; CCJ, SRNSW 5/1107, Pt 12, ppl l, 12, 14
24 CCJ, SRNSW 5/1107, Pt 12, pp9-12. I could not find the number of litres in a ton of seal oil
25 CCJ, SRNSW 5/1107, Pt 12, ppl2-7; Pt 20; Cumpston 1868, p9
26 Hainsworth 1972, p146
27 Probate Case Papers 1812-1827, SRNSW 6/4188, Reel 952
28 SG 29 February 1812, p2a; 9 May 1812 plc; SG 1 Aug 1812, p2a; SG 5 September 1812, p2a; Cumpston, 1968, p26
29 *Index to Sydney Gazette*, Vol 16, p4475; HRA 1, 7, p648
30 SG 15 February 1812, p2a; SG 9 May 1812, plc
31 27 June 1812, p2a
32 Cumpston, 1968, chl, p25; SG 19 September 1812, p2a
33 John Wood, NSWVol 7, No 80

5
CONTRIBUTIONS TO MACQUARIE'S REFORMS

Lieutenant Colonel Lachlan Macquarie became the fifth governor of the Colony of New South Wales on New Year's Day in 1810. He arrived in the colony with his wife Elizabeth (Figures 11 & 12) and his own regiment, and the controversial NSW Corps returned to England. Macquarie found the colony in a deplorable state. He discovered agriculture "in a yet languishing state", "commerce in its early dawn", "the public buildings in a state of decay", and "the few Roads and bridges formerly constructed, rendered almost impassable". And he noticed a population "threatened by famine", "depressed by poverty" and "distracted by faction".[1] Macquarie tackled each of these problems, his building programme especially remarkable. He completed roads, bridges, wharves, churches, schools and charitable institutions, and found ten new towns, including Richmond and Windsor.[2] Noteworthy too, his wish to be the "friend and protector of the honest, sober and industrious inhabitant, whether Free Settler or Convict".[3] Members of the Pitt Family contributed to several of Macquarie's reforms. They also met the Governor and his wife on social occasions.

Macquarie declared invalid the land grants distributed after Bligh's arrest since many went to "persons very undeserving of

Figure 11. Lachlan Macquarie

Figure 12. Elizabeth Henrietta Macquarie

them", although he intended honouring those given from "motives of impartiality and justice".[4] In a shared memorial highlighting their connection to Horatio Nelson, Jemima Pitt, James Wilshire, William Faithfull and Thomas Pitt sought affirmation of their grants received under interim governors Foveaux and Paterson. The Governor confirmed the grants on 1st January 1810.[5] William was "induced to purchase" a further 100 acres, probably his home acres, which he had "cultivated and improved".[6] In September 1810 Thomas Williams loaned William £42 for two months.[7]

Macquarie asked James Wilshire to take charge of the Government Stores at Windsor. To compensate him for income foregone from his tanning and soap concerns, James requested a position as magistrate at Windsor. The post was promised when available.[8] He left for Windsor about February 1810, then at the end of April, Macquarie appointed him Deputy Commissary in Sydney.[9] His salary of £91 5s compared unfavourably with the £150 he paid leather currier, Thomas Cosgrove.[10] While working in Windsor, James's servants in George Street embezzled "upwards of £400".[11] To cushion the loss he chased up an outstanding debt and borrowed money. William Addy agreed to supply James with 20 bushels of wheat. In August 1808 James arrived at the wharf to collect the wheat which he found contaminated with oats and grass seed. He sued Addy for £9 in the Court of Civil Jurisdiction in September 1810. John Redmond, in whose boat the grain arrived, testified the wheat "was very bad indeed". He added, when no one would buy the grain it was "sent back to Addy but he would not receive it". James recovered his £9.[12] In October 1810 James borrowed 12s 3d from Thomas Markwell and £9 1s from Ansley Magrath; the loans payable in three months.[13]

Jemima Pitt wed Austin Alexander Forrest in Richmond on 18th April 1810. With the combined schoolhouse and church not complete until 1812, the marriage probably took place in a temporary building or in Jemima's home. The Reverend Robert Cartwright conducted the ceremony, witnessed by Thomas Matcham Pitt and James Wilshire.[14] The couple married by licence for which Macquarie set the fees at three guineas for the clergyman, £1 0s 6d for the clerk and 5s for the sexton.[15]

Austin, a sea captain, was "an officer of distinguished merit and ability in the East India Company". After retiring he worked for the Calcutta-based company of merchant and shipowner, Robert Campbell. In 1800 he made his first trip to the colony as master and part-owner of the *Hunter*. Campbell came with Austin in the *Hunter* to settle in the colony.[16] Between 1805 and 1808 Austin captained Campbell's ships, the *Sophia, Duchess of York* and the *Sydney*. The ships carried sandalwood, rice, seal oil and skins to and from Bengal, Canton, Fiji, Sydney, Norfolk Island, Bass Strait, the Derwent River and Port Dalrymple (Launceston).[17] As well, he conducted charters for Governor King.[18] Austin settled in the colony after arriving in the *Hibernia* in March 1809.[19] Days after marrying, Austin received £205 for two 80 acre lots at the Field of Mars, east of Parramatta; land granted to Governor John Hunter.[20] Austin bought Swilly Farm, a 100 acres lying on the east side of the Nepean River, just south of the junction of the Hawkesbury and Grose Rivers.[21] (Figure 3) There, Jemima and Austin made their home close by the Woods, Pitts and Faithfulls.

In November 1810 Governor and Elizabeth Macquarie began a tour of the colony's outer settlements. On 30th the Macquaries viewed "the noble River Hawkesbury" at the junction of the Nepean and Grose Rivers, beside the Woods' farm, and "were highly gratified with the sight". The Governor noted where the "Hawkesbury commences ... it is only an inconsiderable stream, and not navigable even for small boats for three or four miles farther down". In the evening the Macquaries camped at the northern end of the Yellow-Mundie-Lagoon. (Figure 3, See Yarramundi Lagoon) The next morning Austin Forrest and several local people joined the Macquaries for breakfast.[22] On the following day, 1st December, Thomas Matcham

Pitt and William Faithfull and other Hawkesbury settlers presented the Governor with an address, congratulating him on his settlement in the colony and thanking him for appointing district magistrate, William Cox.[23]

On the morning of 5th December 1810, Lachlan and Elizabeth Macquarie visited the homes of Mrs Mary Pitt, Mrs Jemima Forrest, Mrs Rebecca Cox, wife of magistrate William Cox and Mrs Jennett Evans, wife of surveyor George Evans.[24] The next day Macquarie selected the site for the township, naming it Richmond after Richmond Hill.[25] (Figure 3) The town was situated on the edge of Ham Common, flood-free ground of more than 5,000 acres set aside for public grazing in 1804.[26] Now Hawkesbury Agricultural College occupies the site. Late in December Macquarie gave surveyor James Meehan guidelines to lay out the streets in Richmond.[27] Macquarie returned to identify sites for the burial ground, church and schoolhouse in January 1811. In February he told Samuel Marsden to consecrate the burial ground as soon as possible.[28] The Reverends Marsden and Cartwright held a meeting to consider erecting the schoolhouse on 18th April. Thomas Matcham Pitt and Austin Forrest attended and both joined the committee. Thomas, Austin and William Faithfull donated money to the building fund.[29]

In September 1811 Lucy Wood sold a house in York Street to William Bagley for £50, the deed witnessed by James Wilshire.[30] Two months later Lucy witnessed a deed James made with William Stewart, buyer of his house in Castlereagh Street in 1805 and captain of the *Cumberland* who found cooper Henry Neale languishing on Campbell Island in 1812. The deed involved Stewart's sloop the *Fly*, with both parties bound to perform "several covenants" for £200.[31] Both men broke the contract and each presented a case to the Court of Civil Jurisdiction. James claimed Stewart owed him £110 10s 7d for "a considerable part" of the wages of the men employed on the *Fly* and for articles supplied, and repairs to the vessel. He admitted owing Stewart £26. William Stewart argued that once James took possession of the *Fly*, he lost opportunities to undertake trips to the Hawkesbury in the grain season and to Bass Strait for seal skins. James won £84 0s 6d, Stewart £60.[32] In the same year and court, James succeeded in four more cases. Plaintiff Thomas Piers Newsham declared his bullock, valued at £40, "came into the hands" of the James who "wrongfully converted it to his own use". The court found James bought the bull. Plaintiff James won £7 14s 6d from William Burgess for goods he sold to the defendant's wife. Defendants John Eyre and Ansley Magrath failed to pay James for promissory notes, Eyre owing £10 10s and Magrath £9 1s.[33] James attended to three other matters in 1811. He raised a bond of £50 for the schooner *Thomas Geordy* delivering troops and stores to Hobart Town.[34] He paid Christopher Airey £19 16s 4d for a farm of 80 acres at Seven Hills.[35] He asked the colonial secretary to supply convict workers for the tannery, particularly a currier to dress and colour leather.[36]

Meanwhile in May 1811 Jemima and Austin Forrest lost one-month-old daughter, Eliza May. In late September Robert Campbell told Austin that Macquarie had "no objection to making a grant of 400 acres of Land on the western side of the Hawkesbury".[37] In November the Forrests informed the public they planned to leave the colony, but before departing a second tragedy occurred.[38] On his way home from Windsor on Christmas Eve, Austin suffered fatal injuries when his horse threw him to the ground near Swilly Farm. At his funeral on the 27th December,

> *a large company of gentlemen assembled, among whom were the Commanders of the India Vessels in port and the principal Merchants to pay the last duties of respect to a highly respectable and meritorious character.*[39] 39

Austin, aged about 48, lies beside Eliza in St Matthew's Cemetery in Windsor. He died without a will. James Wilshire helped Jemima manage his estate.[40]

In honour of Austin, Esther and James Wilshire named their third son Austin Forrest Wilshire. He was born on 15th September 1811 and baptised on 5th March 1812 at St Philip's, Sydney. On the day of Austin's baptism, the Reverend William Cowper conducted a service for Esther, The Thanksgiving of Women after Childbirth. Commonly called The Churching of Women, the service consisted of a psalm and prayer.[41] James Wilshire retired from the Commissariat on 31st March 1812.[42] James's entry in the *Australian Dictionary of Biography* states he had to resign because of his business interests.[43] The author found no evidence for this assertion. Perhaps he resigned because, in reorganising the Commissariat, the London Treasury suspended the pay of officers from 8th January to 31st March 1812 and downgraded the positions and salaries of senior officers.[44] On 3rd January 1812, "to extricate him from impending difficulties", James sold a house on land measuring 290 feet by 45 feet at the south-west corner of his property for £109.[45] "Bred to the business in England", James dedicated himself to his tannery, leather in demand for boots, shoes, clothing, harnesses and saddlery.[46]

Thomas Matcham Pitt was the last of Mary Pitt's Australianbased children to marry. On 15th February 1813 at St John's Parramatta, by licence Thomas wed Elizabeth Laycock, daughter of Thomas Laycock, and Hannah Laycock, nee Pearson.[47] The Reverend Samuel Marsden conducted the marriage in the presence of witnesses, James Wilshire and Rebecca Laycock, Elizabeth's sister. Hannah and Thomas Laycock, Quartermaster in the NSW Corps, arrived with their five children in the *Gorgon* in 1791. Elizabeth was born in the colony in June 1796, the year her father and William Faithfull engaged in the pig-shooting incident.[48]

The Laycocks sent William, Samuel, Elizabeth and Rebecca to England for their education. From Clement's Inn in London in September 1801, Isaac Clementson, guardian of Elizabeth and Rebecca, wrote to D' Arcy Wentworth, "tell Mr Laycock his two girls are hearty and well". In April 1802 William Balmain also wrote to Wentworth from London, "tell Laycock's family I kissed his two daughters they are delightful girls and the boys was (sic) very well a few days ago when I heard from them".[49] Elizabeth and Rebecca returned to the colony with their mother in the *Canada* in September 1810. Meanwhile, the girls' father had died in Pitt's Row (Pitt Street) in December 1809.[50] On the afternoon of 13th December 1810, Governor Macquarie rested for half an hour at the "very neat comfortable well built farmhouse" of Mrs Laycock and her two daughters. The Laycocks were at King's Grove on 500 acres Governor King granted to Hannah.[51] Thomas and Elizabeth Pitt settled on the 200 acres at Richmond Hill. The year before they married, each received a grant 100 acres at Kurrajong, giving George 400 acres to farm.[52]

On 22nd March 1813, by licence, Samuel Marsden married Jemima Forrest and Robert Jenkins of Sydney, at St John's Parramatta with Lucy Wood and Captain Eber Bunker as witnesses. Robert was "attached to Miss Pitt" before she married Austin.[53] Robert was born in 1777 to Robert Jenkins and Mary Jenkins, formerly Warren, who married at St Martin in the Fields, Westminster, London on 29th August 1776.[54] Robert was "a good classical scholar", "conversant with five languages".[55] In July 1809 he arrived in the *Atalanta* to represent London merchant William Wilson.[56] Robert replaced Wilson's former agent, Robert Campbell. Reverend Henry Fulton told Mrs Bligh he suspected Campbell, who supported Bligh, lost the agency after rebels Lieutenant William Minchin and Surveyor Charles Grimes reached London with Johnston's despatches.[57]

In Sydney Cove and at the Hawkesbury, Robert Jenkins sold the *Atalanta*'s cargo which he stored in a warehouse in High Street

(George Street).⁵⁸ Soon he had debts to recover in the Court of Civil Jurisdiction. Robert won cases against: William Kelly for a loan, £100; Michael Hayes for delivered goods, £98 18s 10d; William Hibbart for goods, £20 13s; John Williams for goods, £108 9s 5d; Thomas Sanders for promissory notes, £16; and John White for property, £261 18s 10d. He lost to Thomas Abbott for Treasury bills worth £6 drawn by the paymaster of the 102ⁿᵈ Regiment. In Robert's absence his clerk accepted the Treasury bills, then left the colony!⁵⁹ Robert completed three financial transactions in 1810. In February he gave Henry Kable junior a promissory note for £464 9s 10d.⁶⁰ In June he bought 100 acres at Bankstown for £50.⁶¹ In August he received a loan of £882 from William Gaudry and Henry Kable senior. The loan was for Gaudry's new stone house in George Street, next door to Robert Campbell's establishment beside Sydney Cove, plus property in George Street, land in Chapel Row and 146 cattle.⁶²

In early July 1811, Alexander Bodie, captain and one-eighth owner of the *Frederick*, summoned Robert Jenkins to the Civil Court of Jurisdiction to recover £801 8s 1d. Three owners of the *Frederick* gave fourth owner William Wilson "certain sums" to buy the ship and "a large consignment of goods". After the *Frederick* docked in Sydney Cove on 20ᵗʰ October 1810, Bodie and Robert sold the goods, Bodie at the Derwent, Robert in Sydney on commission. Wilson received all the money, except £801 8s 1d. Robert admitted the debt, possibly caused by Wilson's bankruptcy announced in the *Sydney Gazette* in early August 1811. ("The failure of his agent Mr William Wilson" deprived James Wilshire of three years salary.⁶³) Making matters worse, Bodie lost his sanity in November 1810. At his home in Pitt Street, Robert held a meeting of the medical board which decided the Reverend Marsden, Bodie's brother William and Robert would take control of Bodie's property.⁶⁴ Robert asked Eber Bunker to sail the *Frederick* south to get oil "for the benefit of the owners". The ship left on 30ᵗʰ November 1810 but had not returned before the court case in early July 1811. Robert asked the court to delay payment of debt, or part of it, until Bunker's arrival. Reconvened in late July, the court ordered Robert to pay as soon as possible. By then Bodie had recovered.[65] Robert collected Wilson's debts and put Pitt Street on the market.[66] He set up his own mercantile business.

On 29th November 1811 Robert Jenkins wrote to his mother and sister who were staying in London. General Joseph Holt, "a Protestant Irishman who headed a party of insurgents to defend his country during the Irish Rebellion of 1798", agreed to deliver the letter as he was about to leave for England in the *Isabella*. Shipwrecked on the voyage, Holt did not reach London for two years after the letter was written. Robert began the letter by describing two jobs he had undertaken:

> *The arrival of Captain Brooks here with a cargo from India induced me to offer him my services, which he gladly accepted. Captain Brooks is a very illiterate man, therefore my assistance was to him of first-rate importance, as I conducted the whole of his concerns, introduced my own connections to him, and finally wound up his affairs, amounting to seventeen thousand pounds, by accounting to a penny. For these services I met but a poor reward. Captain B ... allowed me one hundred pounds only for my exertions for ten months.*

The task for Brooks complete, Robert was managing Mr Hannibal Macarthur's cargo which had arrived in the *Isabella*. "Shabbily used" by Brooks, he appreciated "some hundreds of pounds" promised by Macarthur. Robert explained his reasons for remaining in the colony:

> *You will perhaps be surprised to hear me talk of making a home in such a terrible country as New South Wales, but I receive such unfavourable intelligence from England that I really conceive I*

am better here, where I am well known and know everybody, and am well-respected.

He summarized his household arrangements, "I rent a large, handsome house fronting the Harbour. (Obviously, he had moved to Gaudry's place.) My domestics are one convict man and a little boy, a clerk-quite a bachelor's life". He closed the letter with pleasing news. The Court of Civil Jurisdiction had appointed him to audit the accounts of Lord Kable and James Underwood, "an office requiring a man of the soundest judgment and strictest integrity". The "herculean labour" of inspecting "all their books and accounts for eight years back" would take him about six months and earn him about £200 or £300.[67] Robert did not tell his family of his work as a juror, foreman and coroner at inquests.[68] Holt described Robert as "altogether a picturesque figure in early Sydney".[69] (Figure 13)

On New Year's Day 1813, the citizens of Sydney, Parramatta, Windsor and Liverpool presented addresses to mark the third anniversary of Lachlan Macquarie's rule. Robert Jenkins helped frame the Sydney address which praised the Governor's "just, wise, and liberal administration", abundance of food and other goods, construction of roads and townships and "improved system of police". The authors also advised the Governor to develop an export trade and reconsider Government Stores' current method of tender.[70] To commemorate the same occasion, Robert hosted a dinner at his home on 29th January 1813. He erected a roomy tent in the "fancifully decorated" front garden and displayed the British colours. "Nearly 150 gentlemen of the first respectability" sat at tables arranged in an oblong shape attended by Robert and Thomas Matcham Pitt, and other stewards. The band of Macquarie's 73rd Regiment played during the "excellent dinner". Guests toasted the King, Prince Regent, Queen, the rest of the Royal Family, Governors Phillip and Macquarie, religion and virtue, commerce and agriculture, and the intended library.[71] The house at the edge of Sydney Cove was a perfect setting for the occasion.

Figure 13. Robert Jenkins

In July 1813 Governor Macquarie appointed Robert Jenkins one of two magistrates to sit in rotation at the Court of Civil Jurisdiction, which met in Macquarie Street in the new Sydney Infirmary (later Sydney Hospital).[72] Previously, Robert successfully prosecuted several men in this court. For debts resulting from the sale of goods or the issue of promissory notes, he won £5 16s from Thomas Legg, £30 from Thomas Wheeler, £84 0s 4d from William Gore the Provost Marshall, £17 2s 4d from William Jenkins, £33 6s 6d from Charles McIntosh, £11 11s 1d from William Barns, and £41 2s 7d from John Hodges. As well, Captains of the 73rd Regiment, Hugh John Cameron and John Pike had to pay him around £36 and £32, respectively. Hugh John Cameron, on his second appearance, owed £25 6s 8d. Robert also revived and won a previous judgement against John Sanders for £17 14s 4d. The court dismissed Robert's cases against mariners William Parker of England and late of Sydney, and Thomas Folger of Sydney.[73] In July 1813 too, Governor Macquarie consented to Robert taking over Simeon Lord's role of government auctioneer and appraiser, a position he held until 1816.[74]

Unfortunately for the Jenkins, William Gaudry was in financial difficulty. The Court of Civil Jurisdiction ordered the auction of 2 George Street, and although offered on 1st October 1813 it did not sell until at least November 12th.[75] That day, Robert Jenkins bought 11 George Street from merchant Henry Kable.[76] (Macquarie numbered the houses and gave existing and new streets and lanes the names many bear today.[77]) Kable described his property:

> *a commodious Dwelling House with detached kitchen and out-offices, good stable, large granaries, roomy and substantial store-houses, a front retail warehouse and every other convenience suited to a commercial house, the whole in complete repair.*[78]

The home stood on the western side of George Street, bounded on the south by the walled gaol, and on the north by Surrey Lane, which provided access to the houses perched on the rocky slopes above. The lane, which no longer exists, lay under the railway overpass in lower George Street. Jemima and Robert still enjoyed a view of the harbour.

Robert Jenkins completed other property deals around 1813-14. He received a grant of 500 acres in Airds (Campbelltown district).[79] By means unknown, he acquired the 500 acre grant of Charles Fraser in present Chester Hills.[80] He paid Thomas Wheeler £37 for 35 acres alongside the Nepean at Castlereagh.[81] And he traded several properties with cooper William Mannix. Robert sold Mannix one-third and one-sixth parts of post miles (for docking?) at Cockle Bay for £166 13s 4d and £83 6s 8d, respectively. Next, Mannix sold Robert a house on three-quarters of an acre next to Cockle Bay together with a horse called Bobby, cart and harness, stoves, iron hooks, and other articles, all for £250. Lucy Wood witnessed this deed. Curiously, a little later Robert sold Mannix the same Cockle Bay house for £129 6s 2d. Finally, Mannix paid Robert £400 for an unfinished house and outhouses on the corner of George and King Streets.[82]

A general muster took place in October and November 1814, but the land and stock returns have not survived. Inhabitants of the Windsor district assembled at the Windsor Government Stores, the free men of Richmond on 17th October. Land-holders Thomas Matcham Pitt and William Faithfull each had four convicts. In the year of the census, William put his two 25 acre grants in present Ashfield on the market.[83] He also exchanged his less-than-fertile 1000 acres at Liberty Plains for 600 acres at Bunbury Curran in the Campbelltown area and 500 acres named Jordan Hill next to the western bank of South Creek in today's Llandilo.[84] The free women of Richmond gathered for the muster on 20th October with Mary Pitt, Lucy Wood and Elizabeth Pitt arriving together. The women reported their children by number. Lucy acknowledged two children, George, 12 and Sophia, 10. Elizabeth identified one child, George Matcham Pitt born in Richmond on 16th February 1814, his baptism not sighted. Susannah Faithfull stated she had three children, William, 8, Alice Faithfull, born in Richmond on 8th January 1811, and George Faithfull, born on 5th January 1814, probably in Ashfield.[85] The christening of Alice took place on 8th June 1811 at St Matthew's Windsor. On 13th Marnh 1814 at St Philip's, Sydney, the Reverend Cowper baptised George. Cowper also conducted The Churching of Women service for Susannah at which the death of four-year-old Robert Faithfull in August 1812 would occupy her thoughts.

The people of Sydney attended the muster at the Charity School in Castlereagh Street. Robert Jenkins joined the free men and convicts with tickets-of-leave on 9th November 1814. Jemima Jenkins assembled with the free women no longer dependent on stores on 14th November. The Jenkins had five workers, three convict men at Richmond and a free clerk and a convict woman in Sydney. Though born on 26th January 1814, the muster did not list Jemima's first child, Robert Pitt Jenkins. The Reverend Cowper baptised Robert at St Philip's, Sydney, on 20th March. That day, Cowper also performed The Churching of Women service for Jemima.[86] The Wilshires are not in muster although their servants, one convict woman and nine convict men, turned up as their absence "was to be punished with the utmost severity".[87] The year of the muster, and during the rest of the Macquarie era, the five Pitt families delivered many pounds of meat and bushels of wheat to Government Stores.[88]

At muster time Esther Wilshire was pregnant with her fifth child and James Wilshire managed the largest tannery in the colony.[89] The busy couple advertised for a man to undertake plain cooking and gardening in November 1813.[90] Making and selling leather involved several competencies. To begin, James organized a supply of skins and hides, which he sourced from butchers, graziers and his own farms. (On the subject of James's farms, he advertised the sale or lease of the two 40 acre farms at Seven Hills.[91] It appears he sold the farms and replaced them with nine adjacent farms ranging from 30 to 80 acres close to Salt Pan Creek. The creek empties into the George's River.[92]) Next he applied the skills of a fellmonger, chiefly to remove hair from the skins. Then he treated the raw hides with tannin to convert them to leather. Following that he used the skills of a currier to dress and colour the leather. He made soap with the tallow from butchered animals and created glue from soaked scraps of leather. Finally he faced stiff competition in selling his leather, shoes and other wares. In 1814 he had four retail outlets, the house of Bernard Burn in Pitt Street, Longford's place in Parramatta, the property of William Bennett in George Street and R. Lack's shop at 30 Cambridge Street.[93] Also, James, happily exchanged his goods for animal skins, and for spirits and imported goods with sea captains.[94] Macquarie's regiment wore his boots, their price of 8s 6d a pair comparing favourably with the usual 12s charged by shoemakers.[95] Esther also had heavy workload with the birth of her fifth child on 27th February 1815. She named her second daughter Elizabeth Mary Wilshire at her christening at St Johns, Parramatta, on 15th May.

At the Court of Civil Jurisdiction James Wilshire prosecuted customers who failed to pay for goods and return money. From George Crossley he won £12 19s for money and from Laurence May of Windsor £16 14s for goods and money. May insisted he did not receive the goods. However, witness William Beard testified that he weighed the sole leather in the shop and, just before the court case, he heard May offer to pay Mr Pitt. James also won £24 19s 4d from David McKay for sugar and soap and £5 12s from James Derbyshire for soap. On the other hand, William Foster of Lane Cove served James with a writ of £50 for failing to reimburse him for some cows. The plaintiff could not prove his case.[96]

In July 1815 Mrs Mary Reiby announced the sale or lease of her property in Macquarie Street (now Reiby Place) occupied by Robert Jenkins.[97] She also leased Robert a warehouse and house at 99 George Street for two years at £150 a quarter.[98] Clearly, the Jenkins were renovating their place in George Street. Robert sold a wide range of local and imported items such as houses, farms, boats, glass, iron, carpet, textiles, clothing, books, soap, tobacco, alcohol, foodstuffs (tea, Cheshire cheese, spices) and pearl shells and pork from the Society Islands.[99] In the last quarter of 1815, he paid custom duties of almost £30 for imported goods.[100] Cart owners Robert Jenkins and James Wilshire also paid licence fees to defray the cost of the Gaol and Female Orphan School.[101]

Mary Pitt, aged 67, died in the Wilshires' home on 7th November 1815. The funeral service took place on 10th at St Philips, Sydney. Mary was probably buried in the Old Sydney Burial Ground, located where the Town Hall stands.[102] Mary

> *lived highly respected by all who had been gratified in her acquaintance; and died in the arms of her family, in whose remembrance her maternal care and tender solicitude will ever remain a theme of grateful contemplation.*[103]

In 1804, the year before Admiral Lord Nelson died at Trafalgar, he wrote to George Mateham from H.M.S. Victory, "I hope our other friends and relations arrived at last, if not there is long ago an end to all their cares". Nelson enclosed a letter just received from Governor King.[104] Mary's cares had probably ceased. Her children had married, although Lucy was widowed. Mary had 12 surviving grandchildren with a 13th grandchild arriving on the day of her death. Fittingly, Elizabeth and Thomas Matcham Pitt christened their daughter, Mary Matcham Pitt, on 17th December 1815.

In January 1816 Robert Jenkins was appointed a juror in the Governor's Court, his position renewed several times.[105] In this court a deputy judge-advocate and two jurors dealt with claims less than £50 sterling with no right of appeal.[106] Robert and James Wilshire filed cases in the Governor's Court. Some case papers and unrelated judgments survive for Robert. He alleged Daniel Humm, Sergeant of the Veterans Company at Parramatta, owed £30 for goods, William Sherwin of Parramatta £30 for a promissory note and John Norman of Windsor £35 also for a promissory note. Verdicts favouring Robert included Abraham Whittaker for £49 18s 2d, Thomas Clarkson for £5, Joseph Salter for £25, Mary McMahon for £20, Walter Shutt for £34 12s 4d and Joseph Allan for £47.[107] Some case papers and all judgements exist for the lawsuits of James. Plaintiff James won £31 7s from John Howe, £9 1s from Edward Lamb, £26 from John Harris and £16 17s 4d from John Beattie. Beattie had to make two pairs of shoes in a "good workmanlike manner" each week until he paid the debt. Defendant James lost three cases involving promissory notes, £30 to victualler Joshua Holt, £20 to baker James Harman and £27 12s to merchant Robert Campbell Jnr.[108] In the new Supreme Court of Civil Jurisdiction a judge and two magistrates handled claims over £50.[109] In this court Robert Jenkins won cases for unpaid goods, £132 1s 5d from Robert Walton a dealer of Parramatta, £230 from Thomas Gilberthorpe, a farmer of Pitt Town, £100 from Elizabeth Gray a widow of Sydney, and £80 4s 3d from William Fenton of Launceston.[110]

The *Sydney Gazette* announced the birth of the second son of Jemima and Robert Jenkins in George Street on 11th July 1816.[111] He was baptised William Warren Jenkins at St Philips.on 18th August. The couple sought household help, a woman to cook and clean, and a man to drive a cart and clean knives and shoes.[112] Notices Robert placed in the *Sydney Gazette* suggest the birth of William took place in Mary Reiby's five bedroom home at 99 George Street. In April 1816 he informed the public they had moved to 99 George Street after Mrs Reiby returned to Macquarie Street.[113] In March 1817 he announced they had moved to their own premises.[114] During the final months of renovations at 11 George Street, Robert played an important role in setting up the colony's first bank.

In the early months of his administration Macquarie wanted to establish a Colonial Government Bank but the Home Government rejected his proposal.[115] In 1813 the Governor organized coinage for the Colony, a holey dollar worth 5s and a dump worth 15d. Created from the centres and outer rings of silver Spanish dollars, the coins began circulating on the 30th September.[116] Dissatisfied with these arrangements, 17 Sydney traders, aiming to "tackle the currency situation by a kind of 'petty banking'", held the first meeting of the Sydney Commercial Society on 18th October. Robert Jenkins and James Wilshire were on the committee, Robert Vice-President. On 17th November, Macquarie issued a proclamation which "forbade unlicensed assemblies of more than six people, (and) declared it illegal to refuse promissory notes ... or to influence the rate of exchanges between currency and sterling." Forbidden to meet, the Commercial Society issued its own notes, stopping only in 1816 when Macquarie banned all currency notes.[117]

Macquarie invited a group of magistrates, principal merchants, and other gentlemen to address the currency issue at a meeting on 22nd November 1816. Robert Jenkins received an invitation.[118] The meeting approved seven resolutions, the chief ones founding a Colonial Subscription Bank and introducing sterling currency. Needing a minimum of £20,000 to fund the bank, subscribers of £100 were rewarded with the right to vote. One of nine original subscribers, Robert gave £200, the price of two shares.[119] Introducing sterling had implications for the price of labour and the average wage rate. Robert Jenkins, Thomas Matcham Pitt, James Wilshire and others discussed these issues on 25th November at a meeting chaired by Macquarie.[120] Following the meeting Robert sent the Governor an estimate of the cost to keep a convict in food and clothes for a year, £22 2s 4d.[121] Days later a meeting of citizens determined 20s in colonial currency equalled 13s 4d sterling.[122]

The governor consented to the seven proposals of 22nd November which the public approved on 5th December. Subscribers elected a committee of 15 to frame the bank's regulations on 18th December.[123] On 7th February 1817, subscribers approved 50 regulations and elected seven directors, D'Arcy Wentworth, John Harris, Robert Jenkins, Thomas Wylde, Alexander Riley, William Redfern and John Thomas Campbell.[124] The directors met on 12th February and, by March, the Governor had confirmed the bank's charter.[125] The Bank of New South Wales opened in a house in Macquarie Place on 8th April 1817. Robert and James Wilshire had accounts with the new bank.[126] Education of the youth was on Macquarie's packed agenda. In March 1817 Macquarie invited Robert to join a provisional committee on education he chaired.[127]

Meanwhile Robert Jenkins attended the Anniversary Dinner celebrating the arrival of the first fleet on Monday evening 27th January 1817. The dinner was held in the home of Isaac Nicholls at 11 George Street. By a "unanimous wish" of the 40 guests, Robert took the chair. After dinner, the group proposed loyal toasts and sang festive songs. Robert composed words to the tune "Rule Britannia":

Australia

When first Australia rose to fame
And Seamen brave explor'd her shore;
Neptune, with joy, with joy behold their aim,
And thus express'd the wish he bore.
Rise, Australia! with peace and plenty crown'd,
Thy name shall one day be renown'd!

Bright Ceres shall adorn thy land,
And gild thy fields with waving grain;
While roving herds shall o'er thy meads expand,

And range the riches of the plain.
Rise, Australia! etc.

Then Commerce, too, shall on thee smile,
Advent'rous barques thy ports shall crowd;
Well pleas'd, well pleas'd, the Parent Isle,
Shall of her distant sons be proud.
Rise, Australia! etc.

While Europe's Powers, in conflict dire
Exhaust the Flower of armies brave;
Here peace shall flourish, shall flourish - none conspire
With human blood thy soil to lave.
Rise, Australia! etc.[128]

For centuries writers and geographers referred to the South Pacific region as "Australia". The earliest to name the island continent "Australia" in print, were English botanist and zoologist George Shaw in 1794 (*Zoology of New Holland*), and explorer Matthew Flinders in 1814 (*A Voyage to Terra Australis*). On the 21st December 1817 Macquarie recommended "Australia" as the name of the continent. The new name came into general use between 1820 and 1830.[129]

In January 1817 Robert Jenkins received a grant of 1000 acres bordering the north-east bank of Lake Illawarra.[130] To visit the land he rode over the bridle-track on Mt Keira with Mr Charles Throsby Smith; the two forced to cut their way through dense vegetation.[131] Robert called the grant Berkeley after his former place of residence, an estate and market town in Gloucester, England. Around this time Robert engaged in other land deals. He leased property on the corner of Macquarie and O'Connell Streets in Parramatta. He paid £80 for 15 Clarence Street, Sydney. At auction he acquired 30 acres and buildings at Airds, then made over "all Right Title and Interest in the said 30 acres" to John Leighton. Lastly, with

Jemima's permission, Robert exchanged her 500 acres at Liberty Plains for 500 acres D 'Arcy Wentworth owned at Tallowa, east of later Marulan.[132] In July Robert advertised Austin Forrest's Swilly farm and grant of 400 acres for rent.[133]

A series of floods in the Hawkesbury in 1817 caused a great loss of crops and stock and reduced many folk "to a state of starvation".[134] Appeals launched in Sydney and the Hawkesbury raised £500 to feed 500 distressed people.[135] William Faithfull gave £1 and Thomas Pitt a guinea.[136] The donations, plus meat submitted to Government Stores, 4000lbs by Lucy Wood and 3500lbs by William Faithfull, suggest the family at Richmond was not in need.[137] Beyond the reach of the floods in Kurrajong, both Thomas and Elizabeth Pitt had received 100 acres adjoining their previous grants, which they named Trafalgar and Mt Nelson. James Wilshire also got a grant of 120 acres alongside the 400 acres of the Pitts.[138] The five grants were more or less bounded on the east by present Comleroy Road.[139] Thomas Pitt and William Faithfull were jurors for the Hawkesbury district in 1817, the first year the Governor's Court assembled in Windsor.[140] In the Governor's Court in July, Thomas successfully prosecuted Robert Woodley for £13 and Robert Jenkins lost £3 10s to Henry Buttsworth.[141] The case papers related to these judgments have not survived.

During the second half of 1817, the Woods left their sodden farm for Sydney. The move enabled 15-year old George Pitt Wood to begin a four-year apprenticeship with builder James Smith.[142] "A pious man", Smith helped set up the Missionary Society's Wesleyan Sunday Schools.[143] George probably learned his trade on two of Smith's projects. Smith rebuilt St Matthews at Windsor after an unsatisfactory appraisal of the work of architect and builder, Henry Kitchen. And following the death of builder Nathaniel Lucas, Smith took over St Lukes Church at Liverpool in its early stages.[144] Robert Jenkins had a financial stake in the two buildings. Reverend Rowland Hassall and Robert Jenkins backed Smith's contract for

St Lukes with a bond of £500, and James Smith and Robert were trustees for St Matthews.[145] After discovering Kitchen's affairs in an "embarassed state", Robert sued him for £1200 in the Supreme Court of Civil Jurisdiction. To refund Robert and other creditors, the court ordered the sale of Kitchen's land, wheat crop and building materials.[146]

James Wilshire and Robert Jenkins tried to introduce and amend government policies which benefited their businesses and the population at large. In 1815 and 1817 James petitioned the Governor to regulate the tanning industry. He suggested implementing measures from the British Acts, for instance, £30 licences and seven year apprenticeships. He pointed out problems with the trade, including the scarcity of hides, unqualified workers, and unfair competition from fraudulent practitioners. The latter had harmed the public as well as his own business to the extent of "at least £800 a year".[147] The Sydney Magistrates considered licences but decided against control of the industry.[148]

Robert Jenkins was critical of Macquarie's order banning captains of convict ships selling imported goods. Robert and merchant Richard Brooks circulated a memorial in which they stated that the restriction imposed by Macquarie "shackles and injures the Commercial Interests of the infant Colony, by tending to the Establishment of a Monopoly to the exclusive Benefit of a few Individuals". Macquarie suspended the regulation.[149] The chief grievance of merchants became clear: the 350 ton limit on the weight of trading vessels demanded by the East India Company. The governor consented to a meeting of the concerned in January 1819. A committee, which included Robert, was set-up to compose a petition which urged the Home Government to: lower the limit on trading vessels to 150 tons; begin trial by jury; allow spirit distillation from grains; and repeal export duties on oils, skins, wool and timber. Macquarie approved the petition "of all the men of Wealth, Rank and Intelligence", then sent it to the Secretary of

State, Sir Henry Bathurst.[150] Also in Janaury 1819, Robert was re-elected director of the Bank of New South Wales. He resigned in July to join the committee of the Savings Bank set up by Robert Campbell to serve the "industrious poor". Robert was appointed to the Committee of inquiry to examine the original Bank's management.[151]

To celebrate the birthday of Queen Charlotte, Elizabeth and Lachlan Macquarie invited Esther and James Wilshire and Jemima and Robert Jenkins to a ball and supper at Government House on 18th January 1819. (News of the Queen's death in November 1819 reached Sydney in June 1820.) One hundred and seventy guests representing "all the major interests of the Colony" received invitations. The "fanciful and elegant" ambience of the ballroom was achieved with variegated lamps, wreath-encircled columns and chalk sketches of oriental scenes on the walls. Served at 11 o'clock, the supper included "all the elegant varieties of the season". The dancing resumed to the "attractive sound of Pandean Pipes, the shrill tones mellowed by the softer cadences of flutes, claronets (sic), and violins". The guests danced "with uncommon vivacity and spirit until four o'clock in the morning". The guests were "highly gratified with the superior and truly fascinating amusements of the evening".[152] Conveniently before the ball on 10th December 1818, Esther gave birth to a fourth daughter Matilda Pitt Wilshire. A year earlier on 19th February 1817, namesake Esther Wilshire was born. Their baptisms took place at St Philip's, Matilda on 4th April 1818, Esther on 28th February 1819. The day after the ball, 20th January 1819, James transferred 2 Sussex Street by deed poll to William Tristram.[153]

Thomas Matcham Pitt vouched for two servants applying for mitigation of their sentences. Darby Ryan, transported in the *Archduke Charles* in 1813, an employee for three years, "behaved himself sober and honest".[154] John Weston, transported in the *Anne* in 1810, an employee for seven years, "conducted himself much to my satisfaction".[155] In a further act of kindness, Thomas assumed the temporary guardianship of seven-year-old James Scott, "a very nice boy ... quite destitute and a real object of charity". Young James came to the colony with his mother to join his convict father who had arrived on the *Marquis of Wellington* in 1815. James's mother died during their passage from Scotland, their year of arrival and ship unknown. James Scott senior cared for his son until sent to the Coal River for theft in June 1818. Thomas recommended the boy's admission to the Male Orphan School which provided children with shelter, food, clothing and education in the basics.[156] James Scott entered the newly renovated Orphan School in Sydney on 1st January 1819.[157]

"Miss Wood" and "Mrs Wood", almost certainly Sophia and Lucy Wood, spent time at the newly built three-storey Female Orphan School near Parramatta. George Pitt Wood probably worked in this district. Mrs Macquarie was patroness of the school which housed 100 girls from all sections of the colony. On 1st January 1819 Mary Collicott became the school's matron and her emancipated husband Thomas, its master.[158] Before leaving Sydney to take up her appointment, Mrs Collicott arranged for Miss Wood to help her. Because the Macquaries were out of town, Mrs Collicott sought the permission of the Governor's secretary, John Thomas Campbell. He said the proposal presented no obstacles but cautioned the decision was not his alone. Miss Wood lived in as assistant to Mary Collicott. Mrs Wood and Miss Reiby, whose brother had married Mrs Collicott's daughter, often visited, sometimes staying "a month at a time".[159] Through Mrs Collicott Miss Wood asked if she could conduct a boarding school for young ladies. Elizabeth Macquarie rejected the scheme. In August Mrs Macquarie told the Orphan School Committee she heard "that the Orphan children look very ill and also that they are not allowed a sufficient quantity of food". She questioned the Collicotts about the children's rations. She also asked from "where is the food provided from which Miss Wood,

Mrs Wood, and Miss Raby (sic) have been fed". Mary Collicott replied in a polite and contrite manner:

It is with no small concern I find you displeased with my having Miss Wood under my protection, as, permit me to assure you I would not on any account do the least thing that should not meet your approbation ... I should have waited on you with Mrs Wood to have asked your permission to have brought Miss W with me, but you were not in Sydney.

Mrs Collicott commented on Sophia's contribution:

Miss W is I think rather an acquisition than otherwise as she does all she can to assist me in the House and is no expense to the Institution... if it is your wish that Miss W should be removed, I will give Mrs Wood notice that she may try on some other place for her Daughter.

Mrs Collicot also explained Lucy's circumstances. Mrs Wood was keen for Miss Wood to have the position "as she was so unfortunately situated that she had not a house to take her to". Later, in recognition of improved conditions at the School, Mrs Collicott received a bonus of £30. She resigned in January 1821 owing to poor health.[160]

On 28th August 1819 James Wilshire was released from custody to attend his trial at the Parramatta Courthouse. He stood accused of hawking, without a licence, soap and candles and goods not of his making. James had reserved chief constable Francis Oakes to conduct the auction. Oakes had doubts about "infringing the rules" and refused to conduct the auction. James's solicitor, Frederick Garling, suggested Oakes cancelled the auction to attend an inquest. Oakes conceded he had auctioned goods for both James and Robert Jenkins after licences for hawkers were introduced in 1818. Jailer John Beal confirmed Mr Wilshire did not go from "house to house", on the contrary, he used licensed auctioneer Mr Rowe. The case moved to Sydney, where, on 18th September, D'Arcy Wentworth, Simeon Lord, Richard Brooks and John Harris considered the proceedings at Parramatta. They decided the Governor's orders on hawkers and peddlers "to be totally inapplicable to this case".[161]

In 1820 Lucy Wood lived in Sydney; her farm at Richmond leased by John Sherwood.[162] Mrs Wood lived in Macquarie Street. Perhaps Lucy occupied property owned by Robert Jenkins, who, in August 1818, acquired the Green Gate Hotel and two tenements in Macquarie Street, near Phillip Street.[163] Also in 1820, George Pitt Wood petitioned the Governor for 200 acres, next to Lucy's farm:

> *Memorialist is the son of Mrs Lucy Wood widow of John Wood and is a native of this colony. Memorialist is bound an apprentice to Mr James Smith, builder, for the term of 4 years, has now 2 years and 5 months to serve and intends to remain in the Colony. Memorialist has 22 head of horned cattle but has no land or farm whereon to depasture them. Memorialist is now 18 years of age and has not received any land or indulgence whatever from the government. Memorialist hopes the Gov will be pleased to take the same into consideration and grant to Memorialist an allotment of land.*[164]

Three men, two unquestionably associates of Robert Jenkins, wrote recommendations in support of his application. John Piper (formerly NSW Corps, Magistrate) believed George "a sober well-conducted youth of free parents." William Minchin (previously NSW Corps, Principal Superintendent of Police, Magistrate) described George, "a very industrious and deserving young man". The Reverend Fulton (Magistrate, Minister for Castlereagh and Richmond from June 1814) "knew George from childhood ... a very well conducted young man, sober, honest and industrious".[165] George was promised 200 acres at Richmond in March 1821, but his and many other grants were delayed "for want of survey".[166]

During Macquarie's administration the Pitt Family supported charities including the Bible Society, Philanthropic Society, Waterloo Battle Relief Fund, Princess Charlotte Memorial, and the chapel and schoolhouse at Kissing Point.[167] Of special note, the contribution Thomas Matcham Pitt made to the Benevolent Society, formed in mid 1818 for the relief of the poor, distressed, aged and infirm. Many altruistic citizens have supported the society to the present-day. The first meeting of the Hawkesbury Branch took place on 31st December 1818. From the outset Thomas was on the committee and responsible for identifying the needy in the Richmond district. At Government house in Parramatta in January 1819, Macquarie promised land to a delegation (unnamed in the *Sydney Gazette*) from the Hawkesbury Branch. Thomas was at the meeting in the Windsor Courthouse on 6th September 1819 to hear grants of 500 acres at Windsor and Wilberforce announced. Thomas and William Faithfull contributed money to the Society. Robert Jenkins was a committee member, treasurer and collector for the Sydney Branch. Robert and James Wilshire gave money to the Society; James also gave a cow.[168] Participants at a public meeting in June 1820 selected three gentleman of "high respectability and extensive influence" to collect Protestant subscriptions for a Roman Catholic Chapel. Robert was one of the three. Robert and James donated money to the chapel fund.[169]

Sadly, Susannah Faithfull, aged 46, died at Richmond. She was buried on 7th at St Peters Cemetery, Richmond.[170] It appears William took William, nearly 14, Alice, 9 and George, 6 to Sydney since he consolidated store receipts for his wheat and salt pork at the Sydney Commissariat between October 1820 and February 1821.[171] During these months, William junior probably left school to work as a clerk for Robert Jenkins.[172] On a different note, Commissioner John Thomas Bigge, sent from England in 1819 to inquire into the state of the colony, compiled a small list of Richmond landholders. Bigge listed William senior with 1300 acres, 70 cleared for crops, 400 sheep, 80 cattle and 75 hogs.[173] William had increased the acres at Jordan Hill from 500 to 1200. He bought 600 acres at Minto from Simeon Lord, then exchanged the 600 acres for 700 acres beside Jordan Hill owned by Richard Brooks.[174] Comprised mainly of "rich alluvial land", the property enjoyed a frontage of a mile or more to South Creek and a smaller creek.[175] William's home acres account for the other 100 acres.

Less than five months after Susannah's death, on 28th January 1821 Thomas Matcham Pitt, only 39, died of "a severe cold contracted in going home from Sydney; which terminated in a fever". His burial took place on 30th at St Peters, Richmond. The *Sydney Gazette* described George, "a tender and affectionate husband and parent" who was "universally esteemed".[176] Thomas gave his name to Pitt Street in Richmond.[177] A week before he died Thomas made his will, witnessed by Reverend Henry Fulton, Archibald Bell, John Dight and Lucy Wood. He left his property to Elizabeth. He asked her to leave George the 200 acres close to Richmond Hill, Robert the 400 acres near "Curryjong brush" and William the 30 acres on the banks of the Hawkesbury near Windsor. He added, if Elizabeth considered "it necessary for her comfort and welfare to enter into wedlock after my decease", she should divide the horned cattle into six portions for herself and the children.[178] Days after Thomas died, Elizabeth advertised 200 acres for lease.[179] She had her hands full, supervising the farms and rearing George nearing seven, Mary five, Robert three, William Henry almost two and Eliza three months. The youngest three recently born, Robert on 7th September 1817, William Henry on 26th January 1819 and Eliza on 1st November 1820. They were christened at St Peters, Robert in October 1817, William in March 1819 and Eliza in December 1820.

In a tribute to Thomas Matcham Pitt, Esther and James Wilshire named their fourth son, Thomas Matcham Pitt Wilshire. Born on 22nd February 1821, Thomas was christened at St Philips on 23rd April. In the previous January, Commissioner John· Thomas Bigge questioned James about his "considerable tan yard". James told

Bigge in two years he had tanned 1900 ox and cow hides, and yearly about 8000 kangaroo skins and 6000 sheepskins. Asked about the quality of his leather, James replied that the upper leather of his shoes matched the English product and the sole would too, if properly hardened. He told Bigge he cut about 40 pairs of soles from a hide and charged the public 14d for sole leather and 3s 6d for upper leather. However, the government only paid him 1 0d for sole leather and 2s 8d for upper leather. Bigge wondered if he supplied the military with shoes? James said the service men bought his shoes after selling their inferior English ones for between 2s 6d to 3s 6d a pair. He repeated his chief problem, the scarcity of skilled labour, pointing out that in 17 years he had only two curriers and tanners.[180] Well-satisfied with the quality of James's products, the government bought his leather, soap, hair, glue and candles while Sydney Hospital and St Philips Church used his candles.[181] Also in 1821, James got a grant of 500 acres on the banks of the Winburndale Rivulet, north of Bathurst.[182] In support of his request for land, James referred to his large family, his faithful service in the Commissariat for nearly 13 years and the £400 embezzled by servants during his absence from Sydney.[183]

In the early months of 1821, Lucy Wood and George Pitt Wood delivered many bushels of wheat to Government Stores, their store receipts consolidated by Lucy in Windsor and George in Sydney.[184] In April 1821 Lucy received a grant of 175 acres next to the grant of her late husband, John. (Figure 3) She had a long wait as mother Mary recommended her for the grant.[185] Lucy got a new hand, Robert Marchment, who worked for Thomas and Elizabeth Pitt. On Marchment's behalf, Elizabeth sent the Governor a recommendation and a petition signed by the Earl of Marlborough, clergy and inhabitants of Wiltshire.[186] Within days, the Governor granted Marchment an absolute pardon, allowing him to choose his employment.[187] Lucy Wood and William Faithfull applied for a licence to marry on 26th September 1821, intending to marry at St Peters, Richmond, on 29th September. The Reverend Fulton cancelled the wedding once he discovered Lucy was the sister of William's first wife, a restriction lifted in July 1875.[188] The Reverend Cartwright married William and Margaret Thompson of Bringelly on 29th November 1821 at St Luke's, Liverpool. Margaret arrived free in the *Mary* in 1812.[189]

When his regime ended in December 1821 Lachlan Macquarie was a disheartened man. Commissioner Bigge criticised his polices, particularly his promotion of emancipists and his extravagant building programme. Macquarie's masters in England did not appreciate his attainments.[190] Some citizens were discontented, including 13 prominent men Macquarie described as "fractious and dissatisfied". Robert Jenkins was one of them.[191] The admiring Hawkesbury settlers wrote to Macquarie of their "grateful recollections" of "the many advantages" enjoyed under his "wise and mild administration". At their request, the Governor sat for a portrait which still hangs in the Windsor courthouse.[192] The citizens of Sydney lined the shores to farewell the Macquaries on their departure on 15th February 1822.[193]

The Pitt Family contributed to Macquarie's decade of reform.[194] The men worked on committees, acted as coroner, jurors and magistrates, helped develop the first bank, and supported charities. The women produced and reared the next generation. Sadly, though, in these years the deaths occurred of Mary Pitt and her children Susannah Faithfull and Thomas Matcham Pitt, and her son-in-law Austin Forrest. Family events to celebrate included the births of fourteen grandchildren, and the land grants, one to Austin Forrest, two to Thomas Matcham Pitt, two to Elizabeth Pitt, two to Robert Jenkins, two to James Wilshire, one to George Pitt Wood and one to Lucy Wood.

1	HRA I, 10, pp671-2
2	Broadbent, James, and Hughes, Joy, eds, *The Age of Macquarie*, Melbourne University Press and Historic Houses of New South Wales, Victoria, 1992, ch 12
3	SG 7 January 1810, p3a
4	HRA 1, 7, pp 82, 227-9
5	Memorial for Confirmation of Grant, SRNSW, Fiche 4/1822, No 338; *Grants of Land*, Bk 5, Pgs 14, 15, 16, 17, DL
6	Registers of Copies of Wills 1800-190 I, SAG Will 1/1821. See re buying home acres
7	NSW JA Rg., Bk 3, Pg 21, No 143, ML A3610
8	Government and General Orders 5 January 1810- 26 December 1818, SRNSW SZ758, Reel 6038, p4; Letters Sent 28 December 1809- 13 April 1810, SRNSW, 4/3490B, Reel 6002, p38; *Main Series of Letters Received* 28 December 1809 - 27 May 1816, SRNSW, 4/1723, Reel 6042, p125; Letters Sent 28 December 1809-28 December 1813, SRNSW 4/3490B, Reel 6002, p68
9	HRA 1, 7, p327
10	NSW JA Rg., Bk 4, Pg 62, No 14, ML A3610
11	Memorials 1821, SRNSW 1/1827, Fiche 3040, No 151.
12	CCJ, Minutes of Proceedings, SRNSW 5/1103, No 340
13	NSW JA Rg., Rg., Bk 3, Pg 20, No 142; Pg 21, No 144, ML A3610
14	HRNSW 7, p358; Mutch Index, Pitt/Forrest (I assume the Pitt's witness was Thomas)
15	Browning, Yvonne, *St. Peters Richmond, The Early People and Burials 1791-1855*, Browning, Kurrajong, 1990, pp 13, 37
16	*Naval Chronical*, Vol 28, 1812, in BT Biography, A2000, 2, p441; Statham, Pamela, ed., *A Colonial Regiment, New Sources Relating to the New South Wales Corps 1789-1810*, Australian National University, Canberra, 1992, pp382, 368; Colonial Index, Robert Campbell, SRNSW; Houison J, K.S.
17	HRA 1, 5, pp640-l, pp767-8; HRA 1, 6, pp192-4, pp618-9; HRNSW 5, p745
18	Margaret Steven, *Merchant Campbell, 1769-1846*, Oxford University Press, Melbourne, 1965, p38; NSW JA Rg., Bk 1, Pg 109, No 619, ML A3609
19	SG 19 March 1809, plc, 2b
20	NSW JA Rg., Bk 4, Pg 26, No 308; Pg 34, No 377, ML A3610; Naval Chronicle Vol 28, 1812, in BT Biography, A2000, Vol 2, Pg 441; Old Chum (J.M. Forde), *Old Sydney*, ML B248; McNaught, Jean, *Index and Registers of Land Grants, Leases and Purchasers 1792-1865*, 1998, pl23
21	SG 8 March 1817, 2b; County Cumberland, Parish Castlereagh, DL Map

No 10, sheet 1, L/F, 8th ed 1969; Letters Sent 14 April 1810-24 September 1810, SRNSW, 4/3490C, Reel 6002, p72

22 *Lachlan Macquarie,* Governor of New South Wales, *Journals of His Tours in New South Wales and Van Diemen's Land 1810-1822,* Trustees of the Public Library of New South Wales, 1956, pp23-25
23 HRNSW 7, pp464-5
24 *Lachlan Macquarie ...,* 1856,p 30; ADB 1, Cox, Evans
25 HRA 1, 7, p399
26 SG 12 August 1804, plb,c; 27 January 1805, plb
27 Letters Sent 24 September 1810-27 April 1811, SRNSW 4/3490D, Reel 6002, pp55-60
28 *Lach/an Macquarie ...* 1856, pp39-40; SRNSW 4/3490D,R eel 6002,p 97
29 SG 11 May 1811, plc; SG 18 July 1812, plb
30 NSW JA Rg., Bk 5, Pg 72, No 588, ML A3611
31 NSW JA Rg., Bk 5, Pg 179, No 886, ML A3612
32 CCJ, Minutes of Proceedings, SRNSW 5/1108, Nos 402,403;5/1109,No 5
33 CCJ, Minutes of Proceedings, SRNSW 5/1104, No 197; 5/1105, Nos 171, 217; 5/1106, No 16
34 Miscellaneous Records relating to Immigration, Shipping and Trade, Bonds, to the Naval Officer, SRNSW X702, Fiche 3283, pp27-9
35 NSW JA Rg., Bk 5, Pg 77, No 608; Bk 5,Pg 93, No 655, MLA3611
36 Main Series of Letters Received 1811, SRNSW 4/1726, Reel 6043, p264
37 Letters Sent 29 April 1811-28 December 1813, SRNSW, 4/3491, p80
38 SG 16 November 1811, p2c
39 SG 28 December 1811, p2a
40 SG 4 April 1812, plc
41 *BDM, St Philip's Sydney 1809 to 1818, SRNSW, COD 385, p171; The Book of Common Prayer,* The University Press Oxford, London, p217
42 Copies of Letters Sent 29 April 1811-28 December 1813, SRNSW 4/3491, Reel 6002, p216; SG 28 March 1812, pla
43 ADB 2, Wilshire
44 HRNSW 7, pp 569-571; HRA 7, p483; *Memorials 1821,* SRNSW, 4/1827, Fiche 3040, No 151
45 See Ref 11 above; NSW JA Rg., Bk 6, Pg 327, No 128, MLA3614
46 BT Box 20, p3463; Hainsworth, R., *Builders and Adventurers, the Traders and the Emergence of the Colony, 1788-1821,* Cassell Australia, 1968, ch 4, pl32
47 International Genealogical Index, Marriage of Thomas Laycock /Hannah Pearson
48 Laycock, K.G. Laycock, *A Pioneer Australian Family,* 2000, pp8, 10
49 Wentworth Family Pa pers, MLA751, pp61, 89, 90
50 SG 8 September 1810, p2b; MIT Laycock
51 *Lachlan Macquarie ...*, 1956, p37; Johnson, Keith A. and Sainty, Malcolm R., *Land Grants 1788-1809,* Sydney, 1974, p148: SG 7 December 1816, Suppl., pla

52	*Land Grants 1811-1826*, MLA361, CY 736, fr 7; County Cook, Parish Kurrajong , 9th ed. Map 25, DL
53	JRAHS, vol 8, 1923, Suppl., p409
54	International Genealogical Index, Marriage of Robert Jenkins/Mary Warren
55	lllawarra Mercury 27 November 1901, p2b,c
56	ADB 2, Jenkins
57	Banks Papers , Brabourne Collection , Vol 6, p157, MLA78-5
58	SG 6 August 1809, p2c; SG 8 October 1809, p2b
59	NSW Court of Civil Jurisdiction, *Minutes of Proceedings*, SRNSW, 5/1103, Nos 209,210,227,244,276,280,281
60	NSW JA Rg., Bk 4, Pgs 75-6, No 113, MLA3610
61	NSW JA Rg., Bk 4, Pg 20, No 242, MLA3610
62	NSW JA Rg., Bk 3, Pg 151, No 113, MLA3610; Main Series of Letters Received, Bundle 4, SRNSW 4/1725, Reel 6042, pp300-l
63	CCJ, *Minutes of Proceedings*, SRNSW 5/1106, Nos 43, 182; SG 17 August 1812, plb; *Memorials 1821*, SRNSW 4/1827, Reel 6051, No 151
64	Documents Extracted from the Main Series of Letters Received, Papers respecting the sanity of Captain Bodie of the *Frederick*, SRNSW ML Safe 1/53, Item 4, Reel 6040
65	Letters Sent 1808-25, SRNSW 4/3490D, Reel 6002, pp164-6
66	SG 22 August 1812, p2c; SG 21 September 1811, plc,2b
67	JRAHS, Vol 8, Suppl., 1923, pp411-3; CCJ, SRNSW 5/1108, No 96
68	Special Bundles, Coroner's Inquests 1809-12, SRNSW 4/1819, pp9, 27-30, 89, 219-20, 355-6, 381-2, 531,533,635, 637, Reel 6021; Main Series of Letters Received, Bundle 6, 1812, SRNSW 4/1727 Reel 6043, pp31, 33
69	Old Chum (J.M.Forde), Old Sydney, B245 ML
70	SG 2 January 1813, plb, c
71	SG 20 Nov 1813, p2c; SG 16 January 1813, p2c; SG 30 January 1813, p2c,3a
72	SG 3 July 1813, p2a; Government and General Orders 5 Jan 1810-12 to 1814, SRNSW SZ758, Reel 6038, p391; HRA, 1, 8, pp300-301
73	CCJ, *Minutes of Proceedings*, SRNSW 5/1109, Nos 287,336,337,338, 339,342; 5/1110, Nos 254,295,297,511; 5/1111, Nos 58, 82, 91
74	SG 28 September 1816, 2d
75	Main Series of Letters Received, SRNSW 4/1728, Reel 6043, pp139-41; Letters Sent 1808-25 SRNSW 4/3491, Reel 6002, pp506, 516; Government and General Orders 5 Jan 1810-12 to 1814, SRNSW SZ758, Reel 6038, p392; SG 11 September 1813, pld; SG 6 November 1813, pld
76	Memorials 1832, SRNSW Fiche 3048, No 194A
77	SG 27 October 1810, p2
78	SG 6 April 1811, p4c
79	Land Grants 1811-1826, MLA361, CY 736, p8
80	See SG Index re Jenkins Farm at Parramatta on 16 Dec 1815 - item not

found on this date; Bk 9. No 987, DL; GG 1857, Vol 1, p994, 16 Apr; County Cumberland, Parish Liberty Plains, Map 28, Sheet 1, L/F, DL

81 NSW JA Rg., Bk 5, p298, No 1197, ML A3612
82 NSW JA Rg., Bk 6, Pg 4, No 1286; Pgs 7-8, No 1295; Pg 15, No 1311; Pgs 41-2, Nos 1372, 1373, ML A3613
83 SG 22 January 1814, plc
84 Main Series of Letters Received 1814, SRNSW 4/1730, Reel 6044, pp393-395a; Letters Sent within the Colony 1 Jan 1814-19 Jan 1816, SRNSW 4/3493, Reel 6004, p247; SG 28 May 1814, p2d; NSWDepartment of Lands, County Cumberland, 1925, William's land at South Creek was Houston's grant; SRNSW; Registers of Copies of Wills 1800-1901, SAG Will 1/1821
85 Mowle, L.M., *Pioneer Families of Australia*, 5th ed., Rigby, Sydney, 1978, pl 61. (As George Faithfull was born in the district of Canterbury, the Faithfulls were probably living on William's grants at Ashfield)
86 BDM, St Philip's, Sydney, 1809 to 1818, SRNSW COD 385, pl79
87 Baxter, Carol J. ed., *General Musters of New South Wales 1814*, Australian Biographical and Genealogical Record and Society of Australian Genealogists, Sydney, 1987, pp xi, xii, 11, 13, 36, 94, 140, 180,190,205,218
88 See many entries in SG Index 1814-21; Main Series of Letters Received, Bundle 11, 1817, SRNSW 4/1737, Reel 6046, p38; Main Series of Letters Received 1821, SRNSW 4/1748, Reel 6051,pp136,137, 142, 152,155,156
89 Cunningham, Peter, *Two Years in New South Wales*, Royal Australian Historical Society, Angus and Robertson, 1966, p390
90 SG 27 November 1813, p2a
91 SG 7 May 1814, p2c
92 SCCJ, Equity, SRNSW, 3/3974, No 787; 3/3674, No 1182
93 SG 23 July 1814, plc; SG 26 November 1814, p2d. Cambridge and Gloucester Streets were reversed.
94 SG 3 February 1816, plb
95 Main Series ofLetters Received 1818, SRNSW 4/1741, Reel 6047, p44
96 CCJ, *Minutes of Proceedings*, SRNSW 5/1109, Nos 30,189; 5/1110, Nos 202, 203,341
97 SG 29 July 1815, plc; SG 9 September 1815, pld
98 NSW JA Rg., Bk 6, Pg 97, No 1488, ML A3613; SG 27 April 1816, p2d
99 SG 29 June 1814, p2d; SG 19 November 1814, pld; SG 26 November 1814, p2d; SG 11 January 1817, p4a; SG 5 July 1817, plc; SG 18 June 1818, p4b; SG 20 February 1819, pla,b; SG 27 January 1821, p2a; BT Box 13, pp839-41
100 Special Bundles, Naval Officer's Quarterly Reports, 1815-1817, SRNSW X699, Reel 6023, p47
101 BT Box 1 2, pp271- 2
102 *Evening News* 24 October 1896, p9; Browning, Yvonne, *St Peters*

5 Contributions to Macquarie's Reforms

       Richmond, The Early People and Burials 1791-1855, Dennis Browning, Kurrajong 1990, p412. (Note that Mary was not buried at Richmond)
103   SG 18 November 1815, p2c
104   Letter of 14 February 1804, Admiral Lord Nelson to George Matcham, Fearn, Marie A. J., Family of Pitt, ML D80, Item 7
105   Proclamations, Government and General Orders, and Related Records 9 Nov 1814 - 26 Dec 1818 SRNSW SZ759, Reel 6038, ppl71,362
106   GC, Precepts and Warrants 1815-25, SRNSW 4/7856, pp9, 58-60, 107-8
107   GC, Case Papers Heard, SRNSW 4/7860, Nos 58, 59, 173; GC, Judgment Book No 10, 4/7883, Nos 407, 462, 463, 464, 542, 772
108   GC, Case Papers Heard, SRNSW 4/7860, No 150; 4/7861, No 776; GC, *Writs Issued,* 4/7870; GC, Judgment Book No 10, 4/7883, Nos 97,419,421,434,435
109   Concise Guide to the State Archives (S-Y), Supreme Court of Civil Jurisdiction, 1814-1824, pl
110   SCCJ, Judgement Rolls, SRNSW 9/2212, No 36; 9/2222, No 252; 9/2228, No 358; 9/2234, No 472; Judgement Book No 2, 1817-1828, SRNSW 9/922, Nos 36, 252, 358, 472
111   SG 13 July 1816, p2b
112   SG 17 August 1816, p2d
113   SG 27 April 1816, p2d; SG 21 December 1816, 2d
114   SG 8 March 1817, p2b
115   HRA 1, 9, p215
116   HRA 1, 7, pp750-6
117   Hainsworth, 1968, ch 2, pp55-7
118   Letters sent 1808-25, Copies' of letters sent within the Colony 20 June 1816-19 February 1817, SRNSW 4/3495, Reel 6005, pp285-6
119   SG 30 November 1816, p2b; HRA 1, 9, p219
120   Letters sent within the Colony 20 June 1816 - 24 Jan 1818, SRNSW 4/3495, Reel 6005, pp305-7
121   Main Series of Letters Received, Bundle 10, 1816, SRNSW 4/1736, Reel 6046,pp179,179a
122   SG 7 December 1816, plb,c,d, 2a
123   SG 14 December 1817, p2b
124   SG 8 February 1817, p2a; HRA 1, 9, pp227-235
125   SG 22 March 1817, p2a
126   SG 5 April 1817, plb; BT Box 27, pp6292, 6295, 6298
127   SG 15 March 1817, p2a
128   SG 1 February 1817, p2c, 3a,b; JRAHS, 8, 1923 Suppl., p410
129   HRA 1, 9, pp747, 867-9 (Note 84)
130   Indexes and Registers of Land Grants and Leases, SRNSW 7/447, vol 2, Reel 2561, p138, No 1243
131   *Illawarra Mercury* 23 November 1901, p2
132   NSW JA Rg., Bk 6, Pgs 340-41, No 150, ML A3614; Letters Relating to Land, SRNSW 2/7892-93, Reel 1146, 11 Nov 1830; NSW JA Rg., Bk 7,

Pgs 18-9, No 223; Pg 316-7, No 614, ML A3616; NSW JA.Rg., Bk 9, Pg 30, Nos 41,42, ML A3619; NSW JA Rg., Bk 7, Pgs 179-80, No 456, ML A3616

133 SG 5 July 1817, 4b
134 SG 8 March 1817, pla,b; SG 15 March 1817, plc
135 Bowd, D.G., *Macquarie Country*, Library of Australian History, Sydney, rev.ed., 1982, pl8
136 SG 22 November, 1817, p4a
137 SG 1 Feb 1817, p2a; SG 14 June 1817, plb; SG 27 Dec 1817, plb
138 Grants of Land, Town Grants, Leases, Bk 2, Pgs 58, 59, 60, DL
139 County Cook, Parish Kurrajong, Map 25, 9th ed., DL
140 Bigge's Appendix, ML A2131, CY727, p ll8; HRA 4, 1, p230; SG 3 April 1819, plb,c
141 GC Judgment Book No 10, 4/7883, Nos 557, 558
142 SG 14 June 1817, plb; SG 27 Dec 1817, plb; *Memorials of Land 1820*, SRNSW 4/1825B, Fiche 3034, No 801, pp1009-10
143 Hassall Family Correspondence, ML A1677-2, Vol 2, CY913, p286; *Marsden Papers*, Vol 5, p63, ML A1996; BT Box 8, p3500, ML
144 Proclamations, Government and General Orders, and Related Records, 5 Jan 1810-22 Dec 1819, SRNSW SZ1044, Reel 6038, pp8, 84; Government and General Orders and Public Accounts, SRNSW SZ759 Reel 6038, p438
145 Main Series of Letters Received 1817-18, Bundle 12, SRNSW 4/1740, Reel 6047, pp269-70, 278-83; Letters Sent 1808-25, Copies of letters sent within the Colony, 20 April 1820-26 December 1820, SRNSW 4/3502, Reel 6007, p l03; Letters Sent 1808-25, Copies of letters sent within the Colony, 23 January 1818-23 July 1818, SRNSW 4/3498, Reel 6006,pl32
146 SG 10 July 1818, p2b; SCCJ, Judgment Rolls, SRNSW 9/2215, No 75; SCCJ, Judgment Book No 2, 9/922, No 75
147 Memorial of James Wilshire, 14 Jan 1815, BT Box 13, pp903-14; Letter Book, 19 February-26 August 1817, SRNSW, 4/3496, Reel 6005, pl72
148 Main Series of Letters Received 1818, SRNSW, 4/1741, Reel 6047, pp28-34, 38, 43-46
149 SG 21 November 1818, plc; BT Box 18, p2515; BT Box 7, pp2798-2801
150 BT Box 28, pp6887-9; SG 23 January 1819, p3a, b; HRA 1, 10, pp21-3, 809, Note 7
151 SG 9 January 1819, p2b; SG 31 July 1819, plb; SG 19 June , 1819 p2b; SG 17 July 1819, plb; BT Box 28, p6882
152 Macquarie , Elizabeth, *Miscellaneous Papers 1818-1824*, ML MSS 5052, Item 2; SG 23 January 1819, p3a; Broad bent and Hughes , 1992, ch 2, pp29-30; ch 7, p90
153 NSW JA Rg., Bk 8, Pg 99, No 126, MLA3617
154 Petitions 1813-1816, SRNSW 4/1849, Fiche 3173, p67a
155 Peitions 1817, SRNSW 4/1853, Fiche 3182, p365

156 Main Series of Letters Received 1818, List of Children Recommended by Clergy and Magistrates, SRNSW 4/1740, p254, Reel 6047; Letters Sent within the Colony 23 Jan-28 Oct 1819, SRNSW 4/3498, Reel 6006, p283
157 Miscellaneous Records Relating to Education and Clerical Matters, Male Orphan School, 1819-24, SRNSW 4/7208, Fiche 3307, pp3-4; HRA 1, 10, p94
158 SRNSW Colonial Secretary's Index, Mary Collicott
159 SG 7 June 1817, p3b
160 Rules and Regulations for the future management and improvement of the Female Orphan Institution 30 June 1818-15 January 1824, SRNSW 4/403, Reel 6040, pp 29-33, 50, 56
161 BT Box 19, pp2881-9; 2920-1
162 BT, Box 24, p5167
163 SG 16 Dec 1820, p4a; JA Rg., Bk 7, Pgs 156-7, No 428, MLA3616
164 Letters Received Relating to Land Matters 1820, SRNSW 4/1825B, Reel 1068, pp1009-10, No 810
165 ADB 1, Fulton; ADB 2, Minchin
166 Land Grants 1811-1826, MLA361, CY 736, p5a; Concise Guide to State Archives, Court of Claims, SRNSW
167 SG 11 July 1812, plc; SG 3 April 1813, plc, 2b; SG 27 March, 1813, plc; SG 22 January 1814, pla ,b; SG 3 February 1816, plc; SG 2 March 1816, p2d; SG 15 March 1817, p2b; SG 17 May 1817, p4a; SG 16 May 1818, p2b; SG 26 February 1820, pla; SG 29 December 1821, p2a; SG 4 January 1822, p2a
168 Rathbone, Ron, *A Very Present Help*, State Library of New South Wales, Sydney 1994, chs 1,2,3; Walker, William, *History of the Hawkesbury Benevolent Society*, Turner and Henderson, Sydney, 1887; BT Box 7, p2363; BT Box 19, pp2903-4; SG 30 January 1819, p2b,c, 3a,b; SG 11 December 1819, p2b; SG 27 May 1820, p2b,c; SG 22 February 1822, p4a; SG 30 January 1819, p2c; SG 9 May 1818, p2a,b; SG 16 May 1818, p4a; SG 31 July 1819, plc; SG 28 August 1819, plc; SG 18 September 1819, p2c; SG 15 April 1820, p3a; SG 29 April 1820, p2a; SG 3 February 1821, plc; SG 20 June 1821, p2b; SG 8 February 1822, p4c; Howe, George, *Benevolent Society of New South Wales, Abstract of Proceedings*, Sydney 1819; BT Box 8, pp3474-6
169 SG 1 July 1820, p2c; SG 1 December, 1821, p4a; SG 24 May 1822, p4b
170 SG 9 September 1820, p3c
171 Main Series of Letters Received 1821, SRNSW 4/1748, Reel 6051, pp 136, 137, 142, 152, 155; SG 6 January 1821, p2a; SG 24 February 1821, p2b
172 Maxwell, Charles, F., *Australian Men of Mark*, Vol 2, Version 1, Melbourne, 1889, p378
173 BT Box 26, p6083
174 NSW JA Rg., Bk 7, Pgs 159,161,162, ML A3615
175 SG 20 January 1835, p4e; Aus 20 January 1835, p4e; Department

of Lands, Map of County Cumberland 1925, SRNSW. See grants of Houston and Brooks and the back creek

176 SG 3 February 1821, p3a,b
177 Registers of Copies of Wills 1800-1901, SAG Will 1/112
178 Bowd D.G., *Origins of Names of Streets, Parks and Features: Windsor Municipality*, Windsor Municipal Council, 1973
179 SG 10 February, 1821, p2c
180 Bigge 's Appendix, Trade, Public Record Office, London, ML CO 210/129, K, No 2, Reel 117, p7
181 Proclamations,Government and General Orders, and Related Records, SRNSW SZ 1044, Reel 6038, p84; Letters Sent 1808-25, Copies of Letters Sent within the Colony, 8 March 1822 - 28 June 1822, SRNSW 4/3505, Reel 6009, p225; Proclamations, Government Orders, and Notices, SRNSW 4/424, Reel 6039, pp80,125,126,140,414,445; SG 17 February, 1821 Suppl; Main Series of Letters Received 1820, SRNSW 4/1747, Reel 6050, p225; Main Series of Letters Received 1822, SRNSW 4/1759, Reel 6054, p8; SG 8 September 1821 Suppl; SG 24 November 1821 Suppl
182 Land Grants NSW 1811-26, ML 361, CY736; *New South Wales Calendar and General Post Office Directory 1834*, Stephens and Stokes, Sydney, p94
183 Memorials 1821, SRNSW 4/1827, Reel 6051, No 151; Letters Sent 1808-1825, 25 October 1821 - March 1822, SRNSW 4/3504A, Reel 6008, p61
184 SG 17 February 1821, 4a; SG 3 March 1821, p3a; Main Series of Letters Received, 1821, SRNSW, 4/1748, Reel 6051, pp156, 172
185 Miscellaneous Records re Land Grants, Leases, etc., SRNSW 9/2652, p18, Fiche 3266, p18; Grants of Land, Bk 8, Pg 254, DL
186 Main Series of Letters Received, 1821, SRNSW 4/1750, Fiche 3266, pp71-3
187 Colonial Secretary, SRNSW 4/1862, Fiche 3206, p 10.
188 Special Bundles 1800-1825, Applications for marriage by Special Licence 1819-25, SRNSW 2/8305 ppl7-8, Reel 6028; Mutch Index, Wood/Faithfull; Heaton, J.H., *Australian Dictionary of Dates*, George Robertson,Sydney, 1879, Pt 2, p85
189 Baxter, Carol J. ed., *General Muster and Land and Stock Muster of New South Wales 1822*, Australian Biographical and Genealogical Record and Society of Australian Genealogists, Sydney, 1988, p159
190 Broadbent and Hughes, 1992, ch 3, pp46-7; ch 12, ppl58-9
191 Macquarie Papers, Memoranda and Related Papers 1808-1823, ML A772, pl75
192 HRA 1, I 0, p704
193 SG 15 February 1822, p2a,b
194 HRA 1, 10, pp671-701. (See list of Macquarie's achievements)

6
THE GRANDCHILDREN MARRY

During the 1820s four grandchildren of Mary Pitt married, the young women at 16 and 17, the young men at 21 and 24. The newly-weds could access land by grant until July 1831 and by auction for no less than 5s an acre from 1825.[1] The revenue from the auction funded immigration, the population rising from 24,000 to 46,000 in this decade. In 1823 Governor Thomas Brisbane set up the Legislative Council by selecting a small group of men to help him rule the colony.[2] Also in 1823, a new Charter of Justice created a Supreme Court in New South Wales with a chief justice presiding and barristers and attorneys admitted to the bar.[3]

The first grandchild to marry was 17 year-old Sophia Wood, only daughter of John and Lucy Wood. On 28th June 1821 at St Johns, Parramatta, the Henrys' good friend, the Reverend Samuel Marsden, married, by licence, Sophia and Samuel Pinder Henry.[4] The witnesses were James and Louisa Wilshire, and James's sister, Susannah Eyre, who came to the colony in 1812 and married widowed missionary John Eyre.[5] Samuel was the son of the Reverend William Henry and Sarah Henry, née Maben, members of the London Missionary Society based in Tahiti. The Henrys originated from Dublin. Joseph Smith, later Samuel's brother-in-law, described Samuel, "a fine, tall, and stout man" with a "simple and open-hearted" manner.[6]

The parents of Samuel Pinder Henry arrived in Tahiti on the *Duff* in 1797 with the first group of missionaries. The next year tribal wars drove them to Port Jackson, William Henry conducting an itinerant ministry in Parramatta. The Henrys were back in Tahiti shortly before the birth of Samuel on 3rd February 1800. Samuel and his siblings had an unusual upbringing on Tahiti and Moorea in the incompatible cultures of the strict and pious missionaries and the permissive Tahitians. The favourite child of King Pomare II, Tahitian women nursed Samuel and he spoke Tahitian. Further disturbances in the islands saw the Henrys in New South Wales between 1808 and 1811. Samuel's mother died in Tahiti in 1812; the following year his father married a young woman in Sydney. While his father was away, Samuel boarded with mission schoolmaster Davies, but "behaved exceedingly ill, did not mind his lessons at all". In 1814 Samuel, missionary Charles Wilson, settler George Bicknell and King Pomare II spent three months in the Leeward Islands, after a storm carried the whaler *Matilda* to Huahine.[7] (See Figures 4 and 5 for locations of Samuel Henry.) Samuel struggled to conform to the expectations of the missionaries, his troubled conscience obvious in the letter he wrote to Reverend Thomas Hassall on 24th September 1815. He confessed "his long silence was owing to shame on account of what you had heard concerning me", confiding he suffered from "growing pains".[8]

William Henry entrusted Samuel Marsden to select son Samuel's employment on the young man's arrival at Port Jackson in the *Active* in 1816. William suggested Samuel learn carpentry, thinking James Smith might take him for a "moderate fee". Instead, Marsden chose navigation to equip Samuel to command a trading schooner in support of the island missions. Rumours about Samuel's misbehaviour circulated in Sydney. Marsden reported he "improved very fast" and others spoke well of him, especially his "affable manners". Also, Samuel helped new missionaries compile an English-Tahitian dictionary.[9] In 1819 Samuel took up his first position, second mate on the *Haweis*. Launched in Tahiti in 1817 for the Tahitian mission, the brig was jointly owned by the island missionaries, King Pomare II and the Missionary Society in London. By 1820 Pomare had formed a company with George Bicknell and Samuel, the three intending to plant sugar and tobacco and send sugar and salt pork to Port Jackson. When the missionaries found the *Haweis* too small for their purposes, Pomare got all but the two shares obtained by Samuel and Bicknell. As captain of the *Haweis*, Samuel would undertake assignments for Pomare in the Islands and at Port Jackson in return for land on the island of Moorea.[10] In Sydney Samuel received a letter from Pomare which revealed their familiarity:

> *Is your woman in Port Jackson? You don't mean to tell me that good people can acquire mistresses. Now don't go spreading this around. I am just poking fun at you. It had better be a good woman you are sleeping with, if she is not, but just an old hag, you will be the laughing stock here. Do not stay too long in Port Jackson.*[11]

Robert Campbell refused to comply with the missionaries' instructions to release the *Haweis* to Samuel Henry on its arrival in Port Jackson in November 1820. Acting for the London Missionary Society while the Reverend Marsden was in New Zealand, Campbell would take instructions only from the directors of the Society. Aware Pomare wanted a vessel free of restrictions, Samuel engaged merchant and prominent Wesleyan Edward Eagar to buy the *Governor Macquarie*, fit it out, and load it with salt, casks and other produce. Eagar also engaged sugar expert, Thomas Scott, for Samuel.[12] In return for his services Eagar demanded much of Pomare. To meet the cost of the brig and its cargo, Samuel was to return with cargoes of pork. Eagar desired a third or fourth share of the *Governor Macquarie* which was to trade constantly between the Islands and the colony. Eagar would act as Pomare's agent in the colony. Samuel must tell Pomare the *Haweis* was not to trade in opposition to the *Governor Macquarie*.[13] Samuel left in the *Governor Macquarie* in early December 1820.[14]

On Samuel's homeward voyage he stopped for supplies at Ravaivae in the Austral Islands. To his astonishment more than 800 islanders had gathered for Christian worship, "How greatly affecting and delightful was the scene which presented itself!" Samuel observed, "The whole of their gods are mutilated; removed from their Morais (places of worship), and even converted into stools at the entrance to the church". Since no missionary had visited the island, Samuel thought "the great change from idolatry to Christianity the more wonderful". However, Pomare had visited the island about 18 months previously, leaving one of his chiefs to teach reading and writing. A Christian from 1812, the king used all his power to persuade the islanders to remove their idolatry.[15]

In April 1821, Pomare made Samuel Henry sole agent for his cargoes in Port Jackson and elsewhere.[16] In command of the *Governor Macquarie*, Samuel reached Port Jackson with 148 casks of pork, 11 of lard, 9 water casks, a whale boat and two swivels, on 30th May.[17] At once he wrote to the *Sydney Gazette* with news of the "wholly unparalleled and unprecedented" event witnessed at Ravaivae.[18] Then he called on Eagar who thought Pomare had accepted the brig and the cargo on two counts. Samuel told him the king intended sending three cargoes of pork in return for the cargo and brig. And Eagar understood Pomare wanted the vessel repaired. Hoping to stop Pomare and Eagar trading between the islands without reference to the missionaries, Marsden sent for Samuel. He reminded Samuel the son of a missionary should do nothing against the interests of the missionaries who "could not buy a pig nor arrowroot". With Marsden at his side, Samuel tendered the pork at 7d a lb to the Government Stores. The same day, 2nd June, Eagar and several of his men boarded the *Governor*

Macquarie with sticks and bludgeons, forcibly taking possession of the vessel and cargo.[19] Two days later at the Sydney Bench of Magistrates, Samuel accused Eagar of unlawfully taking the cargo. The magistrates dismissed the case.[20]

At the beginning of July 1821, Samuel and Sophia sailed for Tahiti in the *Westmoreland* which Marsden had chartered for Pomare and the missionaries.[21] Before Samuel left the colony, he arranged to sue Eagar in the Supreme Court of Civil Jurisdiction. At the trial in August, Samuel aimed to recover the cost of Pomare's cargo taken by the defendant. He did not deny owing Eagar for the goods supplied despite the merchant greatly inflating certain items according to witnesses Robert Jenkins and Robert Campbell. Eagar claimed he seized the cargo because Pomare breached the "agreed" conditions, particularly the obligation to accept the brig as well as the cargo. Samuel recovered damages of £1208 6s 6d, the difference in value of the cargoes supplied by Eagar and Pomare.[22] In May 1822 Eagar challenged the decision in the Court of Appeals presided over by Governor Thomas Brisbane. Eagar argued Pomare owed him nearly £6000 for the brig, cargo and commission fees. The Governor confirmed the previous verdict, finding Eagar not only made a good profit on his goods by marking them up by as much as 150%, but also possessed the *Governor Macquarie*. However, Eagar won £525, freight costs for the cargo shipped to Tahiti. The Governor commented on Marsden's "wholly indefensible" conduct.[23] In 1827 Eagar appealed to the highest court available, the English Privy Council, which reversed the decision. Samuel was to return the £1208 6s 6d. Pomare II got the brig but had to refund Eagar for the cargo he supplied.[24]

James Wilshire and Robert Jenkins were appointed the two jurors in the Governor's Court in January 1822.[25] The two had been plaintiffs in the court. James won cases against John Doling, who owed £7 10s for goods and a promissory note, and Thomas Clarkson, who farmed for James, owed £6 8s 3d for delivered goods. Robert also succeeded in cases against James Vandercom of Liverpool, butcher George Cribb of the Rocks, John Croaker of Sydney, carpenter Thomas Turner of Sydney, John Hascroft of Upper Minto and William Johnston of George's River. All failed to honour promissory notes valued between £30 and £50.[26] Wives Esther and Jemima applied to the Female Orphan Institution for young female apprentices. In February 1822, Mary Kinsela was placed with Esther and Bertha Loveridge with Jemima.[27] The assignments failed. Mary died later in the year; the Wilshires chided for not communicating properly "relative to her death".[28] Bertha absconded in 1825.[29]

The *Sydney Gazette* of 1st March 1822 announced the *Tiger* had landed a still for Robert Jenkins. The newspaper described the still:

> *It is the first of the kind allowed to be imported into the colony. Two hundred gallons may be distilled at once; which is the size of the still; and a brewing copper is attached, containing 1000 gallons. The still, with its appendages, cost £800.*[30]

Stills became legal on 1st August.[31] A week after the still arrived, the Jenkins "entertained a select company" at dinner. Eight of the party dined in the brewing copper; other guests sat nearby, "content to fare sumptuously".[32] The Jenkins's home was spacious with a hall, eight rooms, a detached kitchen, cellar, harness-room, a three-stall stable, large shed, two chaise houses, and a front and back garden. For his work, Robert had a counting house, large warehouse with a shopfront facing George Street and two warehouses with lofts standing next to the lane.[33]

His apprenticeship finished, George Pitt Wood sailed to Tahiti where he spent most of his first year. On 21st March 1822 he left on the *Queen Charlotte* with sister, Sophia Henry, and brother-in-law and captain of the ship, Samuel Pinder Henry.[34] Marsden helped Samuel buy the brig for Pomare II after the couple arrived at Port Jackson in the *Westmoreland* in December 1821.[35] The King died in their absence.[36] Before the *Queen Charlotte* left, Jemima Jenkins, Lucy Wood at her side, bought food and borrowed money for Samuel from Andrew Frazier, a baker and dealer in foodstuffs in the Rocks.[37] Missionary Williams described the New Zealand leg of their voyage. The *Queen Charlotte* had an easy passage to the Bay of Islands where a week was spent loading timber. At the next port of call, North Cape, the natives were "rather troublesome". The Maori Chief sat in the companionway preventing Mrs Williams and Mrs Sophia Henry going below. A Tahitian on the *Queen Charlotte* pushed him out of the way. "White with rage", the chief took out a knife and threatened to stab the Tahitian who "seized a sword in self-defense". Once separated, the anger of the two subsided. Shortly afterwards the wind dropped and eight or nine large canoes, some carrying 20 to 30 men, came close to the boat. It took the threat of guns to disperse them. The thought of the ship becalmed near the shore all night frightened the passengers, especially the women, wrote Reverend Williams who "prayed in his little cabin". When Samuel went down to tell the passengers a breeze was springing up, their "fears were turned into songs of praise for the very merciful interposition of a gracious God".[38]

On 4th May 1822 Robert Jenkins was on his way home with friends from an auction in Surry Hills. In George Street the horse took fright and threw Robert, "both falling together". Medical help was "of no avail" as he remained in a "state of insensibility". Robert, in his 45th year, would be greatly missed by his family and friends:

> *As a husband, his inconsolable widow has to mourn the loss of an inestimable partner; as a brother, the weeping sisters have to regret their sudden deprivation of an affectionate protector in a land to which they have but lately been introduced; as a father, none could be more tender; as a friend, his urbanity of disposition has been pretty well established during a residence of 14 years amongst us.*

In the public sphere Robert made a major contribution:

> *A merchant of the first rank, possessing and evincing public spiritedness in an eminent degree, Mr Jenkins long rendered the colony of New South Wales the most essential and invaluable services; he was a strictly honourable and honest man; and was ever actively engaged in promoting our colonial prosperity.*[39]

Margaret Steven, biographer of merchant and shipowner Robert Campbell, praised Robert, "the Riley brothers, Alexander Berry and Edward Wollstonecraft, and Robert Jenkins, all brought depth and respectability to Port Jackson".[40] Robert requested a private funeral, "attended only by a few respectable friends if such are to be found in NSW". The funeral took place at St Philips on 6th May, the burial in the Sydney Burial Ground, now Central Railway Station.[41]

Days after the death of Susannah Faithfull, and "knowing the uncertainty of human life", Robert made his will.[42] His witnesses were George and Sophia Wood, and John Wood of Chipping in the Bringelly district, a settler who arrived in 1818.[43] Jemima was sole executor of Robert's estate of £20,000. (William D. Rubenstein, author of *All Time Australian 200 Rich List*, judged Robert the third wealthiest Australian in the years 1788 to 1849.[44]) Robert named Jemima guardian of Robert, eight and William, six. She was to provide their sons with "as good an education as in this colony can be had". His "dear wife" inherited the Sydney properties in George Street and Macquarie Street, other unspecified property, all the merchandise, the bank shares, promissory notes and securities. He also gave her the "full profits of land and stock". He advised her to keep the herd at 1000. When Robert and William reached 21, Jemima was to give them equal shares of the "lands out of Sydney". Robert gave £500 to each of his sisters, Susannah and Elizabeth Jenkins, who arrived in New South Wales in February 1821.[45] Once Jemima received the letters of administration in

May, James Wilshire and John Wood sold the goods at the store in George Street.[46] Architect Henry Kitchen also died in 1822 and, with Robert his chief creditor, Jemima applied to the Supreme Court to administer his estate of no more than £250.[47]

The missionaries asked Captain Samuel Pinder Herny to move members of their group from Moorea to Tubuai in the Austral Islands. Before leaving in the *Queen Charlotte*, first mate Thomas Ebrill told Samuel a pirate captain intended capturing the *Queen Charlotte* at Tubuai. The pirate had seized the brig *Prudence* and renamed it *Arocano*. After reaching Tubai, Samuel invited the captain of the *Arocano* and two of his men to tea on the *Queen Charlotte*, the ruse ensuring their detention. In the evening, Samuel, Ebrill, seven Europeans and 10 Tahitians set out in two boats for the *Arocano*. They confined the six men on-board and Ebrill took charge of the ship. The next morning Samuel rounded up the crew of the *Arocano* on snore. The ships left Tubuai on 27th June 1822, Samuel commanding the *Queen Charlotte* and Ebrill the *Arocano*; the incident reported to the magistrate at Tahiti on 1st July.[48] In Samuel's absence, on 17th June 1822 Sophia gave birth to her first child, naming him William John Wood Henry after his grandfathers. Perhaps this event prompted Samuel to name the Sophia Islands in the Tuamotu Archipelago. He discovered the islands, now the Actaeon Group, while pearl fishing for the missionaries in the *Queen Charlotte*.[49]

In September 1822 local magistrates supervised musters of the population and the land and stock. The free people of Richmond gathered at the local schoolhouse, men on 5th and women on 7th. William Faithfull owned 1350 acres (50 more than Bigge reported?) which supported 37 acres of wheat, 20 of maize, 6 of barley, 121 cattle, 410 sheep, 60 hogs and 9 horses. He had stored 100 bushels of wheat and 400 of maize. Six convicts worked for William. Son William (Thomas in the muster) owned 20 cattle and 100 sheep. Neighbour Elizabeth Pitt held 610 acres, two devoted to a garden and orchard, the rest holding 12 acres of both wheat and maize, three of barley, one of potatoes, 93 cattle, 23 hogs, and five horses. She had set apart 10 bushels of wheat and 70 of maize. A convict helped Elizabeth.[50] At the Governor's Court, Belmont Hill resident William Sims Bell accused Elizabeth of taking his "team of bullocks and 6 milch cows". Although Sims sued Elizabeth for £50, her fine was just £1.[51] Seven-year-olds George Faithfull and George Matcham Pitt attended Richmond School in 1822. George F did not return in 1823; George P stayed until the end of 1824.[52]

The free inhabitants of Sydney assembled at the Courthouse, men on 2nd and women on 10th September. The muster excluded the land and stock of James Wilshire but included James and Esther, their eight children, and live-in helpers colonial-born Mary Roberts and free settler James William Osburn. Esther was pregnant with John Jackson Wilshire who died aged five weeks on 19th December. Also, three-week-old Amelia Jemima Wilshire was buried on 18th May 1824. James employed 26 mostly convict servants. The muster showed Jemima Jenkins living in Sydney with her sons, and housekeeper Lucy Wood and employee William Pitt Faithfull. Jemima owned 2,100 acres, 1200 cattle, 17 horses and 10 acres of wheat. Ten convicts and ex-convicts, nearly all at Illawarra, worked for her. Two servants and "adopted" 13-year old Bertha Loveridge helped in her home.[53] In the July before the muster, William Pitt Faithfull was one of Jemima's witnesses at the Criminal Court of Jurisdiction. William stated he was "in the country" when Edward Stone robbed her stores. On returning, he identified the missing items, three dozen (36) pairs of woollen hose and five pieces of yellow nankeen, valued at 40s. Stone pleaded not guilty, his sentence seven years at Port Macquarie penal settlement.[54]

On 5th October 1822, tenders opened for masons, carpenters and builders interested in finishing Jemima Jenkins's residence in O'Connell Street. The late William Mansel started the house; the plans held at the office of convict architect Francis Greenway.[55]

On his arrival Greenway worked on private commissions and continued to do so once appointed Colonial Architect in 1816. His first major commission was the parsonage at Parramatta built by James Smith. At Macquarie's request, Greenway designed buildings still standing in Macquarie Street, Hyde Park Barracks (1817), Queens Square (1817), Government House Stables, now the Conservatorium (1819), and St James Church (1819-1822).[56] Jemima advertised 11 George Street for rent on 1st November.[57] Her new home stood on the second block at the north end of the east side of O'Connell Street.[58] At auction she paid £200 for the allotment next door, giving her more than half an acre in street.[59] Jemima's place was one of "several excellent specimens of modern architecture" in O'Connell Street.[60]

After an absence of nine months, on 22nd January 1823 George Pitt Wood reached Sydney in the cutter H.M. *Mermaid*.[61] From O'Connell Street he wrote to Governor Brisbane for a ticket of occupation for 2000 acres surrounding his stockyard in the Shoalhaven gullies. The land was near Windellama, between the today's towns of Goulburn and Braidwood. George needed extra pasture because he could not keep the 240 cattle, branded JW and WF, on his grant of 200 acres bordering the Grose River at Richmond. (Figure 3) He also asked for a ticket of occupation at Tomboye in the Braidwood district, where he had 525 cattle and hoped to increase that number by 300.[62] George received 2000 acres at Windellama and 2000 acres at Bumballa, not far from later Marulan. Jemima had secured tickets of occupation for 6000 acres at Tomboye, and 5000 acres at Bumballa, near Robert's 500 acre at Tallowa.[63] Jemima gave William Pitt Faithfull some of her acres at Bumballa positioned alongside 1500 acres he had leased. William soon exchanged the Bumballa land for 2000 acres on the banks of the Shoalhaven to the south of his grant at Boro, "about five miles from Mrs Jenkins' stations" at Tomboye.[64] Jemima also occupied 6000 acres alongside Berkeley.[65] From the start of the colony, unauthorised use of Crown land caused problems. Tickets of Occupation allowing temporary use of Crown land provided the earliest form of regulation.

Jemima Jenkins ran into trouble in selling Robert's still. While Francis Ewin Forbes wanted the still, he proposed unacceptable terms. John Wood of Chipping sold the still to Samuel Terry and delivered the accessories to him. On 27th January 1823 a surprised Jemima found the still and head removed though not the boiler. Forbes sent Jemima a letter in which he admitted delivering the still and head to distiller Robert Cooper out of concern for the still. After checking John Wood had not sold Forbes the still, Jemima issued a warrant for the arrest of Robert Cooper. The Bench of Magistrates dismissed Cooper, the Superintendent of Police finding Jemima agreed to sell the still to Forbes before receiving a better offer from Terry. The evidence of naval officer Vickers Jacob, Jemima's tenant in George Street, did not help her cause.[66] Jemima petitioned the Governor, but he refused to reopen the case.[67] Her business sense prevailed; she advertised "Good old Medoc", red wine from southwest France, at 34s a dozen (12), and "good port wine" at 96s a dozen.[68]

Jemima chased up Robert's debts and a few of her own. On Robert's behalf, in the Governor's Court, she successfully prosecuted Edward Lamb of Sydney for goods and money, John Masterson of Campbelltown for goods and a promissory note, Sydney butcher and publican Mark Bifield for a promissory note, and Parramatta wheelwright Charles Weaver for a debt. Their liabilities ranged from £16 16s to £50.[69] To recover the £230 Thomas Gilberthorpe owed Robert (Court of Civil Jurisdiction 1819), Jemima advertised the sale of 1000 bushels of maize on the defendant's farm at Pitt Town.[70] In the Governor's court Jemima defended a case of Robert's. Victualler Edward Franks sought unpaid rent for a furnished room in his "travelling house" in Hunter Street. Treasurer Robert Jenkins and Mr Eagar paid 10s a week to rent the room for members of the Sydney Reading Room which offered subscribers recent British newspapers, magazines and reviews. Following Robert's death, Jemima found an outstanding account for the plaintiff's purchase of spirits and other goods. Franks told Jemima Robert gave him the goods to compensate for the cost of the room. The court awarded Franks £22 15s for rent and candles. His Honour felt the case should not have come before the court. Franks commented on Robert's premature death, "a circumstance much regretted by an extensive circle of friends". On her own account, in the Governor's Court, Jemima won £5 5s from publican John Dargan of Sydney, £15 from Elizabeth Cullen of Pitt Town and £15 10s from butcher George Cribb of Sydney.[71] Again on Robert's behalf, the new Supreme Court of Civil Jurisdiction ordered surveyor James Meehan to pay Jemima £52 10s 8d for the use of a house, outbuildings and land. [72]

In May 1823 Samuel Pinder Henry brought 80 casks of pork to Port Jackson in the *Queen Charlotte*. Sophia came with her husband.[73] Samuel purchased the 70 ton government cutter *Snapper* for 2000 Spanish dollars, then equivalent to 4s 2d. On the spot he paid $1000 and arranged to pay the balance to Mr Hassall and Solomon Levy in six months. (The holey dollar and dump were withdrawn from circulation in September 1828).[74] However Samuel had not paid for the goods and money Andrew Frazier gave Jemima early in 1822. Frazier sued Jemima for the debt in the Governor's Court in September 1823. The evidence of Lucy Wood "failed to prove the defendant's liability".[75] Samuel and Sophia left Sydney in July.[76] Sophia gave birth to a second son Samuel Pinder Henry II in September. By 1824 the Henrys had made their home at Atinua, on the coral-fringed south-west coast of Tahiti, not far from good anchorage at Mairipehi.[77] On 21st April 1824 the Henrys attended Pomare III's coronation, the first since the Tahitians embraced Christianity, hence an important occasion for the missionaries. About 8000 attended, including the kings and chiefs, governors, district judges and magistrates, from Tahiti, Moorea and the Leeward Islands. The king, aged about 4, lived only until 1827.[78]

James Wilshire was a plaintiff, defendant and juror in the Sydney courts in the early to mid-twenties. In the Court of Civil Jurisdiction, he won £150 and £200 for loans from Samuel Laycock but lost £31 9s to Solomon Levy for a promissory note he signed but failed to honour.[79] At the Governor's Court, Dr Francis Moran filed for damages of £30 from James. Moran had tended and cured James's apprentice James Young with "divers Medicines, medical potions, (and) Plaisters". The court dismissed the case. In this court too, James recovered two debts, £12 2s 2d from Alfred Simms of Bringelly and £50 from James Smith of Parramatta.[80] After the Governor's Court closed in 1824, Quarter Sessions dealt with all crimes except those punishable by death. The grand jurors of the court decided if allegations warranted a full trial and regularly inspected the gaols. James signed the report on the prison in George Street handed down in September 1825. The grand jurors found the prison "generally clean and wholesome" though lacking in security. Also, they noted damp debtors' quarters and debtors subject to moral contamination "from their continued intercourse with common felons". The grand jurors interviewed prisoners. Elizabeth Bridge told them five of her seven young sons lacked proper care after authorities sent her husband to a penal settlement. The grand jurors recommended placing the children in the Orphan School. Another prisoner spoke about the severity of his punishment, prompting the grand jurors to remark on the "present evil arising from any single individual having the power to inflict punishment". The grand jurors inspected the *Phoenix*, the floating prison moored in Lavendar Bay, pronouncing it clean and healthy but lacking clothing and bedding.[81]

"Leather is made by a great variety of individuals; but in greatest quantity and perfection, I believe, by Mr Wilshire of Sydney". It was Peter Cunningham, a surgeon-superintendent of convict transports who spent short periods of time in the colony between 1820 and 1826, who praised the leather produced by James.[82] To store and sell his leather and other goods, in 1823 James had secured 21-year leases on allotments in Parramatta, in Phillip Street, Ross Street and Pennant Street, now Victoria Road.[83] James put two properties on the market. He sold the land at Liberty Plains in September 1824 for £300. And he sold a house and land in George Street, one block removed from Liverpool Street in July 1825 for £165.[84] In October 1825 a fire rose from the kitchen to the upper story of the Wilshires' home. One of the older boys discovered the fire and quickly put it out with the help of four passing gentlemen.[85]

The Wilshire boys achieved good results at the Sydney Grammar School founded by the gifted, but eccentric, Dr Laurence Halloran.[86] William Pitt Wilshire received a silver pen for an unspecified achievement in December 1821.[87] James Robert Wilshire earned a medal for Latin in January 1824 and in mid-year took home a second medal for "rapid progress" in English and Mathematics.[88] In the half-yearly examinations in 1825, Austin Forrest Wilshire won the arithmetic prize and the school recognized his "penmanship".[89] Robert Pitt Jenkins also performed well at the school, winning a prize for his results in the half-yearly examinations in 1824 and a silver medal for Classical Learning in June 1825.[90] William Warren Jenkins studied with Halloran, Dr John Dunmore Lang and William Cape. An avid reader, throughout his life William "devoted much of his time to storing his mind with useful and elevating knowledge".[91] Dissatisfied with the education available, Halloran proposed setting up the Sydney Public Free Grammar school under the patronage of Governor Brisbane. James Wilshire and others who gave £50 became governors for the life of the school. The school, which opened in November 1825 with Halloran as principal, failed through lack of support at the end of 1826.[92]

In March 1825, James Tofield drove Jemima Jenkins and her two sons in a carriage along a narrow road. At the same time, on the same narrow road, Colonial Treasurer William Balcombe was on his way home to O'Connell Street in his carriage after attending the races in Hyde Park. At the Quarter Sessions, Balcombe charged James

Tofield "with having furiously driven the carriage of his mistress" against his carriage, "whereby the lives of His Majesty's subjects were endangered, and some ladies in carriages then passing, were put in serious alarm". The Bench of Magistrates ordered Tofield "to be bound over in good and efficient sureties to keep the peace towards all His Majesty's subjects, and more especially, towards William Balcombe, Esq. for 12 months". The *Sydney Gazette* published Jemima's comments on the incident. She agreed with Tofield's penalty for "furious driving", but thought Balcombe had less to complain about than she did. She complained that Balcombe "had not only the crown but the entire road to himself", whereby he forced her carriage "amongst the bushes on the side of the road, to the great danger of myself and the children".[93] The next year Jemima experienced another coach incident on her way home from the races. When her coach driver came to a standstill "to put down some ladies" at the Wilshires' gate in Brickfield-Hill, the pole of Sir John Jamison's carriage struck against the dickey (seat) of her carriage. Because Jamison's coach driver John Burgess deliberately caused the damage, he was sentenced to three days on the treadmill.[94]

Meanwhile William Faithfull was one of 19 jurors sworn in at the first meeting of the Windsor Court of Quarter Sessions in December 1824. The jurors inspected Windsor Gaol, finding scanty rooms, poor beds and no single cells. Their recommendations included classification of prisoners, extension of solitary confinement and punishment likely to deter.[95] In 1825 William sought farm labourers on three occasions. In January he contacted the Colonial Secretary to complain about the lack of convict workers to harvest his wheat. He told the secretary not to expect grain without help to reap and thrash it. In autumn though, he sold James Hankinson 200 bushels of wheat at 10s 6d a bushel to make bread for the soldiers and prisoners.[96] In August he asked for six men from the last convict ship. In November he wanted help to reap 50 acres of wheat.[97] Margaret and William had a daughter and son, Helen Eliza

Faithfull on 19th March 1824 and James Robert Faithfull on 25th August 1825. Sadly, James died at two.

It appears Lucy Wood first met her Henry grandsons, William and Samuel II, after Sophia and Samuel arrived in the *Brutus* in April 1825. The family lodged at Mrs Waple's place in Pitt Street.[98] Samuel asked Governor Brisbane to cover his expenses for rescuing and supporting the crew of the London based *Policy*, wrecked off Tahiti in May 1824.[99] The Henrys left in the *Governor Macquarie* in August 1825.[100] In April 1826, Sophia visited again, bringing one of her sons and a servant in the *Minerva*.[101] They left in the *Minerva* in June.[102]

Although Richmond village was "flourishing", the marriage of George Pitt Wood and Elizabeth Markwell took place at the temporary church of St Peters.[103] By licence on 9th September 1826 the Reverend John Cross wed George, the only son of Lucy and John Wood, and Elizabeth, second daughter of Maria and Thomas Markwell. Sophia and Henry Hewitt, Elizabeth's sister and brother-in-law, witnessed the wedding. Thomas Markwell gave permission for 16-year-old Elizabeth to marry 24-year old George. According to "family tradition", Markwell gave his daughter 500 sheep and two imported Suffolk Punch horses.[104] Elizabeth's father arrived on the *Scarborough* in 1790 with a sentence of 14 years for theft. Elizabeth's mother was born in the colony to Thomas and Ann Cheshire, née Teasdale, who also came in the Second Fleet transports *Neptune* and *Lady Juliana*.[105] Elizabeth grew up in Richmond, her baptism on 22nd April 1810 one of the first at St Peters.[106] To support his wife, George farmed not only his 200 fertile acres at Richmond but also 300 acres (leased?) in the Hunter Valley on which he grazed 240 cattle and cultivated 55 acres.[107] Early in 1827 George imported three casks of goods from Tahiti.[108] That year, Lucy Wood asked Chief Justice, Francis Forbes (not the Francis Forbes interested in Jemima's still), to settle the long-delayed affairs of her husband, "That the said John Wood

Figure 14. Andrew Gibson

was possessed of Property and left no will in this Colony. That the effects of the said John Wood still remain unadministered". Lucy had charged the estate for a coatee (a short-tailed coat), waistcoats, jackets and trousers.[109]

The *Sydney Gazette* announced the February 1827 marriage of 16-year old Alice Faithfull, the only daughter of Susannah and William Faithfull:

> *By License, on Saturday, the 24th instant at St James' Church, by the Reverend Richard Hill, Andrew Gibson Esq. Assistant-Surgeon to the New South Wales Veteran Company, to Miss Alice Faithful (sic), Daughter of William Faithful (sic), Esq. a long and respected resident of Richmond, niece to Mrs Jenkins, of O'Connell-street, and also to Mrs Wilshire, the wife of James Wilshire, Esq. Brickfield-hill, Sydney; also, niece to Mrs Wood, a respectable resident at Richmond.[110]*

Louisa Wilshire and Captain S. Wright signed the marriage register. Alice received 60 cows, 200 ewes and three rams from her father, and 56 heifers, three brood mares, a horse and a filly from Jemima.[111]

Andrew Gibson was a member of the medical staff of 39th Regiment of Foot when he arrived in the *John Barry* in July 1826.[112] (Figure 14) Andrew was a hospital assistant at the Battle of Waterloo in 1815. He was court-martialled in Halifax in 1821 but readmitted as a hospital assistant in October 1825 and soon rose to assistant surgeon.[113] In July 1827 the Colonial Medical Department employed Andrew as an assistant surgeon, his position backdated to May 1826.[114] For £444 a year, Andrew attended the civil establishment, three veterans companies and the family of Governor Darling. He also practised privately.[115] In September 1827 the Governor sent Andrew to the Shoal Haven to help a veteran injured in a shooting accident. Negotiating the rugged terrain took him several days and although he treated the wound, the soldier died.[116] The Gibsons lived with Jemima. Alice gave birth to Alice Jemima Gibson in O'Connell Street in December 1827.[117]

On applying for land at the "competent of 18, William Pitt Faithfull received the smallest grant of 320 acres on the edge of the Goulburn Plains. Before the land was surveyed, William took advantage of new regulations:

> *Land will be granted in the proportion of one Square Mile or 640 acres for every (£500) Five Hundred Pounds Sterling of Capital, which the applicant can immediately command to the extent of four Square Mile or 2,560 acres.*

Keeping a convict for a year earned the applicant an extra 100 acres.[118] In June 1827 William advised the Land Board he had £2232 in cattle, sheep, pigs, horses, a plough, cart and tools. He had bought 50 cows from Jemima, while his father gave him the rest of his stock. Jemima, his referee, told the Land Board she knew William well. He had lived with her for seven years, and since Robert's death supervised her pastoral affairs. Her nephew was "a very careful young man" of "excellent character". The Land Board observed William, "very tall and stout. .. a modest, unassuming young Gentleman, who has received better Education than could have been expected within the Colony". William received 1280 acres at Coorangangennoe on the edge of the Goulburn Plains.[119] This land was beside 800 acres his father bought for £150 from Thomas Fenton in 1825; the deed witnessed by George Pitt Wood.[120] On the last day of 1827, William's grant was approved.[121]

Plaintiff Andrew Gibson won two trials of assault at the Sydney Quarter Sessions in 1828. Cabinet-maker David Bell rented a small house with an attached workshop adjoining Jemima's place. Bell called on Jemima, pleading hardship and insisting he was usually regular in his rent payments. As Bell had previously broken his word, Andrew asked him to leave. In the evening of 14th January,

Jemima watched Bell walk up and down the street with a stick. She alerted her coachman, Patrick Moran. When Andrew came home, Bell "placed himself before the gate", used violent and abusive language, and refused to let Andrew to pass until "he gave him a good hiding". Andrew called Bell "a blackguard" (scoundrel). With a large stick Bell struck Andrew on the head, knocking off his hat, Andrew deflecting some of the force with his umbrella. Andrew sent the coachman to fetch a constable. Meanwhile, several people arrived on the scene to "prevent further violence". Bell was fined £100.[122] The second episode of assault took place in February. Dr Francis Moran claimed, in the presence of others Andrew stated he "kept low company and was a frequenter of pot-houses (taverns)". Believing his reputation as a gentleman and professional man impugned, Moran rode his horse to O'Connell Street and alighted. He addressed a few words to Andrew, then struck him so hard he fell to the ground. Found guilty of aggravated assault and fined £175, Moran had to keep the peace for 12 months or forfeit a bond of £100.[123]

In 1828 defendant James Wilshire lost a trial of assault at the Sydney Quarter Sessions. The incident occurred at James's "extensive and capacious" property at the end of Bathurst Street, adjoining Cockle Bay. There, in 1826, he began slaughtering and salting meat for the local and overseas market.[124] The new business made sense since James used the by-products to produce leather, parchment, soap, candles and glue. After securing a contract to supply the Government with salted meat, Daniel Cooper and Samuel Terry sent William Klensendorlffe to James's abattoir to supervise killing the beasts and weighing the carcasses. When James asked him to leave, Klensendorlffe replied "in terms not the most courteous" and an argument developed. James struck Klensendorlffe who returned the blow with interest. The judge, though considering James had a right to expel the plaintiff, fined him £1 for using excessive violence.[125] James was both plaintiff and defendant in the Supreme Court of Civil Jurisdiction in 1827-8. He won suits against John

Raine, £59 4s 10d for money borrowed, Thomas F. Hawkins, £30 2s 3d for unpaid goods, Henry D. Owen, £52 1s 8d for a debt, and John Browne, £48 5d for not honouring a bill of exchange. He lost £24 10s 10d on a bill of exchange to Richard Charles Pritchett.[126]

Also in 1828, Jemima Jenkins was a plaintiff and defendant in two cases at the Supreme Court of Civil Jurisdiction. She employed attorney William Charles Wentworth to sue Thomas Horton James over a promissory note offered for horned cattle and goods. The debt probably concerned the 75 acres along the Botany Bay Road which Jemima sold James for £375, the property costing her £230 10s in 1822. The court awarded her £194 2d. Jemima lost £100 to plaintiff John McIntyre for not letting him select the cattle he agreed to buy at the Illawarra.[127] Despite fashionable O'Connell Street and other town attractions, Jemima decided to move to the countryside. In June 1828, she bought Eagle Vale farm near Campbelltown from Daniel Cooper, paying him £3250 for 1605 acres consolidated from various grants.[128] Fully fenced and divided into paddocks, Eagle Vale had a "well-finished" brick house measuring 70 feet by 30 feet with a detached kitchen, dairy, an excellent garden full of fruit trees, men's huts, sheep sheds, a barn and a piggery.[129] At the same time, Jemima sold 11 George Street to Daniel Cooper and Solomon Levy for £3600.[130] The merchants soon sold her place to lessee Alexander Sparke for £4000. The price elicited comments with a familiar resonance:

> *The buildings, with the exception of the store, are only fit to be razed to the ground, and as the store might now be erected for about £1000, Mr Spark has given at least £3000 for the allotment of the ground! Land is not merely land now-a-days, but land appears to be gold.*[131]

The "amiable" Mrs Jenkins retired to her country estate in August 1828.[132]

6 The Grandchildren Marry

A detailed and compulsory census took place in November 1828. At Richmond, Elizabeth Pitt was mother to George, 14, Mary, 13, Robert, 11 and William, 9, and two children fathered by William Scott - John Scott, 4 and Elizabeth Scott, 2. Elizabeth's youngest child, seven-year-old Eliza, lived in Pitt Street with her grandmother, Hannah Laycock. Elizabeth owned 730 (630?) acres, 200 cleared and 70 cultivated, and 250 cattle. She employed five servants including overseer William Scott. William, 26 came free in the *Surry* in 1816 with Margaret Scott, 21 (his sister?), who also worked for Elizabeth.[133] Two more children were born to Elizabeth and William Scott, Augusta Scott in 1831 and Frances Scott in 1833.[134]

Next door to Elizabeth Pitt, William and Margaret Faithfull looked after George 15 and Helen, 4. Margaret had a female servant and William about 12 convict servants. William owned 2190 acres (40 acres more than in 1825?) on which he cultivated 153 acres and grazed 450 cattle, 720 sheep and 16 horses.[135] In 1829 William bought 50 acres and 60 acres in the district of Prospect for £360. By 1830 he had also acquired 30 acres at Toongabbie.[136] In 1828 William joined the Windsor branch of the Agricultural Society of New South Wales, which began in 1822 and is still active.[137]

Close by the Faithfulls and Pitts, Elizabeth and George Pitt Wood lived with their new son, Thomas John Wood. Sadly he died aged six weeks in December. The Woods had also lost their first child Lucy Sophia, aged about two months, in October 1827. Fortunately their third child survived; William Henry Wood, born in November 1829. George owned 270 (200?) acres, 70 cleared and 50 cultivated, 100 cattle and 200 sheep. Four convicts worked for him.[138] By 1825 George was a juror at the Windsor Court of Quarter Sessions. In January 1829 George and William Faithfull judged a "light session of 13 trials for crimes such as uttering counterfeit coin, violent assault on a person and the theft of a shirt."[139]

Jemima Jenkins had settled in her new home at Eagle Vale. Robert, 15 and William, 13 were finishing their education with local clergyman and classical scholar, Thomas Reddall.[140] Jemima owned 9075 acres, 552 cleared and 134 cultivated, 2000 cattle, 320 sheep and 60 horses. She employed 29 men and one woman.[141] Named one of the largest land-holders in the "new country to the south", Jemima acquired most of this land at auction.[142] She paid £500 for 2000 acres beside Robert's 1000 acres at Berkeley, and with the 270 acres Robert purchased from five grantees, the acreage totalled 3270.[143] The estate had a long water frontage to Lake Illawarra.[144] At Bumballa Jemima bought 2000 acres for £1500, while at nearby Tallowa she supplemented Robert's 500 acres with 250 acres for £75.[145] At Tomboye, near present Charleyong, she gave £600 for 1000 acres and called the farm Tomboye Forest.[146] Together, Berkeley, Bumballa and Tomboye accounted for more than 7000 acres. Adding Jemima's 1605 acres at Eagle Vale and Robert's 500 acres near Parramatta, her acreage was more than 9000. Robert had sold the grant of 400 acres west of the Hawkesbury since he advertised only Swilly Farm for let just before his death. Other properties of Robert's turned up in letters Jemima wrote to the Colonial Secretary and in cases she presented to the Court of Claims. These sources revealed she owned an allotment in Macquarie Street, Parramatta (which Robert bought at a sheriff's sale in 1818), 30 acres at the Field of Mars and property in Kent Street, Sydney.[147] Jemima purchased more land in 1831, paying William Laycock £300 for 100 acres in the parish of St George and 100 acres in the district of Botany Bay.[148]

Lucy Wood and William Pitt Faithfull still lived at Eagle Vale.[149] Lucy had advertised her Richmond farm for rent in May, and with Jemima's move impending, advised interested parties to contact the Wilshires at 48 George Street.[150] William superintended Jemima's properties for £150 a year.[151] He found time to improve his grant Pitt Mount. Five convicts helped him clear 800 acres? (See Chapter 7, Ref 11), cultivate 10, and tend eight horses, 219 cattle and 300 sheep. Two convicts worked at Boro.[152] William also occupied 3000 acres adjoining his grant. A new regulation permitted use of crown land bordering the properties of land-holders for a yearly charge of 2s 6d for 100 acres.[153]

Alice, Andrew, and one-year-old Alice Jemima Gibson lived in O'Connell Street.[154] Andrew's office was conveniently located in the surgeons' quarters in the most northerly of the three hospital buildings in Macquarie Street. In the previous July, following the death of four passengers from smallpox, Andrew vaccinated three or four children from the *Bussorah Merchant* at the quarantine station in Neutral Bay.[155] Earlier, in April, he attended the first meeting of the Australian Racing Club held in Macquarie Place.[156] In the same month, Andrew, Alice and Jemima attended meetings of the Parramatta Female School of Industry, which trained young women for domestic service. To aid the school, Andrew gave a cow and Jemima five.[157] In June 1827, to secure a land grant, Andrew gave the Land Board a list of his possessions. His referee, Jemima Jenkins, gave him 56 heifers, a filly, three brood mares and a horse. Andrew bought 50 bullocks, a horse, a chaise and a harness. Also, he owned property in Ireland and life insurance which paid £100 on his death. The Board noted Alice's possessions. Andrew assets of £2510 entitled him to 2560 acres. William Pitt Faithfull agreed to manage Andrew's property until he retired from the Colonial Medical Service in February 1829. The Civil Establishment refused Andrew a pension but the army gave him half pay, £75.[158] Alice and Andrew settled on their grant which they called Tirranna after their parish of Terranna. The grant was immediately north of William Pitt Faithfull's property.[159] Andrew leased 2000 acres on the perimetre of the grant.[160] Appointed a Magistrate of the colony on his retirement, Andrew dealt with minor crimes as well as convict assignment, discipline and tickets-of-leave. The court met in the small, roughly hewn courthouse in today's North Goulburn.[161]

The census records Hester and James Wilshire with their children, Louisa, 22, William, 21, James, 19, Austin, 17, Elizabeth, 13, Esther, 11, Matilda, 9, Thomas, 7 and Joseph, 2. Joseph Wood Wilshire had been born on 1st February 1826 and baptised at St James on 18th April. Needing help wih her large family, Esther advertised for a wet-nurse and a cook in December 1826 and a housemaid in March 1827.[162] James owned 550 acres, 144 cleared, 387 cattle and 12 horses. He employed about 18 men, including four apprentices. Son William also had a servant.[163] Sons James Robert and Austin applied for land grants. Each owned 2000 cattle given by friends and their father, which John Wood kept at the Cox's River. James Robert refused the offer of 320 acres and bond of £500, complaining the land was not worth £80. He reminded the Colonial Secretary of the 1280 acres given to his cousin, William Pitt Faithfull. Seventeen-year-old Austin did not qualify for a grant.[164] On the north-west corner of George Street and Union Lane, James senior set up Emu Inn, the first licencee James Simmons in 1828.[165] By then, James had secured a contract to supply the Government with 160 tons of salted beef. To fulfil the contract, he asked the Colonial Secretary for four butchers and four coopers.[166]

The problem of finding and keeping skilled and honest workers persisted for James Wilshire. His chief annoyance, "petty tanners" taking apprentices he had trained in "the art and mystery of tanning".[167] James did what he could to help good workers. Shoemaker Thomas Lyon was one he helped. Sentenced to seven years in County Chester for stealing geese, Lyon worked for James on his arrival in 1816. Lyon bought land from James which he improved and sold for nearly £300. In 1817 he appealed unsuccessfully for his wife and six children to join him. On the expiry of his sentence in April 1821, the Home Government refused a further request to bring out his family because he had young children and the youngest child was illegitimate. In 1824 Lyon left for England, hoping to return with his family. James gave him a character reference in which he said Lyon was "a Strict Sober Honest Industious Man". After he arrived in England, Lyon sent the reference to Earl of Bathurst with a request to return to New South Wales with his family at his own expense. The 1828 Census does not include the family.[168] James re-employed two convicts with blemished records. He gave Dennis Lynch a second chance after he spent a month on the treadmill for stealing soap. However, thinking it unwise to sanction Lynch's marriage, James refused to approve his ticket of leave. An unnamed convict who committed a "trifling offence" got his job back when he returned to the Colony. In the previous service of James the convict was not only "strictly honest" but also "never drank any intoxicating liquors".[169]

Besides managing his tannery and slaughterhouse and attending to his farms and inn, James Wilshire contributed to the community. He was a steward at the Anniversary Dinner celebrating founding the Colony in January 1827 and vice-chairman for the same event in 1828.[170] He was elected to the Trader's Committee in 1829.[171] Also in 1829, he was a juror at the inquisition into the lunacy of Mrs Esther Johnston, wife of deceased rebel officer George Johnston. Robert Johnston wanted his mother declared insane, hence unfit to manage her estates. The jury found her "insane, but having lucid moments". Her son failed to gain control of her estates.[172] James supported the Benevolent Society, the Sydney Dispensary and the Female School of Industry. Esther and Miss Wilshire also subscribed to the Female School of Industry.[173] For respite from their busy lives, the Wilshires set up a retreat in Surry Hills, west of today's-Bourke Street, near Devonshire Street. The retreat occupied one of eight acres, holding paddocks James bought for £383 in 1829.[174]

William Pitt Wilshire, 21, eldest son of Esther and James, married Catherine Maria Robertson by licence at St James Church in Sydney on 21st February 1829. The Reverend Richard Hill conducted the weddding before witnesses Elizabeth Wilshire, James Wilshire and William Bland of Pitt Street. Christened at Lambeth, Surrey, in July

1812, Catherine Maria, known as Maria, was the daughter of James Robertson, and Anna Maria Robertson, née Ripley. Maria arrived with her family in the *Providence* in 1822; their settlement in New South Wales recommended by friend Governor Brisbane.[175] Maria's father, a jeweller and clock maker, was appointed superintendent of government clocks.[176] Her brother, Sir John Robertson, was five times premier of NSW.[177] The newly-weds settled next door to William's parents at 47 George Street.[178] William earned his living as a clerk in the Commissariat.[179] He started colour painting about 1829 and probably was Australia's first native-born oil painter.[180]

Samuel Pinder Henry continued trading in the Pacific Ocean. In 1827 he clashed with the native people in the Fiji Islands, with several workers fatally wounded. Twice in 1828 he took produce from the Society Islands to Port Jackson in the *Snapper*.[181] For his most ambitious venture, an expedition for sandalwood to Erromanga Island in the southern New Hebrides (Vanuatu), Samuel chartered the 523 ton *Sophia*. First discovered by Peter Dillon in 1825, sandalwood was shipped to China, usually in exchange for tea. Many objects were made from sandalwood: fans, inlaid boxes, ornaments, perfumes, cosmetics, medicines, and incense for religious and ceremonial occasions. George Bennett, a medical practitioner and naturalist, left an account of the voyage. Knowing from a previous visit how hard it was persuading Erromangans to work for European goods, the *Sophia* stopped at Tongatabu in the Friendly Islands (Tonga) to engage 95 volunteers for six months. The ship sailed from Tonga on 3rd August 1829 and a week later reached Wiriau on the western side of Erromanga. Already on the island, a gang of about 19 Tongans who arrived in the *Snapper* then anchored in the bay. The Tongans, one had been clubbed to death, erected a stockade to protect themselves from repeated attacks. Samuel urged the Tongans to establish friendly relations with the island's inhabitants.[182]

6 The Grandchildren Marry

The morning after their arrival, New Zealanders on-board the *Sophia* rowed a boat ashore with gifts of iron-hoops, hoping to make friendly contact with some Erromangans observed on rocks "abreast" the ship. They persuaded one to come aboard and following his favourable treatment, nine spent several hours "perfectly at their ease" on the *Sophia*. That evening the Tongans reported on reaching the interior of the island, a large group of Erromangans attacked them. They captured an injured native. Bennett saw him in the stockade, "looking as if he expected to be killed and eaten". He was set free after they dressed his wounds and gave him presents. On 24th August 1829, about 50 Erromangans joined the Tongans feasting on a shark and, from 26th, worked alongside them. By then, Bennett had realized "that the tribes are almost constantly at war with the other, and the tribe now with us, being routed by another, had taken refuge with our gang". Sure enough, despite expressing gratitude for their gifts, the Erromangans left in three days. The 113 Tongans collected about three and a half to four tons of sandal wood daily, by felling the small but heavy tree, removing the sap, cutting the wood into portable lengths, and carrying the logs to the stockade. One problem they had, "At several places the descent was so steep as to oblige the bearers to throw their loads before them down the steep places and then descend carefully themselves".[183]

On 2nd September 1829 the *Sophia* left Erromanga with the sandalwood. The ship called at Tahiti; reached Hawaii on 16th November 1829; and sailed from Honolulu in late January 1830. The *Sophia* stopped briefly at Rotuma in the Fijian Islands, leaving on 28th February with volunteers, 200 men and 13 women. Despite the captain of the *Sophia* taking every care to disguise the exact location of Errornanga, steerage passengers, a watchmaker and silversmith, made a small sextant and discovered the island's position. The watchmaker disclosed "the secret to the king and chiefs on a liberal compensation being made to him". Two ships beat the *Sophia* to the island, the Hawaiian *Becket* with 179 workers and the privately owned *Dhaule* with about 130 workers from Rotuma. On 6th March the *Sophia* arrived at Erromanga where many imported workers had died and most others suffered from malaria. The expedition leaders decided to "give up this fatal speculation". They kept the workers from Rotuma on-board and removed the sick from shore to ship. On 7 March, Samuel arrived from Tahiti at the helm of the *Minerva*. The small *Minerva* proved most helpful in moving the sick Tongans on to the *Sophia*, the last boat-load coming under attack.[184] In Sydney on 13th November 1830, Samuel reported the loss of 88 of labourers on the doomed expedition.[185] He was about to embark on a government-sponsored expedition to Pitcairn Island.

Grandchildren Sophia Wood, George Pitt Wood, Alice Faithfull and William Pitt Wilshire married in the 1820s. The experiences of Sophia Wood's husband, sea captain Samuel Henry Pinder, are a feature of this chapter. The three couples based in New South Wales began their married lives with grants of land. George Pitt Wood received 200 acres beside the Grose River, William Pitt Wilshire's wife, Maria, 640 acres at Kurrajong and Alice's husband, Andrew Gibson, 2,560 acres just south of later Goulburn. The death of Robert Jenkins in 1822 left intact only one of the marriages of Mary's children, that of the Wilshires.

1	HRA 1, 16, pp380, 864-7 (Note 116)
2	Clark, C.M.H., *Select Documents in Australian History 1851-1900*, Angus and Robertson, Sydney, 1962, Sec 7, pp318-321, Sec 8, p405
3	HRA, 4, 1, pp509-20
4	SG 30 June 1821, p3c
5	SG 9 May 1812, plc; SG 5 September 1812, p2a; Mutch Index, Eyre
6	Gunson, Niel, "Deviations of a Missionary Family", Davidson J.W. and Deryck Scarr, *Pacific island Portraits*, Australian National University Press, Canberra, 1970, ch 2, p40
7	ADB 1, Henry; Gunson, 1970, ch 2, pp35, 6, 39
8	Hassall Family Correspondence, Vol 2, pp217-8, ML A1677-2 Letter 4 Sept 1815

9   Marsden Papers, ML CY A 1 996, Vol 5, pp44-5, 49; Hassall . . . Vol 2, pp285-7, ML A1677-2; Gunson, 1970, ch 2, p39
10 BT Box 28, p7223; SG 3 April 1819, p2b; BT Box 23, pp4825-7; Gunson, 1970, pp40-1; Division of Law, Macquarie University, Unreported Decisions of the Privy Council, on Appeal from the Australian Colonies before 1850, http://www.law.mq.edu.au/pc/EagarvHenry.1827.htm p12
11 Gunson, 1970, ch 2, p41
12 Steven, Margaret, Merchant Campbell 1769-1846, Oxford University Press, Melbourne, 1965, ch 11, pp274-5; See third item at Ref 10, p12; SG 10 November 1821, p2c; Gunson, 1970, ch 2, p41
13 SG 25 August 1821, p3b
14 SG 9 December 1820, p3a
15 SG 2 June 1821, p3a, b; *Journal of Pacific History*, Vol 4, 1969, p72
16 Marsden Papers, MLA1996, Vol 5, p87
17 SG 2 June 1821, p2b
18 SG 2 June 1821, p3a,b
19 See third item at Ref 10, pp 6,7,12,13,17; SG 25 August 1821, pp3b,4b
20 SCCJ, Judgment Rolls, SRNSW 9/2233, No 499
21 SG 7 July 1821, p2b,c
22 SG 25 August 1821, pp3,4a,b; SCCJ, Judgment Rolls, SRNSW 9/2233, No 499
23 SCCJ, Court of Appeals, Case Papers, SRNSW 2/8143, pp131-461; Minute Book, SRNSW 4/6604, pp65-70
24 See third item at Ref 10, pp14,15
25 Main Series of Letters Received, March-June 1822, SRNSW 4/1759, Reel 6055, p8
26 GC, Case Papers SRNSW, 4//7862, Nos 15,58,185,308; 4/7863, Nos 209,273,354,388; GC, Judgement Book No 11, 4/7884, Nos 15,58,185, 209,273,308,354,388
27 Special Bundles and other records, Proclamations, Government and General Orders, 1803-15 Jan 1824, SRNSW 4/403, Reel 6040, p84
28 SRNSW 4/403, Reel 6040, p88
29 SG 21 July 1825, p1c
30 SG 1 March 1822, p2a
31 Government and General Orders 1810-1822, MLA2091, CY 907, pl70
32 SG 8 March 1822, p4c
33 SG 1 November 1822, p3c
34 SG 25 January 1822, 4b; SG 22 March 1822, p2c
35 Gunson, 1970, p42; SG 15 March 1822, p2b
36 SG 15 December 1821, p3a
37 GC, Case Papers Heard, SRNSW 4/7866, No 209
38 SG 24 May 1822, p2c; Hassall...Vol 2, MLA1677-2, CY 920, pp441-4
39 SG 10 May 1822, p3c
40 Steven, Margaret, *Merchant Campbell 1769-1840*, Australian National University, Canberra, 1965, p284

41 Johnson, Keith A. and Malcolm R. Sainty, *Sydney Burial Ground 1819-1901*, Library of Australian History, Sydney 2001, p457
42 Stenhouse N. D. and W. Hardy, Miscellanaeous Legal Papers, ML A102, pp1-6
43 Sainty, Malcolm R. and Keith A. Johnson., eds., *Census of New South Wales, November 1828*, Library of Australian History, Sydney, 1980, p401
44 Rubenstein, William D., *The All-Time Australian 200 Rich List*, Allen and Unwin, Crows Nest, 2004, p13
45 SG 17 February 1821, p2a
46 SG 24 May 1822, p1c; SG 24 May 1822, p1c
47 SG 28 June 1822, p2c; SG 12 April 1822, p2c; Registers o f Copies of Wills 1800-1901, SAG Will 1/145
48 Main Series of Letters Received 1821-22, SRNSW, 4/1753, Reel 6052, pp165-166a; Main Series of Letters Received 1823, SRNSW 4/1765, Reel 6056, pp117-21; SG 16 August 1822,p2c,3
49 Hassall, Vol 2, ML A1677-2, p471; Gunson, 1970, ch 2, p42
50 Baxter, Carol J., ed., *General Muster and Land and Stock Muster of New South Wales 1822*, Australian Biographical and Genealogical Record and Society of Australian Genealogists, Sydney, 1988, ppxi, 159,384,551,571. (Consult family names in the Index (pp587-752) for convict servants)
51 GC Judgement Book, SRNSW 4/7885, Vol 12, No 194; Process Book, SRNSW 4/7887, No 47; Case Papers Heard, SRNSW, 4/78666, No 194
52 SG 29 September 1821, p2c; Miscellaneous Records Relating to Education and Clerical Matters, Richmond School 1822-24, SRNSW SZ1014, Fiche 3307, pp2,6,10,14,18,22,24,26,28,30,32,34,36,38,40,42, 46,50,54,58
53 Muster 1822, ppxiii, 159 (See Thomas Faithful for William Faithfull), 256, 519, 525, 553, 560; (Consult family names in the Index for convict servants; District Constables' Notebooks 1822-1824, SRNSW 4/1219, Reel 1254
54 NSW Court of Criminal Jurisdiction, Special Bundles 1820-24, SRNSW SZ798, Reel 1977, pp 91-103
55 SG 27 September 1822, p1b; SG 13 January 1821, p4b; SG 20 January 1821, p4a
56 ADB 1, Greenway; Broadbent, James, and Joy Hughes, *Francis Greenway Architect*, Historic Houses Trust of New South Wales, 1997, ch 12
57 SG 1 November 1822, p3c
58 NSW JA Rg., Bk 6, Pg 107, ML A3613; SG 27 November 1808, p2c; Grants and Leases of Land, Bk 3c, Pg 9 DL; Bk S, No 469, DL; Thomas, Bryan, Map of Early Sydney 1803-1810, 1979, SRNSW. See lot of John (James) Aicken. The street numbers began on the western side of the street at the northern end and finished on eastern side and northern end of the street. See SG 10 June 1815, Suppl., for No 5 west; SG 13 January

	1821, p2b for No 3 west; SG 10 April 1823 Suppl., p2b for No 18
59	Memorials forwarded by the Commissioner of Claims 1832-1842, SRNSW Reel 1205, No 636; SG 3 May 1822, p3b NB Storer No 15; Bk 39, Pgs 84,142, DL
60	Maclehose, James, *Picture of Sydney and Strangers' Guide to New South Wales in 1839*, John Ferguson, 1939, p89
61	SG 30 January 1823, p4a
62	Memorials 1823, SRNSW 4/1835B, Fiche 3074, No 352, pp1157-8, 1161-3; Land Grants NSW 1811-26, ML A362, CY 736, p5a; County Cook, Parish Kurrajong, 9th ed, Map 25, DL; Letters sent within the Colony 21 March 1823-1 August 1823, SRNSW 4/3508, Reel 6010, p59; Letters sent within the Colony 18 Dec 1823-26 Apr 1824, SRNSW 4/3510, Reel 6012, p410.
63	Memorials 1822 Suppl., SRNSW Fiche 4/1833, No 30; Letters sent within the Colony 28 Nov 1822-20 March 1823, SRNSW 4/3508, Reel 6010. p121; Letters sent within the Colony 18 Dec 1823-26, Apr 1824, SRNSW 4/3510, Reel 6012, pp410, 674
64	Memorials 1823, SRNSW 4/1834B, Fiche 3063, No 104, p633; Letters sent within the Colony 31 July 1823-18 December 1823, SRNSW 4/3509, Reel 6011, p504; Memorials 1824, SRNSW 1/1837A, Fiche 3087, No 327, pp283-90; Copies of letters sent within the Colony 26 April 1824-20 July 1824, SRNSW 4/3511, Reel 6013, p256
65	Memorials 1823, SRNSW 4/1830, Fiche 3048, No 194; Letters sent within the Colony 31 July 1823-8 December 1823, SRNSW 4/3509, Reel 6011, p299
66	SG 27 February 1823, p2b; Main Series of Letters Received, Miscellaneous Jan-Mar 1823, SRNSW 4/1770, Reel 6058, pp147-147a; SG 29 May 1823, p3c; Proclamations, Government and General Orders and Notices, Bundle 16, No 1, 1 Dec 1821-19 Dec 1825, SRNSW 4/424, Reel 6039, p440
67	Letters sent within the Colony 28 Nov 1822-20 March 1823, SRNSW 4/3507, Reel 6010, p406
68	SG 26 August 1824, p4e
69	GC, Case Papers Heard, SRNSW 4/7865, Nos 40, 46, 55; 4/7866, No 117; Judgement Book, SRNSW 4/7885, Vol 12, Nos 50, 46, 55, 117
70	SG 24 July 1823, pla
71	GC, Case Papers Heard, SRNSW 4/7865, No 48; 4/7866, Nos 127; 236; 4/7867, No 321; Judgement Book, SRNSW 4/7885, Vol 12, Nos 48; 127, 236, 321; SG 26 August 1820, p2c
72	SCCJ, Judgement Book 1817-28, SRNSW 9/922, 2/1825, No 15; Judgement Rolls 1817-28, SRNSW 9/5198, 2/1825, No 15
73	SG 15 May 1823, p2a
74	Main Series of Letters Received 1823, SRNSW 4/1765, Reel 6056, pp127-30a, Letters Sent within the Colony 28 Nov 1822-1 Aug 1823, SRNSW Reel 6010, p597; Miscellaneous Records, SRNSW 4/7027,

Fiche 3280, p4; Bennett, George, 'Account of the Islands Erromanga and Tanna, New Hebrides Group', *Asiatic Journal* (Jan-Apr 1832), Vol 7, 1832, p l 20; SG 2 August 1822, p4a, b; State Library of New South Wales Magazine, July 2008, p2l

75 GC, Case Papers Heard, SRNSW 4/7866, No 209; Judgement Book, SRNSW 4/7885, Vol 12, No 209
76 SG 10 July 1823, p2a
77 Gunson, 1970, p42
78 SG 17 February 1825, p3c,d; Hassall,Vol 2, ML 1677-2, pp804-5
79 SCCJ, Judgement Rolls, SRNSW 9/2238, No 555; 9/2244, No 680; 9/5193, No 10; Judgement Book SRNSW, 9/922, Nos 555, 680, 10
80 GC, Case Papers, SRNSW 4/7866, No 114; Judgement Book, 4/7885, Vol 12, Nos 114, 241, 253
81 Sessions Clerk of Peace, Sydney Quarter Sessions Oct 1827-Jan 1828, SRNSW 4/8448; SG 10 February 1825, p3a; Woods, C.D., *A History of Criminal Law in New South Wales, The Colonial Period 1788-1900*, Federation Press, Sydney, 2002, pp56-59; HRA 1, 11, pp97, 582, 892-3; SG 8 September 1825, p3c; Aus 8 September 1825, p2c
82 Cunningham, Peter, Two Years in New South Wales, David Macmillan ed., Angus and Robertson, Sydney, 1966, pp xx, 237
83 Bk 25, Pgs 100, 255, 271, DL
84 Bk A, No 84, DL; Bk C, No 272, DL
85 SG 31 October 1825, p3d
86 ADB 1, Halloran
87 SG 22 December 1821, p3b,c
88 SG 1 January 1824, p2c; SG 1 July 1824, p2b
89 SG 30 June 1825, p2c
90 SG 1 July 1824, p2; SG 30 June 1825, p2c
91 *Ilawarra Mercury* 3 June 1884, p2b,c; ADB 1, Cape, Lang
92 SG 20 October 1825, p3c; ADB 1, Halloran
93 SG 17 March 1825, p5a; 31 March 1825, p3c
94 SG 21 June 1826, p3c
95 SG 2 December 1824, p3a, b
96 HRA 1, 11, pp835-6
97 Main Series of Letters Received, Bundle 27, SRNSW 4/1786, Reel 6063, p121; Reel 6064, 4/1787, pll 7, 4/1788, p118
98 SG 14 April 1825, 1b, p2a
99 Main Series of Letters Received, July -23 December 1825, SRNSW 4/1787, Reel 6064, pp61, 81
100 Aus 18 August 1825, p4a
101 SG 19 April 1826, p2a
102 SG 10 June 1826, p2a
103 Cunningham, 1966, p56
104 Grahame and Frances Cook, Helen Reichenbach, Bob and Fay Markwell, *Leg Irons to Landowners*, 1985, p46

6 The Grandchildren Marry

105 Research of Janelle Cust
106 Yvonne Browning, *St Peters Richmond, The Early People and Burials 1791-1855*, 1990, pp17, 483
107 Letters Received Relating to Land, SRNSW 2/8010, GPW Letter 14 Nov 1827, Reel 1200
108 SG 24 February 1827, p3d
109 Probate Case Papers 1812-1827, SRNSW 6/4188
110 SG 8 March 1827, p3f
111 Letters Received Relating to Land, SRNSW 2/7864, Reel 1130, AG Jun 1827
112 SG 12 July 1826, p2a; HRA 1, 12, p459
113 Peterkin A., and William Johnston, *Commissioned Officers in the Medical Service of the British Army 1660-1960*, Vol 1, Wellcome Historical Medical Library, London, 1968, p259
114 SG 6 June 1827, plb
115 HRA 1, 15, p471; HRA 1, 14, p594; HRA 1, 12, p355
116 SG 6 September 1826, p4a
117 SG 17 December 1827, pp3,4
118 HRA 1, 12, pp378-9
119 Letters Received Relating to Land, SRNSW 2/7854, WPF letters 1827, Land Board Report, Reel 1125
120 Memorials Forwarded by the Commissioners of Claims, SRNSW 2/1777, Reel 1234, No 4; County Argyle, 1907, DL. (See Mangamore parish for land of William Faithfull, senior and junior)
121 Grants of Land, Bk 57, Pg 15, DL
122 SG 21 January 1828, p2b,2e,f; SG 11 January 1828, p3c; Sydney Quarter Sessions, SRNSW 4/8448, No 57
123 SG 21 July 1828, p2d, e; Sydney Quarter Sessions, SRNSW 4/8449, No 46
124 SG 1 February 1826, p2e; SG 27 September 1826, p4e
125 Sydney Quarter Sessions, SRNSW 4/8450, No 60, Pg O, 38/10/1828; Aus 24 October 1828, p3e; SG 24 October; 1828 p2d,e
126 SCCJ, Judgment Rolls, 9/5213, No 57; 9/5218, Nos 84, 11; 9/5233, Nos 36, 43; Judgment Book SRNSW 9/922, 9/5213, No 57; 9/5218; No 84; 9/5218, No 11; 9/5233, No 36; 9/5233, No 43
127 SCCJ, Judgment Roll, SRNSW 9/5232, (2/1828), No 35; 9/5230, (4/1828), No 106; Judgment Book, 1817-28, No 2, SRNSW 9/922, 9/5232, No 35, (?/1828); 9/5230. No 106, (3/1828); Bk S, No 430, DL
128 Bk 21, Nos 889, 890, DL
129 SG 7 January 1828, pp3-4
130 Bk D, No 16, DL
131 SG 16 May 1828, p2e; Bk D, No 36, DL; SG 22 January 1824, p4c
132 SG 20 August 1828, p2f
133 Census 1828, pp 9,303,331,435,471
134 Baxter, Carol J. ed., *General Muster List of New South Wales 1823, 1824,*

	1825, Australian Biographical and Genealogical Record and Society of Australian Genealogists, Sydney, 1999, p5 l O; Mutch Index, Pitt/Scott
135	Census 1828, pp 142,428,463
136	Registers of Copies ofWills 1800-1901, SAG Will 1/1821; Register C, No 336, 338, DL; Letters Relating to Land, SRNSW 2/7854, Reel 1125, WF 15 Feb 1830
137	Aus 26 September, 1828, p3b; SG 12 July 1822, p2a
138	Census 1828, pp402, 439
139	Main Series ofLetters Received, Nov 1824-1825, SRNSW 4/1782, p81b, Reel 6062; SG 17 January 1829, p3a
140	Census 1828, p208; Radi, Heather, ed., *200 Australian Women, a Redress Anthology*, Women's Redress Press, Inc., 1988, p6
141	Census 1828, pp208, 431,467
142	Aus 23 January 1828, p3a
143	Purchases Special Grants Bk 35, Pg 26 DL; Memorials forwarded by the Commissioners of Claims 1832-1842, SRNSW 2/1792, Reel 1205, Nos 603, 627; 2/1793, Reel 1206, Nos 665, 673, 678
144	Bk 19, No 12 DL; Vol 1527, Folios 237-240, DL (See for long lake frontage)
145	Grants of Land, Bk 41, Pgs 32, 36, DL; County Camden, Parish Bumballo, 6th ed., Map 10, D
146	Grants of Land, Bk 42, Pg 4, DL; County St Vincent, Parish Tomboyc, 3rd ed., Map 62, DL
147	SG 5 May 1822 p4a; Letters Received Relating to Land, SRNSW 2/7892-3, Reel 1146, JJ Aug 1832; Memorials forwarded by the Commissioners of Claims 1832-1842, SRNSW, 2/1792, Reel 1205, No 628; 3/1793, Reel 1206, No 651
148	Register E, No 225, DL
149	Census 1828, p402
150	SG 30 June 1828, p4e
151	Census 1828, p142; Letters Received Relating to Land, SRNSW 2/7854, Reel 1125, Land Board Report, AG 12 June 1827
152	Census 1828, pp428, 463
153	HRA 1, 15, p62; SG 17 October 1828, plb
154	Census 1828, pl62
155	Index to SG 1827 -29, Vol 1 *Bussorah Merchant*; SG 4 August 1828 p2a, 3c
156	SG 25 April 1828, p2a
157	SG 4 April 1828, p3c; 14 April 1828, p2d; 16 April 1828, p2d
158	Letters Received Relating to Land, SRNSW 2/7864, Reel 1130, AG Letters 20 Apr 1827, 11 Jun 1827, 6 Oct 1831; HRA 1, 15, p471
159	Grants of Land, Bk 34, Pg 82, DL
160	HRA 1, 15, p62
161	SG 19 February 1829, pla; Aus 31 July 1835, p4c; Wyatt, Ransome T. *History of Goulburn*, Landsdown Press, Epping, New South Wales, 1972,

p67

162 SG 16 December 1826, p3e; *Sydney Monitor* 2 March 1827, p333c
163 Census 1828, pp399 (Though Thomas is not in the Australian copy of the Census, he is in the London copy) 439, 475
164 Letters Received 1831, SRNSW 4/2116, No 7083
165 Email 27 March 2007, Ken Knight to Janelle Cust
166 Letters Received 1828, SRNSW 4/1980, No 4182
167 SG 18 July 1818, pl c; SG 1 September 1821, p4a; SG 14 October 1821, p2c; SG 25 May 1827, p3e,4
168 Colonial Office, Original Correspondence of Settlers, ML CO 201/160, PRO Reel 139, pp351-3
169 Letters Received 1826, SRNSW 4/1899, No 5090; 4/1902.1, 26/5860
170 SG 26 January, 1827, pla; SG 28 January 1828, p2d
171 Aus 27 November 1829, plb
172 Aus 20 March 1829, p3b,c
173 SG 3 April 1823, plb; SG 20 May 1824, p3e; Aus 3 June 1826, p2a; SG 30 May 1828, plb; SG 9 August 1826, plc; Aus 13 April 1826, plb; SG 12 May 1828, plc
174 Old Chum (J.M.Forde), Old Sydney, MLFM 4/7710, C141; Bk D, No 798, DL; Bk 36, No 15, DL; SG 27 September 1826, p4e
175 SG 11 January 1822, p3b; ADB 6, Robertson
176 SG 27 September 1822, p4c; Proclamations, Government Orders and Notices 1 Dec 1821-19 Dec 1825, SRNSW 4/424, Reel 6039, p21
177 ADB, 6, Robertson
178 New South Wales Calendar and General Post Office Directory 1833, Stephens and Stokes, Sydney, See Sydney Directory
179 Records of St James C of E Sydney, SAG Reel 62, Burial 590
180 JRAHS, 1921 vol 7, pt 2, pp l0l -2; Kerr, Joan ed., *Dictionary of Australian Artists*, Melbourne Oxford University Press, Melbourne, 1992
181 "Philology and the South Sea Islands", South-Asian Register, Roger Oldfield ed., No. 4, 1828, p377; Aus 7 May 1828, p2d; Aus 28 November 1828, p3d
182 Shine berg, Dorothy, *They Came for Sandalwood*, Melbourne University Press, Victoria, 1967, ch 1, pl; ch 2, pp16,18; Bennett, George, "A Recent Visit to Several of the Polynesian Islands", *United Service Journal 1831*, Pt 2, p196; Bennett, George, "Account of the Islands Erromanga and Tanna, New Hebrides Group", *Asiatic Journal* (Jan-Apr 1832), Vol 7, 1832, p119
183 Bennett, 1832, ppl19-123
184 Bennett, 1832, pp l 25-28 (See third footnote on p l27 for localities of action; Shineberg 1956, ch 2, p22)
185 SG 13 November 1830, p3b

7
SQUATTING AND ITS PERILS

The land available for settlement lay within the 19 counties drawn up by 1829. Roughly speaking, the boundaries of the approved land were the southern bank of the Manning River, the northern bank of the Murrumbidgee River, and the present western towns of Wellington, Orange and Cowra.[1] The Faithfull, Gibson, Jenkins and Pitt families and many other colonists, occupied large tracts of land outside "the limits of location", a practice known as squatting. The lessees of the squats received handsome rewards but those working the runs, experienced primitive and dangerous conditions.

In 1830 the tannery was thriving with James Wilshire "treating about 15,000 hides a year, producing enough leather to supply the colony's needs and exporting surplus green hides to England".[2] Structures covered the Wilshires' site. The family home, washhouse, workers' huts, rented tenements and probably the old and new stables bordered George Street, Union Lane and Pitt Street. The rest of the site held the tan house, 40 tan pits, bark house, bark mill, currier's shop, wool-loft, two mills, mill house, soap house and storehouse.[3] James secured freehold title for the 2 acres and 2 roods in 1831. Apparently he received the extra land when he set up his tannery.[4] In the early thirties James bought property for his slaughter business. He paid £370 10s for 10 acres in later-named Glebe.[5] And he gave Dr John Dunmore Lang £216 for an allotment across the road from his land in Bathurst Street.[6] The deed for the 2 acres, 3 roods and 30 perches at the end of Bathurst Street were not available until 1838.[7]

The first grandchild of Esther and James Wilshire, Wlliam James Wilshire, was born in Sydney to Maria and William Pitt Wilshire in January 1830. Sadly he died in November. The couple also named their second son, born in February 1832, William James. Ann Thompson nursed William James on her arrival in the *Pyramus* in March.[8] Maria took advantage of the short-lived policy whereby Governor Darling created a special category of grants to "act as an inducement to the Young Settlers to marry". Daughters from large families qualified for a grant if "highly respectable in Conduct and Connexion".[9] Maria selected 640 acres in Kurrajong, beside present Comleroy Road. Brother-in-law Thomas Matcham Pitt Wilshire and solicitor Brent Clements Rodd were trustees for Wilshirehurst.[10]

In early February 1830, still hoping for a further grant, William Pitt Faithfull gave the Colonial Secretary a report of his progress at Pitt Mount. With the help of six convicts and two free servants he had built a slab home, temporary barn, sheep shed and dairy, the value of the buildings, £200. They had cleared 75 acres, cultivated 45 acres and completed two miles of fencing. The stock had increased to 12 horses, 253 cattle and 631 sheep. William owned working oxen and implements of husbandry worth £270 and he held £173 in cash and bills.[11] Pitt Mount was close to the Great South Road and a few miles south of sister and brother-in-law, Alice and Andrew Gibson.[12]

The Gibsons' "neat and cheerful" bark cottage commanded "a very good and extensive view" from its position on the hill. The exposed position of the cottage affected Andrew's health and in two or three years he erected a new home on the flat.[13] On 29th December 1830 the Gibsons entertained dinner guest William Edward Riley, one of the Riley brothers who "brought depth and respectability to Port Jackson". In his journal Riley commented on Alice and Andrew. Alice was "an amusing lass, rather a pretty and pleasing person", and Andrew, "a gentlemanly, well-informed man". Andrew deeply regretted foregoing his medical practice. He held a "commission of the peace, and with Lieutenant McAlister of the mounted Police", sat weekly on the Bench to hear the complaints of settlers and their servants.[14]

Captain Alexander Sandilands of HMS *Comet* arrived in Port Jackson with orders from England to arrange with Governor Darling to move the Pitcairn Islanders to Tahiti. The Pitcairners were the proud descendants of the Bounty Mutineers. Sandilands wanted to take a helper familiar with the islands and Samuel Pinder Henry got the job. (See Figures 4 and 5 for locations Samuel Henry visited.) Darling made the *Lucy Ann* available to transport the Pitcairners and appointed Captain Walpole of 39th Regiment to keep the peace. With Samuel at the helm of *Lucy Ann*, the two ships left Sydney on 27th December. After spending five days at the Bay of Islands, the ships reached Pitcairn's on 28th February 1831. Sandilands and Samuel gave the heads of the families "every information" and, though stressing the voluntary nature of the expedition, all 87 inhabitants decided to move. The *Lucy Ann*, loaded with Pitcairners, yams, potatoes, fruit and household goods, sailed on March 7th escorted by the *Comet*. The ships completed the 600 miles to Tahiti on March 23rd. The Tahitian Queen assigned land to the newcomers and she asked missionary Bicknell to supply them with food for six months. Sandilands told the Governor about Samuel's valuable help:

> *The master of the Lucy Ann, has been diligent in his duty - but I must in a particular manner mention to your Excellency, that as Pilot and Interpreter, I have found Mr Henry most useful, and*

can safely recommend him as a person deserving of every trust being placed in him, in any service connected with the Eastern Pacific Islands.[15]

Samuel received £50 for the job, not enough to forestall a demand for him to appear at the insolvent division of the Supreme Court of New South Wales in October 1831. The case papers are missing.[16] The Pitcairners stayed in Tahiti for just five months. They experienced illness, 12 deaths and homesickness for their "fertile and picturesque isle".[17]

On 17th May 1831 the Reverend John Vincent married by licence Louisa Wilshire, the eldest child of James and Esther Wilshire, and Philip Elliot, at St James Church, Sydney. The witnesses were Louisa's brother, William and sister, Elizabeth. Born in 1805 in Trentham, Philip was the son of Thomas Elliot, and Jane Elliot, formerly Liddle.[18] Philip arrived in New South Wales in the *Prince Regent* in September 1827. He was one of six surveyors, including Sir Thomas Livingstone Mitchell, sent to the colony to boost the staff of the Department of the Surveyor-General.[19] Philip's superior in Newcastle Under Lyme, Thomas Slater, described him, "well qualified to undertake and execute correctly Land Surveying, Planning and Measuring ... and an honest and industrious Young Man". The Secretary of State for the Colonies appointed Philip an Assistant Surveyor on a yearly salary of £200, plus allowances for accommodation and forage.[20]

Soon after Philip arrived he measured 100 acres at Manly Cove.[21] In 1828 he identified the boundary of County Camden for Thomas Livingstone Mitchell's General Survey of the Colony. Philip continued working in the southern districts, surveying farms, rivers and creeks, mountains and towns. He measured the boundaries of farms in the districts of Bong Bong, Goulburn Plains and Nattai River. He traced rivers and creeks such as the Nepean, Shoalhaven, Wingecarribee, Patrick's, Black Bob's, Chain of Ponds and Bargo.

He surveyed sections of the mountain ranges in the south and western section of County Camden. In 1829 he planned the town of Goulburn, now North Goulburn, and measured allotments for veterans close to the town. That year, in November, he sent his superiors a list of six "highly regarded" convicts he hoped to keep in his service.[22] Louisa selected her marriage grant of 960 acres on the Goulburn Plains, just south of William Pitt Faithfull, the trustees for Trentham Park her brothers, James and Austin.[23] Near Louisa's grant, Philip leased 640 acres at £1 a year.[24]

Early in 1830 Philip Elliot was transferred to the Roads Department to form a road over the Blue Mountains to Bathurst.[25] Once he set up a base camp near Collitt's Inn at Harley Vale, Philip asked if the Bridge Party could build him "a small cottage" His request rejected, his superiors "expected (him) to live in a tent as a surveyor ought to do". Road gangs at Harley Vale, Mt York, Blackheath and O'Connell's Plains carried out the backbreaking work of clearing timber, quarrying rock and building retaining walls. Finding difficulty in managing the convicts and "now in charge of the whole works", in April from Mt York Philip wrote two letters to the surveyor general. In the first letter he explained, "I am much at a loss to know how I am to deal with runaways and others in the Gangs". In the second letter he complained about a contractor who left workers without food for three days. Had Philip not bought wheaten meal, "a great many" would have run away. In 1831 Philip superintended works on "the Great South Road leading to Argyle and the Southern Districts". He was not far from home at Myrtle Creek (Picton in 1841).[26]

Appointed a Justice of the Peace in January 1830, Philip Elliot judged cases before the Stonequarry (Picton) Bench of Magistrates.[27] In the September before his appointment, Philip was a witness in the case of Mary Harroll, charged with drunkenness and gross disorderly conduct. A servant to Mrs Wild, Mary was "repeatedly insolent" and "excessively saucy". Mrs Wild's son, John, called

Philip from his bed at 1.30 am. The two men found the defendant "in a state of nakedness and quite drunk" in the dairy where she "remained ... , drinking and singing till the morning". Mary was sentenced to three months in the third-class of the Female Factory. Philip's servant, William Starsmord appeared before Henry Colden Antill and Philip for absence without leave, a common offence. One Friday evening, Philip's overseer ordered the prisoner to take two letters for Mr Elliot about eight miles to Campbelltown. Although told to return by noon Saturday, it was 9 o'clock in the evening before he turned up. A rumour circulated that, while away, he was "drunk and kicking up a row". The judges ordered the prisoner to spend seven days in solitary confinement. Twice in 1833 William Pitt Faithfull's servant, Joseph Smith, was convicted of absconding in Philip's district. On both occasions Smith was sent to the Goulburn Plains for a decision on his punishment.[28]

On 6th April 1832 Philip Ellliot asked for a fortnight's leave to conduct "private business of a very serious nature requiring my presence in Sydney". Thirteen days later, 19th April, Louisa gave birth to Thomas Wilshire Elliot at her former home in George Street. Unfortunately she lost her second son on his birthday, 10th May 1833.[29] During Louisa's confinements, Philip surveyed land, roads and a new town. He measured grants, farms and crown land at the Illawarra, Berrima, Dapto, Shoalhaven, Wollongong, Red Bank Creek, Mulgoa, Stonequarry, Burragorang, The Oaks and Bargo. He planned new roads in the Illawarra and Camden districts and, once completed, he had to meet Governor Bourke at Appin or the Illawarra to show him the work.[30] He also documented features of the Wollongong town reserve, selecting the best sites for the church, school, gaol, courthouse and hospital. On 2nd May 1833 Philip submitted this project, which Governor Bourke approved in November.[31] He followed up with detailed plans of the 40 acre glebe and laid out sections of Wollongong in allotments.

7 Squatting and Its Perils

William Pitt Faithfull and Andrew Gibson were the Pitt Family's first squatters in 1833. The south bank of Murrumbidgee already settled, the brothers-in-law took their stockmen and cattle to the Monaro district in the Southern Alps. Polish biologist, John Lhotsky, recorded their presence. William squatted at an unknown location, Yuiquimbiang.[32] Andrew occupied the grasslands near present Kiandra, the area called Gibson's Plains for many years.[33] At Gibson Plains in 1834, one of Andrew's servants died in a heavy snowstorm and many of his cattle perished.[34]

Andrew Gibson also took advantage of the new regulations allowing the purchase of land. At Tirranna he bought 810 acres and 897 acres, while to the north-west at Narrawa in County King, he purchased bordering lots of 646 acres and 1034 acres.[35] The cost of the four lots, £846.15, offset with mortgages.[36] As well, he leased land near Tirranna.[37] In January 1834 Andrew resigned as magistrate. Having spent five years on the Bench, he wanted to devote more time to "natural history and to comparative anatomy".[38] Andrew's interest in these topics evident in the "natural curiosities" he sent to the United Kingdom and his subscription to Gould's *Birds of Australia*.[39] The focus for Alice was her young sons, Thomas Jamieson Faithfull Gibson born in December 1830 and Andrew Faithfull Gibson in March 1833.

Doctor Gibson kept in touch with medical matters. In late June 1832 he aided Governor Richard Bourke after his horse fell on top of him during his "first journey into the interior".[40] The Governor stayed with the Gibsons in their cottage on the hill.[41] Bourke noted the site of Goulburn was low-lying and subject to flood so he ordered a survey of higher ground to the south. The new town, on which the present town is based, opened in 1833.[42] The Colonial Secretary, Alexander Mackay, asked Andrew to monitor the health of Daniel Geary, lately constable on the Goulburn Plains. Geary suffered a serious wound to his left arm "in an encounter with a desperate gang of Bushrangers" in the Bathurst district in October 1830. Though the arm improved, it was still "paralytic and unserviceable" in July 1832. A year later in his final report, Andrew recorded the "permanent nature" of the injury.[43] Andrew was appointed a consultant on cattle and sheep diseases in 1833.[44] At the request of Governor Bourke, in 1835 he and others completed a report on the epidemic of Catarrh (Influenza) among sheep in Argyle and bordering counties.[45] About the same year, Andrew won the contract to build the hospital and surgeon's quarters in the new town. When the cost of the project exceeded the tender, the Treasury criticised Governor Bourke for not adhering to regulations.[46]

Master Gibson expected his servants to behave properly. He discovered servant widow Eliza Walton, 14 and veteran soldier widower William Wychellow, 43 had published banns for their marriage without his consent. Andrew explained that Eliza, solicited by Wychellow, "in the first instance refused him, and afterwards was induced to accept him ... to get out of Bondage, and to avoid punishment for a theft to which she was accessory in my House." Andrew was "seriously assaulted" when he tried to discourage the ex-soldier "from forcibly attempting to obtain access to my servant". Taken into custody for assault, Wychellow was freed "upon voluntarily writing an admission and humble apology". The Governor consented to the marriage at Sutton Forrest in 1831. Andrew was not in the "least doubt" Eliza practised "some deception to obtain consent to a second marriage", such as forging documents of her first husband's death. In 1837 Wychellow had sold his farm near Goulburn "through dislike of her disorderly and immoral conduct and returned to England". Eliza married a "respectable blacksmith" in 1839. Before long she was taken into custody for burglary then sent to the Female Factory. Veteran soldier Christopher Wharmby complained to the Governor that Andrew Gibson cancelled Sarah Moreton's ticket of leave to prevent her marrying him. Andrew said Mr McAlister cancelled her ticket of leave for "living in open prostitution with the said Wharmby".

Sarah had received the ticket of leave for "good conduct", but Andrew decided her subsequent behaviour did not entitle her to a continuation of this leniency. The reason for Andrew's action:

> *Notwithstanding repeated admonitions from me, she .. .latterly lived with Memorialist Wharmby immediately in view of my residence to the annoyance of my family, and bad example to my servants obliging me to bring her conduct before the Bench and to prosecute her as I did.*

Soon after these events, in 1832, Wharmby married, but not Sarah Moreton. Andrew did not oppose servants marrying as he recently approved the marriage of two servants "deserving of the indulgence". However, he thought "it would constitute the greatest insubordination" if he "allowed (female servants) to believe that they might marry whom, and when they pleased in defiance of their master and without reference to their conduct whilst in his service".[47]

Andrew harshly punished his servants for misconduct. Whittaker got 50 lashes for "quitting sheep as shepherd". Cleary received 14 years and 50 lashes for "making away with a keg of rum at harvest". Servant Charles Smith also received 14 years and 50 lashes for "neglecting the letters". Joseph Smith, in strife for "losing 109 sheep", got seven years and 50 lashes.[48] Appreciating well-behaved servants, Andrew pleaded for "any indulgence in my power" for long-serving convict Robert Gregson whose "former errors are repented, and his conduct fully reformed".[49]

Again in June 1834, Samuel Pinder Henry arrived at Pitcairn's Island, this time in the Pomare captained by brother-inlaw, Thomas Ebrill. The missionaries asked them to return George Nobbs to Pitcairn's Island. From 1828 Nobbs had been teacher and preacher on Pitcairn's. In 1832 Joshua Hill arrived, calling himself Lord Hill and claiming the British Government sent him. The intruder "assumed a power and exercised a severity, and even cruelty at Pitcairn's Island quite unauthorised". Hill ejected Nobbs from his house and position as teacher, seized his muskets, and deprived him of medicine when ill with dysentery. He also flogged Nobbs for setting up a mock trial in which he portrayed Hill as judge, juror and executioner. Eventually Nobbs and two others fled the island. Hill had a few supporters, especially those Nobbs criticised for setting up a distillery on their return from Tahiti. Hill's followers alleged an arrogant Samuel Henry "tried all he could to corrupt our women, both married and single, he being a married man himself".[50] Similarly, in the mid-twenties missionary Elijah Armitage wrote, Samuel lived "in hopen sin with the native wemin though a wife & children & she traviling with him".[51] Sophia had given birth to Lucy Ann in September 1827, Alfred in June 1828, Sophia in September 1830 and Alice in November 1833.

Regretfully, Elizabeth Pitt lost son, 15-year old William Henry Pitt in on 27th June 1834. Six months later, on 1st January 1835, Elizabeth died aged only 38, leaving George not yet 21, Mary 19, Robert 17 and Eliza 14. George inherited the 200 acres at Richmond and William's 30 acres near Windsor, and Robert the 400 acres at Kurrajong. Hannah Laycock, who died in Sydney Hospital in May 1831, left grand-daughter, Eliza, her home in Pitt Street as well as the family bible and other personal belongings.[52]

Elizabeth and Thomas Pitt's elder daughter, Mary Matcham Pitt, married her cousin Thomas William Eber Bunker Laycock at St Matthews, Windsor, on 31st August 1835. The Reverend Robert Maunsell conducted the wedding which Edward and Margaret Inall of Richmond witnessed. Thomas was the son of Isabella Laycock, née Bunker, and Captain Thomas Laycock, brother to Mary's mother. In 1810 Captain Laycock left for England with 102nd Regiment of Foot, formerly the NSW Corps. In January 1815 Thomas was born at Halifax, Nova Scotia, his father serving there with 98th Regiment of Foot during the 1812-1814 war against the Americans. The family returned to the colony in the *Fame* in 1817.[53] Thomas lived on the east bank of Putty Creek on 100 acres granted to his grandmother, Hannah Laycock.[54] Mary gave birth to her first two children in Richmond, Thomas Laycock in July 1836 and Elizabeth Laycock in October 1838.

Less than a month after his sister's wedding, on 22nd September 1835 George Matcham Pitt, eldest son of Thomas and Elizabeth Pitt, married Julia Johnson at St Matthews, Windsor. (Figures 15 & 16) The Reverend Henry Stiles married the couple in the presence of witnesses A. Black, Hannah Polack and Robert Aull. Julia was born to John Johnson, and Mary Johnson, née Moore, in Sydney in January 1815. Mary Moore, sentenced to seven years, arrived in the *Aeolus* in 1809. John Johnson, a potter, came in the *Anne* in 1810 with a sentence of 14 years. In 1829, four years after Julia's father died in Sydney, her mother married widower Robert Aull and took her family to live with Robert in Richmond.[55] Julia settled with George on his 200 acres near Richmond Hill. George understood his grandmother, Mary, called her 100 acres, Pitt Farm, and his father, Thomas, his 100 acres, Nelson's Farm.[56] George named the combined grants Bronte.[57] The name derives from the Sicilian title Duke of Bronte awarded to Horatio Nelson in 1799, with Nelson allowed to use the title in 1801.[58] Julia and George lost first child, three-month-old Thomas Matcham Pitt in October 1836.

Returning from its second surveying voyage to South America, H.M.S. *Beagle* berthed at Matavai Bay, Tahiti for 10 days in November 1835. Captain Frederick William Beechey, of the Royal Navy, introduced Samuel Pinder Henry to Robert FitzRoy, surveyor (map-maker) and captain of the *Beagle*. Beechey, who visited Tahiti in 1826, told FitzRoy, "Mr Henry was born upon the island, and had never visited England, yet a more English countenance, or more genuine English ideas, I have seldom met with in any part of the world". Samuel supplied FitzRoy with "nautical intelligence" and other useful information. He met naturalist Charles Darwin

Figure 15. George Matcham Pitt

Figure 16. Julia Johnson Pitt

who, impressed by the Tahitians, credited their good conduct to the efforts of the missionaries. He ate breakfast on the *Beagle* and joined in other activities with Darwin and the crew. On 26th November Samuel farewelled the *Beagle* bound for New Zealand and Australia. Samuel and Sophia were "about to make a journey to some distance" with "a favourite son", possibly 13-year old William, "undertaking a new and difficult mission at Navigator's Island" (Samoa).[59] William Henry thought son Samuel experienced a "saving conversion" in 1835. Apparently Samuel and Sophia had a stormy relationship throughout the thirties.[60]

Four months after the *Beagle* left, Samuel Pinder Henry enjoyed the company of another Englishman, medical practitioner Frederick Bennett. A member of the Royal Geographic Society and actively interested in the Zoological Society of London, and the Devon and Cornwall Natural History Society, Bennett sailed around the globe for three years on the whale ship *Tuscan* to follow his scientific interests. On 27th March 1836 Samuel rode his horse to Papeete to collect Bennett to view the natural and historical features along the west and south-west coasts of Tahiti. Bennett admired the "extreme beauty" of the scenery with its "profuse vegetation", "splendid varieties of ferns", "verdant heights", "caverns which perforate precipitous cliffs" and "springs of fresh water rising from the sea". Samuel stirred Bennett's interest in the history of the area, "spots we passed possessed a local interest which the kindness and intelligence of my companion did not permit me to disregard". Sites viewed included the ancient morais "sacred groves of idolatry" (huge piles of coral blocks) and "the scene of the decisive battle, fought in 1815, between the idolatrous and Christian Tahitians".

Around 6.00 pm the two men reached "Mr Henry's residence at Atinua, where the kindest hospitality obliterated fatigues, and enhanced the pleasures of the past day". Bennett had time to explore the "beauties of Atinua", the chief building the Henrys' home. It was "a neat and convenient dwelling erected at the foot

7 Squatting and Its Perils

of some pastured hills ... surrounded by cultivated lands, which include the largest sugar plantation on the island". (The sugar was "of a superior kind and of a remarkably fine flavour".[61]) Groups of native huts mingled with the "superior habitations" of mechanics, most of whom were English and American. Cattle, swine and poultry strolled, the scene "orderly and domesticated". Bennett could imagine being at a respectable English farm had not the "plumy cocoa-nuts and broad-leaved bananas destroyed the illusion".[62]

About 1836 Jemima Jenkins acquired two squats on the southern bank of the Murrumbidgee River set up by sons of Wicklow rebel, Hugh Byrne.[63] Brewarrena was a sheep station near Grong Grong, east of the later town of Narrandera. Bangus was a cattle station bounded on the east by Adelong Creek, south of the small settlement of Gundagai. Robert Pitt Jenkins's name was on the licences.[64] While Robert looked after the runs, Jemima "took a quiet interest in the affairs of Campbelltown, signing petitions favouring improved roads, schools and churches".[65] Finding it impossible to prevent the unauthorised expansion of the Colony, in 1836 Governor Bourke legalised squatting by issuing £10 yearly licences to depasture stock on land outside the 19 counties.[66] To police the rules, the Governor appointed seven full-time Commissioners of Crown Lands in May 1837, with William Pitt Faithfull one of six added to the list in September.[67]

On 9th May 1836 Esther Wilshire, aged 49 or 50, died at her home in George Street following a short illness lasting three weeks. The Reverend Richard Hill of St James Anglican Church buried her in the Sydney Burial Ground on 13th May.[68] Esther left James and nine children. Her youngest, Thomas, 15 and Joseph, 10, attended the King's School in Parramatta in 1834-5, three years after the school started.[69]

The second son of Esther and James Wilshire, James Robert Wilshire, married Elizabeth Thompson by licence at St James Church on 13th August 1836. The minister was William Yates, the witnesses James Wilshire and Joseph, Susannah and Anne Thompson. Elizabeth was the third daughter of Joseph Thompson, a linen draper, and Mary Thompson, née Brown. The Thompsons arrived in the *James Harris* in May 1834.[70] James and Elizabeth made their home at Mimosa Cottage built on James senior's land in Pitt Street. The cottage, named for the mimosa or wattle tree which produced the tannin used in preparing leather, backed on to the tannery where James worked with his father.[71] Elizabeth gave birth to two children in the thirties, James Thompson Wilshire in April 1837 and Emily Elizabeth Wilshire in December 1838. Emily died a year later.

At the end of 1836, the Town Surveyor asked James Wilshire to set back his fence in George Street. With the ascent at Brickfield Hill levelled at this time, James appealed to Governor Bourke for the administration to bear cost of the work He pointed out the scarcity and high price of labour, the limited number of convicts he could employ, and the value of his leather industry. Also he told the Governor he supplied India and settlements along the coast of New Holland, including Van Diemen's Land.[72] Clearly, the tanning business explains James Robert's visit to Van Dieman's Land in the *Guardian* in January 1835.[73] James Robert Wilshire followed his father in the role of steward at the Anniversary Dinner in January 1837.[74] That year in August, Austin Forrest Wilshire and Frances (no surname recorded) had a son, Austin Forrest Wilshire, but he died in Berrima at 16 months.[75] James senior contributed £60 to the fund for the Church of St Andrew. The Cathedral was erected between 1837 and 1886, with James appointed Honorary Secretary to the Cathedral Trustees.[76] As well, James subscribed to the Patriotic Fund and the fund for the statue of Governor Bourke.[77] Despite these gifts, in November 1837 he borrowed £500 for three years from Willliam Faithfull, securing the loan with the George

Street property occupied by son William.⁷⁸ And before the decade ended, James made £285 on the land in Bathurst Street previously owned by Dr Lang.⁷⁹

The year 1837 proved difficult for surveyor Philip Elliot. Early in the previous year, he refused to accompany Thomas Mitchell to "the Interior", feeling "quite unprepared for so long an excursion". Instead, he worked on roads in the Illawarra district including "the path up the mountain". Also, he surveyed farms, grants and crown land at Jervis Bay, the "Kangaroo Ground", Crook Haven, George's Basin, Bulli, Dapto, Kiama, the Illawarra and County St Vincent in the south-east. Then Philip's productivity declined, with only four farms measured in the four months leading to February 1837. Asked to explain his "neglect of duty", he offered three reasons: two weeks of wet weather; the time taken to travel 450 miles with slow bullocks; and unheeded requestions for equipment. Governor Bourke wanted the Wollongong town fully laid out and a start made on Kiama, including the road leading to it. Philip's superiors, dismissing the idea he had "too much work in hand", gave him "a detailed account" of the tasks and requested a time frame for their completion. Philip said he could probably complete the work in two months once he received the tracings, provided the articles requisitioned in January reached him in good repair. Philip received the equipment in July, minus the tracings, tents, camp table and other items. Asked in August to explain his neglect of the allotted tasks, Philip answered on 16th September. Since neither the tracings nor all the equipment arrived for the Wollongong and Kiama jobs, he measured and mapped in County St Vincent. On 30th October 1837 Philip asked for 10 days leave to attend "an interview with His Excellency the Governor, on business of the greatest importance to me". The next day he was dismissed.⁸⁰

Philip's job was near-intolerable. It involved much field work, extensive travel over rough terrain, copious paperwork (maps and plans, weekly and monthly reports, requisitions), staff shortages, inadequate equipment and primitive living conditions.[81] Needing another source of income, Philip paid £300 for about 211 acres in the south-east corner of Appin Parish, bordered in the east by the George's River.[82] There, in present St Helens Park, the Elliots set up their home, Stanhope. The suburb has an Elliott Place, and though wrongly spelt, the street is probably named after the Elliots. To make a living, Philip farmed the acres in Appin, Louisa's land in Goulburn and a temporary lease of 1280 acres in County King.[83]

Again in 1837 William Pitt Faithfull sought more crown land, claiming his assets in 1827 justified a maximum grant of 2560 acres. The letter revealed he had changed the name of his property to Springfield in recognition of the springs supplying the Mulwaree Ponds.[84] The estate straddled the ponds, "round or oval basins, of from 20 to 200 feet in diameter, or length, excavated or sunk in the superfices of an alluvial soil, which is commonly of a rich kind, fed by subterraneous springs".[85] In 1835-7 William increased Springfield to more than 5600 acres. He bought 610 acres from James Mcfarlane, 750 acres from William Roberts, and 770 acres, 952 acres and three 640 acre lots from the Crown. On the other hand, he sold the northern halves of two adjacent 640 acre lots on the northeast boundary of his estate. He also bought 100 acres near Berrima.[86] To cover costs of over £1500, William raised a mortgage on five Springfield lots, including his primary grant.[87] He held the licence for the Monaro run in 1837-8; then let it lapse.[88] At least 34 convicts worked for William.[89] He had the company of George, who, helped by a labourer and errand boy, looked after the stock on their father's 800 acres.[90] Alfred Smith of Richmond described George, "a tall, nice young fellow".[91]

Andrew Gibson also increased his acreage in 1836-8. Close to his original grant, he paid the Crown £264 for 1056 acres and £204 10s for 818 acres, and he gave £1100 for 2000 acres in the estate of Judge John Stevens.[92] To the north of Tirranna, Andrew procured the unworked 100 acre grants of six soldiers, including those of

Wychellow and Whannby, though he shared Whannby's land with William Bradley.[93] At Narrawa Andrew purchased 640 acres for £160.[94] As well, he bought town allotments, five in Auburn Street, Goulburn, three at £1 and two at £1 6s 8d, and six in Marulan priced between £10 and £15.[95] Andrew employed at least 44 convicts.[96] Despite owning 11,000 acres, the unoccupied land west of Tirranna beckoned so Andrew paid for a licence for a squat in the "Western Lachlan" in May 1838. He surrended the lease on the Kiandra run.[97] Alice looked after their six children, the latest arrivals Susannah Jane Gibson born in March 1835, Frederick Faithfull Gibson in January 1837 and William Faithfull Gibson in December 1838.

A valuable member of the community, Andrew gave evidence on the difficulty of securing constables to the Committee on Police in 1835.[98] In 1836 he participated in the Goulburn committee for Southern Association for the Suppression of Stock Stealing.[99] That year too, he returned to the Magistrate's Bench.[100] In 1837 he joined the Protestant Committee at Goulburn, one of several district committees set up in opposition to Governor Bourke's proposal for National schools similar to the Irish scheme. In these schools children studied textbooks free of dogma but with a Christian framework. The proposal displeased Anglican Bishop, William Broughton and other Protestant clergy.[101] Andrew, William and George supported Broughton.[102] In 1838 Andrew was appointed trustee for deposits in the Savings Bank at Goulburn.[103] Throughout the thirties, Andrew and William Pitt Faithfull had contracts with the Commissariat to provide supplies for government organizations stationed in Argyle and counties convenient to their homes and squats. Parties supplied included His Majesty's Troops, the Mounted Police, surveying groups, road parties and prisoners.[104] William continued supplying the government in the forties.[105] At Tirranna and Springfield, the brothers-in-law built flourmills and made them available to neighbours.[106]

Early in 1838 Maria and William Pitt Wilshire left 47 George Street to live on Maria's 640 acres in Kurrajong.[107] With them were Frederick Robertson Wilshire born in March 1837 and six-year-old William James Wilshire. The couple lost eight-week-old Maria Wilshire in June 1834. Partial to the name Maria, they called their next daughter, Maria Janet Wilshire, when she arrived in October 1839. Before leaving Sydney, William annoyed his father. In October 1835, following seven years at the Commissariat, William advertised a wine and spirit store. Two months later he advertised a leather and soap manufactory, promising "parties may depend on a more regular supply than the market...heretofore affords". He continued selling wine.[108] In June 1836 James gave William his 120 acres at Kurrajong. Seven months later he sold the land for £75.[109] After William left Sydney, James let the public know he would not accept responsibility for his son's debts or orders.[110] William applied for a position as a land commissioner at Richmond, his application stressing the role's importance in a district inhabited by "the lowest description of settlers".[111] This attitude explains William's frequent clashes with his servants and his many appearances as plaintiff and defendant in the Windsor Court. For instance, with four males and one female in William's service, two ran away to present affidavits to the police at Windsor. William Coughlan and Patrick Whalan claimed their master withheld their rations, physically mistreated them and used abusive language such as "bloody Irish wretch". At the court, William, who strongly defended his behaviour, accused the two of perjury. He also criticised the conduct of the hearing. The magistrate, Samuel North, decided "Mr Willshire (sic) is not temperate in the management of his convict servants".[112]

In April 1838 George Matcham Pitt and William Scott took possession of Crown Land on the Lower Gwydir (Moree district), leaving George Bull in charge.[113] At the end of the year, George applied for "a license to depasture Crown Lands Beyond the Limits of Location", in the district of "Brisbane". To support his application, George told the Colonial Secretary he was married with a child, a house and 200 cattle.[114] William Scott's name was on the licence issued in July 1839.[115] By then, Julia had given birth, not only to George Matcham Pitt in October 1837, but also to Jessie Pitt in January 1839.

Towards the end of the thirties black-white relations on the frontiers of settlement deteriorated creating dangerous conditions for squatting. In February 1838 George Faithfull set off from Goulburn with plans to squat in the Ovens River district, not far south of the Murray River. He took about 35 servants in two parties, at least three flocks of sheep and a herd of cattle, their gear and supplies hauled in oxen-drawn drays. George and his men travelled along the main south road through today's towns of Yass, Gundagai, and Albury, leaving supplies at Bangus. Finding the grazing land at the Ovens already occupied, George decided to move further south along the Port Phillip Road. First, though, he visited the fabled Oxley Plains to the south-east with servants and stock, intending to catch up with the other party at the Broken River near present-day Benalla. William's overseer, George Crossley, and 17 men, headed south along the main road with about 3472 sheep and 395 cattle.[116] Crossley and his servants reached the Broken River on Friday 7th April 1838. Relations with the Aboriginal men were cordial. Crossley's party gave the Aborigines food and showed them how to use firearms. The Aborigines displayed their skill with spears. Before long, Crossley's party noticed missing sheep, a slayed lamb and spears in the reeds beside the river. On Wednesday morning 11th April 1838, Crossley decided to move his men towards the Goulburn River, near present Seymour. He sent the four shepherds to start the sheep while he yoked the oxen to the drays. Hearing a cry of "murder, a man is speared", Crossley and others ran to help the shepherds who were fleeing spear-throwing natives. Thomas Bentley fired a shot in the air. One native "fell". More shots followed. At least 150 Aborigines advanced from all directions and 40 or so began ransacking the drays. The visitors fled, hounded by natives.[117] Seven servants lost their lives, two of William's and five of George's, namely, Thomas Bentley, John Bass, James McCann, John Hargreave, John Fanning, Joseph Smith and Edward Laycock.[118] When news of the incident reached George Faithfull in the evening of 11th April 1838, he had camped between the Ovens and Broken Rivers after leaving cattle on the Oxley Plains. The next morning George found the badly injured Will Read about four miles from the camp site. Overtime he returned to the camp site to bury the bodies, reload the drays and find the stock. The survivors fled to several runs, Crossley and two others finding refuge at the station of John Clark on the Goulburn River on 13th. Clark thought the three were bushrangers until earliest mailman on the Port Phillip Road, John Bourke, recognized Clark as William's overseer. Clark gave Crossley his best horses to ride to Melbourne. In the Melbourne Police Court on 14th, Lieutenant G.B. Smyth JP examined Crossley. Smyth followed Crossley and a party of Mounted Police to the massacre site. On 22nd Smyth took evidence from George and several survivors recovering at the camp George set up on Lieutenant Colonel White's run at the Ovens River. Convict John Clay stated his employer, George Faithfull, "always treated the natives well".[119] Late in April, George began building a homestead at the Bontherambo Plains near later Wangaratta but natives forced him to abandon the site.[120]

Letters from brother George and overseer George Crossley alerted William Pitt Faithfull to the massacre. On 23rd April 1838 Andrew Gibson sent the "melancholy intelligence" to Governor Gipps. Within a week William had organized supplies and set off to help George. At Bangus on 3rd May, he met two of his servants who escaped the massacre. After giving their master a full explanation of the events at Broken River, William sent Andrew a letter containing the information. At the Ovens on 8th May, William asked the Colonial Secretary for servants to replace the murdered men and the runaways. At the massacre site William collected the drays and his sheep. George and William lost about 200 sheep.[121]

Governor Gipps heard news of the massacre in late April 1838. Soon after, he directed a party of Mounted Police and Yass magistrate, Richard Hardy, to investigate the causes of the "lamentable occurrence" and bring the offenders to justice. The party searched for 41 days and "returned without seeing a native".[122] On 9th May 1838 Police Magistrate, George Stewart, left Goulburn with police commander Lieutenant Waddy and about 12 policemen. His instructions were "to enquire on the spot into all the circumstances of the case, particularly the circumstances that preceded the murders". On 22nd May Waddy's group arrived at Colonel White's station at the Ovens to find White and George Faithfull, expecting an attack, had abandoned the run. Stewart's party also spent many fruitless days searching for the Aborigines.[123] In June Andrew Gibson cancelled William's contract to supply food and forage for surveying parties in the Goulburn district.[124] At the Ovens in August William lost another servant, George Graham, who was moving sheep hurdles. William found Graham's body bearing the wounds of a tomahawk and spear marks on his head and arms.[125] Early in 1839 Aborigines captured one of George's shepherds, stripping him of all his clothes and keeping him for several days before he escaped.[126]

What motivated the Aborigines to attack the Faithfull party? In his report of June 1838 Magistrate Stewart concluded, "it would appear from the evidence obtained from some of the survivors of Mr Faithfull's men, that the outrage was committed solely for motives of plunder".[127] Lady Jane Franklin heard the stockmen gave "some offence".[128] Educator G.W. Rusden questioned survivors of the attack, who told him Faithfull's men refused to pay for the "sexual services" of the native women. However, the evidence differed on the presence of women.[129] William Pitt Faithfull believed the natives "were distressed for food from the scarcity of kangaroos, and in consequence, tempted to seize flour". William offered this motive early in 1839 when an expert witness before a committee of the Legislative Council considering amendments to the Squatting

Act in response to the spread of settlement. The committee recommended setting up a special constabulary, the Border Police, under the control of the Commissioners of Crown Lands.[130]

On returning to Springfield at the end of 1838, or later, William Pitt Faithfull discovered five servants had absconded.[131] He gave his attention to developing a good flock of sheep, a project started in 1835 with the purchase of 20 Collaroy Saxon rams. In the year he returned from the Ovens, William bought 10 rams from William Macarthur's Camden Park. In the early years too, he bought 960 ewes of all ages from the reputed flock of Mr Hassall. William "was one of the first in his part of the country to recognize the importance of breeding from none but pure-bred and high-class sires".[132] William and his father invested in town allotments. William junior paid £21 and £22 for allotments of more than half an acre in Bourke Street, Goulburn. William senior outlaid £27 for 53 perches in Macquarie Street, Parramatta.[133]

Meanwhile on 11th July 1838, Matilda Pitt Wilshire, with the consent of her father, married her cousin William Warren Jenkins at St James, Sydney. Matilda was the fourth daughter of Esther and James Wilshire, William the younger son of Jemima and Robert Jenkins. By licence Reverend Steel married the couple in the presence of witnesses Matilda's father, James, and her sister, Esther. Jemima allowed William Warren to use Berkeley Estate, "exceedingly choice land in a compact block". Earlier, she gave him 60 acres and 80 acres in Appin, the origin of the land unknown.[134] With the help of convicts, William built a brick cottage with clay found on Berkeley.[135] The first child of William and Matilda, William James Robert Jenkins, was baptised at Jemima's church, St Peters, Campbelltown, on 15th October 1839. By then, the couple were in their new home.

The next marriage in the Pitt Family also involved cousins, Eliza Pitt, younger daughter of Thomas and Elizabeth Pitt, and Austin

Forrest Wilshire, third son of James and Esther Wilshire. On 14th February 1839 at St Peters, Campbelltown, the Reverend Richard Taylor conducted the wedding by licence before witnesses Robert Pitt Jenkins and Esther Wilshire. The place of the marriage suggests Eliza Pitt lived with Jemima. Eliza made out the deeds for her 19½ perches in Pitt Street in Austin's name.[136]

Before the wedding, Lucy Wood left Eagle Vale to live at Richmond.[137] She would become more involved with her seven grandchildren. Six were born in the thirties, George Wood in July 1831, John Thomas Wood in November 1832, Sophia Wood in June 1834, Lucy Wood in March 1836, Robert Markwell Wood in November 1837 and Alfred Sherwin Wood in April 1839. Lucy secured the deeds for two acres in the "highlands" in December 1838. (Figure 3) She explained the grounds for owning the plot in her letter to the Colonial Secretary on 3rd June 1835. Governor Bligh promised her the land because "destructive floods" swamped her farm "on the lowlands". Since Bligh's time she had "retained peaceable and, uninterrupted possession" of the allotment, which she had "cleared and fenced ... and built thereon" and rented to George Howell, the elder.[138]

On her journey from Port Phillip to Sydney, Lady Jane Franklin, wife of John Franklin Governor of Van Dieman's Land, met George Faithfull in the Ovens district on 15th April 1839. Approaching Tarcutta on 24th April, Franklin "met the wonderful sight of a cart, with one horse & 2 men, carting some bags, belonging to & going to Mr Faithful's (sic), from Goulburn to the other side of the Murray". On 5th May Lady Franklin arrived at Tirranna in the carriage Andrew Gibson sent to collect her at the Breadalbane Plains. She lunched with the Gibsons, and afterwards walked in their garden, which, despite the effects of the third year of drought, had a profusion of plants such as roses, honeysuckles, asparagus, apples, gooseberries and many espaliers. Behind the house a series of courts were "formed by 'pretty servants' offices', the 'whitewashed stables with centre pediment' and a handsome pigeon house". (Figure 17) Franklin returned to the Gibsons after breakfast on 6th May. Andrew took her up the hill for a view over Goulburn. Next, he showed her the old and new towns. She noted 100 or so houses, many stores, a bank, hospital, old courthouse, mail coach office, three inns, and the recently built large brick Episcopal Church of St Saviour's, the Bishop insisting the church occupy a central position in the town! William Pitt Faithfull joined the Gibsons and Jane Franklin at dinner where they discussed the incident at Broken River. Lady Franklin described William, "a giant in size", and Andrew, "a man about 40-pale or sallow, head or neck a little awry-gentlemanly, quiet & gentle in manner". Andrew told Franklin he was "a Presbyterian by birth, but an Episcopalian by habit in the army & by preference tho' a subscriber to both churches". Andrew explained the Presbyterian minister was "excessively zealous & had something of the old Covenanter about him". Lady Jane commented, "I think Dr Gibson thought it too much". Franklin learned 11-year old Alice Jemima Gibson attended Mrs Harvey's school in Sydney.[139]

In the later months of 1839, the Crown Lands Commissioners visited the family squats except George Matcham Pitt's station in the far north-west. On 18th August Henry Bingham called at the Oxley Plains' lease of George and William Faithfull. Extending for 50 miles in superior open and forest country between the Ovens and King Rivers, the run carried 9 horses, 1214 cattle and 3921 sheep. Twentythree residents, including superintendent, George Faithfull, lived in good slab huts.[140] George was the only squatter in the family to live permanently on his run.

Henry Cosby recorded two squats in the Lachlan district held by Andrew Gibson. On 26th September 1839 he visited Andrew's "bush station", Boggydillon, bordered by Caragabal Creek and situated between today's towns of Grenfell and West Wyalong. The station's empty slab huts and two stockyards signalled the presence

Figure 17. Tiranna Homestead

of Aborigines. The men had moved with the stock to the "head station", Boga Bogalong. On 10th October Cosby reached Boga Bogalong, a 40 mile run close to later Grenfell, which supported 1600 cattle, 7 horses, and 5 acres of cultivation. Eleven residents, including superintendent James Smith, lived in bark huts.[141] Nearer to home Andrew had more trouble. At Grabben Gullen, on the highroad from Wheeo to Goulburn, three outlaws confronted his shepherds and fired two shots at his superintendent, Oliver Fry. Previously, Fry had disarmed and captured the bandits at the Narrawa farm, but they escaped and returned to the Goulburn district for "the avowed purposes of seeking revenge". In November 1839 Andrew posted a reward of £50 for the three men, two of them "well-known as notorious bushrangers".[142] Bushrangers overran the country in 1839.[143]

Bingham reached the Jenkins's Murrumbidgee run, Bangus, on 4th November 1839. Extending over ranges and plains for 50 miles, the station held 1250 cattle, nine horses and 10 acres of cultivation. Twelve people slept in slab huts, their supervisor Leighton Robertson.[144] Workers had abandoned Brewarrena after the Wiradjuri declared war in the Narrandera district by killing Dennis Denay on 8th January 1839. Ticket-of-leave holder Matthew Donovan had just returned to Brewarrenna from the muster at Yass when he discovered the Denay's body close to the stockyard. His hut plundered and burnt, Denay had seven spears in his body and tomahawk wounds to his head. Donovan recalled Denay "was particularly fond of the blacks and always very kind to them". Jemima offered a reward of £20.[145] On Commissioner Henry Cosby's second visit to the Narrandera the district in early May, he discovered the natives had speared 22 cattle at Brewarrena since January 1st. Although the Aborigines speared many cattle, they murdered few white people.[146]

Esther Wilshire, third daughter of Esther and James Wilshire, wed widower Henry Rawes Whittell by licence on 11th November 1839 at St James, Sydney. Reverend George N. Woodd conducted the ceremony, which Esther's father James, and her sister Elizabeth, witnessed. Henry was born in Chester, England, in November 1805, to Charles Whittell, a doctor and member of the Royal College of Surgeons, and Hannah Whittell, née Rawes.[147] Henry left West India Dock in the *Camden* on 11th April 1838, "a fine a Day as ever was out of the heavens". The brig's passengers, missionaries on their way to the Islands, devoted much time to morning and evening prayers, sermons, and lessons in the native language. The *Camden* took a pilot on-board at the Heads before anchoring at Pinchgut Island at midnight on 10th September.[148] In the colony Henry practised medicine and witnessed coroners' inquests and inquiries made by Justices of the Peace.[149]

The Faithfulls, Gibsons, Jenkins and Pitts squatted on crown lands "beyond the limits" at the Monaro, Ovens River, Murrumbidgee River, Lachlan Basin and Gwydir River district. For a small outlay, the squatters earned rich rewards. However, those living on the runs experienced extreme temperatures, floods, droughts and hostility from displaced Aborigines. During one of most notorious squatting incidents dubbed the "Faithfull Massacre", Aborigines killed seven servants of William and George Faithfull.

---

1   HRA 1, 17,pp424-28, 776-7
2   Hainsworth, D. R., *Builders and Adventurers*, Cassell Australia, Sydney, 1968, ch 4, p133
3   Registers of Copies of Wills 1800-1901, SAG Will 1/1222; L A & V P 1865, 2, p838
4   Town Grants A, Bk 29, Pg 71, DL; SMH 8 September 1928, p3g
5   Bk E, No 551, DL; Supreme Court of NSW, Equity, 3/3974, No 787, re 10 acres in Glebe
6   Bk F, No 115, DL
7   Town Grants Bk 48, Pg 75, DL
8   GG 1832, p193, 13 Mar
9   HRA 1, 14, pp385-6; HRA 1, 15, p149

10	HRA 1, 16, p793; Bk 197, Pgs 93-99, DL; County Cook, Parish Currency, Map 13, DL
11	Letters Received Relating to Land, SRNSW 2/7854, Reel 1125, WPF 4 Feb 1830
12	Stephens and Stokes, *NSW Calendar and Directory 1834*, Sydney, p85
13	Russell, Penny, ed., *This Errant Lady*, National Library of Australia, Canberra, 2002, ch 6, p97-8; (See Ref 14 below)
14	Jervis, James, "The Journals of William Edward Riley", JRAHS, Vol 32, 1946, pt 4, pp259-60
15	NSW *Governors'Despatches and Enclosures 1830-1831*, ML A1267-12, pp963-75; HRA 1, 14, pp741, 941-2, Note 210; HRA 1, 16, pp48-52; HRA 1, 16, pp259
16	HRA 1, 16, p49; Aus 7 October 1831, p3e
17	HRA 1, 16, pp688-9; Bennett, Frederick D., *Narrative of a Whaling Voyage Round the Globe From the Year 1833 to 1836*, Richard Bentley, London 1840, Vol 1, ch 3, pp51-2
18	Philip Elliot, NSW 04884
19	Aus 28 September 1827, p3a; HRA 1, 14, p l 77
20	HRA 1, 13, pp124-5; HRA, 1, 14, p338
21	NSW Governor's Dispatches, Aug-Dec 1835, ML A1214, CY 650, p641
22	Surveyor General, Letters Received from Surveyors, Letters Received from Philip Elliot 24 Mar 1828 - 1 Oct 1841, SRNSW 2/1534, Reel 3064; HRA 1, 15, p321; Surveyors Field Books, SRNSW 2/4931, Reel 2627, Elliot
23	Letters Received Relating to Land, SRNSW 2/7851, Reel 1123, LE 25 Jul 1831, 11 Aug 1831, 26 Sept 1839, 1 Aug 1840; GG 1839, Vol 1, p628, 25 May; Purchases Special Grant, Bk 35, Pg 339 DL; County Argyle, Parish Mangamore, Map 22, DL
24	GG 1834, Vol 1, p276, 8 Apr
25	NSW Governor's Dispatches, Jan-Apr 1831, ML A1208, CY 541, pp734, 736,989
26	Surveyor General, Correspondence, SRNSW 4/2430, Surveyor General, 38/5921; Surveyor General, Letters Received from Surveyors, Philip Elliot 24 Mar 1828 - 1 Oct 1842, SRNSW 2/1534, Reel 3064, June 1831
27	Aus 10 March 1837, p2d
28	Picton Bench Books, SRNSW 4/7572, Reel 671, 21 Sept. 1829; 4/5627, Reel 672, 30 Jan 1832, 21 Mar 1833, 1 Aug 1833
29	Bk 108, No 214, DL, re son born 10 May 1833
30	Surveyor General, Letters Received from Surveyors, Letters of Philip Elliot, Mar 1828 - 1 Oct 1841, 2/1534, Reel 3064; Select List of Maps and Plans SRNSW 5959,W.1.828; 5080 R.1.818; 5082,R.2.818; 5083, R.3.818; 1871, C61.730
31	GG 1834, Vol 2, p820, 28 Nov
32	Lhotsky, John, *A Journey to the Australian Alps 1835*, p105
33	SMH 25 February 1860, p7f

34	*Sydney Monitor* 25 October 1834, p3b
35	Purchases Bk 32, Pg 39, DL; Purchases Bk 44, Pgs 8, 9, 61, DL; County Argyle, Parish Terranna, 5th ed., Map 42, DL; County Argyle, 1907, Map, DL; County King, Parish Wallah Wallah, 1921, Map 43,
36	Gibson, Andrew, Bill of Exchange, ML MSS Ag 20; Bk K, No 859, DL
37	GG 1834, Vol 2, p918, 20 Oct; GG 1835, Vol 1, p319, 19 May
38	Letters Relating to Land, SRNSW 2/7864, Reel 1130, AG 8 Jan 1834
39	SG 10 March 1828, p2e; Aus 10 July 1841, 3d
40	Wyatt, Ransome T., *History of Goulburn*, Lansdown Press, Epping, NSW, 1972, p310; GG 1832, p 149, 27 Jun
41	Russell, 2002, ch vi, p981
42	GG 1833, p107, 27 Mar
43	HRA 1, 16, p245; HRA 1, 17, pp6, 183
44	Hogan Papers 1830-1836, p36, ML A663
45	Bennett, George, Andrew Gibson, William Sherwin, *Reports on the Epidemic Catarrh or Influenza prevailing Among the Sheep in the Colony of New South Wales in the Year 1835*, Stephens and Stokes, Sydney 1835, pp33-9
46	HRA 1, 18, pp85-7
47	Letters Received, Miscellaneous Persons F-K, SRNSW 4/2495.1, Reel 2220; Wichelton/Walton NSWV1831 1135 15, Wharmby/PalmerNSW V1832 1127 16
48	Wyatt, 1972, pp60-1
49	Despatches to the Governor of New South Wales, July to Dec 1840, p328, ML A1283
50	Brodie, Walter, *Pitcairn s Island and the Islanders in 1850*, Whittaker & Co., London 1851, pp 174-210
51	Gunson, Niel, "The Deviations of a Missionary Family", Davidson J. W., and Deryck Scarr, *Pacific Island Portraits*, Australian National University Press, Canberra, 1970, p43
52	Registers of Copies of Wills 1800-1901, SAG Will 1/503
53	Laycock K.G., Laycock, *A Pioneer Australian Family*, 2000, p27
54	Registers of Copies of Wills 1800-1901, SAG Will 1/503; County Hunter, Parish Gullongulong, 1964, Map 17, DL
55	Indents of Convict Ships 1806-1811, SRNSW 4/4004, COD 139, pp297, 328; John Johnson, NSW V 1 825 6490 2B; Aull/Johnson, NSW V 1 829 4527 3B
56	Registers of Copies of Wills 1800-1901, SAG Will 4/10756
57	Smith, Alfred, *Some Ups and Downs of an Old Richmondite*, Nepean Family History Society, Emu Plains, 1991, p88
58	Hibbert, Christopher, *Nelson, a Personal History*, London, Penguin, 1995, pp 194, 417
59	Robert FitzRoy, *Narrative of the Surveying Voyages of His Majesty's Ships Adventure and Beagle Between the Years 1826 and 1836*, Vol 2, Colburn, London 1839, ch xxii, pp524, 527; ch xx iii; pp542-3, 553, 537;

Vol 3, ch xx, pp491,493; Beechey, Frederick W., *Narrative of Voyages and Travels to the Pacific and Beering's Strait, In the Years 1825, 26, 27, 28*, Colburn and Bentley, London, 1851, Vol 1, ch 9, p299

60   Gunson, 1970, pp42-3

61   Bennett, George, "A Recent Visit to Several of the Polynesian Islands", *United Service Journal* 1831, Pt 2, p 196

62   Bennett, Frederick D., *Narrative of a Whaling Voyage Round the Globe From the Year 1833 to 1836*, Richard Bentley, London 1840, Vol 2, ch 2, pp37-42, 48-9

63   Gammage, Bill, *Narrandera Shire*, Gammage, 1986, pp30. (See p49 for map of Brewarenna); County Wynyard NSW, 1908, Map DL. (See river frontage for Bangus)

64   Treasury, Certificates for Depasturing Licenses 1837-38, SRNSW 4/91, 38/91, Reel 5067; GG 1837, Vol 1, p ll9, 30 Jan

65   Liston, Carol, *Campbelltown The Bicentennary History*, Allen and Unwin, 1988, p46

66   GG 1836, Vol 2, pp745-6, 1 Oct

67   GG 1837, Vol 1, p362, 9 May; GG 1837, Vol 2, p650, 18 Sept

68   SG 12 May 1836, pp3,4; Records of St James Anglican Church Sydney, SAG Reel 136, fr 78

69   Yeend, Peter, ed., *The King's School Register 1831-1999*, 3rd ed., The Council of the Kings School Parramatta, 1999, p486

70   Vessels Arrived, Jan to Jun 1834, SRNSW COD 28, 4/5206

71   Registers of Copies of Wills 1800-1901, SAG Will 1/1222, re JRW's house in Pitt Street; *New South Wales Calendar and Post Office Directory 1835*, Stephens and Stokes, Sydney. (See Sydney Directory)

72   James Maclehose, *Picture of Sydney and Strangers' Guide*, 1839, p69; Town Surveyor, SRNSW 4/2382.3, 51/1837

73   Aus 16 January 1835, p2a

74   Aus 13 January 1837, p3d

75   Austin F Wilshire NSW V 1837 227 21; Austin Wiltshire (sic) Vl838 3236 22

76   Aus 27 October 1837, p3d

77   Aus 16 August 1836, pp3,4; Aus 5 December 1837, p2f; 15 May 1838, p3e

78   Bk M, No 54, DL

79   Bk P, No 10, DL

80   Letters Received from Surveyors, Philip Elliot, Mar 1828-1 Oct 1841, SRNSW 2/1534, Reel 3064; Surveyor General, Correspondence 1838, SRNSW 4/2430, 38/5921

81   Governor's Despatches, Jan-Apr 1831, ML A1208, CY 541, p 1 063ff, See Ref 79 above; HRA 1, 17, p422

82   Bk M, No 52, DL; Primary Application 6529 DL; Bk 0, No 430, DL; County Cumberland, Parish Appin, Map 2, 4th ed., DL. See SE corner of the parish for grants of Fair, Davis and Barnett

7 Squatting and Its Perils

83 Letters Received Relating to Land, SRNSW 2/7851, LE 26 September 1839, Reel 1123; GG 1834, p276, 8 Apr
84 Letters Received Relating to Land, SRNSW 2/7854, Reel 1125, WF 10 July 1837
85 Lhotsky, John, A Journey from Sydney to the Australian Alps, 1835, pp25, 26,85
86 Purchases Bk 32, Pg 226, DL; Bk J, No 200, DL; Bk L, No 56, DL; Purchases Bk 63, Pg 62, DL; Purchases Bk 64, Pgs 126, 127, DL; GG 1836, Vol 2, p924, 27 Nov; Purchases Bk 65, Pgs 15, 164, DL; Bk M, No 507, DL; County Argyle, Parish Mangamore, 4th ed., Map 22, DL; County Argyle 1907, DL
87 Bk L, No 411, DL
88 Treasury, Certificates for Depasturing Licenses 1837-38, SRNSW Reel 5067, 4/91, 37/331; Commissioners of Crown Lands, Itineraries, SRNSW Reel 2748, X815, 29 July 1839-24 Nov 1840. No lease for;William's squat in the Manaro
89 Butlin N.G., Cromwell C.W. and K.L., Suthem, eds., *General Return of Convicts in New South Wales in 1837*, Australian Biographical and Genealogical Record and Society of Australian Genealogists, Sydney, 1987, p718
90 GG 1837, Vol 2, p775, 30 Sept
91 Smith, Alfred, 1991, p88
92 Purchases Bk 64, Pg 19, DL; Purchases Bk 63, Pg 28, DL; Grants Bk 57, Pg 75, DL; Reports of the Commissioners of Claims c1825-55, SRNSW 2/1752, Case 44, Reel 1209; Court of Claims Registers 1836-1921, 2/2369, Case 44, Reel 1249
93 Grants Bk 58, Pgs 13, 29, 30, 39, 40, DL; Grants Bk 59, Pg 151, DL
94 Purchases Bk 69, Pg 47, DL
95 Town Purchases Bk 202, Pgs 84, 85, 87, 88, 90, DL ; Town Purchases Bk 208, Pgs 52, 53, 54, 58, 59, 60, DL
96 Census 1837, p721. See Gibson
97 Treasury, Certificate ofDepasturing Licenses , SRNSW Reel 5067, 4/91, 128/38; Commissioners of Crown lands, Itineraries and Returns, Monaro 29 July 1839-24 Nov 1840, SRNSW, X815. (No lease for AG's squat in the Monaro)
98 Aus 31 July 1835, p4c
99 Aus 11 March 1836, ple
100 GG 1836, Vol 1, ppl, 2 Jan; GG 1838, Vol 2, pl083, 8 Dec
101 HRA 1, 18, pp466-70; ADB 1, Bourke
102 Aus 27 Jan 1837, p3c
103 GG 1838, Vol 1, p99, 3 Feb
104 GG 1832, pp428-9, 27 Nov; GG 1836, Vol 1, pl25, 8 Feb; GG 1936, Vol 2, p984, 27 Dec; GG 1837, Vol 1, pl 6, 27 Dec 1836, GG 1837, Vol 1, pl69, 7 Feb; GG 1839, Vol 1, p353, 25 Mar, Vol 2, pl 440, 18 Dec; Letters Received from Miscellaneous Persons, SRNSW 4/2404.3, Reel

	2212, 38/13376, 38/3461
105	GG 1844, Vol 2, p1591, 15 Dec; GG 1845, Vol 2, p1327, 19 Nov; GG 1846, Vol 1, p358, 30Apr
106	Third Foot Regiment (Buff) Papers 1826, MLA 338, p82
107	Miscellaneous W, 1838, SRNSW 4/2408.1, 33/12264
108	Aus 6 October 1835, p3f; *New South Wales Calendar and General Post Office Directory, 1836, 1837*, Stephens and Stokes , Sydney. (See Sydney Directory); Aus 29 December 1835, p4b
109	Bk K, No 818, DL; Bk K, No 840, DL
110	Aus 4 December 1838, p3c
111	Miscellaneous W, 1838, SRNSW 4/2408.1, 38/12264
112	Bench of Magistrates Windsor, Judgement Book 1837-44, SRNSW 4/5695, Reel 2390, pp68, 72, 73, 87, 90; Letters Received, PoliceWindsor 1839, SRNSW 4/2470.2, Reel 1191, 29 Dec 1838, 5 Jan 1839; Police , Windsor, SRNSW 4/2587.5, 42/356
113	Treasury, Letters Received 1847, SRNSW, 4/2788, Wm Scott 47/4126
114	Letters Received 1826-49, Miscellaneous Persons M-Y, SRNSW 4/2406.4, Reel 2213, 38/3985
115	Treasury, Certificates for De pasturing Licenses 1839-40, SRNSW Reel 5068, 4/92, No 2
116	Bride, Thomas Francis, Letters from Victorian Pioneers, Heinemann, Melbourne, 1898, No 4, p219; Letters Received SRNSW 4/2423.3, 38/5770, 4/2415.2, 38/5757; HRV 2A, pp314, 325
117	HRV 2A, pp314-317, 328-9, 333; Russell, 2002, ch vi, pl0l; Letters Received, SRNSW 4/2423.3, 38/5759; SMH 21 May 1838, p2b,c
118	HRV 2A, pp319, 325; Letters Received, SRNSW 4/2423.3, 38/5759; Census 1837, p205, No 8580; Re Joseph Smith, see Picton Bench Books SRNSW 4/7573, Reel 672, 21 Mar 1833, 1 Aug 1833
119	HRV 2A, pp315-317, 318-319, 322; *Australasian* 26 September 1896, p601; NSW and Victoria, Miscellaneous Papers 1817-73, CY907, pp 315-7, ML A1493
120	BT, Box 26, p6083
121	HRV 2A, pp325, 329, 321; Letters Received, SRNSW 4/2415.2, 38/5757, 38/5758; *Sydney Monitor* 9 May 1838, p2e; *Sydney Monitor* 14 May 1838, p3a
122	HRA 1, 19, pp398, 510
123	HRV 2A, pp226-8, 332; SMH 19 May 1838, p2a
124	Letters Received, SRNSW 4/2415.2, 38/6517
125	Letters Received, SRNSW 4/2423.3, 38/9268; HRV 2A, p334
126	Aus 7 March 1839, p2e
127	HRV 2A, p333
128	Russell, 2002, ch iii, p54
129	Connor, John, *The Australian Frontiers Wars 1788-1838*, University of New South Wales, Sydney, 2002, p ll7; HRV 2A, pp 315-5, 329
130	Aus 7 March 1839, p2e,f; HRV 6, pp222-3

131 GG 1838, Vol 1, p294, 10 April; p465, 12 June; p476, 19 June; GG 1838, Vol 2, p567, 24 Jul; p l080, 4 Dec
132 Brown, George, A., *Sheep Breeding in Australia*, 2nd ed., Walker and May, Melbourne, 1890, p313
133 Town Purchases Bk 206, Pgs 77, 78, DL; Town Grants Bk 48, No 49, DL; GG 1838, Vol 1, p 19, 5 Jan
134 Bk 114, No 418, DL
135 Barwick, Kathleen H., *History of Berkeley New South Wales*, Illawarra Historical Society, 1963
136 Miscellaneous 1839, SRNSW 4/2459, 39/6510; GG 1834, Vol 2, p862, 2 Dec
137 Letters Received Relating to Land, SRNSW 2/8010, Reel 1200, LW 12 Jan 1839
138 GG 1839, p211, 12 Feb; SRNSW 2/8010, Reel 1200, LW 3 June 1835
139 Russell, 2002, ch iii, p71, ch vi, pp96-101
140 Commissioners of Crown Lands, Itineraries and Returns, Murrumbidgee 1838-47, SRNSW Reel 2748, X812, p6
141 Commissioners of Crown Lands, Itineraries and Returns, Lachlan, 1839-40, SRNSW, Reel 2748, X813, pp l,5, note p17 for 1840; County Bland, Parish Caragabal, 3rd ed. Map 19, DL; County Forbes, 1908, DL
142 GG 1839, Vol 2, p l300, 19 Nov
143 Clark, C.M.H., *Select Documents in Australian History 1788-1850*, Angus and Robertson, Sydney 1962, p291
144 Commissioners of Crown Lands, Itineraries and Returns, Murrumbidgee 1838-47, SRNSW Reel 2748, X812, 16
145 Letters Received, Police-Yass 1839, SRNSW, 4/2470.4, Reel 1912, 39/2101, pp4-22; GG 1839, Vol 1, p132, 23 Jan
146 Gammage Bill, *Narrandera Shire,* Bill Gammage for the Narrandera Shire Council, 1986, pp33-34; Gammage Bill; "The Wiradji War 1838-1840"; *The Push from the Bush*, No 16, Oct 1983, pp3-17
147 Family of Whittell 1925, ML Z D80, Item 10, Sheet 1, CY774
148 Morgan, Robert, Journal Book, Brig *Camden*, Missionary Service, 1858, ML B277-B281, CY 1209
149 Aus 2 March 1839, p2g; GG 1839, Vol 1, p290, 25 Feb

8
THE GRANDCHILDREN'S GENERATION CENTRE STAGE

In the 1840s the grandchildren's generation occupied centre stage by taking important roles in their communities and raising the greatgrandchildren. Convict transportation ended in 1840 and while many hailed this act because it improved the Colony's reputation and its attractiveness to migrants, others deplored the loss of cheap labour. Between 1840 and 1844 depression gripped the Colony, resulting in low prices, unemployment and insolvency. Despite unpromising times, Governor George Gipps introduced democracy by setting up the election of a majority of members of the Legislative Council and launching municipal councils. Five grandsons represented the Pitt Family on these bodies.

On New Year's Day 1840, horses, men, women and children crowded the "little town" of Goulburn for the horseraces. The Gibsons and William Pitt Faithfull were present. William took part in the highlight of the day, the three mile hurdle race, his sturdy six feet plus frame dressed in a crimson jacket and black cap. He gallantly rode the light-heeled Daylight, successfully negotiating the first three of six hurdles, the horse crashing at the fourth. William fell, but "all up and no harm". Sensibly, William took the role of steward at Goulburn's new racecourse later in the year.[1] He served the community in several other roles: a magistrate from 1839 to 1842; a Justice of the Peace in 1843; a member of the district committee of the Australian Immigration Association in 1840; and a participant at a meeting in Sydney to oppose partitioning the colony in 1841.[2] The focus shifts to William's father, the depression, no doubt, responsible for his uncharacteristic behaviour. William sold 80 acres at Mittagong for £200 and surrendered a mortgage of £570 on three buildings in Brougham Place, Sydney.

Two incidents demonstrate the drawbacks of Henry Whittell's medical practice. Coach-owner Thomas a'Beckett died rather suddenly while in Henry's care. After conducting the post-mortem on a'Beckett in March 1840, Henry and partly qualified Mr Oliver were charged with illegally dissecting a body, the complaint initiated by Constable Daniel Sharply. During the inquest into a'Beckett's death, Henry threatened to contact the Governor which annoyed the coroner who decided to exclude Henry from the inquest into the death of his patient Mrs Catherine Kennedy. The coroner relented; he was willing to seek Dr Whittell's advice on the cause of Catherine's death, but the jury, certain the effects of alcohol caused her death, did not need the doctor's opinion. Fortunately the charges against Henry and his assistant were dismissed.[3,4] In the second incident, Henry treated friend Robert Cooper for 11 months before the distiller left for England without paying his bill. Henry took the matter to the Supreme Court. Cooper's lawyers argued Henry should not expect payment because he often dined at Ormonde Hall (Paddington). On the advice of a medical witness, who considered 10s a fair charge for a consultation, Henry won £3.[5] Although patients' medical and social circumstances determined doctors' fees, Henry's offer of free medical service for the poor every morning from 8 to 9 o'clock would be most welcome.[6]

James Wilshire, aged 70, died at his home on 9th September 1840. He was buried beside Esther at the Sydney Burial Ground on the 12th.[7] Sons James and Austin, and son-in-law William Warren

8 The Grandchildren's Generation Centre Stage

Jenkins managed his estate of about £6000. Louisa inherited the most southerly lot in George Street and the site of the workers' huts on the south side of Union Lane. William's legacy was the house he occupied at 47 George Street. The executors discharged the mortgage on 47 George Street and William raised his own mortgage.[8] James gave the tannery to James Robert and Austin. James Robert could keep his home in Pitt Street. Austin received property in George Street. James had already given James Robert and Austin the place next door. James bequeathed Elizabeth, Esther and Matilda the family home and the retreat and acreage in Surry Hills. Thomas and Joseph inherited three properties, one each in Union Lane, Pitt Street and George Street. Thomas's property in George Street traded as Emu Inn under licence to William Dargin.[9] A section on the north side of Union Lane was to feed, clothe and educate the five youngest children, until Joseph turned 21. Then the five children, plus Louisa, were to share the property. Both niece Elizabeth Weiss and nephew Alfred Eyre got a tenement on the north side of Union Lane. (Figure 18) Grandsons William James Wilshire and Thomas Elliot inherited 60 acres each in the St George district. Income from all other property, the residual estate, was to support the five younger children. James gave Matilda the piano and music books.[10]

Less than two weeks after the death of James Wilshire, on 22nd September 1840, Andrew Gibson died at Tirranna in his early 40s. William Somersby buried him on 27th, probably at Tirranna. Andrew had not fully recovered from injuries suffered at the Battle of Waterloo. In May 1839 Lady Franklin wrote notes on Andrew's condition:

> *He is in indifferent health, produced he thinks by the climate which affected him when living at his station on the hill. He has been better since he came down, but seldom free from rheumatic pains in head - sometimes up all night from them - has taken great quantities of laudanum, to injurious excess, so*

as to sometimes seem stupefied - found it necessary to leave this off a great deal.[11]

The *Australian* commented, Andrew had "for many years discharged the duties of an active and useful magistrate".[12] Andrew gave his name to Gibson Street in Goulburn. Alice inherited Andrew's estate of £10,000, but if she married, the children got the estate. Andrew asked Alice to give their 21-year-old sons livestock to the value of £1000 and their daughters £1000 in cash at the same age, or earlier if they married with consent. Andrew's executors were Alice, George Faithfull and Stuart Alexander Donaldson. Andrew named William Pitt Faithfull an executor in his will of 1837, Donaldson replacing him in the codicil dated July 1839. Andrew empowered the male executors to sell his real or personal estate for the benefit of Alice or the children.[13] Three weeks after Andrew's death, on 17th, October, Alice gave birth to her seventh child, Septimus Faithfull Gibson.

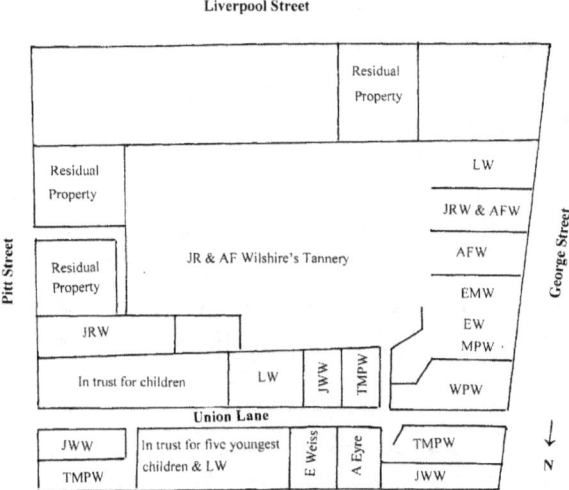

Figure 18. An approximation of the George Street Complex of James Wilshire in September 1840

A third event in September 1840, George Matcham Pitt gave Julia a wedding gift of one rood and three perches near The Terrace in Windsor Village, paying £50 for the allotment.[14] On George's mind, the Pitt Street property Hannah Laycock left to her son William Laycock. Hannah had directed William to leave the 26 perches to his sister Elizabeth, and she to her five children by Thomas Pitt.[15] Laycock's actions after Elizabeth's death upset George. Laycock gave Charles Smith a 40-year lease on the property for a down payment of £100 and a yearly rental of £30. Smith, on the other hand, had to find and provide Laycock's board.[16] At the Court of Claims in November 1840 George confirmed the Pitts future right to the property. James Robert Wilshire, who supported George's claim, was trustee of Hannah's property.[17] Although Laycock did not die until 1853, during the forties Mary Matcham Laycock "sold" her fifth share to Austin Forrest Wilshire for £200, and Austin "bought" half of William Pitt's portion from George.[18] George, Robert and Austin leased the shops and houses in Pitt Street and gave most of the rent to William Laycock.[19]

"In perfect health" at 64, Lucy Wood made her will in Sydney on 8th July 1841. Nephews William, James and Thomas Wilshire were her witnesses.[20] Lucy saw daughter Sophia Henry and Miss and Master Henry in the early months of 1841, their arrival unrecorded. They left in the brig *Star* on 1st June 1841.[21] A Mr Henry left Sydney in early March in the *Shepherdess*, bound for America. Did he repeat his actions of the previous year? In the first quarter of 1840 Samuel "collected" horses at Valparaiso, which he sold in Tahiti for £90 to £120 a head.[22]

On 15th July 1841, Bishop William Broughton consecrated the attractive stone St Peters Church of England, Richmond, in the presence of "all the respectable families in the town or neighborhood".[23] Parishioners discussed building the church at a public meeting in the old Richmond schoolhouse back in October 1835. At this meeting chaired by Samuel Marsden, William

Faithfull and George Pitt Wood joined the planning committee. The two contributed to the building fund, William £40, George two guineas.[24] The Faithfulls and Pitts paid £2 10s for five pew seats in the first year of the church. Family members continued to support the church. William was the warden from 1842-7, George in 1851. Mrs Faithfull gave a guinea to the organ (finished 1849) fund, George two guineas. George donated five guineas to the gallery (finished 1855) fund.[25]

George Pitt Wood attended the new Wesleyan Methodist Church once it opened in Richmond in August 1842.[26] Elizabeth and George and their nine children, including Ellen Maria born in October 1840 and Mary Ann in July 1842, lived at Oatlands, probably George's 200 acres. A servant assisted Elizabeth with housework while five labourers, just one a convict, helped George with his crops, pigs and cattle, plus cattle belonging to Lucy.[27] A skilled horseman like many in his generation, George attracted a fine of £5 for "riding furiously".[28] Elizabeth's father Thomas Markwell, who died in September 1841, bequeathed 20 breeding ewes to his Wood and other grandchildren. The will of Markwell revealed his close association with George Matcham Pitt and the family of wife, Julia. Markwell's executors included George Matcham Pitt and John Crowley, husband of Mary Johnson, Julia's sister. Also, Markwell gave mourning suits to Mr and Mrs George Matcham Pitt, Mr and Mrs John Crowley, and Julia's mother and stepfather Mr and Mrs Robert Aull. And widower Markwell gave £20 to Julia's mother "for her attention and kindness" to his 11-year-old daughter, Mary Ann.[29]

Jemima Jenkins, aged 59, died suddenly at Eagle Vale on 22nd March 1842. She was buried beside Robert in the Sydney Burial Ground on 27th.[30] Jemima died intestate. In keeping with his father's instructions, heir-at-law Robert transferred Berkeley to brother William in January 1843. William raised £1000 on the estate.[31]

8 The Grandchildren's Generation Centre Stage

On 28th July 1842 William Faithfull lost his second wife Margaret Thompson aged 53. The Reverend Stiles buried her in St Peters Cemetery on 31st July. In the year of Margaret's death, two more distressing and related events occurred at William's farm, Mt. Pleasant.[32] In October armed men entered William's home, confining the occupants in a room before ransacking the house. The thieves expected to find a large sum of money but left disappointed. At the Quarter Sessions, three of those involved were found guilty.[33] Late in December fire destroyed William's barn and stacks. William considered the act wilful, "having recently prosecuted, to conviction, a band of notorious robbers". He offered a reward of £100, while the Governor recommended a free pardon for any prisoner of the Crown providing information leading to a conviction.[34] It was also in 1842 that son William Pitt Faithfull borrowed money to buy land. In May he bought two parcels of 640 acres in the parish of Quilago in the east, his primary grant securing a loan of £2000. In September he bought a 640 acre farm in the Scone district with £ 1000 borrowed on one of his 640 acre lots. The Australian Trust Company lent him £1000 for four years on six parcels of Springfield in October 1843.[35] That year, sheep sold for 6d and 7d.[36]

The depression affected the finances of James Robert and Austin Forrest Wilshire. In September 1842 the brothers borrowed £3000 from Alice Gibson.[37] The previous year Austin raised £2000 on the three-storied brick house he built on Hannah Laycock's land in Pitt Street. He rented the house for £365 a quarter.[38] Austin had also borrowed £1000 from William Pitt Faithfull on his property in George Street.[39] Lack of money did not deter James and Austin's plan to develop the George Street frontage. The pair paid Louisa £868 for her place in George Street.[40] Also they gave Esther and Matilda £707 apiece for the land either side of the family home. The three sisters had partitioned 48 George Street, Elizabeth taking the house and letting it for a peppercorn rent to George Cooper Turner.[41] The financial circumstances of James and Austin probably account for an "agreement" the Wilshire children made in January 1843. The unseen agreement apparently involved shared management of their father's residual estate. These holdings included sections of the George Street Complex, the Darling Harbour Complex, property at Parramatta and acreage in the districts of Glebe, Salt Pan Creek and Bathurst. In Sydney alone, the brothers had 49 properties to rent, 14 in Union Lane, 13 in Pitt Street (2 rows) and at least 22 in Bathurst and nearby streets.[42]

Despite the economic crisis, the Legislative Council incorporated Sydney as a city on 20th July 1842.[43] Appointed an assessor in September, James Robert Wilshire updated citizens' rolls in preparation for the city's first elections. Given his contact with citizens, it was not surprising to find James proposed a candidate for the forthcoming election. He acknowledged the honour, then unexpectedly volunteered his personal failings, poor English, no knowledge of the Corporation Act, "excessively indolent" and "exceedingly bad tempered".[44] The voluntary vote, confined to men occupying property valued at £25, took place on 1st November, a holiday. Voters selected four councillors in each of six city wards with James successful in Phillip's ward. Afterwards "a number of athletic Australians" hauled James in his carriage to his home.[45] On 9th the 24 councillors elected six aldermen, one being James. With two aldermen chosen from Phillip's ward, James agreed to represent Macquarie ward.[46] James was a steward at the celebratory dinner on 10th November.[47] His first task was chairing the committee which searched for suitable offices for the "Town Hall". From four possible buildings identified by the committee, the council preferred Pultenay Hotel in York Street, between present Market and Druitt Streets.[48]

Governor George Gipps considered the 24 city councillors "good men of business" rather than gentlemen of "wealth or station". Gipps therefore recognized just one esquire on the list of councillors and their occupations he sent to England.[49] The *Sydney Morning*

Herald singled out four esquires from the six aldermen. James Robert Wilshire was not on either list.[50] Offended by the *Herald*'s lack of respect for his brother, William Pitt Wilshire sent a letter of objection to the *Australian*, which had recorded all councillors as esquires. The letter also contained advice for James. He should "discharge the duties of a City Councillor with disinterestedness, and with a patriotic zeal for the welfare of that City which appears destined to be the greatest in the Southern World". And he should remember the example of his father in performing his "duties of an executor with rigid justice and honesty of purpose". The signature on the letter, *sub umbra*, is Latin for in the shade or shadow.[51]

Far from the new City of Sydney, in the Isle of Pines, New Caledonia, a horrifying event overcame 21-year-old William Henry, eldest child of Sophia and Samuel Pinder Henry. (Figure 4) Captain Thomas Ebrill and helper William Henry reached Sydney in the *Star* in March and October 1842. On the second trip Ebrill arrived with sandalwood from the Isle of Pines about 8th October. He left for the Isle of Pines about 20th October with sundries and 5 passengers, including William Henry.[52] Soon after ship reached Vao on 1st November, the island chief implemented his plan to attack the visitors. On 2nd about 30 local people boarded the *Star* with their weapons. They killed Ebrill with an axe sharpened on the ship's grindstone. With the intentions of the inhabitants clear, the 17 members of the *Star* spread about the ship, some fleeing below, others climbing the masts. By the 3rd William and two Samoan teachers were the only survivors. Led to see the chief, the three met his son who offered his left-hand and "Greetings". When William responded he was axed to death. Later, the teachers were murdered. The local people cooked and ate some bodies as well as plundering and burning the *Star*. Ta'Unga, a native of Raratonga in the Cook Islands, who studied with the missionaries and spent some months in New Caledonia in 1842, suggested two possible motives for the massacre. Fear of foreigners bringing disease and death to the island, which caused the teachers to flee the island in the *Star* with Ebrill. And retaliation for assaulting the Chief's sons during a bartering incident.[53] After losing his son, Samuel Pinder Henry worked from Papeete, mainly as a pilot. He was always helpful in transporting the missionaries and native teachers to their destinations.[54] In the forties Sophia gave birth to Lucy Sarah Henry in April 1840, Lucy Ann Henry born in 1827 probably died, Sarah Roseanna Henry in April 1843, Joseph Henry in July 1844, Caroline Henry in May 1846 and Henry Henry, who died at birth, the year unrecorded.

For the family based in the New South Wales, marriages and politics dominated the year 1843. At the new church of St Peters, Richmond, on 25th March by licence Thomas Matcham Pitt Wilshire wed Helen Eliza Faithfull with the consent of her father. Thomas was the fourth son of Esther and James Wilshire, and Helen, the only daughter of Margaret Faithfull and second daughter of William Faithfull. Reverend Arthur Wallis conducted the ceremony in the presence of witnesses Elizabeth Mary Wilshire and William Pitt Wilshire. Thomas and Helen, a "good living young woman", lived in Chippendale.[55] Thomas worked in the tannery. Thomas William Faithfull Wilshire arrived in February 1844.[56]

Also at St Peters, Richmond, William Faithfull married third wife Maria Bell by licence on 13th June 1843. The minister was Reverend Joseph Kidd Walpole and the witnesses Rebecca and Eliza Cox of Mulgoa. Born at Cheshunt in Hertfordshire, England in May 1795, Maria was the eldest child of Archibald, and Maria Bell, née Kitching. Ensign Archibald Bell and his family arrived with the 103rd regiment in the *Young William* in July 1807. The Bells settled at Belmont on Richmond Hill.[57] (Figure 3)

Richmond residents Sam Boughton and Alfred Smith recorded two incidents featuring William Faithfull. (Figure 19) William suspected his servants stole his sucking pigs. Since the pigs usually disappeared on Saturday night, William visited the servants' hut on

Figure 19. William Faithfull

Sunday morning, hoping to discover what they were preparing for dinner. The cook had a pig boiling in a three-legged pot. On seeing William approach, he pulled off his shirt and placed it on top of the pot to suggest the weekly wash. William did not discover the pig, or so Boughton's story goes.[58] Alfred Smith recalled William, over seventy, urgently wanted to reach Sydney in his gig driven by his servant "Red Bill". Gigs were light two-wheeled carriages pulled by one horse and, in those days, considered "aristocratic turnouts". On his way home from Londonderry with a load of wood, Smith saw William and his servant near Richmond Village, looking for the lynch pin to reconnect the wheel to the carriage. Smith took them to his place where he found a substitute pin.[59]

Electing 24 of the 36 members of the New South Wales Legislative Council in July 1843 introduced a measure of democracy. The Governor could overrule councillors' decisions and the vote was restricted to men occupying property valued at £20.[60] To prepare for the elections, the colony was divided into 13 electoral districts, with William Pitt Faithfull appointed returning officer for Argyle. William's responsibilities included the accuracy of electoral rolls, selection of clerks and deputies, erection of booths and declaration of poll results.[61] William Pitt Wilshire, and some time later, James Robert Wilshire, announced their candidatures for the united counties of Westmoreland and Cook, which embraced Richmond and districts to its west. Their names were missing from the poll results in June 1843.[62]

The month after the election, the Legislative Council launched district councils.[63] Three grandsons received appointments, William Pitt Faithfull warden of Argyle, Robert Pitt Jenkins councillor for Berrima and William Warren Jenkins councillor for the Illawarra.[64] The Jenkins's brothers were trustees of their local Churches of England, Robert for Campbelltown in 1843, William for Dapto in 1842.[65] William was also chairman and treasurer of the Illawarra to Berrima Road Committee, which aimed to make the route less "circuitous" and the mountain road "passable". He organized meetings of the committee and the public, collected subscriptions, and requested convict labour. In December 1842 citizens thanked him for "his attention, ability and spirit in continuing his exertions in favour of the proposed road".[66] In 1843 William kindly provided land on Berkeley for the project of philanthropist Mrs Caroline Chisholm. She arranged with the people of the Illawarra for 23 needy families to clear and work about 30 acres free of rent for six years.[67]

The city councillors voted James Robert Wilshire mayor in place of first mayor, insolvent John Hosking, on 25th September 1843.[68] Following the second city elections on 8th November, the councillors again elected James their mayor.[69] The grandfather of James's wife, Elizabeth Wilshire, was mayor of Daventry in Northampton in 1783.[70] With "uneasiness" James accepted the mayor's allowance of £600.[71] As Mayor, James occupied three roles: Chairman of the Council, Justice of the Peace and Chief Magistrate of the city.[72] James also served on committees of the Benevolent Society, the National School Society and the Sydney Dispensary.[73]

Austin Forrest Wilshire was another on the payroll of the City Council. Elected an assessor for Phillip's ward in August 1843, he won yearly elections for the position up to 1847.[74] As a basis for levying rates, assessors recorded the name of the owner and the ratepayer, described the property (use, construction materials, number of rooms and levels, dimensions, condition), and ascribed the property an annual value.[75] Besides working for the City Council, James and Austin traded as JR and AF Wilshire. They produced leather, parchment, soap, and candles, and exported tallow, soap and candles. However, in 1844 the partners finished fell mongering and made no more dip-candles, soap and parchment. Making mould candles ended in 1849 or 1850.[76] Problems with their properties increased their workload. For example, an employee stole eight dozen kangaroo skins from the tannery and a fire badly damaged a rental house in Bathurst Street.[77] With their limited funds, James and Austin paid £8 15s at auction for 640 acres in County King where they leased 640 acres.[78] Meanwhile, their wives produced the children and managed the households.

Eliza, wife of Austin Forrest Wilshire, gave birth to Austin Thomas Wilshire in October 1841, Edwin James Wilshire in June 1843, and Thomas Matcham Pitt Wilshire in February 1844. After the birth of Austin, Eliza advertised for "a woman servant to cook and wash for a small family" and soon after the birth of Thomas, "a girl to take care of a child, and who can work well with her needle".[79] It appears Thomas died early. The family still resided in Chippendale, in Bank Street, near Botany Road.[80]

Elizabeth, wife of James Robert Wilshire, gave birth to Mimosa Sarah Wilshire in March 1840, Clara Sophia Wilshire in June 1841, Matilda Elizabeth Wilshire in August 1842 and Mayor Joseph Wilshire in February 1844. Not long after Mayor Joseph's birth, Elizabeth advertised for a cook and laundress.[81] Eldest child, James Thompson Wilshire, attended Mr Peter Steel's Infant Training School in Pitt Street. In December 1843, following the annual school examinations, Dr John Dunmore Lang presented six-year-old James with a prize for reading. Mayor Wilshire sat on the stage with Dr Lang.[82] Elizabeth was secretary of the Dorcas Society which helped poor married women with clothes and other items and, if needed, a midwife during their confinement.[83] The family continued to live in Mimosa Cottage, close to the tannery.[84]

Robert Pitt, second son of Elizabeth and Thomas Matcham Pitt, married neighbour Sarah John, by licence on 6th September 1843 at St Peters, Richmond. Henry Stiles conducted the wedding, witnessed by John Johnson of Richmond and Ann John of Kurrajong. Sarah was born at Richmond in December 1820 to John William John and Sarah Harvey who married in Sydney in April 1818. Sarah John's grandfather was Welshman John William John who came in the *Albemarle* in 1791 with a sentence of seven years.[85] Her other grandparents proved elusive. When married, Robert lived at Kurrajong working his 400 acres known as Trafalgar, adjoined on the east by the farm of Sarah's father.[86] Robert was "a big man, considerably over 6ft in height", and, though taller than brother, George, who was also over six feet, he was not as outgoing. Robert also possessed a "large mental capacity, and a high and pure moral character".[87]

The last of the marriages in 1843 took place in Wollongong by licence on 10th November between Robert Pitt Jenkins, elder son of Jemima and Robert Jenkins, and Maria Louisa Adelaide Plunkett. To cater for their religious differences, Chaplain Matthew Meares conducted a Church of England service at the schoolhouse and Reverend John Rigney a Roman Catholic service at the church of St Francis Xavier. For the Church of England service the witnesses were William Warren Jenkins and P. Plunkett, and for the Roman Catholic service, P. Plunkett, Julianne Plunkett and John Burke. Maria Louisa, known as Louisa, was the daughter of Captain Patrick Plunkett of the 80th Regiment, and Francis Louisa Plunkett, formerly Brown. The Plunketts arrived in the *Lloyds* in July 1837.[88] Robert gave Louisa Eagle Vale. The trustees were William Warren Jenkins and Louisa's second cousin, attorney general, John Hubert Plunkett.[89]

Before marrying, Robert Pitt Jenkins increased his acreage. At Bomballa he added 2050 acres which consisted of two parcels of Crown Land and a reassigned grant, the three properties sharing boundaries with Jemima's 2000 acres. By the way, though the parish is "Bumballa", the name of Robert's estate was spelt in different ways, including "Bomballa", the variant used in this story. At Tomboye Robert purchased 645 acres near Jemima's 1000 acres. The Crown Land at Bomballa and Tomboye cost £523 15s.[90] Louisa settled with Robert at Bomballa. She "played exquisitely on the harp" and may have been the Mrs Jenkins who paid Conrad Martens for art lessons in December 1850.[91]

On 20th January 1844, by licence, William Pitt Faithfull wed Mary Deane at St James Church, Sydney. (Figures 20 & 21) The Reverend Robert Allwood conducted the ceremony before witnesses T. Parsons of Liverpool and Maria Faithfull of Richmond. Born about 1813 in Devonshire, Mary was the daughter of Thomas Deane, and Ann Deane, née Pidsley. Mary, her mother Ann, brother Robert, sister Ann, nephew Master Edgar Deane and relative Mister Robert Dean arrived in the cabins of the *William Metcalf* in August 1838.[92]

In Macquarie Place the Misses Deane opened a boarding school to provide young ladies with "a rare occurrence in scholastic education" for 70 guineas. Subjects taught were "Polite Learning", English, French, history, geography, and plain and ornamanental needlework. The sisters also offered elective subjects, music, drawing, dancing, Italian, writing, arithmetic and the "use of globes". William met Mary at the school when visiting his nieces, Alice and Susannah Gibson.[93] After paying the mortgage on Springfield, William presented much of the estate to Mary, the trustees George Faithfull of the Ovens and Robert Deane of Sydney.[94] The Deanes' School, then at Miller's Point, closed and Mary, her mother, sister, and nephew moved to Springfield.[95] Mary gave birth to her first child, William Percy Faithfull, at Springfield in October 1844. For his new family, William built a two-storey stone Georgian homestead adjacent to the cottage.[96] Austin Forrest Wilshire repaid William's loan of £1000 in April 1845, a fitting time.[97]

On Thursday 4th July 1844, "a horrid attempt at murder" occurred at the Richmond farm of Elizabeth and George Pitt Wood. Elizabeth, looking after ten children following the birth of Thomas George Wood in November 1843, bore the brunt of the sordid affair. The perpetrator, Levi Brett, was "a quiet, harmless and hard-working

Figure 20. William Pitt Faithfull

Figure 21. Mary Deane Faithfull

man" who had served the Woods for 15 years. He lived in a hut on the farm with Catherine McGowen who arrived on the *Pyramus* in 1836. On the Sunday 30th June, Elizabeth noticed Brett "did not appear in his usual manner; he did not appear drunk, but he came up from his hut wringing his hands and crying; he said they would swear away his life and liberty". Elizabeth directed her eldest son, 14-year old William, to watch Brett. When George arrived home in the evening, he spoke to Brett, "who seemed to be more pacified". On Tuesday Brett was required as a witness at the Parramatta Quarter Sessions. Elizabeth did not think "he was in a fit state to go", so before George left for Putty, she asked him to take Brett to the constable or to Mr Bell's. Brett left Bell's place for the Parramatta Court. It was Wednesday 3rd July before Brett presented his evidence, though he was incoherent. Early Thursday afternoon, Kitty asked Elizabeth for her bonnet, saying she "was going to leave Brett as she had no business stopping with a madman". After leaving Elizabeth, Kitty met Brett and the two returned to the hut. Near dark, as Kitty made the bed, Brett told her it was "the last bed she would ever make", then he propped a pitchfork against the door and took a knife from the table. Kitty escaped towards the Woods' home, only to trip and fall. Brett caught up with her. He put his knee on her chest and cut her throat, severing her windpipe and oesophagus, but missing the main arteries and nerves. From the verandah Elizabeth heard a strange noise "which she thought must be the blacks". A tribe had headquarters at Belmont. The children told her Kitty made the noise. Elizabeth asked Jesse Weston to fetch Kitty and make her a bed. Elizabeth sent for Mr James Bell and he returned with Constable Joseph Williams. Dr John Selkirk arrived about midnight. He "pronounced the wound fatal, stating nothing could be done for it". In the following days, doctors Henry White, Lewis Whitaker and William Stewart were in constant attendance. Although one of the doctors sutured the "edges of the wound", it was hard to feed Kitty as the "water gruel" flowed out of the wound. Kitty lingered in the Woods' home until 24th July.[98]

Held at the Woods on Tuesday 30th July 1844, the inquest "excited much interest". The Coroner found Catherine McGowen died of the effects of a wound inflicted with a sharp instrument by Levi Brett who was not "in a sound state of mind", the temporary derangement thought caused by drugs, probably tincture of opium. Days before the attack Brett claimed James Hatcher poisoned him and William Carver shot him. The police found tincture of opium on Hatcher's premises and Carver pleaded guilty to threatening Brett. Tried for "wilful murder" at the Supreme Court in Darlinghurst on 10th October 1844, Brett pleaded insanity. Found not guilty, the court remanded him for the Governor's decision, freedom or the Lunatic Asylum.[99] Before this event, Samuel and Sophia Henry made the trip to Sydney with four children. Again, documentation exists only for their departure in the *Sarah Ann* early in February 1844.[100]

Between April and August 1844 Mayor James Robert Wilshire chaired public meetings of the Mutual Protection Association which aimed to restore employment and fair wages for thousands of tradesmen and labourers. For the meeting James conducted in late May he received compliments, "we have never yet attended a public meeting, where the objects in view were so steadily adhered to". To address the plight of the workers, the Association sent petitions to the City Council, the Legislative Council and the Governor. The petitions recommended relief measures: withdrawing convicts from public works and re-employing them in the interior; opening new public projects; suspending labourers and tradesmen immigrating; and moving poor families on small farm allotments.[101] Also with the working-class in mind, the City Council lead by James petitioned the parliament in June 1844 to lower the municipal franchise from £25 to £10.[102]

While acting for the impoverished workers, Mayor Wilshire wrote two lengthy petitions to the Legislative Council on the topics of municipal revenue and police administration. Before outlining the petitions, the revenue for the year in question is indicated.

The Council collected £5,259 16s 10d in rates and £3,032 12s 4d in Police Office fees and market tolls. The takings formed the City and Police Funds. The Government topped up each fund with £5000, a sum restricted to the amount raised in rates. The first petition of 5th August 1844 sought extra income for the City Fund to upgrade the city's sewers, streets, paving, lights and water supply. The suggested sources of income, the licence fees charged publicans, auctioneers, carters and others, as well as fees, fines and forfeitures levied at the Police Office with some exceptions. The second petition of 21st August 1844 demanded financial and administrative control of the city police. Financially, the Council expected to make its own decision on police expenses, based on estimates of the number of police needed. Administratively, the Council wanted to appoint and dismiss police, and regulate their duties.[103] The Legislative Council approved the reports but failed to carry out the recommendations.[104]

A highlight of James Robert Wilshire's term in office was the Mayor's Fancy Dress Ball. Held on Wednesday 21st August 1844 in the recently renovated Victoria Theatre in Pitt Street, the women requested the ball. The 700 or so guests wore "a vast variety of costly and magnificent garbs and costumes of all nations". Spectators filled the gallery. "A tableau vivant, a series of living pictures of different ages and countries", represented the theme of the ball. The scene was one of "gaiety and splendour"; "the eye of the spectator wandered from object to object with ever-varying pleasure". Boards placed across the stage increased floor space. The workshops behind the stage were transformed into an elegant refreshment room, with meats (turkey, fowl, duck, ham, tongue), salads, pies, cakes and biscuits available throughout the evening. Thomas Wilshire, the mayor's secretary, looked after the arrangements for the music and dancing, and formally introduced the guests to Mayor James and Mayoress Elizabeth. James Thompson Wilshire was the Mayoress's "Little Page". Most of the Wilshire family attended, Joseph Wilshire wearing a costume of the reign of Edward VI, Miss (Elizabeth) Wilshire, Matilda Pitt Jenkins, Thomas Wilshire's wife Helen, and Esther and Henry Whittell. Members of the Eyre and Thompson families and the newly married Faithfulls were there, too. Guests of high social-standing included Governor and Lady Gipps, and the Secretary and Treasurer of the Colony. The bands of the theatre and 99th Regiment provided music. Quadrilles, waltzes and gallopades began soon after 9.00 pm and continued until 6.00 am. Aborigines performed on stage for the first time, "One of these sable heroes, arrayed in a tattered blanket, enlivened the audience vastly on one occasion by brushing into the centre of a circle of waltzers, and giving a ludicrous facsimile of an Aboriginal dance". The ball was a great success, "It was impossible any party could go off more pleasantly". Moreover, "it was very gratifying to observe all classes mixing familiarly together".[105]

The day before the ball, the *Australian* published a tribute to Mayor James Robert Wilshire. The item first appeared on 6th August 1844 in the *Port Phillip Herald*:

> *As a member of City Council, Mr Wilshire has been constant in his attendance, and zealous in the performance of his public duties. As Chief Magistrate of the City, he presides in Petty Session, and on the Bench daily in the Police Court. He has been chairman of several important committees whose reports, especially those of the Lighting and General Police Committees, were adopted with marked approbation by the Council... and though he has no pretensions to oratorical display, he has a competent share of intelligence and sound sense, with an exceedingly unassuming and amiable disposition. His political sentiments are liberal and independent... In all the relations of private life, he is esteemed by those who know him; and in his public capacity, both as Magistrate of the City, and President of the Council, the impartiality and firmness of his administration entitle him to the respect of the cornrnunity.*[106]

The *Sydney Morning Herald* did not share the political views of James. He accused the *Herald* of criticising him "at every opportunity", but the editors insisted they bore him no ill will and thought him a "virtuous and responsible fellow-citizen".[107] At the end of James's term as mayor, he and Austin were appointed Justices of the Peace and Magistrates.[108] Several newly elected members of the City Council used the civic dinner in December "to throw out very broad hints" to the new Mayor to follow his predecessor in holding a fancy dress ball.[109] The grateful citizens of the city presented Mayor Wilshire with a gold chain.[110]

Henry Whittell could not keep his family on the income from his medical practice. Henry and Esther lived in premises in Pitt Street before moving to the corner of Elizabeth and Liverpool Streets just before the birth of Matilda Hannah in October 1842. Wanting a place of their own, Henry paid William Charles Wentworth £450 for a house bounded on the north by Francis Street and west by College Street, at the southern end of Hyde Park.[111] After Henry built a new brick house facing College Street, he owed £650 on his home and £400 on Esther's inheritance.[112] When second child Charles Whitten arrived in October 1844, Henry was a coal merchant.[113] Setting up the new business required much capital. Henry leased the Ebenezer Coalmines at Lake Macquarie and engaged two miners. He bought a barge, two ballast boats, a diagonal boat and a schooner, and rented wharves. Fortunately, he secured a Government contract to transport coals from Newcastle to various public offices and establishments in Sydney.[114] Henry found time to appear as a medical witness and lecture the Total Abstinence Society on "The Effect of all alcoholic liqueurs on the human system is of the same injurious and destructive character".[115]

William Warren Jenkins's term as councillor on The Illawarra Council ended in April 1845 but, satisfied with his performance, citizens elected him in mid 1846.[116] William contributed to his community in other ways. From early in 1844 he and brother Robert were Justices of the Peace and Magistrates.[117] William was a steward at the Wollongong races held 28-30th August 1844.[118] He attended the first meeting of the Illawarra Agricultural and Horticultural Society and was on the committee which organized the first show in January 1845.[119] In his leisure hours William enjoyed outdoor pursuits. He liked dogs and was a "splendid horseman":

On making a daring attempt to cross Broughton's Pass (between Mount Keira and Appin) on horse back, while travelling to see his mother on her death-bed, he narrowly escaped losing his life.

There was a flood running at this treacherous place... and had it not been for his expertness and excellent knowledge of horsemanship, he would have been swept over the fatal rocks, as several others were from time to time.

William loved walking and enjoyed rowing the waters of Allan's Creek, Tom Thumb Lagoon and Illawarra Lake. He was an "athletic young man, majestic in stature, powerful in physical capability".[120]

At Berkeley with sister Matilda Pitt Jenkins, Louisa Elliot gave birth to Elizabeth Ella Louisa Elliot on 13th February 1845.[121] Philip Elliot was a "principal contributor" to the Appin Church of St Mark the Evangelist consecrated in 1843. Also, he was a trustee for the 2 acres and 2 roods set aside for the schoolhouse. The church, burial ground and school were erected on a 40 acre glebe granted to the Church of England in November 1842.[122] In Camden in May 1844, Philip and several citizens organized a public meeting to consider new regulations for the runs on Crown Land.[123] Mindful of his own need for land, Philip bought 40 acres at Oallen in the Braidwood district and leased 640 acres in County King.[124]

Louisa Jenkins was also away from home, in Surry Hills, for the birth of her first child Alice Frances Jemima Jenkins in April 1845. The events described in this and the next paragraph, indicate the

Jenkins's home was under construction. In November 1844 Robert issued a warning to settlers in the habit of trusting unprincipled convicts. He gave the caution after a ticket-of-leave holder, ordered to bring a dray loaded with property from Sydney to Robert's home near Marulan, hawked Robert's goods along the road. On arrival at Berrima, the convict aroused the suspicion of Henry Foster, the Governor of the Gaol, who spoke to the police. The offender was locked up before his trial at the Bench of Magistrates.[125] Between 1844 and 1847 Robert borrowed £2272, securing the loans with several properties, including the second block in O'Connell Street, on which Jemima had built "four handsome cottages". He also sold the 37 perches in north Kent Street for £410.[126]

The Jenkins were living in Campbelltown where Robert, in carrying out his duties as magistrate, "frequently overlooked the impropriety" of chief constable of the district. The situation escalated in October 1845 when Robert learned convicts were working for settlers instead of repairing the local bridge. On his way to Campbelltown, Robert noticed a convict grubbing in a field near the bridge so he asked Constable McAlister to investigate. Later, McAlister approached Robert's carriage "with his arms akimbo". He spoke to Robert "in a very disrespectful manner", failed to address him as "sir", and refused to visit the convict gang until the next day. Robert reprimanded McAlister and threatened to report his disgraceful conduct to the Governor. The constable complained to the Governor who referred the matter to the Campbelltown Bench. Justices of the Peace, James Macarthur and William Howe responded, "we are of the opinion that the demeanor of the Chief Constable towards the Magistrates is frequently abrupt and wanting in proper courtesy". The justices added, "we have felt it to be our duty to caution McAlister not to lay himself open to any complaint."[127] Built on a "lofty piece of table-land", Bomballa commanded "an enchanting and most picturesque view".[128]

It is time to look in on the Faithfulls, George on the Oxley Plains, Alice just south of Goulburn town, and William on the edge of the Goulburn Plains. First the reflections of bachelor George Faithfull on his continuing trials with the Aborigines, "I and my men were kept for years in a perpetual state of alarm. We dared not move to supply our huts with wood or water without a gun, and many of my men absconded from my service." George recalled the day he ended the warfare, "Some hundreds of painted warriors with the most dreadful yells" challenged him and two of his stockmen as they rode along the banks of river. The first reaction of the three was to retreat, but the natives showered them with spears. George's horse fell into a large hole, a spear barely missing him. His predicament signalled a general onslaught, "the natives rushed on us like furies, with shouts and savage yells". Unable to repel the Aborigines, George resorted to firing his double-barrelled gun. The hostilities continued from 10 in the morning until four in the afternoon. "We were slow to fire, which prolonged the battle, and 60 rounds were fired, and I trust and believe many of the bravest of the savage warriors bit the dust." The way the women and children fearlessly moved forward to pick up the spears for their men surprised George. He took home a boy and found him "very useful" once tamed. George believed the attention he gave the boy deterred his tribe "committing further wanton depredations upon my property". The Government threatened to hang anyone who shot a native and "resorted to the most contemptible means to gain information against individuals". Squatters were often falsely accused of destroying the "savages". The accusations "instead of doing good, did much evil. People formed themselves into bands ... and then ... the destruction of the natives really did take place".[129]

Widow Alice Gibson leased baker John O'Brien two of Andrew's allotments in Auburn Street, Goulburn. In return for erecting shops and houses to detailed specifications, Alice offered O'Brien long-term leases at nominal rents.[130] To comply with Andrew's will, executor George Faithfull witnessed the deed in July 1845.

Andrew's other executor, Stuart Alexander Donaldson, renounced his right to manage the will in April 1844.[131] Alice enrolled her sons at The King's School at Parramatta, Andrew attending from 1843 to 1848, Thomas in 1848, and Frederick and Septimus from 1847 to 1849.[132]

In January 1846 Warden William Pitt Faithfull called for tenders to repair five bridges on the Great South Road between Bungonia and Marulan.[133] His duties as warden ended in July when he replaced William Bradley, member for Argyle, in the Legislative Council. About 70 took the opportunity to meet William at Mendleson's Inn. Captain Gore thought William a worthy representative with the right credentials for the position, "he has been known to us all for a long service of years, and on all occasions he has shown his interests to be connected with that of the whole community". The group assembled in the courthouse and elected William unopposed.[134] When the new session of Parliament began on 8th September, Hannibal Hawkins Macarthur, nephew of John Macarthur, and the Colonial Secretary, Edward Deas Thomson, introduced William to the house.[135] The parliament met in a chamber built on the north end of the most northerly of the three hospital buildings in Macquarie Street. The state legislature still occupies the enlarged and modified building.[136]

William did not stand for re-election after the Parliament dissolved in June 1848.[137] He would see more of Mary and their children, four-year-old William Percy Faithfull, George Ernest Faithfull born in April 1846 and Henry Montague Faithfull in June 1847.

James Robert Wilshire bought a house beside Elizabeth Bay at Potts Point on nearly an acre in present Macleay Street. The house, which he bought in May 1846, stood just north of Alexander Macleay's Elizabeth Bay House. It belonged to Emma and Joseph Potts, who gave their name to Potts Point.[138] For the insolvent Potts, James paid the Bank of Australia £1400 and gave Emma £150 to replace her wedding gift.[139] Elizabeth Mary Wilshire moved into Mimosa Cottage.[140] Sadly, James's wife, Elizabeth, aged about 35, died of consumption on 13th August 1846.[141] Alderman Robert Wilshire, who was born in September 1845, died two months after Elizabeth, leaving James with James, nine, Mimosa, six, Clara, five, Matilda, almost four, and Mayor, two.

Soon after Joseph Wood Wilshire turned 21 on 1st February 1847, James Wilshire's executors distributed several properties in the George Street Complex. Joseph and Thomas Matcham Pitt Wilshire got their properties in Union Lane, George and Pitt Streets.[142] Louisa, Elizabeth, Esther, Matilda, Thomas and Joseph obtained their small portions of land on the north side of Union Lane.[143] Louisa received the property on the south side of Union Lane which had been in trust, an arrangement probably enshrined in the 1843 agreement.[144] (Figure 18)

A man of property, Joseph Wood Wilshire married Anne Osborne by licence on 26th February 1847 in the schoolhouse in St Michael's Parish, Wollongong. Reverend Meares conducted the wedding and the witnesses were J. Osborne of Garden Hill and Henry Osborne of Marshall Mount. Born about 1827 in Strabane, County Tyrone, Ireland, Anne was the third daughter of surgeon John Osborne, of the Royal Navy, and Mary Osborne, formerly Clarke.[145] The Osbornes came to the colony in the *James Pattinson* in February 1836.[146] Joseph and Anne began their married life at Anneville on the Garden Hill property of Anne's parents just west of Wollongong town. Looking ahead, Anne had a stillborn daughter in February 1848 and a son Osborne Wilshire in May 1849.[147] Also, Joseph was a member of the Wollongong Church of England School Board from the start of 1849.[148]

Meanwhile, George Matcham Pitt had been active in his community. In May 1845 he was appointed to the committee of the Hawkesbury Agricultural Society. In August he attended the public meeting of members of the Church of England held at the Church of England School in Windsor. Those present, including William Faithfull, decided to set up the Hawkesbury and Nepean Branch of the Church of England Lay Association for New South Wales. In 1846 George carried out four tasks. Like his father, he joined the Committee of the Hawkesbury Benevolent Society. At the Hawkesbury Races he was a steward. He joined the citizens' group pressing for a road to Bathurst from Windsor and Richmond, a cause supported by brother, Robert. And he collaborated with others to get the deeds for the Richmond Common.[149] In May 1847 George was appointed a trustee for the Windsor branch of the Savings Bank of New South Wales.[150]

George's wife, Julia Pitt, was the hardworking mother of eight children after giving birth to five in the 1840s. Julia Eliza Pitt was born in November 1841, Edwin Pitt in February 1844, Stewart Pitt in April 1846, Harry Austin Pitt in October 1847 and Robert Matcham Pitt in December 1849. Stewart died in infancy. Building a new home for his growing family probably explains the £500 George borrowed on Bronte in January 1847; the loan paid in October 1851.[151] George's sister, Mary Laycock, and sister-in-law, Sarah Pitt, were also busy with their children born in the 40s. Additions to Mary's family, Robert Laycock born in July 1840, Henry Laycock in July 1843, Andrew Laycock in July 1845, Isabella Eliza Laycock in March 1847 and Emily Jane Laycock in March 1849. The Laycocks saw George Matcham Pitt when he visited his lease of 950 acres at Putty.[152] Sarah's first arrivals were Anne Pitt in May 1844, Sarah Pitt in June 1845, William Pitt in June 1847 and Emma Pitt in July 1849.

William Faithfull, about 73, died on 16th April 1847 at his Richmond home then named Lakeville.[153] Two days later he lay at rest beside wives Susannah and Margaret in St Peters Cemetery. To manage his estate of £4000, William chose sons William and George, and nephew-in-law George Matcham Pitt whom he forgave a debt. The estate included 100 acres at Lakeville, 1200 at Jordan Hill, 800 at Goulburn, 30 at Toongabbie, 50 and 60 at Prospect and premises in Macquarie St Parramatta. Also, he had acquired 60 acres in the parish of Londonderry and he paid £300 for 180 acres in the parish of Nepean in January 1844. Maria received Lakeville and the income from investments. Alice inherited the acres in Londonderry, and Lakeville was hers after Maria's death. George got the farm at Jordan Hill. William gave Helen Eliza the piano and the properties at Toongabbie, Prospect, the Nepean, and Parramatta. Before his death, William sold his stock to his children. For example, William junior paid his father £2000 for 9000 sheep, 200 cattle and 50 horses.[154] Clearly, this stock grazed the 800 acres next to Springfield which William senior bequeathed to grandson William Percy Faithfull. Maria's sister, Matilda Bell, received £50. William rewarded his servants, Thomas Riley with £10 and Mary Smith with £5.[155] Faithfull Street, Richmond, was named in memory of William.[156] Just eight days after her father's death, 24th April 1847, Helen Eliza Wilshire, née Faithfull, aged 23, died in Pitt Street South. The Reverend W.H. Walsh buried her on 26th; the cemetery unrecorded. Helen left husband Thomas Matcham Pitt Wilshire and three-year-old Thomas William Faithfull Wilshire.

On 29th May 1847, the Reverend Ross married James Robert Wilshire and his first wife's sister, Sarah Thompson, at the Pitt Street Congregational Church. By this illegal but sensible union, Sarah was both aunt and stepmother to James's children. James and Austin faced a financial crisis which James attributed to depreciation in the value of hides and tallow on the London market.[157] James, Austin and Eliza owed $6130 on five mortgages. Having just paid his 1843 mortgage on six Springfield lots and sold his farm near Scone for £450, William Pitt Faithfull lent James £500 and Austin and Eliza £1000.[158] To reduce his debt, James sold his Elizabeth Bay home for £2000, though he owed the bank half this sum.[159] He auctioned his elegant household furniture, a superior cabinet pianoforte, a select library of books, plates, plated goods, china and glass, and a fashionable carriage.[160] James and Austin persuaded creditors Flower, Salting and Company to delay payment on their loan of £1130 for 12 months.[161] Despite debts their families grew. Eliza, wife of Austin, had fourth child Emily Eliza Wilshire in February 1845, Isabel Eliza Wilshire in September 1846 and Alice Emily Wilshire in August 1848. Emily Eliza died in January 1846. Sarah, wife of James, gave birth to her first child Alfred Theodore Wilshire in September 1849. James and Sarah had returned to Mimosa Cottage. (Figures 22, 23, 24)

Henry Rawes Whittell was declared insolvent on 29th September 1847 with a debt of £903. He experienced setbacks, a steep rise in the cost of mines and a partnership that did not eventuate.[162] Embarrassed at the state of his finances, Henry assigned College Street to his lawyers for the benefit of his creditors.[163] Esther's family came to the rescue. Henry redeemed the mortgage on Bathurst Street with a loan of £400 from the estate of Esther's father.[164] And at the final meeting of creditors in April 1848, James Robert Wilshire paid £114 10s 8d for the last of Henry's assets.[165] Henry transferred his home to the mortgagees in July 1850 and the family moved, probably to 202 Elizabeth Street.[166] Henry persisted as a coal merchant and attended coroners' inquests.[167] Happily, Esther gave birth to Thomas Alfred Whittell in September 1847 and Esther Whittell in August 1849.

In a bid for a greater share of his father's estate, William Pitt Wilshire filed a Bill of Complaint in the Equity division of the Supreme Court on 18th April 1847. Executors James and Austin represented their siblings in the case. James made three points in their defence: his father's wishes expressed in the will; his father's "dissatisfaction at the large claims for pecuniary assistance, which the said complainant had made upon him"; and his father's personal estate barely covered his debts, funeral and testamentary expenses.[168] Following many legal manoeuvres, on 9th May 1848 the court awarded William the residual property in Pitt Street which

Figure 22. James Robert Wilshire

Figure 23. Austin Forrest Wilshire

Figure 24. Eliza Pitt Wilshire

included the allotment on the corner of Pitt Street with a large frontage to the south side of Union Lane.[169] (Figure 17) The two sides had resolved "all matters of difference", William agreeing to suspend his complaint and abandon all title to the rest of the residuary estate. William withdrew the original Bill of Complaint on 27th October 1848. Soon after, Darling Harbour was partitioned into 26 allotments for eight of the Wilshire children.[170] (Figure 25)

Just before withdrawing the Bill of Complaint, William had the misfortune to lose his wife. On 12th October 1848, Maria, aged 36, died of a "severe illness" lasting five days.[171] The Reverend W. R Walsh buried her on 14th October but did not record the cemetery. Maria died at 3 Gloucester Terrace, Macquarie Street, where she lived with William, William James, 15, Frederick, 10 and Maria, almost eight.[172] About the beginning of 1845, the family left Kurrajong and rented Wilshirehurst, with its six rooms, three measuring 17 feet by 14 feet, detached kitchen, stables, coachhouse, dairy and garden.[173] William still owned 47 George Street; he had it mortgaged for £250.[174] He wasted no time in selling 10 properties in Pitt Street including the large allotment facing Union Lane which he had subdivided.[175]

New regulations for squatters were in place. Fourteen year licences replaced yearly ones, although delays in surveying resulted in yearly renewal for some time. The licence fee of £10 increased for runs carrying more than 4000 sheep or 640 cattle, an extra 1000 sheep or 160 cattle costing £2 10s.[176] Disputes over ownership and boundaries were settled at Boga Bogalong, Bangus and Brewarrena, and many other stations.[177] George Faithfull also struggled to protect his squat:

> *No sooner was all fear of the blacks dissipated than the whites became almost as great a nuisance in edging in their applications and claims for portions of our runs... Unfortunately, the Government gave too willing an ear to them...; they readily*

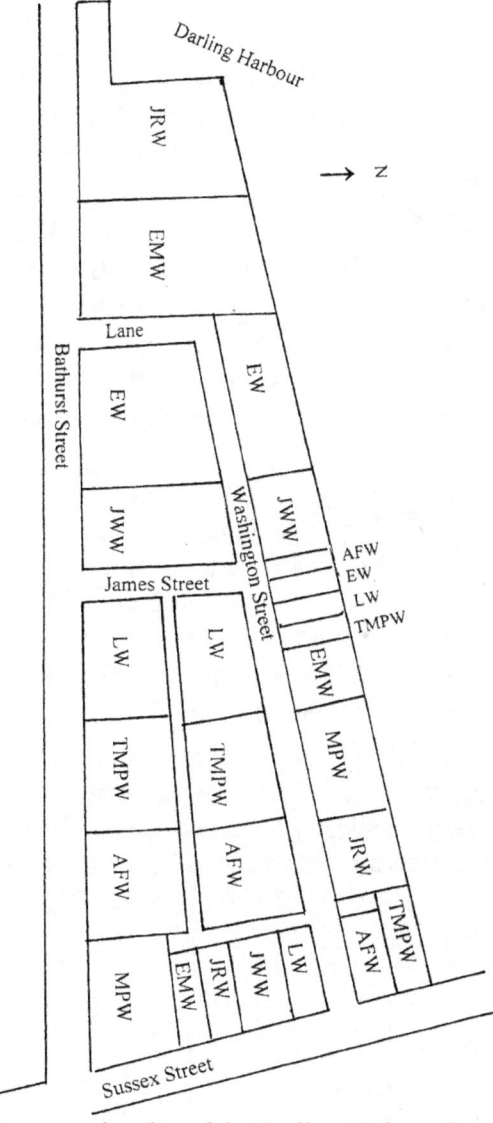

Figure 25. An approximation of the Darling Harbour Complex of the Wilshires in November 1847

deprived us of portions of our runs to give them to other squatters.[178]

The *Government Gazette* of September 1848 records the name, location, size, and ideal stock capacity of the runs. In the Gwydir River district, George Matcham Pitt leased 72 square miles called Coorar after the creek bounding part of his property. The run maintained 1500 cattle.[179] In the Lachlan Basin Alice Gibson leased Boga Bogalong and Bland, formerly Boggydillon. County Bland was named in honour of Andrew's good friend, Dr William Bland.[180] The 75,520 acres of Boga Bogalong supported 6000 sheep, while Bland, a heifer station, held 1000 cattle on its 44,800 acres.[181] (Alice also bought two 640 acre lots in County King, and 640 acres and 1240 acres in County Argyle.[182]) Robert Pitt Jenkins leased Bangus and Brewarrena but he had applied to transfer Brewarrena to William Pitt Faithfull. Boasting a frontage of about eight miles to the Murrumbidgee, the 45,000 acres of Brewarrena grazed 8000 sheep. Bangus also carried 8000 sheep on its fertile 25,000 acres which extended west from Adelong Creek along the south side of the Murrumbidgee River.[183] Beyond the Murray River, George and William Pitt Faithfull jointly leased Oxley Plains, a run of 92,000 acres near later Wangaratta, with frontages of about nine miles to the Ovens River and 26 miles to King River. The squat sustained 2500 cattle or 8000 sheep. George also leased Heifer Station, a run of 25,600 acres at Buffalo, the site of modem Myrtleford, bounded by the Buffalo River for 10 miles and the Ovens for four miles. Heifer Station supported 500 cattle.[184]

About October 1848, Louisa and Robert Pitt Jenkins moved to Bangus with three-year-old Alice and Robert Augustus Jenkins, born in Sydney in December 1846. The change of address plus the further £2300 Robert borrowed, suggested renovations at Bomballa were incomplete.[185] Robert "attended the Gundagai Court in his magisterial capacity, and from the ability and experience he appears to possess, his residence as a magistrate will be a great acquisition to the neighborhood".[186] The Wagga Wagga Bench of Magistrates also benefited from the services of Robert, and those of William Pitt Faithfull. Owing to his concern about Gundagai's development, Robert sent the Colonial Secretary letters on siting the courthouse, watch-house and lock-up.[187] At Bangus Louisa gave birth to Herbert Frederick William Edmond Jenkins in July 1849 and Ernest George Jenkins in October 1850.

William Warren Jenkins divided Berkeley Estate into portions for tenants to farm. Two tenants accepted special conditions in return for a moderate rent. David James paid £5 a year to lease an unspecified number of acres for eight years. William asked David James to erect boundary fences within three years.[188] Schoolmaster John McPhail leased an acre to build a public house at Charcoal Creek, beside the road from Wollongong to Dapto and Kiama. William expected him to erect a brick building valued at £200 or more. Joseph Wood Wilshire witnessed the deed with McPhail. The schoolmaster rented a further 10 acres for 21 years, but failed to complete the lease.[189] William's tenants "found him kind and considerate in the extreme". In Matilda too, they found "a sympathising friend and generous benefactor".[190] Matilda gave birth to seven children in the 1840s, Robert Thomas Jenkins in September 1840, Matilda Jemima Jenkins in March 1842, Louisa Helen Jenkins in August 1843, Ellinor Maria Jenkins in April 1845, Emily Annie Jenkins in February 1847, Frederick Jenkins in February 1848 and Alice Elizabeth Jenkins in March 1849.

James Robert Wilshire's term of office on the Sydney Council expired in November 1849. Before retiring, he proposed extending the franchise to all adult males occupying rateable property, his catchcry "no taxation without a vote".[191] James campaigned for the seat of Robert Lowe in the Legislative Council. The previous year he chaired the group working to elect Lowe, a highly intelligent and eloquent barrister. Henry Parkes made his political debut as secretary of the group and in Parkes James found a political ally.[192] The political leaning of James was liberal or "orthodox radical" in contrast to conservative, although no political parties existed.[193] James promised to reform the electoral system and land policies, oppose transportation and support national education. To reform the electoral system, he proposed extending the vote to all men, shortening the terms of parliament from five to three years, and providing greater representation in populous districts. To reform land policies, he would amend the long leases and low rents granted to squatters and reduce the high cost of Crown Land.[194] Lowe and Henry Parkes backed James. He also had the support of the Constitutional Association, which organized two anti-transportation protests in June 1849 following the arrival of 250 convicts in the *Hashemy*, a cause James supported in the 1850s.[195]

In a contest where less than a quarter of the electors voted, James Robert Wilshire lost decisively to Dr William Bland.[196] At the declaration of the poll, the other unsuccessful candidate, Adam Bogue, said Wilshire's defeat demonstrated:

> *that no gentleman, however competent and eligible to become a candidate, who had been put forward by a secret society whose best exertions were used for the propagation of communist and socialist principles, would hope to succeed.*

James was not present to refute Bogue's criticism, but Parkes, who gained a hearing with difficulty, denied he was a communist.[197] James had more disappointing news. The Slaughter Houses Bill of 11th October 1849 banned offensive trades operating within the city's limits from 1st January 1860.[198]

In the 1840s Mary Pitt's adult grandchildren and their spouses occupied centre stage. The women bore about 57 great-grandchildren and reared most of them while managing their households.[199] The men financially supported their families and served as committee members, trustees, justices of the peace, magistrates, councillors, alderman, warden, mayor and parliamentarian.

1	Aus 7 January 1840, p4a,b; Aus 8 August 1840, p3b; *Goulburn Evening Penny Post*, 25 April 1896, p2e
2	HRA 1, 22, pl6; GG 1844, Vol 1, p298, 15 Feb; Aus 10 December; 1840, p3c; Aus 6 February 1841, pp2, 3
3	Bk T, No 58, DL; Bk U, No 244, DL
4	Aus 12 March 1840, p2b; Aus 21 May 1840, p2e
5	SMH 26 July 1842, p2c
6	Index to SMH January 1842-January 1845, Vol 12, p365l. Reference to HRW's free medical service for poor not found. (See Table of Fees: http://www.medicalpioneers.com/colonial.htm)
7	Aus 10 Sept 1840, p2g
8	Register T, No 784, DL; Bk T, No 890, DL
9	Email 27 March 2007, Ken Knight to Janelle Cust
10	Registers of Copies of Wills 1800-1901, SAG Will 1/1222
11	NSW Vl840 1022 24A; Griffiths, Glynde Nesta, *Some Southern Homes*, National Trust of Australia, NSW, 1976, pp52-3; Russell, 2002, ch vi, pp96-7
12	Aus 1 October 1840, p3d
13	Registers of Copies of Wills 1800-1901, SAG Will 1/1295
14	Bk T, 319, DL; Bk 32, No 171, DL
15	Registers of Copies of Wills 1800-1901, SAG Will 1/503; GG 1838, Vol 2, p931, 29 Oct, p931
16	Reg H, No 662, DL
17	Court of Claims, Register of Cases, SRNSW 2/2370, Reel 1249, Case 779; Court of Claims, Reports of the Commissioners of Claims, c1835-55, SRNSW, 2/1765, Reel 1218, Case 779
18	Bk 9, No 953, DL
19	Bk 15, No 651, DL; Bk 20, No 55, DL
20	Registers of Copies of Wills 1800-1901, SAG Will 1/2803
21	Aus 3 June, 1841, p2a
22	Aus 6 March, 1841, p2a; Aus 16 April 1840, p2g, 3a
23	Bowd, D.G., *Macquarie Country*, Library of Australian History, Sydney, rev. ed., 1982, p72
24	SG 26 November 1835, plb
25	Browning, Yvonne, *St. Peters Richmond, The Early People and Burials 1791-1855*, Browning, Kurrajong, 1990, pp20, 23-6, 28, 93
26	Mary Ann Wood, NSW V1842, 484, 54; Bowd, 1982, p86

27   Census of NSW, SRNSW Reel 2223, X951, No 1100, pl01 The extra female child may have been Lucy.
28   Bench of Magistrates, *Windsor Judgement Book 1837-1844*, SRNSW Reel 2390, No 27, p36
29   Registers of Copies of Wills 1800-1901, SAG Will 1/1299
30   SMH 5 April 1842, p3c
31   Bk 3, No 252, DL. See for 3270 acres at Berkeley. Surprisingly Berkeley was mortgaged until WWJ's death: Bk 3, No 576, DL; Bk 19, No 93, DL; Bk 19, No 12, DL; Bk 30, No 194, DL; Bk 36, No 542, DL; Bk 96, No 212, DL; Bk 314 No 53, DL
32   SMH 3 April 1843, p3c
33   SMH 17 Oct 1842, p2h
34   SMH 4 Jan 1843, p2h; Police-Windsor, SRNSW 4/2587.5, 42/9722; GG 1843 Vol 1, pp5,6, 2 Jan
35   Bk 1, No 222, DL; Map County Argyle, NSW, 1907 DL; Bk 1, No 94, DL; Bk 1, No 971, DL; Bk 5, No 412, DL
36   Clark, C.M.H., *Select Documents in Australian History 1788-1850*, Angus and Robertson, Sydney, 1962, p292
37   Reg 3, No 93, DL
38   Reg Y, Nos 281, 282, DL; Bk S, No 157, DL; Bk R, No 361, DL
39   Bk 8, No 686, DL
40   Bk X, No 535, DL
41   Bk 14, No 850, DL; Reg 15, No 376, DL; Bk 1, No 390, DL; Reg 2, No 196, DL
42   Supreme Court of New South Wales, Equity, SRNSW 3/3975, 788. See for agreement of l't Jan 1843; LA & VP, 1865, 2, p838; SMH 1844, p3d; SRNSW 3/3974, No 787 See for number of properties.
43   SMH 4 August 1842, p4; SMH 5 August 1842, pp3d-h, 4; SMH 6 August 1842 p2a,b
44   GG 1842, Vol 2, p l 317, 3 Sept; Aus 14 September 1842, p2a; Aus 30 Sept 1842, p3f; SMH 16 September 1842, pp2-3
45   GG 1842, Vol 2, pl 677, 11 Nov; Aus 2 November 1842, p2c
46   Aus 11 November 1842, p2d,e
47   SMH 12 November 1842, p2f,g
48   Bertie, Charles H., *The Early History of the Sydney Municipal Council*, Sydney, 1911, ch 7, pp65-67
49   HRA 1, 22, pp376-7
50   SMH 10 November 1842, p2a
51   Aus 18 November 1842, pp2-3
52   Aus 17 March 1842, p2a; SMH 8 October 1842, p2a; SMH 20 October 1842, p2a
53   Crocombe, R.G. and Marjorie, *The Works of Ta'Unga, Records of a Polynesian Traveller in the South Seas, 1833-1896*, Australian National University Press, Canberra, 1968, ch 4; Shineberg, Dorothy, *They Came for Sandalwood: a study of the Sandalwood trade in the south-west*

Pacific, 1830-1865, Melbourne University Press, 1967, pp43-44, 207-208; Cheyne, Andrew, *The Trading Voyages of Andrew Cheyne 1841-1844*, Australian National University Press, Canberra, 1971, pp146-147; SMH 20 April 1843, p2a; SMH 29 September 1843, p2a

54 Gunson, Niel, "The Deviations of a Missionary Family", Davidson, J.W. and Deryck Scarr, eds., *Pacific Island Portraits*, Australian National University Press, Canberra, 1970, p43
55 Smith, Alfred, *Some Ups and Downs of an Old Richmondite*, Nepean Family History Society, Emu Plains, 1991, p88
56 Thomas W. F. Wiltshire (sic), NSW V 1844 326 28. See TMPW, tanner, living at Chippendale
57 Browning, 1990, pp 173-174
58 Broughton, Sam and others, *Reminiscences of Richmond*, Newspaper Cuttings, c1903, p78
59 Smith, 1991, p88
60 Clark, 1962, pp335-40, 365-67
61 GG 1843, Vol 1, pp635-7, 4 May; GG 1843, Vol 1, p613-17, 1 May
62 SMH 7 January 1843, p1f; SMH 23 January 1843, p2f; SMH 26 May 1843, p2e; SMH 22 June 1843, p2c
63 GG 1843, Vol 2, Suppl., pp959-66, 26 Jul
64 GG 1843, Vol 2, pl 047, 14 Aug; GG 1843, Vol 2, pl097, 24 Aug; GG 1843, Vol 2, p1118, 28 Aug
65 GG 1843, Vol 1, p437, 17 Mar; JRAHS, Vol 28, Pt 2, pp151-152
66 Letters Received, SRNSW 4/4560.2, Reel 2255, 42/8869; SMH 28 December 1842, p2b,c; Aus 16 December 1842, pp3,4; SMH 19 December 1842, p1c; SMH 21 December 1842, p1e ; SMH 28 December 1842, p3,c,d; SMH 30 December 1842, p1,c,d
67 JRAHS, Vol 28, Pt 5, pp282-3
68 GG 1843, Vol 2, pl 249, 26 Sept; SMH 26 September 1843, p2c-f
69 SMH 10 November 1843, p3b
70 *Port Phillip Herald* 6 August 1844, p4b
71 Aus 18 November 1842, p2b; SMH 10 November 1848, p2d
72 GG 1843, Vol 1, p1,2 Jan; GG 1843, Vol 2, p1381, 24 Oct
73 SMH 31 July 1844, p2e; SMH 21 October 1844, p2g; Low, Francis, *The City of Sydney Directory for 1844-5*, Facsimile , Library of Australian History, North Sydney, c1975, p142
74 GG 1843, Vol 2, pl 030, 10 Aug; GG 1844, Vol 1, p379, 2 Mar; GG 1845, Vol 1, p259, 3 Mar; GG 1846, p315, 5 Mar; GG 1847, Vol 1, p272, 2 Mar
75 Sydney City Archives, Assessment Books, 1845-1950, Information Leaflet
76 Low, c1975, p115; LA, V&P 1865, 2, fr 838; SMH 1 July 1844, p2c; SMH 7 Sept 1844, p2a; SMH 6 Jan 1845, p2a
77 SMH 5 December 1844, pp3-4; SMH 6 Dec 1844, p2f; 78 SMH 15 March 1843, p3f
78 GG 1845, Vol 2, p937, 27 Aug; GG 1846, Vol 1, p737, 5 June

79	SMH 5 October 1842, pp3-4; SMH 22 March 1844, p3e
80	Low, c1975, p115
81	SMH 13 April 1844, p3d
82	SMH 23 December 1843, p3c
83	SMH 8 July 1843, p3d; Low c1975, p142
84	Low, c1975, p115
85	Baxter, Carol J. ed., *General Musters of New South Wales, Norfolk Island and Van Diemen's Land 1811*, Australian Biographical and Genealogical Record and Society of Australian Genealogists, Sydney, 1987, p68; Baxter, Carol J. ed., *General Muster List of New South Wales 1823, 1824, 1825*, Australian Biographical and Genealogical Record and Society of Australian Genealogists, Sydney, 1999, p294; Mutch Index, John Harvey
86	County Cook, Parish Kurrajong, 9th ed., Map 25, DL; County Cook, Parish Curren cy, 7th ed., Map 13, DL
87	Broughton, c1903, p154; *The Hawkesbury Herald* 4 December 1903, p16c; Watson, James, Newspaper Cuttings, Australian Pioneers, p42
88	Vessels Arrived 1837, SRNSW, 4/5212, COD 34. No 133
89	Bk 5, No 455, DL; Molony, John N., *An Architect of Freedom*, Australian National University Press, Canberra, 1973, pxiii
90	Purchases of Land, Bk 68, Pgs 179, 217, 218, DL; Grants of Land, Bk 59, Pg 239, DL; GG 1839, Vol 2, p1429, 14 Dec; County Camden, Parish Bumballa, 6th ed., Map 10, DL; County Camden, 1915, VGS, DL; County St Vincent, Parish Tomboye, 3rd ed., Map 62, DL. For the spelling of "Bomballa" see: Ford, W and F., *Official Post Office Directory for New South Wales 1851*, Sydney, pxxx vii; Bk 62, No 461, DL; *Goulburn Herald* 2 November 1867, p5e
91	*Narrative of the Wreck of the SS "Royal Charter"*, Batson and Atwater, Sydney 1884, p15; Conrad Martens Notes 1835-1856, p156, DL MS 142; Kerr, Joan ed., *The Dictionary of Australian Artists*, Melbourne University Press, 1992, p402
92	Vessels Arrived 1838, SRNSW, 4/5213, COD 35, No 200
93	National Museum of Australia, Friends, Vol 17, No 3, Sept 2006, pp10-12
94	Reg 6, No 307, DL
95	SMH 8 March 1844, p4g; *Friends*, Vol 17, No 3, Sept 2006, p12
96	*Springfield*, Meares and Associates, Sydney 2000, p2
97	Register 8, No 686, DL
98	SMH 2 August 1844, p4b; Census 1837, p404; *Hawkesbury Courier* 11 July 1844, p2c; Broughton, c1903, p49; *Hawkesbury Courier* 1 August 1844, p2c;
99	*Hawkesbury Courier* 10 October, p2c
100	SMH 9 February 1844, p2a
101	SMH 25 October 1843, p3a; *The Guardian* 20 April 1844, pp1-2b; *The Guardian* 18 May 1844, p76 a,b; *The Guardian* 25 May 1844, pp81-83; *The Guardian* 1 June 1844, p89c; *The Guardian*, 7 August 1844, pp183,

	184b; *The Guardian* 17 August 1844, pp180c,d, p183, 184a,b; *The Guardian* 24 August 1844, pp185-8a,b
102	The Guardian 22 June 1844, p113c
103	Wilshire , James Robert, Letters to W.C. Wentworth ... on the subjects of Municipal Revenue and Police Administration , D.L., Welch , Sydney, in *Great Britain and Ireland, Parliamentary Papers*, Vol 41, 1841-44, Pts 14, 15, 1844, ML; HRA 1, 22, pp363-364; HRA 1, 23, p326; *The Weekly Register* 15 June 1844, p637b; *The Guardian* 15 June 1844, pp105d, 106a; SMH 10 May 1844, p2f,g
104	*The Weekly Register* 28 September 1844, p162a-c
105	SMH 23 August 1844, p2c-g; SMH 12 May 1843 p3; Aus 23 August 1844, p603c-f; *Hawkesbury Courier* 1 August 1844, p2b; *The Weekly Register* 3 August 1844, p57b; The Weekly Register 24 August 1844, 92-4
106	Aus 20 August 1844, p591 d,e; *Port Phillip Herald* 6 August 1844, p4a,b
107	SMH 26 September 1843, p2c,d; SMH 30 Sept 1843, p3a; SMH 13 Dec 1844, pp2g-3a
108	HRA 1, 24, p41
109	SMH 13 December 1844, p2d
110	Bertie, 1911, ch 5, p49
111	SMH 10 October, 1842, p3b; SMH 15 September 1842, p1b; Reg 5, No 69, DL; Reg 5, No 562 DL
112	Bk 18, No 992, DL. See for new brick building; Register 5, No 565, DL; Register 6, No 657, DL
113	Charles Whittell, NSW V1844 309 58
114	Insolvency Register 2, SRNSW 2/8811, No 1683; GG 1847, Vol 2, p 1354, 9 Dec; GG 1846, Vol 1, p82, 17 Jan
115	GG 1846, Vol 1, p82, 17 Jan; SMH 4 July 1844, p3d
116	GG 1845, Vol 1, p427, 17 Apr; GG 1846, Vol 1, p672, 1 Jun
117	GG 1844, Vol 1, p79, 6 Jan; GG 1844, Vol 1, p298, 15 Feb
118	SMH 7 August 1844, p2b
119	SMH 23 April 1844, p2f,g; McCaffrey, Frank, *First Century of the Diarying in New South Wales*, Sydney and Melbourne Publishing Co., 1909, pp83-4
120	*Illawarra Mercury* 3 June 1884, pp2,3
121	SMH 17 February 1845, p2e
122	Butler, B.N., *St Mark the Evangelist Anglican Church, Appin, 150 years of Ministry 1838-1988*, pp5,7,8; GG 1842, p1755, 23 Nov; Register of Grants, Bk 334A, Pg 8, DL
123	SMH 26 April 1844, p3d. See new regulations in GG 1844, Vol 1, p508, 2 Apr
124	Police, Bungonia 1846, SRNSW 4/2738.6, 46/909; GG 1847, Vol 1, p674, 16 Jun
125	SMH 18 November 1844, p2g; SMH 30 November 1844, p2e
126	Bk 6, No 149, DL; Bk 9, No 987, DL; Bk 12, No 323 DL; Bk 8, No 817

	DL; Letters Received Relating to Land, SRNSW 2/7892-3, Reel 1146, JJ 3 Oct 1831; Bk 11, Nos 928, 929, DL; Bk 12, Nos 255, 279, 557, DL
127	Police, Campbelltown, SRNSW 4/2699.7, 45/7880
128	*Goulburn Herald*, 2 November 1867, p5e
129	Bride, Thomas F., *Letters from Victoria Pioneers*, Heinemann, Melbourne 1898, pp219-21
130	Bk 10, No 412, DL; Bk 12, No 360, DL
131	Bk 9, No 665, DL
132	Yeend, Peter, ed., *The King's School Register 1831-1999*, 3rd ed., Council of the King's School, Parramatta, 1999, p177
133	SMH 31 January 1846, 5e
134	SMH 24 July 1846, p2e-g; GG 1846 Vol 2, p923, 27 Jul
135	*Hawkesbury Courier* 10 September 1846, 2b; SMH 9 September 1846, p2c
136	http://www.cityofSydney.gov.au/aboutSydney/historyandarchives/ SydneyHistory/HistoricBuildings/ParliamentHouse.asp
137	SMH 13 July 1848, p1g, 2b
138	Bk 15, No 629, DL
139	Bk 15, No 787, DL
140	Low, Francis, *Low's Directory of the City and District of Sydney for 1847*, Grocott, Sydney, 1847, p93
141	SMH 14 August 1846, p3f
142	Bk 15, Nos 916-919, DL
143	Bk 45, No 23, DL
144	Bk 15, No 916, DL
145	SMH 2 March 1847, p4a
146	Mowle, P. C., *Pioneer Families of Australia*, 5th, ed. L.M. Mowle, Rigby Australia, 1978, p295
147	SMH 18 May 1849, p4c
148	GG 1849, Vol 1, p66, 12 Jan
149	*Hawkesbury Courier*, 15 May 1845, p2b; *Hawkesbury Courier* 7 August 1845, p3a,b; *Hawkesbury Courier* 12 February 1846, p2b; *Hawkesbury Courier* 5 March 1846, p4b,c; *Hawkesbury Courier* 20 August 1846, p2c; *Hawkesbury Courier* 10 September 1846, p3b
150	GG 1847, Vol 1, p525, 12 May
151	Bk 12, No 142, DL; Bk 21, No 915, DL. Margaret Betts believes she lives in the third home built on Bronte.
152	GG 1843, Vol 2, p 1 052, 24 Jul; GG 1844, Vol 1, p684, 9 May
153	Smith, 1991, p88
154	Bk 11, No 495, DL
155	Registers of Copies of Wills 1800-1901, SAG Will 1/1821; Reg 6, No 325, Primary Application, Miscellaneous Bk 63, No 21740, DL
156	Bowd, D.G. *Origins of Names of Streets, Parks and Features: Windsor Municipality*, Windsor Municipal Council, New South Wales, 1973
157	*Empire* 3 April 1856, p4f

158 Register 13, No 312, DL; Register 14, No 2, DL; Register 14,210, DL; Register 15, 376, DL; Register 15, No 493, DL; Bk 13, No 50, DL; Bk 14, No 156, DL
159 Register 15, No 788, DL
160 A Catalogue of Elegant Household Furniture ... to be Sold by Auction ... 19th December 1848, Kemp and Fairfax, Sydney, 1848, pp911-918, ML 018. PA 1
161 Register 16, No 791, DL
162 Insolvency Register 2, SRNSW 2/8811, No 1683
163 Register 13, No 170, DL; GG 1847, Vol 2, p1047, 29 Sept; GG 1847, Vol 2, p1148, 20 Oct; GG 1847, Vol 2, p1331, 1 Dec; GG 1847, Vol 2, p1354, 9 Dec; GG 1847, Vol 2, p1439, 30 Dec; GG 1848, Vol 1, pl 83, 2 Feb
164 Bk 18, No 456, DL
165 GG 1848, Vol 1, p390 18 Mar; Bk 16, No 795, DL
166 Bk 18, No 992, DL; SMH 17 August 1850, pp5-6
167 GG 1849, Vol 1, p90, 10 Jan
168 Supreme Court of New South Wales, SRNSW Equity, 3/3974,No 787; 3/3975, No 788; 3/3674, No 1182
169 Bk 15, No 292, DL
170 Register 15, Nos 681,706,707,708,713,714,715,716, DL
171 SMH 19 Oct 1848, p4d
172 Letters Received, Miscellaneous Persons W, SRNSW 4/2862.3, Reel 2276, 49/1573
173 *Hawkesbury Courier* 2 January 1845, p3c
174 Bk 13, No 679, DL
175 Bk 15, No 574, DL; Bk 15, No 620, DL; Bk 15, No 621, DL; Bk 15, No 790, DL; Bk 15, No 793, DL; Bk 15, No 830, DL; Bk 16, No 245, DL; Bk 16, No 680, DL
176 HRA 1, 25, pp432-3
177 GG 1849, Vol 1, p373, 5 Mar; GG 1849, Vol 2, pl 004, 4 Jul; GG 1849 Vol 1, pp375-6, 5 Mar; GG 1850, Vol 2, pp1637-8, 19 Oct
178 Bride, 1898, p22 l
179 GG 1848, Vol 2, p1175, 9 Sept
180 SMH 26 July 1935, pp9-10
181 GG 1848, Vol 2, p1311, 27 Sept
182 GG 1848, Vol 1, p784, 12 June; GG 1849, Vol 2, pp1151-2, 21 Jul
183 GG 1848, Vol 2, p1365, 30 Sept; Letters Received 1848, SRNSW 4/2808.2, Reel 2272, 48/3034, 48/3772
184 GG 1848, Vol 2, p1094, 26 Aug
185 Bk 16, No 909, DL; Bk 18, No 66, DL
186 *Goulburn Herald* 14 October 1848, p4b
187 *Gormly Notes 1825-1958*, ML MSS 672/3, Pt 1, p7; Pt 3, pp25,29, 31,32,36
188 Bk 23, No 428, DL
189 Bk 18, No 830, DL; Bk 40, Nos 745, 746, DL

190 *Illawarra Mercury* 3 June 1884, p2d; *Illawarra Mercury* 30 May 1876,p2e
191 SMH 23 October 1849, p2e; SMH 2 November 1849, p2e; SMH 24 October 1848, p2c
192 SMH 26 November 1849, p1b; SMH 11 July 1848, p1d; ADB 1, Lowe, 2, Parkes
193 Roe, Michael, *Quest for Authority in Eastern Australia 1835-1851*, Australian National University, Melbourne, 1965, ch 4
194 SMH 19 December 1849, pp1d, 4e-g
195 *Bells Life in Sydney and Sporting Reviewer* 22 December 1849, p2c,d; SMH 12 June 1849, p2d-f; SMH 19 June 1849, pp2d-3b
196 SMH 20 December 1849, p2d
197 SMH 22 December 1849, p2e,f,g
198 SMH 18 September 1849, p2c; SMH 12 October 1849, p2c; LA, V&P 1865, 2, fr 829
199 The number of great-grandchildren depends on the accuracy of the New South Wales birth and baptisms records as well as the information on the Henrys of Tahiti. Three great grandchildren born to the Woods in the forties are recorded in Chapter 9.

9
UNTIMELY DEATHS

The Colony prospered after the discovery of gold in the Bathurst district in February 1851. The new wealth spurred economic growth, immigration and political reform. Important political developments included Victoria (1852) and Queensland (1859) separating from New South Wales, and New South Wales achieving self-government in 1856.[1] Remarkably, three grandsons of Mary Pitt served in the new parliament. Communications progressed, the first steamship arriving from England in 1852, the railway between Sydney and Parramatta opening in 1855, and electric telegraph linking the eastern cities before the end of the decade.[2] For the Pitt Family, early deaths cast a shadow over the 1850s.

In the second week of January 1850, "an accident of a fearful nature nearly happened to Mr W Faithfull JP and Mr R Jenkins JP". William safely negotiated the Murrumbidgee River between Wagga Wagga and Bangus. Robert and a "little boy" followed, but the two horses pulling Robert's gig "turned down the stream". As Robert couldn't swim, he jumped out and grabbed the branch of a tree. The waves washed the boy out of the gig and William rescued him. While the gig was recovered, the horses drowned.[3]

The transfer of Brewarrena to William approved in August 1849 may account for the excursion.[4]

City cousin, William Pitt Wilshire, was secretary of the Australian Society of Artists for its first quarterly meeting held at the Royal Hotel in Pitt Street in March 1850.[5] The rules of the Society stipulated submission of at least one original sketch each three months, with the first sketch due on 6th May. At the July meeting members decided to display their work in December, meanwhile, the Society collapsed.[6] William, a juror, failed to attend the court in June. Accused of frequent absence, he protested in the *Sydney Morning Herald*. In three years he had just three absences, the most recent caused by advance notice of four weeks.[7] A correspondent suggested using a diary. William countered, forgetting to consult his diary was as likely as overlooking the note he placed on the mantelshelf in his studio.[8] James Robert Wilshire also missed jury duty; his fine of £2 excused. He filed an affidavit which explained the unintended absence was the only session missed in seven years.[9]

James Robert Wilshire remained politically active and closely associated with Reverend Doctor John Dunmore Lang, champion of the radicals once Robert Lowe left for England. In response to the "crisis" in the Colony, and helped by James, Henry Parkes and others, Lang founded the Australian League. The members of the League aimed to unite the five Australian colonies (which included Tasmania and South Australia) into the "Great Australian Nation", ensure transportation ended, promote immigration and win independence for the colonies. James chaired the first meeting of the League at Lang's Australian College in Jamison Street on 26th April 1850. He also chaired the provisional committee of the League when launched in July.[10] Lang campaigned for a seat in the Legislative Council, promising to extend the franchise, oppose transportation, support general education and set up a university.[11] James chaired his election committee and Henry Parkes was his secretary. Lang won the seat on 1st July 1850.[12] He asked the parliament to appoint a select committee to inquire into allegations that he acted contrary to regulations in organizing immigration to Moreton Bay and Port Phillip while in England in the late forties. After refusing Lang's request, the Council passed a resolution critical of him.[13] Lang announced his resignation. James organized a meeting which condemned the Council's action. Lang kept his seat.[14]

Although no convict ships had arrived since the *Hashemy* in 1849, many colonists feared transportation would resume. Their apprehension increased on learning Governor Charles FitzRoy had informed London authorities that newspaper accounts of the antitransportation meetings held in June 1849 exaggerated the number and respectability of those present.[15] The day the Herald published the Governor's criticisms, 9th August, James Robert Wilshire chaired a protest meeting. A committee of the meeting developed resolutions representing four sentiments: an indignant dissent from the covert movement of certain parties in the interior who supported transportation; a strong sense of public insecurity while orders in council remain unrevoked proclaiming New South Wales a penal settlement; a want of confidence in the present local government; and a prayer to recall Charles FitzRoy.[16] At Circular Quay on 12th August, Lang and Parkes moved resolutions while James bravely proposed removing the Governor.[17] On 16th September at Old Barrack-Square, citizens approved a petition and motions opposing transportation which insulted present colonists and made the Colony unattractive to migrants. A petition, resolutions and report of the meeting were sent to the Secretary of State in London.[18] James joined the management committee of the newly formed NSW Association for Preventing the Revival of Transportation.[19]

In September 1850 the citizens of Goulburn asked their warden, William Pitt Faithfull, to conduct a public meeting with the aim of petitioning the Legislative Council to revoke the order authorising transportation. During the meeting William disclosed he supported the scheme as a member of the Legislative Council but had since changed his mind. The Legislative Council called for an end to transportation on 1st October 1850. The British Government finally abolished transportation in Eastern Australia in 1852.[20] William addressed Governor FitzRoy when he toured Goulburn in early December 1850. The Governor commented on "the increasing prosperity of this important town".[21]

Alice Gibson held the first of many picnic race meetings on a paddock at Tirranna in 1851. The event originated in racing contests the Gibson boys conducted with their neighbours, the Chisholms of Kippilaw, in the Christmas holidays.[22] With a few pounds collected for prizes, Alice bought items, mainly for the ladies, such as thimbles, necklets, broaches, chains and lockets. She provided lunch and dinner for her guests. The race club was officially registered in 1855 with Alice's second son, Andrew Faithfull Gibson, taking the roles of club secretary and treasurer.[23] Alice increased her acreage, buying 60 acres in the parish of Terranna for £2 an acre, and five lots totalling 193 acres near Andrew's land in County King for £1 an acre.[24] As well, she leased 640 acres in County Argyle and nearly 6000 acres in County King.[25] The eldest daughter of Alice, Alice Jemima Gibson wed James Donaldson in Sydney in July 1851. James was brother to Andrew's executor, Stuart Alexander Donaldson.

Three properties changed hands in the George Street Complex in 1851. Their finances improved with the export of 1115 casks of tallow, James Robert Wilshire and Austin Forrest Wilshire paid £1250 to brother, William Pitt Wilshire, for his house in George Street. They took over his mortgage which had a year to run.[26] William also sold a property in Pitt Street for £750.[27] James paid Louisa £100 for the allotment housing the workers on the south side of Union Lane.[28] James and Austin owned all their father's properties in George Street except for the family home. Preparations for their business venture almost complete, James followed his political ambitions.

At the request of nearly 200 electors, James Robert Wilshire campaigned for the seat of Eastern Camden in September 1851. His wide-ranging policies included: reforming, enlarging and consolidating the Colony's institutions; extending suffrage; voting by ballot; developing a system of national education; building railways; improving roads, bridges and other public works; and ending transportation. James lost to local candidate Henry Osborne.[29] James announced his candidacy for the City Council then operating under amended legislation which empowered citizens to elect the mayor as well as the aldermen.[30] On 4th December 1851 nine men contested three vacancies for aldermen. James was successful. After his election, James raised the issue of his removal from the Commission of Peace. He suggested his audacity in proposing the removal of the Governor accounted for his omission from the list of Justices of Peace published in October 1851. Brother Austin and cousins William Pitt Faithfull, Robert Pitt Jenkins and William Warren Jenkins were on the list.[31]

The battle for mayor proved tougher. Opponents thought James "ultra radical" and a "seven-and-sixpenny tanner of hides backed by the Hunter-street toyman", namely, Henry Parkes. James heard rumours "to the effect that three years ago I was insolvent and that I then made a false and dishonest statement of my affairs, to induce my creditors to take a composition". Nevertheless, he "succeeded in the midst of great difficulties in paying the full amount of his liabilities". James believed he could restore his tarnished reputation if he won the office of Mayor for then he could prove his worth as Chief Magistrate of the City. Though supported by Parkes, Lang and a large group of friends, he came a distant second to George Hill. His health poor, Hill was unable to take office and the unpopular William Thurlow stayed on as Mayor.[32] Days later, Councillors James Robert Wilshire and William

Piddington objected to Thurlow's illegal conduct, failing to give due notice of meetings. Councillor George Thornton rejected their criticism. James, he said, was "impertinent" and remarkable for his "buffoonery".[33]

Nine months separated the deaths in Tahiti of Sophia Henry, and Samuel Pinder Henry, Sophia at 47, and Samuel at 52. (Figure 26) Sophia, the only daughter of John and Lucy Wood, died on 3rd September 1851 "after a short but painful illness".[34] On 9th June 1852 Samuel died, allegedly of alcoholism.[35] At Samuel's death, their children ranged in age from 28 to 6, with two married. Samuel Pinder Henry II wed Isabella Brine Orsmond in Tahiti in 1848 and Sophia Henry junior wed James Greer in Sydney in 1849. At the end of his life Samuel had regrets judging by the letter his father, William Henry, wrote to Reverend Lang in October 1850:

> *He (Samuel) being of a weekly constitution and frequently unwell when among the islands, and having in consequence to be kept at home and deprived of the advantages of the Mission School, has come behind in learning: nor did he show much concern about his deficiency... until within the last year in which he has evidently a very considerable change and alteration in his views and sentiments, and attendance on the means of grace, and for some time past he has manifested and expressed an earnest desire to be prepared for the ministry and with this view proposed being placed under you, which has led to the step we are now taking.*

Samuel delivered the letter from his father's home in Ryde.[36] Samuel was renowned for his good manners and comfortable relations with Polynesians, including Pomare II and other Society Island chiefs. Niel Gunson wrote, Samuel Henry "belongs ... to a generation of sea captains who made a profound impact on the development of the South Sea Island communities".[37]

Figure 26. Samuel Henry

Between the deaths of the Henrys, Thomas Matcham Pitt Wilshire lost his life at the early age of 31. Thomas, fourth son of Esther and James, died on 5th March 1852 at Louisa Creek, southwest of Mudgee, the site of gold diggings.[38] He was buried on 9th in St John the Baptist Cemetery, Mudgee.[39] Brother Joseph applied to manage Thomas's estate of about £1200.[40] Joseph also assumed the guardianship of eight-year-old Thomas William Faithfull Wilshire.[41] Thomas and Joseph were close; both had lived and worked at Berkeley.[42] In 1852 William Pitt Wilshire and his sons William and Frederick also fossicked for gold, probably at Louisa Creek with Thomas. William and his sons were "fairly successful as they also were in getting rid of what they won".[43]

About 30th March 1852 Governor FitzRoy stopped overnight in Goulburn on his way to the goldfields at Braidwood. The next day he inspected the Goulburn gaol before setting out for "the beautiful residence of William Pitt Faithfull, Esq. Springfield".[44] Springfield also impressed Englishmen Samuel Mossman and Thomas Bannister on their visit to Goulburn, possibly in 1852. "There are few places that will bear comparison... It possesses almost every advantage in position, climate, in the lay of the land, the richness of the soil." The estate had an "appearance of order and comfort" with its fenced-in paddocks near the homestead and outbuildings. The silos were deep wells cut into solid rock, one containing 1500 bushells of wheat. The cottage-style home had several additions. The perfect garden was planted with various fruit trees such as apple, pear, peach, nectarine and loquat.[45]

There was anything but "an appearance of order and comfort" at Bangus about midnight on 24th June 1852. That night, weeks of torrential rain in the Snowy Mountains culminated in a great swell in the Murrumbidgee River. The Gundagai district flooded with devastating results: 89 of the 250-300 inhabitants killed; 160 affected; and 71 buildings destroyed.[46] The superintendent of Bangus and his family were rescued from the roof of the kitchen in a rowboat. On 29th June the superintendent wrote to Robert from the woolshed:

> *I am sorry to inform you of the great destruction that has been done to your house and premises by a great flood that was here on Friday night last. The water rose to the ceiling of your house, carried away the wheat rick, coach house, and a great deal of the fences; destroyed all the provisions in the store, tea, sugar, salt, and soap. Your furniture will be all destroyed unless you come up at once, and save your property from destruction. There is one foot of mud on the boards of the verandah and the storeroom and offices.*[47]

Robert cleaned and repaired Bangus. He was asked to dispense relief to the residents of Gundagai, but the "requested instructions re distributiqn of the fund" had not arrived before he left Gundagai on 29th March 1853.[48] On 26th April 1853 Alfred Frederick Jenkins was born at Bomballa. Before the flood Robert sold 500 acres at Eagle Vale for £1000. He gave Bomballa to Louisa.[49]

The conduct of city mayor, William Thurlow, continued to annoy James Robert Wilshire. This time the mayor's irregular use of the city funds irritated him. James and Daniel Egan, leading a group of councillors, sought a special meeting late in June 1852. The issue unresolved, the councillors considered taking legal action.[50] On July 14th James took out an injunction to restrain mayor and treasurer Edward Lord. Six days later in the Supreme Court, the mayor argued he used emergency powers to avoid delay in Council business caused by lapsed meetings of the Improvement and Water Committees. The judgment on 31st July confirmed James's position, "that the Mayor has not the power contended for". Council rules required at least three council members and the town clerk to sign payments. James won the case although he paid the court costs. The judge told James he should have prosecuted the case not as a private citizen, but on behalf of the Council or a group of councillors.[51] The day James got the injunction, the Legislative Council appointed a committee to consider the future of the City Council. In spite of the committee recommending reform of the poorly functioning body, the parliament decided on its suspension. Three commissioners replaced the elected members of City Council.[52]

Lucy Wood died at Richmond on 26th November 1852 at the timely age of 75. Her burial took place two days later in St Peters Cemetery, Richmond. Lucy owned goods worth £150 and about 287 acres at North Richmond. She gave George Pitt Wood his father's grant of 100 acres, the 10 acres John bought, and her grant of 2 acres. Sophia Henry got Lucy's grant of 175 acres, 50 head of cattle and her mother's personal effects.[53] Sophia's son, Samuel Pinder Henry, 11, applied for his mother's share of the estate through his brother-in-law, attorney James Greer.[54]

By April 1853 the increasing prosperity of the colony had helped James and Austin Wilshire pay their mortgages of the late forties and one from 1851. William Pitt Faithfull was paid "long since".[55] Their financial position was still precarious on three counts. They had borrowed money from the estate of brother, Thomas. Alice Gibson's loan of 1842 was not redeemed until August 1854. The annual profit of the "not half worked" tannery averaged £1779 15s 9d.[56] Yet James and Austin carried out their grand plan, erecting three large stone commercial buildings facing George Street.[57] (Figure 27) Before starting, the brothers improved the layout of the buildings. They paid Elizabeth £616 for the family home and she gave them £500 for the land next door, previously owned by Matilda.[58] Since James lived on site and Austin in Pitt Street, Redfern, the two could closely supervise the project while their wives cared for the new arrivals.[59] Sarah gave birth to Emily Rebekah Wilshire in March 1851 and Sarah Jane Wilshire in February 1852. In February 1853 Sarah had another daughter who died in the following April. Eliza gave birth to George Pitt Wilshire in September 1850, Percy Wilshire in February 1852 and

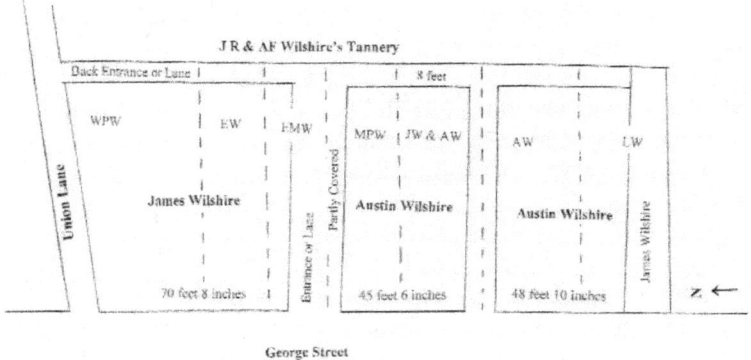

Figure 27. Plan of Wilshire Place

Emma Mary Wilshire in August 1853. George Pitt Wilshire died in December 1851.

In July 1853 Henry Whittell bought the Wilshires' family retreat and eight acres in Surry Hills. He gave both Matilda Pitt Jenkins and Elizabeth Mary Wilshire £750 for their third shares.[60] The Whittells made the retreat their home. Henry also bought six lots at Darling Harbour, one from Elizabeth Mary Wilshire for £140, two from Louisa Elliot for £282, and three from Joseph Wood Wilshire for £472.[61] Joseph had partitioned two of his three Darling Harbour blocks with one divided three ways to create six lots. Similarly, Louisa subdivided the largest of her four lots to make five. She had sold her other three lots.[62] The site at Darling Harbour was ideal for a coal contractor and dealer, with coal in demand and well priced.[63] Even so Henry had debts.[64] However, the family grew, Esther giving birth to Alfred Whittell in June 1851, who sadly died two years later, Elizabeth Whittell in October 1853, Louisa Whittell in September 1855 and Henry Rawes Whittell in June 1857. Louisa Elliot's son Thomas Wilshire Elliot wed Ann Sampson in Sydney in July 1854.

On 3rd August 1853 James Robert Wilshire left his sickbed to chair a public meeting. Four to five hundred opponents of the proposed Act for self-government attended the meeting in the Royal Hotel. A committee of the Legislative Council drafted the bill after the Secretary of State for the Colonies invited New South Wales, Victoria, Van Diemen's Land and South Australia to design their own constitutions. Outrage greeted the bill. The prospect of an Upper House of nominees was especially unpopular. Critics feared it would evolve into an English House of Lords given the proposal for hereditary titles with the titled electing the Upper House. Also causing offence, the unjust distribution of electoral seats heavily favouring country and squatting interests.[65] At a second meeting on August 15th, 2,500 people crowded into the Victoria Hotel in Pitt Street. James sat on the platform. The meeting sent the Legislative Council several resolutions, including a request to delay the second reading of the bill. William Charles Wentworth, head of the committee that prepared the bill, labelled opponents "dirty, paltry, ruffians". Following a resolution passed at the earlier meeting at the Royal Hotel, the New South Wales Constitutional Committee was set up to "resist that flagrant attack on the public liberty". James was on its committee.[66] A further public meeting held on 5th September near Circular Quay attracted a crowd of about 5000, "unquestionably the most orderly and determined, if not numerous body of colonists ever assembled for a political purpose in this Colony". On this "delightfully propitious" day, James sat on or near the speakers' platform. Those assembled agreed to ask Her Majesty and the Imperial Parliament for a Legislature with both houses based on popular suffrage and a fair distribution of electoral seats.[67]

William Pitt Faithfull was also caught up in the constitution debate. On 20th August 1853 Goulburn magistrates and others asked their warden to convene a meeting in response to Wentworth's accusation that the silence of citizens implied their agreement with his constitutional plans. William missed the meeting. At the next meeting in early September he took the chair following an exchange of views on his absence. During the meeting William admitted his general agreement with Wentworth's proposal. His views clashed with those who called the meeting. They opposed the arrangements for the upper house, the two-thirds majority needed to alter the constitution, the limited franchise and the exclusion of ministers of religion from parliament. The meeting sent a petition of dissent to the Legislative Council. Diplomatic William praised the "harmony and good feeling" that pervaded the meeting.[68]

The Governor of the new colony of Victoria, Charles La Trobe, asked pioneers to record their time of settlement and early experiences. On 8th September 1853 George Faithfull dutifully identified his time of arrival, described the massacre and recounted his struggles with black and white trespassers. Earlier chapters covered George's experiencies in the 1830s and 1840s. In the 1850s the gold-diggers troubled him:

> *the ephemeral grubber of the day, sets up his claim to the right, not only of the auriferous metal in the bowels of the earth but to the grass upon the earth, and that, too, free from all restraint, tramping under foot the rights of the pioneer squatter-rights gained by discovery and by conquest.*[69]

In 1853, George was appointed a magistrate.[70]

Also in the year 1853, the deaths occurred of Elizabeth Wood, 43, and husband George Pitt Wood, 51. Elizabeth, née Markwell, died on 25th June, George, only son of Lucy and John Wood, on 24th September. The couple was buried in the Markwell vault at St Peters Cemetery, Richmond, Elizabeth on 28th June and George on 26th September. They left 13 children including Alice Elizabeth Wood born in June 1845, Susanna Wood in March 1847, and Henry Austin Wood in April 1850. Elizabeth also gave birth to

Henry Austin Wood in March 1849 and James Edward Wood in November 1852. Both died within a month of their births.

Soon after the death of his wife, George Pitt Wood made his will, naming Elizabeth's brothers Thomas and John Markwell trustees and executors, and guardians of his 11 under-age children. For George's six daughters and sons Alfred and Thomas the income from Wood's Farm was to be invested and paid to them at 21 or when married. Eldest son, William Henry Wood, who married neighbour Ann Crowley in 1847, was to live on the farm and inherit the household goods, farm utensils, pigs and crops. He had to maintain and educate Sophia, Lucy, Ellen, Mary, Alfred, Thomas and Henry as well as apprentice the boys. When the last child turned 21 or married, a half share of the farm was for William and quarter shares for third son John and youngest son Henry. William's share was subject to him paying £150 to Robert at 24. John had to put aside £20 for six years to clothe and apprentice Robert. Since John drove a team over the mountains, he also got two working horses, a dray and harness.[71] Second son George, who married neighbour Caroline Aston in June 1853, inherited John Wood's 10 acres, but had to pay William £8 rent for 10 years. Lucy's two acres on the Highlands and George's 200 acres were placed in trust, the two acres for Susanna, the 200 acres for Alfred and Thomas; the income from the land would provide their upkeep.[72] After the deaths of George and Elizabeth the rest of their children married. Some wed in Richmond: Lucy Wood to William Farlow in 1854, John Thomas Wood to Mary Ann Aston in 1856, Robert Markwell Wood to Louisa Baines in 1858, and Susanna Wood to Thomas Hawkins in 1869. Others married elsewhere: Sophia Wood to Robert Lamrock in Sydney in 1860, Alfred Sherwin Wood to Catherine Mary Ferguson in Maitland in 1862, Mary Ann Wood to James Grant in Balmain in 1864, Henry Austin Wood to Catherine Gilleth in Sydney in 1870, Alice Elizabeth Wood to James Hope in Penrith in 1871, and Thomas George Wood to Jane Matilda Howell in Orange in 1874.

Life had been up and down for William Warren and Matilda Pitt Jenkins. Happily William displayed the best blood stallion and best blood mare at the local Agricultural Society Show back in January 1851.[73] In August 1853 William was appointed warden of the Illawarra Council following Alick Osborne's resignation.[74] Sadly the Jenkins lost two children. Charles Matcham Jenkins, born in November 1850, died in January 1852, and Esther Ada Jenkins, born in January 1853, died in the following May. During these years Anne and Joseph Wood Wilshire lived with Matilda and William at Berkeley. There, Anne gave birth to Thomas Herbert Wilshire in June 1851, Henry Clarke Pitt Jenkins Wilshire in April 1853, he died in August, and Beatrice Louisa Wilshire in May 1854. Soon after the birth of Beatrice, Joseph bought 278 acres and a "capital" residence near Wollongong, the property part of the Garden Hill Estate formerly owned by Anne's parents.[75] Seller Henry Gilbert Smith lent Joseph £4000 of the asking price, £7000; the loan guaranteed with Joseph's properties in Pitt and George Streets.[76] The Wilshires left Berkeley to live at Garden Hill.

In Spring 1853 William Pitt Wilshire had his gig fixed. Finding the work unsatisfactory, he offered 10s for the repairs instead of the agreed cost of £3. The Brickfield Hill repairers refused to release the gig. William contacted the police who issued a search warrant and wheelwright Thomas Lane was taken into custody for theft. The court dismissed the charge.[77] Elder son, William James Wilshire, sold his mother's 640 acres at Kurrajong. The justification for his action, his father had not used the land.[78] William senior recovered the property.[79] William James rightfully sold the 60 acres near Botany Bay inherited from his grandfather.[80] Although farming did not interest William senior, he would enjoy the Exhibition of Natural and Industrial Products of New South Wales held at the Australian Museum at Hyde Park in November 1854. The finest articles were shown at the Paris Exhibition in the following May. The display of more than 300 pictures included two oils by William, *A Party of Travellers overtaken by the Simoon in the Desert* after Scottish artist David Roberts, and a portrait, the person depicted not named in the catalogue.[81] Also appealing to William, the Sydney Sketching Club which began about April 1855, with William secretary and Conrad Martens, president. The club admitted those with "a certain degree of competency to sketch from nature" and aimed for selfimprovement through "friendly criticism".[82]

Robert Pitt Jenkins enlarged his home at Bangus into a spacious inn with 10 rooms and wide verandahs. "Finished in a style unsurpassed by any other inn on the road", the inn opened in July 1854 under manager John Levitt.[83] Built where the main south road crossed Adelong Creek, the inn captured the trade of the gold-diggers flocking to Adelong where the precious metal was discovered in 1853.[84] In 1855 Robert sold 866 acres at Eagle Vale for £2470 and rented the brick house on 100 acres. Eagle Vale had excellent facilities, an eight-roomed house, butler's pantry, china closet, kitchen, servants' rooms, offices, stores, dairy, laundry, coach-house, stable and gardener's cottage.[85] Robert also sold 60 acres ofJemima's at West Bargo for £240.[86]

In the first half of the 1850s George Matcham Pitt completed several land deals. Brother Robert and George bought, price unknown, one and a half acres in the Highlands in May 1850. (Figure 3) They sold the land in September 1853 to Tom Homery for £30.[87] In passing, George gave Ben Mortimer £5 for recovering the body of a Tom Hornery from the Yarramundi Lagoon.[88] (Figure 3) Wife Julia's brother?, builder John Johnson, paid George £60 for Julia's allotment in Windsor town.[89] George made a handsome profit on 32 acres extending from the Hawkesbury River to the lagoon, buying the farm for £800 and selling it three months later for £1050.[90] George transferred Coorar to another lessee in September 1854.[91] He replaced the distant squat with Lower Gerawhey, 19,200 acres in the Wellington district.[92]

George Matcham Pitt continued to support community causes. He gave £10 to St Paul's College, the first college affiliated with Sydney University established in 1850, with lectures starting in 1852. William Pitt Faithfull, James Robert Wilshire and Austin Forrest Wilshire also made donations to the college, William £100, James £50 and Austin £50. George participated in the Annual Meeting of the Windsor Hospital in January 1855. In the following May he was a steward at the two-day Hawkesbury Race Meeting.[93] Appointed a commissioner of the Richmond Road Trust in December 1854, George held the position until at least the end of 1862. The trust collected tolls on the Blacktown Road, repaired roads and bridges, and rented the Richmond ferry and punt.[94] At some stage George leased the punt from Maria Faithfull for three years at £100 a year. Soon after taking the lease, and about to go "to his station up country", he negotiated terms with the owners of a new punt. Later, he leased the wharf and because the conditions of the lease required the lessee to own the old punt, Maria sold it to him for £90. This arrangement also went astray, the Government auctioning the wharf 21 months before the lease expired. Alfred Smith recalled his time at the punt with George, "I knew him very well - and a grand old man he was. He was my boss for three years at the punt, and during that time I always found it a pleasure having anything to do with him".[95]

In December 1854, at the motion of John Dunmore Lang, James Robert Wilshire chaired a meeting at the Royal Hotel. About 500 constituents had gathered at the hotel to hear Heury Parkes report on his first session in the Legislative Council.[96] James joined Parkes and Lang in the Legislative Council after William Thurlow resigned. At a public meeting held on 10th January 1855 in the Lyceum Hotel in York Street, Lang, Parkes and others spoke in support of James. Although not a powerful orator, he was an earnest worker who successfully ran the election campaigns of Robert Lowe and Dr Lang. He had been active in the anti-transportation movement and displayed singular "moral courage" in confronting the Governor over the issue. He had also promoted "democratic" policies such as universal suffrage, removing the squatters' land monopoly, ending state support for religious denominations and setting up national schools. Following his unanimous endorsement, James addressed the assembly, his slogan, "the people are the sources of all power".[97] He was elected unopposed on 24th January 1855. At the post-election meeting, Parkes remarked on James's election, "I can only say that I congratulate you on the soundness of the choice you have this day made. You will never have occasion to regret the decision". The words of Parkes appeared in the *Empire* on the page announcing the departure of FitzRoy.[98] Wilshire, Lang, Parkes and others presented the new governor, Sir William Denison, with a petition which asked him to dissolve the Legislative Council because it approved the unpopular Constitution Bill.[99]

At the post-election meeting, Henry Parkes remarked his colleague of seven or eight years, James Robert Wilshire, "had denied to himself his ordinary relaxation and pleasures of his own fireside in order to help promote the general interest of the country".[100] Those deprived of his company, Sarah and his nine children including Louisa Alma Wilshire born in February 1855. The family saw even less of him with the buildings in George Street under construction. James confirmed the windows were on site when questioned on his attitude to free trade during the election campaign. He was asked, "Did he send to England for sash windows instead of getting them made in the colony"?[101] To help finance the project, James sold for £315 an allotment at Darling Harbour, his other two were Sarah's wedding gift. On the other hand, James and Austin found £150 to pay cousin, Alfred Eyre, for his land in Union Lane.[102] Also the Wilshires decided to sell three allotments in the town of Parramatta, the 500 acres in the Bathurst district, and the nine farms near Salt Pan Creek. Again division of the family property caused dispute. In the Equity Division of the Supreme Court on 18th July 1855, the Wilshire children, except William, filed a Bill of Complaint which challenged the right of nephew Thomas William Faithfull Wilshire to the share of his father, Thomas Matcham Pitt Wilshire. Henry Brown, headmaster of the City Grammar School, was guardian of Thomas during the court case. The court awarded Thomas an eighth share of his grandfather's property. The Certificate of Partition was not issued until October 1858.[103]

On 22nd October 1855, George Faithfull, son of Susannah and William Faithfull, died at 41 on the Oxley Plains, near Wangaratta, "deservedly regretted by all who know him".[104] He did not make a will. His estate of £20,000 included the farm at Jordan Hill and acreage at Wangaratta and much property in Melbourne. Those benefiting from his estate were brother William Pitt Faithfull, sister Alice Gibson, and nephew Thomas William Faithfull Wilshire, son of late half-sister, Helen Eliza Wilshire, née Faithfull.[105]

In December 1855 news reached Sydney that Queen Victoria had approved the Constitution Bill giving New South Wales control over its domestic affairs through an elected Legislative Assembly and an appointed Legislative Council. Called responsible government, the term describes a political system in which the cabinet and ministry hold office subject to the sanction and control of the Parliament. In turn, the Parliament is accountable to the people through elections.[106] James Robert Wilshire campaigned for one of four Sydney seats; his political statement released on 14th January. He asked for support based on his past performance of public duties and his participation in events where important principles were at stake. He reminded voters of his early advocacy of liberal views, fearlessly expressed and acted on. For example, he worked to extend the franchise, end transportation and stop the land monopoly. More recently, he opposed undesirable features in the Constitution Bill, the nominated upper house, the two-thirds majority required in both houses to alter the constitution, the clause excluding clergymen and the "extravagant pensions" granted to retiring officers in the previous administration. If elected, James promised to reform land policy and reinstate elections for the city council (achieved in 1857).[107] He was one of four "fit and proper" persons endorsed to represent the city at a public meeting on 23rd January. James thanked the meeting for associating his name with the other three, Henry Parkes, Charles Cowper, son of clergyman William Cowper, and Robert Campbell, son of merchant and shipowner Robert Campbell, all members of the previous parliament.[108]

Dubbed "the bunch", the four campaigned as a group, a tactic devised by Lang. The clegyman planned to get the four "honest" and "liberal" men elected by defeating the Attorney General, John Hubert Plunkett, "a consistent supporter of bad government" according to Cowper. The four met in the Exchange hotel on the corner of Margaret and George Streets, where, from their committee room on the first floor, they addressed supporters on the street below. James was "very ill" and unable to attend the meeting of followers on 10th March 1856.[109] Two days later at Hyde Park, Robert Stewart proposed James as a candidate. In the forties Stewart first noticed James, "acting for thousands of starving people in the city". James had begged the government to open the closed public works and supported an increase of 6d in workers' wages.[110] Brother William Pitt Wilshire backed Plunkett, while brother-in-law Henry Whittell supported James.[111] On 13th March "the bunch" won the four Sydney seats, James overtaking Plunkett by 101 votes to place fourth. James said it was "impossible for him to express his grateful sense of the honour conferred upon him... He had lost many friends, but he gained others". After the official results were declared at Hyde Park on 20th, the four returned to the Exchange Hotel to thank their supporters. Owing to lameness, James took his gig, while the others walked arm-in-arm. It seems James had suffered a stroke.[112] On December 19th, Henry returned the £115 James paid for his assets at his final insolvency meeting. The next day Henry sold Esther's land in Union Lane for £264.[113]

William Pitt Faithfull and Robert Pitt Jenkins were appointed to the Legislative Council for five years on 13th May 1856.[114] William

Warren Jenkins declined the offer of a seat in the Upper House because he "had clear and decided views on all political questions... but... had neither taste nor inclination for the stormy atmosphere of the politician".[115] The Legislative Council occupied a prefabricated iron church, imported from Glasgow, hastily erected on the southern side of the north wing of the hospital in Macquarie Street. The Legislative Assembly took over the chamber on the north side used by the original Legislative Council.[116] The present New South Wales Parliament incorporates these buildings.

Crowds of eager spectators gathered to watch Parliament open at noon on Thursday 22nd May 1856. The *Sydney Morning Herald* confirmed the presence of William Pitt Faithfull, Robert Pitt Jenkins and James Robert Wilshire on that momentous day. Their families received invitations. The afternoon began with signing the roll and swearing the oath of allegiance. Next, the President of the Upper House, Sir Alfred Stephen, addressed both houses in the new chamber. Once the Legislative Assembly elected speaker Daniel Cooper on 23rd, Governor Sir William Denison spoke to the parliamentarians.[117] When the Legislative Assembly met in the late afternoon of 23rd, Parkes hoped to discuss a petition tabled by Plunkett's supporters who claimed the four city members gained most of their votes by "illegal, fraudulent, and unconstitutional means". Plunkett withdrew the petition, but Parkes, sure no evidence of wrongdoing would emerge, felt the matter warranted investigation.[118] Staggered election days and plural voting enabled Plunkett to win Argyle and Bathurst.[119]

While electioneering, James Robert Wilshire filed a case for trial in the Equity division of the Supreme Court. He challenged directors, E. Knox, Clark Irving and Ralph Robey, to answer for the financial affairs of the Australian Sugar Company's sugar works and offices in Canterbury, Liverpool Street, and Parramatta Road. The judge considered only the Canterbury premises as the directors used their own funds to buy the other two establishments. The company's troubles began in 1843-4 when the directors engaged in share dealings designed to avoid insolvency. James refused to give up his share or contribute to the company. The judge found the directors "dealt with the shares of the company in a way unwarranted by the deed of settlement, and in a way in which... they derived advantages which the other shareholders... did not share". On 8th April Justice Roger Therry ruled James had a right to 1/125th of the company's assets from principal actors Ralph Robey and Clark Irving. But he pointed out the case with its "mass of documentary evidence", much of it "calculated to embarrass" rather than to "aid inquiry", cost much more than the sum contested.[120]

In a break from parliamentary duties in July 1856, William Pitt Faithfull entertained Daniel Henry Deniehy, orator, writer, barrister, and radical politician. Deniehy's favourable impressions of Springfield follow. William took his gig to Goulburn to collect Deniehy who spent three nights and two days "very pleasantly" in William's "magnificient domain". The men enjoyed each other's company, "Walking together over the hills and spacious plains of lordly Springfield, we spoke together even about his most private affairs as though we had known each other twenty years". William impressed Deniehy, "Faithfull is a grand specimen of an Australian, built on a scale of giant proportions, but with a mind honest, simple and gentle as a child's". Deniehy's description of William's personality was widely endorsed.[121] Eldest son, 11 year-old Percy Faithfull, was "one of the noblest looking children" Deniehy had ever seen. William's heart was "entirely wrapped up in having his children mentally cultivated; they had hitherto enjoyed the rare blessings of a home education, the grandest training of all, from their mother and aunt". The Deane women were "ladies in the truest sense of the word, cultured, amiable, and kind, and though each has the reputation of being as proud as Juno, I got on with them charmingly".[122] Hostess Mary had four young children under five, Reginald Faithfull born in January 1850, Florence Faithfull in November 1851, Robert Lionel in February 1853 and Augustus Lucian Faithfull in April 1855.

Robert Pitt Jenkins surrendered the lease on Bangus in 1856 after using his pre-emptive right to buy 173 acres surrounding the inn for £1 an acre. The next year he sold the inn on 2 acres for £900.[123] In 1858 Robert increased Bomballa to 6500 acres by paying £1566 for 1740 acres from the estate of Dr Patrick Hill. He also sold the house at Eagle Vale and 608 acres for £2500.[124] Louisa and Robert had seven children, following the births of Augustus Patrick Jenkins in September 1855 and Warren William Jenkins in October 1857. (The name of Robert's youngest son suggests Robert's brother, William Warren Jenkins, was known as "Warren". The directories of the 1830s also list him as "W. Warren Jenkins".[125]) With its beautiful grounds of stately English trees, a profusion of camellias, and a large orchard "stocked with the choicest fruit-trees", Bomballa provided a beautiful setting for the family.[126]

Meanwhile, William Pitt Wilshire displayed seven pictures at the third exhibition of the Society for the Promotion of Fine Arts held at the Sydney School of Mechanics in January 1857. He exhibited an *Aboriginal woman*, speaker of the Legislative Assembly *Sir Daniel Cooper*, Roman noblewoman *Beatrice Cenci* (after Zucarelli?), *Laughing Boy* (after Frans Hals?), *Cottage Girl* (after Thomas Gainsborough?) and two of artist *Sir Joshua Reynolds*. James Robert Wilshire lent the exhibition his portrait by Richard Noble.[127] In July William's brothers and cousins received recognition for their talent, magistrates dispensing the law. Those appointed were James Robert Wilshire, Austin Forrest Wilshire, Joseph Wood Wilshire, William Pitt Faithfull, Robert Pitt Jenkins and William Warren Jenkins.[128]

On 22nd December 1857 James Robert Wilshire and his political allies met their constituents at the Prince of Wales Hotel. Parkes had resigned his seat in December to give full attention to his newspaper the *Empire*. William Bede Dalley, an impressive young man of Irish parents, replaced Parkes. The meeting was rowdy and unruly. Cowper, twice premier during the parliamentary session, spoke with difficulty. (Incidentally, Andrew Gibson's executor, Stuart Alexander Donaldson, was the first premier but Cowper defeated him after about 11 weeks.) Dalley followed Cowper with "a long and desultory speech". Third and fourth speakers, Campbell and Wilshire, retired after struggling to address the assembly.[129] The *Sydney Morning Herald* taunted James Robert Wilshire. "Alas, poor Robert! ... the idol of the multitude, where is he? Mr Wilshire might expect that no Public Assembly where the Irish were in any force would forget him."[130] Was James called "Robert" to distinguish him from his father?

Once again James Robert Wilshire and three colleagues campaigned to capture the Sydney seats. The four set up headquarters in the Criterion Hotel on the corner of King and Castlereagh Streets.[131] James met his supporters at the Friendship Fountain in Brickfield-Hill where he announced his policies, equalising electoral districts and further changes to the land laws.[132] At a gathering in Hyde Park to select candidates, Mr B. James proposed James Robert Wilshire. Having known James Robert for 15 or 16 years, the proposer thought him a man of "independence, integrity and consistency".[133] On 5th January 1858 eight candidates contested four seats, Cowper placing third, Campbell fourth, Dalley fifth and James seventh. The *Empire* remarked, "the extraordinary result... admits of no popular interpretation whatever". Predictably, the defeat delighted the conservative *Sydney Morning Herald*, "the hideous Bunch... has been finally demolished".[134]

On 23rd March 1858, on the advice of the Executive Council, the Governor appointed James Robert Wilshire and four others to the Legislative Council.[135] The five were introduced to the parliament in April. To the delight of James, the Cowper ministry had launched the Electoral Law Amendment Act. The bill gave almost all adult males over 21 the right to vote, introduced the secret vote, and changed electoral boundaries to more closely match the population, although the pastoral vote was worth twice the urban vote. Strong opposition from some in the upper house delayed the Bill until 24th November 1858.[136] In the previous June, James became a trustee of the Savings Bank of New South Wales.[137]

James Robert Wilshire put politics aside to partition Wilshire Place in October 1858. James claimed the largest building, plus the rest of Louisa's property, Austin Forrest Wilshire the two smaller buildings.[138] (Figure 27) The two had accounts to pay. Austin sold two properties at Darling Harbour, one to Henry Whittell for £786.[139] James mortgaged Wilshire Place and Louisa's property for £5000.[140] Surprisingly, in June 1857 James had borrowed £3000 to buy a house on nearly an acre at Potts Point beside Elizabeth Bay, not far from his first home.[141] Sarah gave birth to Robert Pitt Wilshire in Pitt Street in February 1857 and Esther Phoebe Wilshire at Potts Point in January 1859.

Financially secure by the fifties, William Pitt Faithfull enlarged his estate and built a stately home. He purchased about 3290 acres in his own parish of Mangamore and the adjoining parishes of Terranna, Qualigo and Gundary. Most of the 30 to 569 acre lots cost £1 an acre.[142] While visiting his two stations in the Ovens district in January 1857, William "met with rather a severe accident... slipped and fell on his hip, which received such injury as to cause considerable lameness".[143] Jeremiah Rogers managed Brewarrena. When Rogers completed 25 years of service in 1878, William gave him 6883 acres at the back of the squat.[144] Between 1858 and 1860 William built an "Italianate Villa" at Springfield.[145] (Figure 28) The villa was home to nine children including Constance Mary Faithfull born in July 1857 and Frances Lilian Faithfull in June 1859. Remarkably, all the Faithfull children survived. Although William hoped to safeguard his children's "purity by obtaining a polished domestic tutor", his four older boys attended the King's

School.[146] And Monty, if not his brothers, studied at Reverend W.H. Savigny's Collegiate School at the Cook's River.[147]

Alice Gibson invested in more land in the mid to late fifties. In County King she purchased 3 lots, 31 acres at Gibson's Big Flat for £1 an acre, and 34½ acres and 35 acres for £117.[148] In County Argyle Alice bought land in three locations. At the reserve for the village of Tirrannaville, seven small parcels amounting to 36½ acres cost her £150. On one of these allotment she built a church in memory of Andrew.[149] North of Tirranna, 45 acres and 98 acres, three roods, cost her £215 17s 6d.[150] And near the Tirranna Racecourse, she paid £1 an acre for 63 acres and 110 acres, three roods.[151] Alice kept the leases for Bland and Boga Bogalong, and won the tender for the Mugga Swamp in the Lachlan district in 1858.[152] Two more children of Alice had married, Susannah Jane Gibson to Richard Blomfield in February 1855 and Thomas Jamieson Faithfull Gibson to Josephine Lett in February 1859. In July 1856, James Donaldson, husband of eldest child, Alice Jemima, died of a severe cold complicated by "inflammation of

Figure 28. Springfield House

9 Untimely Deaths

the kidneys". A fever he suffered in California some years earlier left him weak. James, formerly an agent of the General Screw Company's steamships, "was a man of singular amiability and kindness".[153]

George Matcham Pitt launched a stock agency in 1858. First, he bought an auctioneer's licence.[154] Second, in tandem with Thomas Sullivan, he leased three runs in the Wellington district, Garagary 22,400 acres, Gunningbar 16,000 acres and Wamerawa 16,000 acres, though he surrendered Lower Gerawhey.[155] Third, he paid £665 for 67 acres close to Fullager's saleyards, on the Western Road at today's Blacktown.[156] Fourth, after giving Julia 53 acres in the Windsor district and 1 rood and 30 perches in Richmond town to replace her marriage gift, he sold the properties, the first in 1859 for £74, the second in 1860 for £20.[157] In September 1857 George and Lewis Duncan Whitaker lent Gwydir squatter Francis Townsend Rusden £5000 for five years, the loan secured with Bangheet squat and 3000 cattle. George would regret the loan although Rusden redeemed it in 1860.[158] Julia finished her family with the births of Colin Pitt in October 1851, Charles Bryan Pitt in March 1854, Frederick Septimus Pitt in March 1856, who died in April, and Eva Laura Pitt in May 1857. Eldest son, George Matcham Pitt, qualified as a Licensed Surveyor in February 1859.[159] In December, the month before George the younger married Elizabeth Town, his father gave him 19½ perches in Lennox Street, Richmond. He paid £56 for the allotment in 1856.[160] The couple made their home at Sunnyside in North Richmond. Second son, Edwin Pitt, attended The Kings School from 1856 to 1859.[161]

At Trafalgar Sarah Pitt had a "narrow escape" from death in the "prime of her life". On picking up a piece of wood, a snake bit her hand. To treat the snakebite, Robert used the methods adopted by the Aborigines, but in sucking the poison from Sarah's wound, his own body became infected and "he was in a more precarious state" than his wife. The sound teeth and gums of the black people prevented the poison entering their bodies. Although a doctor attended, the Aborigines' help "in a great measure saved their lives". You could not "meet a more jolly woman than Mrs Robert Pitt". Robert was "very cheerful", "good-natured", "genial" and "strictly honorable in his dealings with either great or small". A "noted pedestrian", he "would think nothing of walking 40 miles a day".[162]

The couple completed their family with the births of Henry Pitt in 1851, Thomas Matcham Pitt in September 1853, Robert Essington Pitt in December 1855, George Wilshire Pitt in April 1858, Clara Elizabeth Pitt in July 1860, and Ada Mary Pitt in July 1864. Ada, their 10th child, died aged 14 months.

At Putty Mary Matcham Laycock gave birth to her last two children, Mary Matcham Laycock in April 1855 and George Laycock in November 1858. Like Sarah Pitt, Mary had a tenth child who died in infancy. At the race meetings in Richmond, husband Thomas and three others put £50 apiece on a race, the winner taking the lot. Often away droving, Thomas bought stock for "the men in Sydney". A "horse fancier", Thomas owned some fine mares.[163]

Once Wollongong became a municipality in February 1859, William Warren Jenkins's term as warden ended. He had performed his duties, "which embraced a great deal in regard to roads and other matters", with "considerable vigour and public usefulness".[164] Justice of the Peace, Joseph Wood Wilshire, campaigned for the new Wollongong Council. He improved his chance of election by attending district meetings, one conducted by the Wollongong branch of the British and Foreign Bible Society chaired by William Warren Jenkins, and another called to examine the possibility of a new steamer for Wollongong.[165] Joseph asked for support based on his long residence in the district and the attention given to his duties as magistrate.[166] He adopted the political slogan, "economy in our expenditure, with due regard to efficiency".[167] On 29th March 1859 fifteen competed for nine places, Joseph placing sixth.[168]

Following the election he joined the committee formed to consider all matters concerning the wharf.[169] At Garden Hill Anne gave birth to Edith Annie Wilshire in August 1856, Ernest Henry Wilshire in February 1858 and John Matcham Wilshire in June 1859. Garden Hill proved too costly. By 1858 Joseph had sold 178 acres in four parcels for nearly £4300.[170] He also raised a further mortgage on his properties in Pitt and George Streets.[171]

Alice, eldest child of Louisa and Robert Pitt Jenkins, stayed with a great aunt in Paris to finish her education. In June 1859, about a year after Alice arrived in Paris, the aunt informed Robert and Louisa a revolution might develop. Following this news, the couple planned to meet their daughter in London, then tour the Continent. Before leaving, Warren William Jenkins, not yet two, died on 1st August. Robert sent William Warren Jenkins his overseas address, his letter mentioning his despondency over his son's death as well as his fear of the sea voyage.[172] Robert and William Pitt Faithfull witnessed the scene after the *Dunbar* crashed into the cliffs near the Gap on the night of 20th August 1857 with the loss of all but one of the 120-125 passengers and crew. At daylight citizens watched bodies "being washed to and fro in the ledges of the rocks".[173]

On 16th August 1859 Robert Pitt Jenkins made his will, his executors brother William, friend William Pitt Faithfull and brotherin-law William Edmond Plunkett.[174] The same day port authorities cleared the steamer *Telegraph* for its trip to Melboume.[175] Intending to travel in the mail steamer Salsette, Robert heard the *Royal Charter* took only 59 days on its passage from Liverpool to Melbourne. On the upper deck at the stem of the *Royal Charter*, he paid for two cabins separated by a bathroom. Just before the ship sailed, William received letter in which Robert described the *Royal Charter* as a "truly magnificent vessel".[176] (Figure 29) On 26th August, under the command of Thomas Taylor, the 2719 ton, fast, luxurious, iron-hulled steam clipper departed for Liverpool with a cargo of gold, copper, hides and wool. The passengers, numbering about

404, included Robert, Louisa, Robert, 13, Herbert, 10, Ernest, 8, Alfred,6 and Augustus, 4.

After 58 days at sea, the *Royal Charter* approached Queenstown in the Cove of Cork (Cobh) on Monday morning 24th October. A pilot ship put ashore about 14 passengers and collected letters addressed to relatives. Around 1.30 pm the ship left the coast of Ireland with about 390 passengers and a crew of about 112, the captain promising to have them in Liverpool within 24 hours. (Figure 30) Tuesday 25th October dawned grey and bleak touched by a light but favourable wind. Close to Bardsley Island off the Caernarvon coast, eleven riggers transferred to the clipper from steam tug *United Kingdom*. By 1.30 pm the *Royal Charter* was abreast of Holyhead, a small island off the west-coast of Anglesey Island. A strange haze hung over the land and the sky looked strange. Unknown to the people on the *Royal Charter*, a tempest had struck Devon and Cornwall. The wind freshened during the afternoon, and with most of its sails stowed, the vessel progressed slowly northward. About 6.00 pm the ship rounded the north-west corner of Anglesey. Attempts to secure a pilot were unsuccessful. Conditions deteriorated as *Royal Charter* moved along the north coast of the island. In the gale-force winds and mountainous seas, the 200 horsepower auxiliary engine of the *Royal Charter* had little impact. By then several passengers were anxious. The captain took charge of events on the deck at 8.45 pm. At 9.00 pm the ship passed the north-east corner of Anglesey. The wind changed direction from South-East to East-North-East at 10.00 pm. By 11.00 pm a hurricane had developed and, thereafter, the ship was out of control.

The only chance of preventing the ship being driven on to the coast of Anglesey was to anchor. Released at 11.00 pm, the port anchor broke under the strain at 1.30 am. The starboard anchor, freed at 2.30 am, also snapped. Some first-class passengers tried to sleep. Others, reassurred by the captain, stayed in the saloon. About 3.00 am on Wednesday 26th October, the captain decided to

9 Untimely Deaths

Figure 29. *Royal Charter*

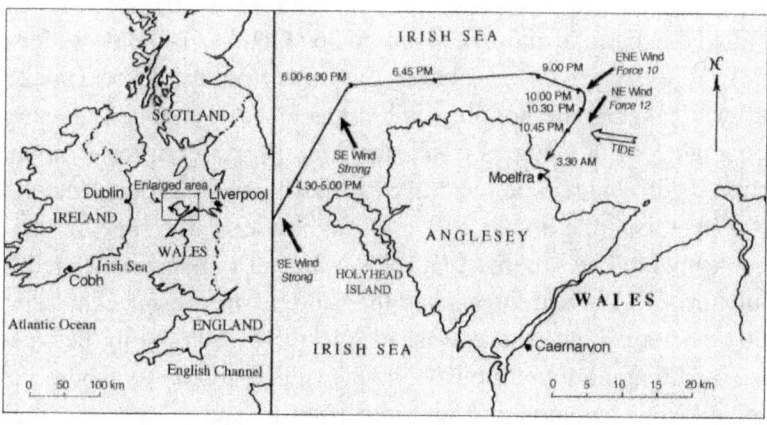

Figure 30. Route of the *Royal Charter* 25-26th October 1859

reduce resistance by cutting down the three tall masts. He ordered passengers to stay below out of harm's way. At 3.30 am, with the mainmast nearly cut away, conditions forced the ship on to a sandy beach north of the village of Moelfra on the east coast of Anglesey. A pronounced shudder and thump shook the whole frame of the ship, throwing the passengers off balance. It took an hour to topple the foremast which fell into the sea about 4.30 am. Before work started on the mizenmast, the top half fell, making a hole in the deckhead of the saloon. From then on, waves washing over the deck entered the ship and drenched the frightened passengers. With the deck breached, the water washed passengers into the sea. Conditions on the ship were appalling:

> *The sounds of the distress signals, the crashing as the masts were hacked away, the violent pounding of the ship on the ground, the lurching that sent the passengers reeling and staggering, and the water that came in through broken skylights and the holes in the deckhead, produced terrible scenes below, particularly among the families with small and helpless children.*

When dawn broke about 6.00 am on 26th October 1859, passengers noticed the *Royal Charter* barely 25 yards from the shore. Breaker after breaker, some possibly as high as 60 feet, pounded the ship. Seaman Joseph Rodgers, swept back and forth between ship and shore, got a light line ashore with the help of the local people. Rodgers used the line to pull across a hawser (large rope or small cable), which he secured to a rock. A bosun's chair was rigged to the hawser. A few crew reached the shore by the bosun's chair, but 60 or 70 awaiting rescue washed into the sea. Probably between 6.30-7.00 am, a tumultuous wave drove the ship on to submerged rocks. Many women and children tried to swim ashore in their heavy clothing. Then the ship broke in two. Scores of passengers lost their lives: some fell into the chasm; many were swept into the sea; and others jumped overboard.

9 Untimely Deaths

About 39 men survived, mainly those staying on the ship. Few drowned; rocks or floating pieces of wreckage fatally injured most passengers. The two enquiries held in November cleared the design of the ship, and the captain, who did not survive. A gale of "unexampled fury" caused the wreck.[177]

In England to tour the Continent, William James Robert Jenkins, eldest son of William Warren and Matilda Jenkins, awaited the arrival of his relatives. With no address for his cousin, William found Alice on his second day in Paris. She already knew of her great loss. From Brighton on 17th November 1859, William wrote to tell his father he had spent three harrowing days at Moelfra trying to identify the bodies and belongings of his relativys. He found nothing.

News of the wreck reached Sydney in January 1860. William Pitt Wilshire composed a poem lamenting the loss of the Jenkins' family. It read, in part:

> *Far on a hill, where the hush'd winds are still,*
> *Fair forms of children once frolic'd at will,*
> *And a mansion is there, with gardens fair,*
> *And mother and sire dwelt happily there.*
> *Notes of sweet music oft gladden'd that home,*
> *But the harp in the hall now stands alone;*
> *The strings of the lyre will be heard no more.*[178]

A servant chaperoned Alice on the ship sailing *Donald McKay* which arrived in Sydney in March 1861.[179] Alice lived in Sydney with her Plunkett relatives. She inherited her father's estate of £60,000, including 6509 acres near Marulan, 1645 acres at Charleyong, premises in Sydney in O'Connell (2 lots) and Macquarie Streets (4 lots), 500 acres near Parramatta, 173 acres at Adelong, and 100 acres at Cooks River.[180]

Figure 31. Matilda Pitt Wilshire Jenkins

Figure 32. William Warren Jenkins

Life moved on for William Warren and Matilda Pitt Jenkins. (Figures 31 & 32) Matilda had completed the family with the birth of tenth child Alfred Matcham Jenkins in September 1857. In 1860 the couple built a second storey on their hilltop home.[181] (Figure 33) To help fund the addition Matilda sold her property at Darling Harbour to Henry Whittell for £790 in June 1859.[182] A "magnificent estate", Berkeley extended from the base of the Kembla or Round Mountain on the west to Lake Illawarra on the south.[183] William shared his good fortune by giving away five parcels of land on Berkeley. One example, the acre he provided for a Presbyterian School. By 1851 the school had begun with William on the School Board and a school-inspector. In 1861 the Presbyterian Minister paid William 40s for the land on which he built a church.[184] A second example, the two acres and subscription of £50 William donated in 1856 for a school in present Lake Heights. That year

Figure 33. Berkeley House

in July, supporters of the temporary school petitioned the Board of National Education for assistance to build a permanent school and schoolhouse. Meanwhile, the residents of the Berkeley and Five Island Estates raised £400 to erect a school with the help of a grant from the Board of National Education. Berkeley Public School opened in January 1858 with William on the School Board. The school operates to this day in George Street, Berkeley.[185] A third gift, the acre contributed for a Church of England and burial ground on Berkeley in March 1862.[186] Other causes benefiting from William's charity, the Irish Famine Fund, the Patriotic Fund for the relief of War Widows and Orphans from the Crimean War, the Manchester Operatives' Fund Relief and the Indian Relief Movement.[187]

In the 1850s the Pitt Family experienced at least 25 deaths. At 75 Lucy Wood's death was timely and the 11 infant deaths typical of the period. Untimely deaths included Sophia and Samuel Henry, Thomas Matcham Pitt Wilshire, George Pitt and Elizabeth Wood, George Faithfull, Robert and Louisa Jenkins and their five sons, Robert, Herbert, Ernest, Alfred, and Augustus. On a brighter note, the grandsons participated in the governance of the colony. William Pitt Faithfull, William Warren Jenkins, James Robert Wilshire and Joseph Wood Wilshire, served on their local councils as wardens and aldermen. James Robert Wilshire, William Pitt Faithfull and Robert Pitt Jenkins were members of the first self-government in New South Wales.

1	Clark, C.M.H. *Select Documents in Australian History 1851-1900*, Angus and Robertson, Sydney, 1962, pp1,515-6; Clark, C.M.H. *Select Documents in Australian History 1788-1850*, Angus and Robertson, Sydney, 1962, p377-8
2	Cathcart, Michael, *Manning Clark's History of Australia*, Melbourne University Press, Victoria, 1993, p234; Clark 1955, p94
3	*Goulburn Herald* 12 January 1850, p6a
4	GG 1849, Vol 2, p1167, 7 Aug
5	SMH 24 March 1850, p1d
6	SMH 3 May 1850, p1d; SMH 29 June 1850, Suppl., p1c, SMH 13 July

1850, p1c. Kerr, Joan, *The Dictionary of Australian Artists*, Melbourne, Oxford University Press, Melbourne, 1992, p862

7   SMH 8 June 1850, p3f
8   SMH 11 June 1850, p3e; SMH 12 June 1850, p3c
9   SMH 7 June 1850, p2f
10   SMH 30 April 1850, p1d; SMH 16 July 1850, p3b; SMH 4 May 1850, p1c
11   SMH 28 June 1850, p3g; SMH; 29 June 1850, Suppl., p1c
12   SMH 2 July 1850, p1e; SMH 9 July 1850 p1d,e
13   SMH 7 August 1850, pp2b-3d; SMH 15 August 1850, pp2b-3b; SMH 22 August 1850, pp2b-3b; SMH 24 August 1850, p1d; SMH 26 August 1850, p3d
14   SMH 28 August 1850, p3d,e
15   SMH 9 August 1850, p3a,b
16   SMH 10 August 1850, p3e
17   SMH 13 August 1850, pp2b-3a
18   SMH 16 September 1850, pp1c,7c; SMH 17 September 1850, p1d; SMH 18 September 1850, pp2,3,6a-d,7; SMH 24 September 1850, p1c
19   SMH 1 October 1850, p1d
20   SMH 7 September 1850, p1c; SMH 16 Sept 1850, p6
21   SMH 4 December 1850, 3b; SMH 6 Dec 1850, p3a
22   *Dalgety's Review*, 1 February 1905, Newscuttings File, Tirranna NSW, ML; Griffiths, Glynde, N., *Some Southern Homes of New South Wales*, Shepherd Press, 1976, National Trust of Australia, p53
23   SMH 9 January 1930, pp12-3
24   Bk 86, No 200, DL; County Argyle, Parish Terranna, 5th ed, Map 42, DL; Alice's 60 acres were part of the lo t with 140 acres; Bk 80, Nos 216-220, DL
25   GG 1852, Vol 2, p1616, 16 Oct; GG 1850, Vol 2, p1861, 20 Nov; GG 1850, Vol 2, p1325, 14Aug; GG 1851, Vol 1, p1009, 9 Jun
26   *Empire* 4 January 1851, p2d; Bk 21, No 504, DL; Bk 21, No 506, DL
27   Bk 21, No 115, DL
28   Bk 22, No 91, DL
29   SMH 14 September 1851, p7c; SMH 23 Sept 1851, p2f
30   SMH 7 November 1851, p1e; SMH 31 May 1850, p2a,b
31   *Empire* 8 December 1851, p3c,d; *Empire* 16 December 1851, p2e; GG 1851, Vol 2, pp1722-3, 1725, 25 Oct
32   *Bell's Life in Sydney and Sporting Review* 8 Nov 1851, p2b; *Empire* 13 December 1851, p1b; SMH 15 December 1851, p3b,c; SMH 16 December 1851, p2f
33   SMH 30 December 1851, p2e; SMH 31 December 1851, p2e
34   SMH 3 December 1851, p3g
35   SMH 31 August 1852, p3d; Gunson, Niel "The Deviations of a Missionary Family", Davidson, J.W. and Scarr, Deryck, eds., *Pacific Island Portraits*, Australian National University Press, Canberra, 1970,

ch 2, p43
36 *Papers of Rev J D Lang*, ML A 2226, CY 893, Vol 6, pp504-5; ADB 1, William Henry, resettled in Sydney in 1848
37 Gunson, 1970, ch 2, p40
38 SMH 1 April 1852, p3c
39 Thomas M. P., Wilshire, Mutch Index
40 GG 1852 Vol 1, p526, 23 Mar; Registers of Copies of Wills 1800-1901, SAG Will 1/2377
41 Legal Documents of Minter and Simpson and Co., Abstract of Title of Trustees of Thomas William Faithfull Wilshire, ML MSS UNCAT, Item 141A, re JWW guardian of TWFW
42 See first item at Ref 40
43 JRAHS 7, 1921, Vol 7, Part 11, p102
44 SMH 31 March 1852, Suppl., p4a
45 Mossman, Samuel and Bannister, Thomas, *Australia Visited and Revisited*, London 1853, pp187-8
46 NSW Legislative Assembly, Hansard and Papers, Gundagai Flood Sesquicentenary, 25 June 2002
47 SMH 8 July 1852, p2b,c
48 *Goulburn Herald* 6 Aug 1853, p2g
49 Bk 21, No 969, DL; Bk 22, No 322, DL; Bk 22, No 323, DL
50 *Empire* 29 June 1852, p1442; *Empire* 7 July 1852, p 1170 b,c
51 *Empire* 15 July 1852, pp1198e, 1199a; *Empire* 22 July 1852, p1222d,e; *Empire* 2 Aug 1852, p1260 a,b
52 NSW Legislative Council, Votes and Proceedings, 1852, 2, frs 1107-1173
53 Registers of Copies of Wills 1800-1901, SAG Will 1/2803
54 GG 1854, Vol 2, p165, 19 Jan
55 Empire 3 April 1856, pp4-5; Bk 24, Nos 805, 806, 862 DL; Bk 25, No 453, DL; Bk 26, No 865, DL; Bk 36, No 16 DL; Bk 36, No 17, DL
56 LA, V&P, 1865, 2, frs 837-8; Bk 77, No 438, DL
57 Bk 61, No 984, DL; SMH 8 September 1928, p13g, re stone buildings
58 Bk 26, No 516, DL; Bk 26, No 517, DL
59 Ford, W. & F, *Sydney Commercial Directory 1851*, Facsimile, Library of Australian History, North Sydney, 1978, p153
60 Bk 36, No 15, DL; Bk 45, No 128, DL
61 Bk 25, No 218, DL; Bk 25, No 217, DL; Bk 19, No 761, DL; Bk 25, No 307, DL
62 Reg 16, No 190, DL; Bk 18, Nos 698, 699, DL
63 SMH 17 August 1850, p5f,g; SMH 31 Dec 1853, p3e; Ford, W & F, 1978, p150
64 Bk 18, No 459, DL; Bk 20, No 538, DL; Bk 25, No 759, DL
65 SMH 4 August 1853, p2e,f,g; *Empire* 4 August 1853, pp2594g-2595
66 *Empire* 16August 1853, pp2634-5 a-d; *Empire* 17 August 1853, p2638be; SMH 18 August 1853, p1e
67 *Empire* 7 September 1853, pp2710b-22712b-f; SMH 4 August 1853,

	p2e-g
68	SMH 7 September 1853, p2d, e
69	Bride, Thomas F., *Letters from Victorian Pioneers*, Trustees of the Public Library of Victoria, Melbourne 1898, p222
70	Despatches from the Governor of Victoria, Jan-Dec 1852, MLA2341, CY 1492, p725
71	*Windsor and Richmond Gazette* 26 August 1893, p4c
72	Registers of Copies of Wills 1800-1901, SAG Will 1/2771
73	SMH 21 January 1851, p3b
74	GG 1853, Vol 2, p1333, 5 Aug 1853
75	Bk 35, No 184, DL
76	Bk 33, No 364, DL
77	SMH 19 October 1853, pp4,5
78	Bk 31, No 324, DL
79	Bk 173, No 764, DL, See for WPW owning the 640 acres
80	Bk 26, No 901, DL
81	*Empire* 14 November 1854, pp1f, 2d; Paris Exhibition Commissioner, Catalogue of the Natural and Industrial Products of New South Wales, Sydney 1854, Reading and Wellbank, Sydney 1855, p79
82	Kerr, 1992, p862; SMH 7 February 1856, p4c,d; *Illustrated Sydney News* 21 April 1855, p185a
83	*Goulburn Herald* 8 July 1854, p1b; *Goulburn Herald* 11 July 1857, pp5-6
84	County Wynyard, Parish Baugus, 7th ed., Map 3, DL
85	Bk 36, No 939, DL; Bk 37, Nos 786-88, DL; Bk 38, No 365, DL; Bk 39, No 523, DL; Bk 39, No 541, DL; *Goulburn Herald* 11 February 1854, 3c
86	Bk 39, No 83, DL
87	Bk 28, No 422, DL
88	Smith, Alfred, *Some Ups and Downs of an Old Richmondite*, Nepean Family History Society, Emu Plains, 1991, p89
89	Bk 32, No 171, DL
90	Bk 32, No 724, DL; Bk 34, No 346, DL
91	GG 1854, Vol 2, p2083, 11 Sept
92	LA, V&P, 1859/60, 3, p664
93	*Empire* 3 Nov 1853, p2931 b,c; SMH 27 January 1855, p5b; SMH 10 February 1855, p3e
94	GG 1854, Vol 2, p2498, 4 Dec; GG 1857, Vol 2, p1789, 1 July; GG 1858, Vol 2, p1598, 31 Dec 1857; GG 1862, Vol 1, pp1153-4, 31 Dec 1860
95	Smith, Alfred, 1991, pp5, 689
96	*Empire* 19 December 1854, p4d
97	*Empire* 9 January 1855, p1e; *Empire* 11 Januaiy 1855, pp4e-5a
98	*Empire* 24 Jan 1855, pp4,5
99	*Empire* 2 February 1855, p1d, 4b,c; *Empire* 7 February 1855, pp4e-5; SMH 7 February 1855, pp4d,e-5a-d
100	*Empire* 11 Jan 1855, p4g

101 Bk 61, No 984, DL; *Empire* 11 April 1855, p5a
102 Bk 34, No 115, Bk 70, No 60; Bk 39, No 38, DL
103 Supreme Court of NSW, Equity, SRNSW 3/3674, No 1182; *Empire* 8 Jan 1855, p1e
104 *Argus* 26 October 1855, p4e
105 Supreme Court of Victoria, Administration, 1/844
106 Cathcart, 1993, Bk 4, ch 5, pp273-5; Clark, 1962, Item 10, p353 http://australianpolitics.com/democracy/terms/responsiblegovernment.shtml;
107 *Empire* 15 Jan 1856, p2d
108 SMH 24 Jan 1856, pp4d-5, 6d
109 SMH 16 January 1856, p6a; *Empire* 5 April 1856, pp4,5; *Empire* 11 March 1856, pp1d, 4d-f
110 *Empire* 13 March 1856, p6d-f; SMH 13 March 1856, pp3c-5c; SMH 14 March 1856, p4c,d
111 SMH 12 March 1856, p2b,c
112 *Empire* 21 March 1856, pp4c-5e, 6a,d; SMH 21 March 1856, pp4a-5d; Registers of Copies of Will 1800-1901, SAG Will 1/4876
113 Bk 47, No 469, DL; Bk 70, No 304, DL
114 GG 1856, Suppl., p1366, 13 May
115 *Illawarra Mercury* 3 June 1884, p2d
116 See Ref 136 in Chapter 8
117 SMH 20 May 1856, p4d,e; SMH 23 May 1856, pp2c-5b
118 SMH 24 May 1856, pp4,5,10; *Empire* 23 May 1856, pp2-4; GG 1856, Vol 1, p1232, 24 Apr
119 GG 1856, Vol 1, p1368, 13 May
120 Supreme Court of New South Wales, Equity, SRNSW 3/3653, No 1039
121 121 MacAlister, Charles, *Old Pioneering Days in the Sunny South*, 1907, p175
122 Martin, E. A., *Life and Speeches of Daniel Henry Deniehy*, George Robertson and Co. (Ltd), 1884, pp8-9
123 LA, V&P 1859, 3, p670; Bk 189, No 2, DL; Bk 52, No 971, DL
124 Bk 62, No 641, DL; *Goulburn Herald* 11 December 1858, p1f; County Camden, Parish of Bomballa, 6th ed., Map 10, DL. See Dr Hill's properties Bosworth and Glenshea; Bk 58, No 669, DL. The acreage sold by Robert at Eagle Vale exceeds Jemima's purchase in 1828 by more than 300 acres.
125 *New South Wales Calendar and General Post Office Directory 1834, 1835, 1837*, Stephens and Stokes, Sydney. See Directories
126 *Goulburn Herald* 2 November 1867, p5e
127 SMH 12 January 1857, p5c,d,e; Society for Promotion of Fine Arts in Australia, Fine Arts Exhibition at the Mechanics School of Arts, Sydney, Exhibition Catalogue for January 1857, The Empire General Steam Printing Office, Sydney, 1857, ML 707/S; Kerr, 1992, p862
128 GG 1857, Vol 2, pp1353-4, 1357, 1 Jul
129 SMH 22 December 1857, p4a,b; SMH 23 December 1857, pp4f-5d;

ADB 4, Donaldson
130 SMH 24 December 1857, p4a
131 SMH 1 January 1858, p1a
132 SMH 4 January 1858, p3a
133 SMH 15 January 1858, p3b, 4a
134 *Empire* 16 January 1858, p4b; SMH 16 January 1858, p4a,c
135 GG 1858, Vol 1, Suppl., p537, 23 Mar
136 SMH 10 April 1858, p8b,f; Clark, 1962 (1851-1900), Sec 3, ch iii, pp374-77
137 GG 1858, Vol 1, p927, 10 June
138 Bk 61, No 984, DL
139 Bk 62, No 395, DL; Bk 77, No 580, DL
140 Bk 58, No 997, DL
141 Bk 48, No 385, DL
142 GG 1850, p1192, 17 Jul; GG 1853, Vol 2, p 1384, 26 Jul; Bk 161, No 496, Nos 497-499, DL; Bk 167, Nos 1881-1884 DL; County Argyle, 1907, DL; County Argyle, Parish Mangamore, 4th ed. Map 22, DL; County Argyle, Parish Qualigo, 7th ed., Map 37, L/F; County Argyle, Parish Gundary, 6th ed., Map 16, DL
143 *Goulburn Herald* 17 Jan 1857, p4b
144 *Goulburn Herald* 6 June 1857, p5a; Gammage, Bill, Narrandera Shire, Gammage, 1986, ch 7,p82
145 *Springfield*, Meares and Associates, Sydney 2000, p2
146 Martin 1884, p9; Yeend, Peter, ed., *The King's School Parramatta*, Register 1831-1999, The Council of The King's School Parramatta, p153
147 Maxwell, Charles, F., *Australian Men of Mark*, Vol 2, Version 1, Melbourne 1889, Appendix, p2
148 Bk 122, No 3866, DL; GG 1855, Vol 1, p587, 2 Mar. This purchase is uncertain as the relevant lines were unclear
149 Bk 101, No s 119-125, DL; Griffiths, Glynde Nesta, *Some Southern Homes of New South Wales*, National Trust of Australia NSW, 1976, p54
150 Bk 107, No 76, DL; Bk 117, No 2631, DL
151 Bk 158, Nos 2669-70, DL
152 LA , V&P, 1859-60, 3, p666; GG 1858, Vol 1, p731, 3 May
153 SMH 22 July 1856, p4f
154 GG 1858, Vol 1, p180, 30 Jan
155 LA & VP, 1865-6, 3, frs 272-4; GG 1859, Vol 2, p2180, 1 Oct
156 Bk 58, No 920, DL; Keavey, Kay, "'The Boudoir' Had a Grand Piano", *The Australian Womens Weekly*, 25 March 1970, p12; Bk 90, No 416, DL; SMH 27 Aug 1861, pp17-8
157 Bk 144, No 1596, DL; Bk 63, No 276, DL; Bk 68, No 197, DL; GG 1859, Vol 2, p2001, 1 Sept
158 Bk 69, No 268, DL; GG 1858, Vol 1, p772, 10 May
159 GG 1859, Vol 1, p255, 1 Feb
160 Bk 43, No 620, DL; Bk 68, No 882, DL

161 Yeend,Peter, ed., *The Kings School Parramatta Register 1831-1999*, 3rd ed., The Council of The King's School Parramatta, 1999, p363
162 Broughton, Sam, and others, *Reminiscences of Richmond NSW*, c1905, pp 152, 154; Smith, Alfred, 1991, p126
163 Smith, Alfred, 1991, pp 106, 130
164 GG 1859, Vol 1, pp452-3, 22 Feb; *Illawarra Mercury* 3 June 1884, p2d
165 *Illawarra Mercury* 11 January 1858, p2d, *Illawarra Mercury* 18 January 1858, p2d
166 *Illawarra Mercury* 24 March 1859, p2c,d; *Illawarra Mercury* 11 January 1858, p3e
167 *Illawarra Mercury* 17 March 1859, p4d
168 *Illawarra Mercury* 31 March 1859, p2e
169 *Illawarra Mercury* 21 April 1859, p2d
170 Bk 43, No 580, DL; Bk 44, No 373, DL; Bk 53, No 464, DL; Bk 74, No 692, DL
171 Bk 60, No 475, DL
172 *Narrative of the Wreck of the SS Royal Charter*, By a Niece of One of the Lost, Batson and Atwater, Sydney, 1884, Pt ii, pp8-10,14; Kennedy, A., *Royal Charter*, McGlashin and Gill, Dublin, 1860, ch 9, p110
173 SMH 22 August 1857, Suppl., p1a,b; *Empire* 23 August 1857, p4e
174 Registers of Copies of Will 1800-1901, SAG Will 1/4673
175 SMH 17 August 1859, p4a
176 Niece of One of the Lost, Sydney, 1884, Pt ii, p9
177 Mc Kee, Alexander, *The Golden Wreck*, Hodder and Stoughton, Kent, England, 1988
178 Niece of One of the Lost, Sydney, 1884, Pt ii, pp10-15
179 Inward Passenger Lists, British Ports, Public Record Office Vic, Fiche 188, pp9-10
180 Registers of Copies of Will 1800-1901, SAG Will 1/4673; Bk 105, No 666, DL; Bk 106, No 256, DL; Bk 107, Nos 30, 31, DL; Bk 107, No 249, DL; Bk 123, No 480, D; Bk 123, No 582, DL; Bk 131, No 392, DL; Bk 149, No 655, DL; *Goulburn Herald* 2 November 1867, p5e
181 Barwick, Kathleen H., *History of Berkeley New South Wales*, Illawarra Historical Society, 1963, p3
182 Bk 62, No 396, DL
183 *Australian Town and Country Journal* 6 September 1879, p484
184 Bk 75, No 471, DL; GG 1851, Vol 1, p34, 10 Jan; GG 1852, Vol 1, p333, 16 Feb
185 Barwick, 1963, pp5,9; NSW Department of Education and Training, *Government Schools of New South Wales 1848-1998, 150 years*, 5th ed., 1998, p31
186 *Illawarra Mercury* 10 June 1884, p2f
187 *Illawarra Mercury* 3 June 1884, p2d

10
THE GREAT-GRANDCHILDREN TAKE OVER

As their parents aged or died, the great-grandchildren replaced their aged or deceased parents in business and domestic affairs. The greatgrandsons ran the family farms and firms, Berkeley, Bronte, Pitt, Son and Badgery, Putty Farm, Springfield, Trafalgar, Tirrana, Whittell's Coal Business, and Wood's Farm. Other great-grandsons found their own jobs, architect, bank manager, barrister, butcher, civil engineer, company manager, doctor, farmer, inventor, merchant, solicitor, stipendiary magistrate, surveyor and wheelwright. The great-grandaughters produced and reared many great-great-grandchildren and managed their households. Between 1860 and 1912, the period this chapter covers, the main developments were free, compulsory and secular education in 1880, the Commonwealth of Australia in 1901, and the vote for women in 1902. Reformer James Robert Wilshire recommended nondenominational education in the 1840s and federation of the colonies in the early 1850s.

The grandsons continued to support their communities. In 1860 George Matcham Pitt spoke at the Hawkesbury Benevolent Society. In 1861 he was appointed a magistrate.[1] The year 1861 also saw four grandsons elected to their local school boards, Robert

Pitt for Kurrajong south, William Warren Jenkins and Joseph Wood Wilshire for Wollongong, and great-grandson Andrew Faithfull Gibson for Tirranna.[2] William Warren Jenkins gave £200 to the building fund for St Michaels Church, Wollongong and he was warden of the church after it opened in November 1862.[3] On the other hand, William Pitt Faithfull resigned from the Legislative Council in May 1861. His honesty prevented him keeping the seat when Charles Cowper "sought to pack the Upper House with members favourable to the policy of his Government".[4]

The second son of Esther and James Wilshire, James Robert Wilshire, 51, died of "paralytic neuralgia" in his home at Potts Point on 30th August 1860. He was buried with his parents in the Church of England section of the Sydney Burial Ground on 2nd September.[5] Eight days after her husband's death, Sarah gave birth to Austin Henry Wilshire at Port's Point.[6] James left Sarah and 13 children, all under-age except James Thompson Wilshire, a student at Sydney University.[7]

James Robert Wilshire died intestate.[8] Wife Sarah renounced her right to manage James's estate of £3000 in favour of eldest son, James Thompson Wilshire, who declined the offer. Instead, James, Sarah, and her brother Samuel Thompson, formed a trust: to pay the mortgages; provide Sarah with an income to keep and educate the children; and divide any remaining real estate among the children once Austin Henry Wilshire reached his majority.[9] To compensate heir-at-law James for refusing his father's property, Sarah gave him her two allotments at Darling Harbour, the two affirming their shared affection.[10]

James Thompson Wilshire executed the deed of partition for the residual estate of his grandfather, James.[11] That done, some family members sold their properties. James Thompson Wilshire (in place of his father, James Robert), Austin, Esther, Matilda and Joseph got £1000 for the 500 acres near the township of Peel, north of

10 The Great-Grandchildren Take Over

Bathurst. Joseph made £60 on a half an acre in Phillip Street, Parramatta. Elizabeth realised £125 on farms at Salt Pan Creek and Punchbowl. Austin received £300 for two farms at Salt Pan Creek.[12]

Sadly, 40-year old Eliza Wilshire, wife of Austin, and second daughter of Thomas Matcham and Elizabeth Pitt, died of "puerperal convulsions" at home, on 5th February 1861. That day she gave birth to a daughter who did not survive. A contagious streptococcal infection, Puerperal Fever claimed the lives of many women at childbirth. Reverend J.D. Brennan buried Eliza in Randwick Cemetery on 7th. She left Austin, 19, Edwin, 17, Isabel, 14, Alice, 12, Percy, nearly nine, Emma, seven, Lucy Pitt Wilshire, four, born March 1857, and Arthur Wilshire, three, born May 1858. Also, in July 1855 Eliza had given birth to Marian Elizabeth Wilshire, but she died aged four and a half months. The family lived in Glenmore Road, in the newly proclaimed Municipality of Paddington. Austin was the Returning Officer for the first council elections held in May 1860.[13] He spent 1861 "clearing up and selling out" the tannery.[14]

As the estate of James Robert Wilshire did not produce enough income to support his family and pay the mortgages, the trustees sold some of his property in August 1862. Austin Forrest Wilshire paid £2945 for half the tannery site, half the property in Union Lane previously owned by Alfred Eyre, Louisa's land holding the workers' huts, a cottage and land in Liverpool Street, and the land behind Mimosa Cottage. The trustees also made £1000 on the house at Potts Point. They kept Mimosa Cottage, the building in Wilshire Place and Lousia's part-property in George Street.[15] In March 1864 Sarah paid the mortgage of £5000 on Potts Point, then negotiated a mortgage of £4,700 on Wilshire Place and Louisa's place next door.[16]

Drover and cattle buyer, Thomas William Eber Bunker Laycock, was also in debt. Declared insolvent on 9th August 1862, Thomas credited his misfortune "to the fact of having from time to time purchased cattle and losing by the resale thereof'. He voluntarily surrendered his estate when Samuel Dight of Singleton began preparations to recover £451 10s owed for 100 cattle in the Supreme Court. George Matcham Pitt had given him £200. And James Rochester loaned him £500 at 9% on Putty Farm in November 1860.[17] All told, Thomas owed £2555 10s 6d. He had assets of £1370 5s, 200 head of cattle on Mr Hoskinson's station, three horses, 15 pigs, farm implements and furniture. Before the final insolvency meeting in March 1863, Thomas tried to sell Putty Farm, cattle and other goods, but with little interest shown he got a mere £25.[18] The Laycocks remained in Putty. They probably rented Putty Farm from Rochester.[19] In 1860-1 Thomas found £538 to buy 538 acres at Putty, the deeds for the 28 allotments in the names of sons Thomas, Robert, Henry, Andrew and George.[20] Robert did not enjoy his land for long. Aged only 25, he died of injuries received in a fall from his horse on New Year's Day 1866.

Four sons of Mary and William Pitt Faithfull attended the King's School, Percy from 1859 to 1863, George from 1858 to 1864, Monty from 1860 to 1864 and Reginald from 1862 to 1864.[21] Their schooling finished, on 6th February 1865 the two older boys, Percy and George, set off for Sydney in a four-in-hand, accompanied as far as Goulburn by the younger two, Monty and Reginald. Not far from the Springfield gate, bushranger Ben Hall and his mates, John Gilbert and Johnnie Dunn, bailed-up the young men. (Gilbert and Dunn had just robbed two mail coaches.) Though holding little firepower, Percy a single-barrelled rifle and George a small revolver, the Faithfulls resisted the attack.[22] Allegedly they said, "we had never dared face our mother had we allowed ourselves to be captured by the bushrangers".[23] In 1876 the four received a gold medal inscribed, "Granted for gallant and faithful services, William Percy Faithfull, George Ernest Faithfull, Henry Montague Faithfull and Reginald Faithfull". The medal is in the National Library of Australia.[24] William struggled with a different problem, protecting the acreage at Brewarrena. William and his neighbour

10 The Great-Grandchildren Take Over

lost the exclusive use of two large waterholes declared reserves on 30th December 1865. Two days later, William's lease expired and the selection regulations of the Robertson Land Acts proclaimed early in 1862 came into force. The acts sanctioned conditional purchase of squatters' land, whereby anyone able to pay 5s deposit on £1 an acre could select between 40 and 320 acres. Despite exercising all means at his disposal to defend the run, including the pre-emptive right to select four acres for every £1 spent on improvements, William secured just 16,194 of the 45,000 acres.[25]

On 8th February 1865 great-grandson Thomas Whittell, proprietor of his father's coal business, suffered a nasty accident. The burst boiler of a two-horse power steam engine, used to cut chaff and wood, injured Thomas and two employees. Thomas was "dreadfully scalded by the steam and water" on several parts of his body.[26] Two weeks later, 21st February 1865, Thomas's father, Henry Rawes Whittell, aged about 59, died of "epilepsy" and "exhaustion" at home, Bourke Street, Surry Hills. On 23rd Henry was buried in the Independent Cemetery at the Sydney Burial Ground. He left Esther, Matilda, 22, Charles, 20, Thomas, 17, Esther, 15, Elizabeth, 11, Henry, seven, and Emily born in November 1861. Henry died intestate and Esther administered his estate of £2000.[27] In the three years following Henry's death, Esther cleared much of Henry's debt.[28] She subdivided and sold the land surrounding the family home for £1659.[29] To compensate Elizabeth Mary Wilshire for £500 Henry borrowed in May 1844, Esther gave her sister a house and land in Esther Street, Surry Hills.[30] And she paid Australian Mutual Provident £2573 and brother Austin £1726 by selling five of the eleven lots at Darling Harbour.[31]

On 9th September 1865, at St Patrick's, Sydney, the Reverend J. McEnroe married Alice Frances Jenkins, only surviving child of Robert and Louisa Jenkins, and Charles Hubert de Castella. Alice's guardian, William Edmond Plunkett, consented to the marriage which George Rowley and Eliza Bradburn witnessed. Charles

Hubert was born on 27 March 1825 in Neuchatel, Switzerland, to Jean-Francois Paul de Castella and wife Eleanore Camille de Riaz. Alice met Hubert on accompanying an aunt to Melbourne to visit the Anderson family into which Hubert's brother Paul had just married. Seeking his fortune, Paul came to Australia in the Royal George in November 1849, Hubert joining him in Melbourne after arriving on the *Marlborough* in March 1854. Paul bought Yering Station of 30,000 acres in present Yarra Glen, not far from Lilydale. Hubert purchased the 15000 acre cattle station Dalry next to Yering Station but returned home for family reasons in January 1856 in the *Anglesey*. While away, Hubert's partner in the cattle business sold Dalry. Hubert came back in the steam-driven *Great Britain* in August 1862.[32] He bought part of Yering and, though intending to farm sheep, planted 100 acres in vines. The sale of Alice's inheritance over almost 20 years enabled Hubert to expand St Hubert's vineyard. At the 1880 Melbourne exhibition he won a trophy given by the Emperor of Germany for a "product showing the greatest aritistic or industrial progress". Hubert was also a talented artist. And he travelled widely and wrote three books on his "adopted country".[33] Alice and Hubert had five sons and five daughters, Francois Robert, Ernest Charles, Louisa Madeleine, Hubert Max, Alice Maria, Nathalie Cecile, Claire, Jean, Clothilde and Claude Louis.[34] Former marathon runner, Robert de Castella, is a descendant of Francois Robert. Leaving his oldest son in charge of the vineyard, Hubert went home to Fribourg, Switzerland in the *Salazie* in October 1886.[35] Alice and her younger children joined Hubert, the children adapting well to their lessons in French. On medical advice, Hubert (and Alice?) returned to Australia in November 1906 but he died in October 1907.

A local resident often met "one very interesting old gentleman", William Pitt Wilshire, in the Kurrajong district in the sixties. He thought William "was possessed of a superior talent, being no mean artist and a frequent contributor to the Sydney press, principally on topics of the day". One of William's topics "was the advocation of

10 The Great-Grandchildren Take Over

a railway to Kurrajong, which was much to the point, and always read with interest". Of interest to the resident, William's "model of a double-keeled ship, which... claimed attention from some of the shipbuilders in England". The resident related an "amusing incident" which took place on a cold wet day after William returned from a walk with his book and umbrella. A "great reader", he loved getting near the fire with his book so took up a position at the corner of his large open fireplace. The cook had a piece of corned meat boiling in an old three-legged iron pot, a peach pie or similar dessert in the camp oven, and a sirloin of beef revolving on the spit. Not keen to tell his master he was in the way, the cook piled wood on the fire. William opened the umbrella to shield himself from the heat. The cook reduced the fire to prevent William's dinner burning.[36]

The children of Maria and William Pitt Wilshire had married by the late sixties. Elder son William James Wilshire wed Rosalie Ada Pettingell in 1855. In the late fifties and early sixties, William James was Secretary of the Steam Navigation and Pilot Board and a Sublieutenant in the Volunteer Naval Brigade.[37] About 1866 he began managing the Royal Hotel in George Street, the site of Dymocks Bookshop; a position he held for many years.[38] W.A. Roberts recalled, "I can see him now in my mind's eye, arrayed in a frock coat, silk hat, and so forth, standing in the vestibule speaking to his visitors".[39] Younger son, Frederick Robertson Wilshire, was appointed a Police Inspector in 1862.[40] The next year he married cousin, Lavellete Mary Maria Robertson. Daughter Maria Janet Wilshire married John Bibb in 1867. John, and others, tested the railway before it opened in 1855.[41]

The stock agency of George Matcham Pitt progressed steadily in the sixties and early seventies. In 1861 George and Julia borrowed £4,500, funds for the business, no doubt.[42] That year George took on a partner, Thomas Sullivan. They worked in an office in George Street, Sydney and sold their fat sheep and cattle at Fullager's yard, at present Blacktown.⁴³ In 1864 Pitt and Sullivan leased two extra runs in the Wellington district, Salisbury Plains and Back Gangary. George put the stock agency on hold to campaign for the seat of Windsor in 1864. William Walker beat him by eight votes.⁴⁴ The partners were selling stations as well as stock by 1865, but the partnership had ended by 1867.⁴⁵ Son Robert Matcham Pitt, an engineer by training, joined his father in 1871 and the firm listed as GM Pitt and Son.⁴⁶ George and Robert used saleyards at Blacktown and Homebush. George sold his land at Blacktown for £505.⁴⁷

Three children of George and Julia Pitt married in Richmond during the sixties, George Matcham Pitt junior to Elizabeth Town in 1860, Jessie Pitt to William Mylan Nicholas Garling in 1868 and Julia Eliza Pitt to Henry Septimus Badgery in 1869. About October 1869 George and Julia Pitt left Richmond to live at Manly.⁴⁸ The people of Richmond missed George's genial company which he enlivened with amusing anecdotes and apt quotes from Robert Burns, William Shakespeare and Lord George Gordon Byron. Asked to say grace at a banquet, flanked by a doctor and a lawyer, George remembered the words of an eminent statesman:

> *From doctors' pills*
> *And lawyers' bills*
> *Good Lord deliver us!*⁴⁹

George leased Fairlight, a large stone house "replete with every convenience" surrounded by 33 acres overlooking the harbour. The residence belonged to Henry Gilbert Smith, "the father of Manly". The Pitts attended St Matthew's Church of England.⁵⁰ At a public meeting on 15ᵗʰ November 1870, Julia joined the committee of the Parochial Association set up to promote the church and parish school.⁵¹ George contributed to his new district. He was appointed to the Manly Public School Board and chaired a public meeting called to consider the "disgraceful condition" of the road to Manly from Middle Harbour. He sold tickets for Grand Amateur Concert

10 The Great-Grandchildren Take Over

in aid of the Cricket Club. And he was a trustee of the reserve near the wharf.[52]

Meanwhile, Austin Forrest Wilshire attended to his debt on Wilshire Place. In the sixties he sold two Darling Harbour properties for £1160 and worked as a merchant at Wilshire Place. [53] These actions helped him pay a mortgage of £4000 on Wilshire Place.[54] Again, he tried to secure compensation for the loss of the tannery. Through influential politician Henry Parkes he petitioned the Parliament for £3500 in March 1865. On May 10th Austin and three others gave evidence to a select committee chaired by Parkes. The committee decided Austin's concerns deserved "consideration by the Government". Next, in June 1867 Austin sent Premier James Martin a letter which he hoped all members of the parliament, including Henry Parkes, would read. The statement with the unseen letter read, "if private interests are to be sacrificed without compensation there is no member of the community who may not, in some way or other, be made to suffer".[55] Then he made his boldest move. On 11th October 1870, Austin sold the tannery site, the land behind Mimosa cottage and property beside Liverpool Street. He made £3500 on the deal.[56] One of the two buyers also bought land on the north side of Union Lane, one lot from Elizabeth Mary Wilshire for £200 and the other from Joseph Wood Wilshire for £75.[57] A new undertaking for Austin and his second son Edwin James Wilshire was their election as aldermen for the new municipality of Penrith in June 1871.[58]

Alice Gibson hosted the Tirranna races for the last time in 1871. The racegoers expressed their gratitude, "the club heartily desires to express to Mrs Gibson its thanks for all the courtesy she has shown, and the things she has so considerately and so generously and so well done for members". The Tirranna Picnic Race Club celebrated its 75th anniversary in January 1930.[59] Alice used conditional purchase to select several allotments of land in County King. However, she sold 72 acres for £72 in the parish of Terranna.[60]

She relinquished the squat in the parish of Bland in 1866 but kept Boga Bogalong until 1878.[61] By the early seventies, six of Alice's seven children had married. Two wed in 1862, second son Andrew Faithfull Gibson to Annie Campbell and widow Alice Jemima Donaldson, to Andrew Finlay. Fifth son Septimus Faithfull Gibson married Annie Marie Chisholm in 1865. Third son Frederick Faithfull Gibson wed Mary Cunningham in 1873.

Influenced by their mother, three sons of Mary and William Pitt Faithfull graduated from Sydney University with Bachelors and Masters of Arts, Percy in 1868, George in 1869 and Monty in 1871.[62] Percy became a barrister, George, a civil engineer, and Monty, a solicitor.[63] Monty was also a fine cricketer for the University and Albert Clubs.[64] Robert qualified as a doctor. Reginald managed Springfield and later ran Brewarrena. Youngest son, Lucian, took charge of Springfield in 1871 just as wool prices began to surge.[65] William bought more land in County Argyle, much of it in the parishes of Quilago and Gundary. And he paid £124 for Louisa Elliot's marriage grant of 960 acres.[66] A feature on Springfield in the *Australian Town and Country Journal* on 24th January 1874 revealed William owned more than 20,000 acres, 12,000 of the best sheep in the country and 700 excellent shorthorn cattle.[67]

William Pitt Wilshire spent time in the early seventies painting and inventing. In March 1872 he exhibited four oil paintings under the patronage of the New South Wales Academy of Art. Three were originals, *Randwick Race Course*, *Robertsons Point* (Watsons Bay), and an unfinished view from *Hyde Park*, while the fourth was a copy, *Maternal Caresses* (after Mary Cassatt?).[68] William invented "an entirely new method" of preserving joints of fresh meat which he trusted would result in trade with England. In June 1872 he told Henry Parkes of the discovery and asked the Commissioner of Railways to reduce the cost of carrying the meat by train from Richmond. William devised a scheme for Sydney's water supply. The Water and Sewage Bill pending, in October

10 The Great-Grandchildren Take Over

1874 he asked Parkes how to apply for membership of the relevant board. He wrote to Parkes from 225 Albion Street, Surry Hills.[69]

In Kurrajong William Pitt Wilshire fathered four children with a young woman, Margaret Hornery, although he would not give them his name. Elvina Hornery arrived in May 1863, William Matcham Hornery in April 1870, James Albert Hornery in October 1872 and Catherine Maria Hornery in October 1875. In 1877, the year Margaret Hornery married Albert Packer, William sold Wilshirehurst for £50 to daughter Maria's husband, John Bibb. Later, he conceded Maria's right to just a third of Wilshirehurst, cancelled the deed and refunded his son-in-law.[70] Son William James was Secretary of the Marine Board in 1872. Son Frederick Robertson had positions at Berrima, Visiting Justice of the Peace at the gaol, Police Magistrate, Clerk of Petty Sessions, Agent for the Sale of Crown Lands, and District Registrar for Births, Deaths and Marriages.[71] At Scone, cousin James Thompson Wilshire was Clerk of Petty Sessions, District Registrar for Births, Deaths and Marriages and Registrar of the Small Debts Court.[72]

Joseph Wood Wilshire of Mangerton, West Wollongong, was elected alderman of the Wollongong Council on 6th February 1874. Next, he stood for mayor with "no private ends to serve". He promised "economy in our expenditure with due regard to efficiency, will regulate my conduct". And he pointed out he performed his duties as magistrate in an "attentive manner". When Council met to elect the mayor, Alderman Lahiff proposed Alderman Wilshire. Lahiff stated Joseph previously performed the duties of mayor "very efficiently, and he had no doubt he would do so again". Unanimously elected to mayor, Joseph took the chair and thanked the Council "very sincerely for the honour".[73] No evidence of Joseph's earlier election as mayor was found. Elected an alderman in February 1865, Mayor Joseph Wilshire signed the Receipts and Expenditure Statements of the Wollongong Municipality for the half years ending on 31st December 1865 and 1866.[74]

Politics aside, Joseph sold two properties, one on the corner of Union Lane and Pitt Street for £500 in 1868, the other facing George Street for £3325 in 1873. Before selling the properties, he paid the mortgages.[75] Wife Anne devoted her time to the children, including Reginald Clarke Wilshire born in October 1861, Laura Maud Wilshire in October 1863, Granville Wood Wilshire in November 1866, and twelfth and final child, Harold Burnell Pitt Wilshire in July 1870.[76] No longer Joseph's ward at 23, Thomas William Faithfull Wilshire wed Jane Brabazon Ruthven in March 1867 at St. Matthias, Paddington.

George Matcham Pitt accepted an invitation to a fishing expedition at Broken Bay in Captain Heselton's newest steamer, *Mystery*. On Friday evening 20th March 1874 the *Mystery* anchored at the Basin in Pittwater. At daylight the *Mystery* steamed outside Broken Bay Heads where the guests spent a good morning's fishing for snapper before moving into quieter waters for breakfast. After breakfast three groups formed, one to shoot Wallabies, another to fish, and the largest to view the scenery on Brisbane Water and further up the Hawkesbury. The fishing party caught snapper weighing over 25lbs. On Sunday the *Mystery* re-entered Sydney Heads and, in the sheltered waters of the harbour, the guests enjoyed an excellent dinner. George toasted the health of Captain Heselton and his family. As well, he congratulated Heselton on his management of the steamers and the hospitality extended to the group. The *Mystery* docked at Circular Quay after a "most agreeable trip".[77] Memories of George in Manly were of a "portly" man, wearing a "straw boater hat", sitting on "the deck of the Manly steamers, full of fun, and cracking jokes to other passengers".[78] The month of the fishing trip, George, brother Robert, and cousin Austin Forrest Wilshire, sold their property in Pitt Street for £6000.[79]

About August 1874, George Matcham Pitt moved to Kirribilli Point, giving him easier access to his offices in the Bank Chambers at 80 King Street and a wonderful view of the harbour. Initially,

10 The Great-Grandchildren Take Over

George leased Holbrook House, then in January 1876 he paid £3200 for the beautiful house on about 2¾ acres.[80] Holbrook is now a short street in the suburb of Kirribilli. On special occasions George returned to Manly. On 16th March 1875 George attended the dinner honouring the departing Captain Heselton and his long association with the Manly steamers. George proposed a toast to the prosperity of Manly.[81] On 28th February 1876 he was vice-chairman at the banquet celebrating the arrival in Manly of telegraphic communication. Son Robert Matcham Pitt attended, too.[82] Robert lived in West Esplanade, Manly, in his new home, Hill-Side, built on one of two choice lots costing £500.[83] He had married Marie Emilie Eugenie Blanchard, "a very pretty little woman of French descent", in Sydney in 1874.[84] At the first public auction of land held at Manly on 28th April 1877, George and Robert paid £2640 for land on the southern side of the Corso, probably in today's Wood Street, Stuart Street and Addison Road. After subdividing the land, the two sold the allotments over several years; the mortgage discharged in less than a year.[85] In 1882 George took a similar course of action, paying £3245 for allotments in Victoria Parade, Wentworth Street, Darley Road and Asburner Street, Manly.[86]

Matilda Pitt Jenkins, fourth daughter of Esther and James Wilshire, died of the effects of two strokes at Berkeley on 27th May 1876. In poor health for two or three years, 57-year-old Matilda bore her illness with "calm submission and Christian fortitude". On Sunday 4th June the Reverends Thomas Campbell Ewing and J. Stone conducted her funeral which was "largely attended" by their tenants. She was buried in the cemetery on Berkeley. Matilda died intestate, her estate worth £7930 10s.[87] The *Illawarra Mercury* published a tribute to Matilda:

> *The many amiable qualities of the deceased lady will be held in life-long remembrance by all who enjoyed the pleasure of her acquaintance, and by none outside the circle of her family will her death be more deeply regretted than by the many tenants*

of the Berkeley Estate, who ever found in her a sympathising friend and generous benefactress.[88]

William "lamented very keenly" Matilda's death. In the year Matilda died, Dr John Dunmore Lang visited William. Lang remarked, "it was a pleasure ... to meet one so well read and conversant with literary and other topics". William owned a large library which he used to achieve a cherished goal, inspiring a love of reading and learning in his offspring.[89] Four children had married, William James Jenkins to Susan Bowen in 1869, Louisa Helen Jenkins to Johnson King in 1871, Frederick Jenkins to Minnie F.E. Atkinson in 1874 and Alice Elizabeth Jenkins to Walter Robertson also in 1874.

At 62, Mary Matcham Laycock, elder daughter of Thomas and Elizabeth Pitt, died suddenly on 15th July 1878. The coroner at Wollombi confirmed she died of heart disease. Her death certificate records her burial on 17th in "Putty Cemetery". Thomas was away, seeking his fortune at Laycock's Folly, his mine on the Gulgong-Mudgee goldfields.[90] Mary left four daughters and four sons. She saw her daughters married, Elizabeth to James Farlow in 1859, Isabella to James Gillespie in 1872, Emily to Oliver Cobcroft in 1876 and Mary to James Timmins in 1875. When James Timmins died or left the marriage, Mary partnered William Thirgood about 1879.

In February 1878 George Matcham Pitt and Robert Matcham Pitt were elected aldermen, George for the Municipality of East St Leonards and Robert for the recently declared Municipality of Manly. Both served long terms on their respective councils, George alderman for a year and mayor for five years, Robert alderman for 10 years.[91] George frequently expressed his views on public affairs in short letters to the press, "often coming down with sledge-hammer blows upon public men".[92] He "took a lively interest in North Sydney" and "to his energy and sustained effort North

10 The Great-Grandchildren Take Over

Sydney, in large measure, owes its water supply... which was laid in flexible pipes across the harbour between Dawes and Milson's Points".[93] Alderman Robert was active on issues such as the leasing arrangements for Manly wharf, the frequency of ferries, the control of local reserves, the condition of Pittwater Road and the need for a new Public School.[94] Robert played a prominent part in planting the Norfolk pines for which Manly was so famous. He transferred the western portion of his land, now part of Manly Park, to the Council for a small fee and in return received life membership of the Manly Cricket Club.[95] George was back in Manly to speak at the opening of the Oddfellow's Hall on 8th March 1879. Also, he was a member of the official party that drove in the first pole for the Public Baths at Little Manly on 21st May 1870.[96]

The year of George Matcham Pitt's election as mayor, 1879, Henry Septimus Badgery, husband of Julia Eliza Pitt, joined George and Robert in the stock and station agency, which then traded as Pitt, Son and Badgery.[97] In the previous year, George appeared before a Committee of the Legislative Assembly considering whether to establish public sale yards in the metropolitan area. George stressed the need for new yards, for preference at Homebush, as the Homebush yards were soon for sale while the yards at Annandale had closed.[98] When the Flemington Sale Yards opened in 1882, George set up his head office next to the yards and bought bordering land to hold stock.[99] Three more children of Julia and George had married. Charles Brian Pitt wed Ada Perry in 1878 in St Leonards. Charles was admitted a solicitor in September 1876.[100] Colin Pitt married Louisa Madeline Dowdell in 1879 in Hobart. Colin, who worked for his father, was an outstanding bowler for Albert and Manly Beach Cricket Clubs.[101] Edwin wed Julia Johnson (Julia Pitt's niece?) in February 1881 in Richmond. George gave him an allotment in Windsor Street, Richmond on his 21st birthday in February 1875.[102] Edwin lived at Bronte and there built a "fine modem cottage".[103]

On 14th April 1881, 66-year-old Thomas William Eber Bunker Laycock died at Putty of "diarrhoea". He was interred on 15th at "Putty". K.G. Laycock believes Thomas and Mary are buried on Putty Farm. Thomas did not leave a will. On 25th January 1879 his sons Thomas, Henry, Andrew and George Laycock paid £100 for Putty Farm at the auction of James Rochester's estate.[104] After their father's death, George married Ada Cobcroft in 1882 and Andrew wed Mary Jane Thorley in 1884. The Laycock boys were great cattlemen. Thomas raised pigs which he drove to market. Andrew was a noted breeder of stud cattle who exhibited stock at the Sydney Show.[105] Their names appear on many lots on both sides of Putty Creek in the parish maps of Gullongulong and Tollagong.[106]

In November 1881, soon after Sarah Wilshire's youngest child Austin Henry Wilshire reached 21, the trustees put James Robert Wilshire's property on the market, the proceeds for his children. Louisa's small property in George Street sold for £3,600.[107] The trustees auctioned Mimosa Place for £3000.[108] Sarah Wilshire and her unmarried daughters, Emily Rebekah, Phoebe Esther and Sarah Jane, paid £8000 for the large building in Wilshire Place.[109] Sarah and her daughters lost no time in selling the southern half of the building for £14,300.[110] With this money Sarah paid the mortgage on Wilshire Place.[111] Several children of James Robert Wilshire had married: Mimosa Sarah and Henry Walter Campion in 1877 in England, Clara Sophia and William Henry Quodling in 1868, Mayor Joseph and Catherine Mary Anastasia Bowes about 1875 in Fiji, and Alfred Theodore and Marianne Smith in 1877. Matilda Elizabeth Wilshire, aged only 36, died on 26th January 1879 at her stepmother's home, Havilah Lodge in Darlinghurst Road, Woolloomooloo.[112]

Louisa Elliot, 77, eldest child of James and Esther Wilshire, died of "senile decay" at Appin on 9th July 1883. Philip, 74, died before her of "paralysis" at Appin on 18th August 1879. The couple, and daughter Elizabeth Ella Elliot, who died in May 1871, were buried

10 The Great-Grandchildren Take Over

in the cemetery of St Mark's the Evangelist Church in Appin, Louisa on 12th July and Philip on 20th August.[113] Philip died intestate, his estate of £800 administered by his only surviving child, Thomas Wilshire Elliot, who lost his wife Mary Ann Sampson in 1871.[114]

William Warren Jenkins's concern for the community endured. He took "a zealous and sturdy interest in every parliamentary election" held in the district. In 1873, he attended "the first great public meeting held... for the purpose of formulating the agitation in favour of a railway between Illawarra and Sydney". He supported local ventures, giving £100 for "an experiment of shipping of butter to England" and buying £100 of shares in the South Coast and West Camden Co-operative Company. Just a few months before his death, William donated a special prize of five guineas to the Wollongong Agricultural Society, "which he supported liberally for many years".

About the time his son-in-law, Johnson King, Commissioner of Crown Lands, died in a buggy accident near Cooma, January 1883, William Warren Jenkins lost his vigour.[115] Sixty-seven-year-old William, younger son of Robert and Jemima Jenkins, died of "dropsy" on 6th May 1884. The Reverend J. Stack buried him in Berkeley Cemetery on 7th. Looking ahead, once Sydney Burial Ground was resumed for Central Railway, Robert and Jemima Jenkins were buried at Berkeley on 2nd September 1901, the exhumation witnessed by their grandson, Alfred Matcham Jenkins.[116] Family, tenants and the community admired William. He treated his family with "kindness and indulgence, perhaps even to a fault". He was ''tender-hearted to all who had to do with him in connection with his estate". The community held him "in high repute for his kindness and hospitality".[117] All told, William "may be accepted as a fine specimen of the old English gentleman".[118]

Sons William James Jenkins and Robert Thomas Jenkins, and friend Mr William Taylor, managed William Warren Jenkins estate of £67,000. His real estate consisted of 3,500 acres at Berkeley, Matilda's property on the corner of Sussex and Bathurst Streets, and about 53 acres at Mt Keira. William gave eldest son, William James, Nudjia, his home on Berkeley, with an option to extend the acreage. William Warren granted use of the home to Robert, Matilda, Ellinor, Emily, Alfred and Louisa Helen King, for as long as it suited Robert and two of his sisters. Five years after William's death, Robert could buy the house and homestead paddock of 168 acres, plus land close by. William authorized the trustees to sell the estate if most of the children agreed, although he hoped to keep Berkeley intact. He specified each child's share of the income, whether from the whole farm or the 30 dairy farms.[119] Three of William's children married after his death, Robert to Agnes Ewing in 1885, Alfred to Bessie Waldron also in 1885 and Emily to Anthony Denny in 1890. The year Emily married, the executors sold most of the estate in parcels.[120] It was April 1904 before they sold the choicest land, 304 acres bordering the lake and 211 acres near the railway and the South Coast Road.[121] The sale of Berkeley residence and surrounding paddock followed the death of Robert Thomas Jenkins in 1913.[122] The residence was demolished in February 1940. Nudjia, a safe and protected place, is now a museum at 83 Cummins Street, Unanderra.[123]

George Matcham Pitt lost wife Julia, née Johnson, at Holbrook, Kirribilli, on 2nd August 1886, her death at 71 caused by "natural decay". Julia's burial took place at St Peters, Richmond, on 3rd. She lived to see her son, widower Edwin, elected alderman for Richmond in February 1885 and its mayor in February 1886.[124] She was not alive when Pitt, Son and Badgery became a Limited Company with approved capital of £100,000 in 1888.[125] The same year in St. Leonards, daughter Eva Laura Pitt married Angelo Tornaghi, whose father was a native of Milan and a clockmaker of some repute.[126] Son Robert left Manly after selling Hill-Side, and Leona, the home he built next door, for £6000 in December 1888.[127] At Wentworth Falls Robert built a beautiful house; naming

10 The Great-Grandchildren Take Over

it Coorar after his father's first squat in the Moree district.[128] Coorar is now part of Blue Mountains Grammar School.

The only daughter of William and Susannah Faithfull, Alice Gibson, died at 77 of "general decay" at Tirranna on 27th January 1888. Alice lies at rest on acre at Tirranna. In 1884 she gave the trustees of Andrew's estate, David Peter Dickson and Alex James Dodds, £20 for the acre.[129] Alice lost William Faithfull Gibson at Caragabal in the Grenfell district in 1874 and Septimus Faithfull Gibson at Goulburn in 1879. Five children survived Alice, Alice Finlay, Thomas Jamieson Faithfull Gibson of Burrumbuttick near Albury, Andrew Faithfull Gibson who had built on Tirranna, Susannah Blomfield, and Frederick Faithful) Gibson who bred thoroughbred horses and Hereford cattle on land he bought on the south bank of Caragabal Creek.[130] Sons Andrew Faithfull Gibson and Frederick Faithfull Gibson controlled Alice's estate of £52,705. She devised Frederick two farms owned by her father, Lakeville and Ropes Farm measuring 60 acres, six allotments (36½ acres) at Terranna Village, and another 60 acres near the village. She gave Andrew the 63 acres and 110 acres near Tirranna Race Course. On reaching their majority Alice's grandsons, George Faithfull Gibson and Norman Gibson, each inherited six acres at Gardner's Reach near Toorak, meantime, the property was to support them. Other grandchildren received money, George Gibson Donaldson £2000, Stuart Donaldson £50 yearly, Minnie Finlay £1000 and Lily Finlay £1000. Alice divided the rest of her real and personal estate, including the properties in Goulburn town and Tirrannna, equally between sons Thomas, Andrew and Frederick, and daughter Susannah Blomfield.[131] Tirranna was still home to Andrew Campbell Gibson, grandson of Alice, at his death in October 1945.[132]

What became of Alice Gibson's North Richmond home? As laid down in the will of her father, Maria Faithfull left Lakeville to Alice who gave it to her son Frederick Faithfull Gibson. Childless on his death in 1913, Frederick bequeathed Lakeville to his nephew

Norman Gibson, son of Andrew Faithfull Gibson. In June 1914, Norman sold Lakeville to Norman Cox of Richmond for £1400.[133] Today the farm of 105 acres, 3 roods and 20 perches is in four sections.[134]

In May 1888 Esther Whittell cleared a debt of £4000.[135] At the same time she made £2820 on the six remaining properties at Darling Harbour.[136] She had moved to Westow Cottage in Audley Street, Petersham after selling her home in Bourke Street in 1882 for £840.[137] Back in June 1875, daughter Louisa died of consumption leaving Esther with seven children. Five had married, Charles to Ellen Elizabeth Turner in 1868, Thomas to Elizabeth Watson in 1873, and after Elizabeth died, Clara Amelia Keating in 1883, Esther to Frank M. de Meyrick in 1881, Elizabeth to Bartin Haigh in 1877 and Henry Rawes Whittell to Amelia Annie Menzies in 1884.

Sister-in-law and close friend, Sarah Wilshire, also lived in the western suburbs, in Emu Street, Burwood.[138] James Thompson Wilshire lived with his stepmother when elected an alderman for Burwood in February 1885 and its mayor in 1886-7.[139] James also represented Canterbury in the Legislative Assembly of the New South Wales Parliament from February 1889 to June 1891.[140] His political career mirrored that of his father. An "exceedingly charitable man", James served on the boards of many charitable institutions including the Home for Incurables, Institution of the Deaf and Blind and Mission to Seamen. An early advocate of cremation, he was a member of the Cremation Society.[141] James, eldest son of James Robert and Elizabeth Wilshire, married Alice Quodling in 1893. Three of his half-siblings, Sarah Wilshire's children, had married, Louisa Alma Wilshire to Samuel Barff in 1882, Austin Henry Wilshire to Hephzibah Maude Stewart in 1888 and Sarah Jane Wilshire to Walter McLean in 1891.

10 The Great-Grandchildren Take Over

Approaching 80 and mentally alert, William Pitt Wilshire took exception to the editorial in the *Sydney Morning Herald* on 26th January 1886, "The little band of marines and prisoners gathered round the British flag, under the command of Captain Phillip, were in reality the forefathers of the (present) energetic and prosperous race". In a letter to the Herald, William complained about the "atrocious falsehood fulminated by the leading journal of the Colony". Ignored, he "took what little revenge" he could by publishing "In Memoriam" notices for his parents, the submission highlighting his parents' connection to high-ranking people. James Wilshire arrived in 1800 and died 1840. He was certified Acting Deputy Acting Commissiary by Governor Macquarie, to the Rt. Hon. The Lords Commissioners of His Majesty's Treasury, dated 25th October 1810. Hester Wilshire, wife of James Wilshire, formerly Deputy-Commissary, died 1836. Youngest daughter of Mary Pitt (née Mary Matcham) who with her family emigrated in 1801 with letters of introduction from Edmund Nelson and his son-in-law George Matcham.[142] About 1886 William painted an Aboriginal family camped at Watson's Bay. (Figures 34 & 35) William, eldest son of James and Esther Wilshire, died at 81 of "sciatica" on 12th March 1889, at 171 Albion Street, Surry Hills. The Reverend T.W. Unwin buried William on 13th at the Church of England Cemetery at Rookwood. William did not leave a will. His eldest son, William James, administered his estate of £500.[143] Three of his children with Margaret Hornery married, Elvina to John McCabe in 1881, William to Charlotte Isobel Clarke in 1896 and Catherine to Herbert Case also in 1896.

Still without compensation for the tannery, Austin Forrest Wilshire contacted Henry Parkes on three more occasions. He wrote to Parkes in December 1879 from Winbourne Mulgoa, in March 1881 from Willow Lodge Bridge Road Pyrmont, and in November 1888 from Hillston Forest Lodge. He criticised Parkes' failure to initially advise him that the Government could not interfere with Acts of Parliament. And he complained about the "mere trifle" he

Figure 34. William Pitt Wilshire

10 The Great-Grandchildren Take Over

Figure 35. Camp of "Blanket", by William Pitt Wilshire

got for the "old place" (tannery site etc.) compared to £32,000 the Government spent on the Police Offices.[144] Central Police Station, which faces Central Street (Union Lane), is run by Corrective Services for those on remand. Central Court, finished in 1892, fronts Liverpool Street and backs on to the remand centre. Considering Wilshire Place in George Street, an article by W.M. Faithfull and H.R. Wilshire in the *Sydney Morning Herald* of 8th September 1928 states, "the remains" of the old stone buildings "are being demolished to make room for work in connection with... the city underground railway." However, Elizabeth Mary Wilshires' small allotment is free of any structure. In the early 1980s to recover rates the City of Sydney Council sold 27 Central Street, the two metre laneway running behind the George Streeet buildings for £98,705. The balance, £150,000, belongs to the estates of James Robert Wilshire and Austin Forrest Wilshire but relatives had not claimed the money by 3rd November 2008.[145]

On 28th May 1889, 77-year-old Austin Forrest Wilshire, third son of Esther and James Wilshire, died of "cirrhosis", "albuminuria" and "ascites" in Pyrmont Bridge Road, Glebe. He was buried in Randwick Cemetery on 29th. Son Edwin handled his estate of £33,778. Austin divided "the land and houses" equally between his eight children. The two buildings in Wilshire Place were not free of debt.[146] Six of his children had married, Austin Thomas Wilshire to Frances Broughton in 1865, Edwin James Wilshire to Ada Hosking in 1869, Alice Emily Wilshire to Francis Lord junior in 1871, Isabel Eliza Wilshire to Edward Ruthven in 1875, Emma Mary Wilshire to Edward Hughes in 1885 and Arthur Wilshire to Annie Rutledge in 1887.

A third family member died in 1889, Mary Faithfull, nee Deane, aged 76. Following seven years of illness, Mary died of "neuralgia and heart dilation" on December 10th.[147] The Reverend Alfred Puddicombe buried her on 12th at Springfield. Three sons had married, William Percy Faithfull to Emma Geary in 1878, Henry

10 The Great-Grandchildren Take Over

Montague Faithfull to Emily Buckland in 1874 and Robert Lionel Faithfull to Jessie Alice Gibson, grand-daughter of Alice Gibson, in 1888. Sadly son Reginald Faithfull died of tuberculosis in June 1882.

In the 1890s six grandchildren died, the first, Joseph Wood Wilshire, youngest child of Esther and James. On 8th August 1893 67-year-old Joseph succumbed to "chronic cirrhosis of kidneys" and "uraemic coma". Joseph died in Pitt Street, Redfern, where he had lived there since 1877, the year he sold his last acres at Wollongong.[148] The Reverend E.S. Wilkinson buried him at Rookwood Cemetery on 10th• Joseph left £1354 to his daughter Beatrice Louisa Wilshire.[149]

August 1893 was also the month Mary Pitt's great-grandson John Thomas Wood, son of Elizabeth and George Pitt Wood, died of Bright's disease at North Richmond on 18th. John "had been an honest, industrious and hardworking farmer, and was universally respected by everyone". His was "probably the most numerously attended funeral (20th) ever held in this part of the district".[150] John ran an orchard at Oakford, the grant of his grandfather, John Wood. He owned the whole farm after buying eldest brother butcher William Henry Wood's half for £900 in 1867, and youngest brother wheelwright Henry Austin Wood's quarter for £100 in 1872. John also paid a nephew £165 for 16 acres adjoining Oakford in 1885.[151] The last generation of Woods raised on the grant were the children of John Thomas Wood and wife Mary Ann Aston. They were Charlotte Elizabeth Wood/Allen (1857-1904), Eva Laura Wood/Markwell (1860-1928), John Rowland Wood (1863-1947), Henry Aston Wood (1865-1945), Clara Caroline Wood/Allen (1868-1932), Edith May Wood/Ives (1872-1935), Frederick William Wood (1874-1876), Fred Hamilton Wood (1877-1951), Frank George Wood (1880-1938) and Arthur Sherwin Wood (1885-1934).[152] John bequeathed the farm to his wife, Mary Ann.[153] Mary Ann remained at Oakford until daughter Edith May married in 1910. Then she lived with Edith at Oakleigh in Slade Street, Naremburn, until her death in August 1914. Mary Ann's executors, sons Frederick, Frank and Arthur, sold Woods' farm of 129 acres in June 1919 for £2,225.[154] At present the farm is in five sections with one section incorporated in the grounds of St John of God Hospital (previously Belmont).[155] The Woods and their neighbours at the junction of the Grose and Hawkesbury "were noted for their hospitality". Their names "will never be forgotten by those who knew them". Among them "you would never go astray", nor would you be "in want of a meal".[156]

William Pitt Faithfull, eldest son of William and Susannah Faithfull, died peacefully of "senile decay" at Springfield on 24th April 1896 at the advanced age of 89. Daughters Florence and Frances Lilian nursed William and son doctor Robert attended him. The Reverend William Goulburn buried William at Springfield on 26th. The *Goulburn Evening Penny Post* remarked, William "has lived uprightly and honestly as a private individual, and has performed all the duties incident to his station in a manner that best serves his country". The *Post* commented, William was "held in great affection as an employer".[157] Faithfull Street in Goulburn recognizes William's contribution.

In 1890 William Pitt Faithfull made his will, his executors George Ernest Faithfull of Brewarrena, Henry Montague Faithfull of Sydney and Augustus Lucian Faithfull of Springfield. At William's death, his estate was £335,253. Augustus Lucien, who had married Ethel Joplin in 1895, inherited Springfield. William made the residence and surrounding square mile available to his unmarried daughters, Florence, Constance Mary, and Frances Lilian, until the last of them married. Frances Lilian married William Hugh Anderson in February 1898. William had 'previously given son William Percy property in Victoria which he sold for about £10,000. Robert Lionel received 100 acres near Berrima and 1160 acres in County Georgiana. George Ernest inherited Brewarrenna

10 The Great-Grandchildren Take Over

and Henry Montague, Jordan Hill. William settled £10,000 and property in Randwick on each of his daughters. He bequeathed the children, except for Augustus Lucian and George Ernest, 640 acres at Wangaratta, two allotments in the town of Wangaratta, and a house and store in Elizabeth Street, Melbourne. William gave the rest of his estate, including stocks, shares and trusts, to his children apart from Lucian and George.[158]

William's descendants, the Maple-Browns, offered Springfield for sale in December 2004. They sold the big homestead and nearby cottages on 800 acres but kept the second homestead and 7000 acres with the idea of setting up a more efficient farming unit. The Maple-Browns gave about 2000 objects from Springfield, "a treasure trove of pastoral life", to the National Museum of Australia in Canberra.[159]

On 12th October 1896, George Matcham Pitt, eldest son of Thomas Matcham and Elizabeth Pitt, died at Holbrook, Kirribilli. Bright's disease claimed George in his 83rd year. His "leaden coffin encased in polished cedar and richly mounted" was shipped across the harbour and carried by train to Richmond. Relatives, many old residents of Richmond, Windsor and Kurrajong, and representatives of the commercial life of Sydney attended the burial service at St Peters on 18th. The *Richmond Gazette* noted, "General regret is expressed throughout the district at the loss of so valuable a citizen".[160] "A grand man, full of mental and physical vigour", George had a "burly form", "voice like thunder", "breezy nature", "big heart", "genial laugh", and "kindly greeting" for all his acquaintances and friends. A final tribute to George, "A more honourable gentleman you would not wish to meet".[161]

George Matcham Pitt made his will in April 1891, adding codicils in November 1894 and December 1895. He gave control of his £11,832 estate to Charles Bryan (George's spelling) Pitt, and to Robert Matcham Pitt who "renounced all his right and title to the

Probate and Execution" of the will.[162] George gave Holbrook to Robert's wife, Marie Emilie Eugenie Pitt. As George owed £4,000 on his home, he gave Marie the "option" of paying 4% interest for ten years or paying the full amount "at any earlier period". George bequeathed Bronte to banker Edwin's three children, Julia Eva Pitt, Irene Emilie Pitt and Edwin Pitt the younger. George junior inherited the 30 acres near Windsor as well as duelling pistols given to his father. The trustees were to invest £1000 for Darcy and Ida Garling, the children of daughter Jessie Garling who died in October 1887. George planned to give £1200 and allotments in the towns of Parramatta and Windsor to Julia Badgery before she died in July 1894. The trustees were to invest £1500 for Edwin, £1200 for Harry, and £1500 for Colin. Charles got £200, selected books, the bookcase, violin, razors and watch. Eva received £500 "free from the control of any husband of hers". George gave friend Philip Francis Adams, former Surveyor-General, an adze, niece Emily Johnson £200 and housekeeper Ms Snedon £50. Three institutions received £100, the Benevolent Asylums at Windsor and Sydney, and the Randwick Asylum for the Destitute. In February 1897 probate was granted to Charles Brian (Charles's spelling) Pitt of Sydney, Solicitor.[163] Pitt Street in Windsor is named after George.[164]

What happened to the 200 acres settled by the Pitt Family in 1802? The executors released Bronte to Mary's great-great-grandchildren Julia Pitt, Irene Pitt, and Edwin Pitt the younger, in December 1906. At her death in January 1908, Julia gave her third of Bronte to her brother and sister.[165] Edwin and Irene sold Bronte to Richard Dowle for £3625 in December 1919, a year after the death of their father Edwin senior.[166] In 1927 Dowle leased part of the farm for 33 years to the Nepean Sand and Gravel Company; the lease renewed in 1950.[167] Richard Dowle transferred the property to Harold and Henry Dowle in 1929.[168] Four years later the Dowles partitioned the 200 acres, Henry taking Pitt Farm and Harold, Nelson's Farm.[169] From this point the histories of the two farms differ. Four more families owned Pitt Farm before subdivision of the property.[170] The

10 The Great-Grandchildren Take Over

fifth title-holder sold 30 acres in 1852 and 75 acres in 1953.[171] The owners of the 30 acres partitioned the land into two 15 acre lots in 1958.[172] The owner of the 75 acres sold 20 acres in 1954 and 55 acres in 1959.[173] The 55 acres has since been divided into three.[174] Pitt Farm is now in six portions.[175] Vegetables grow on the hill, the flats support vegetables and turf, while some land is uncultivated and overgrown.[176] Nelson farm fared better. The fifth owners, William and Mary Betts, paid £23,179 for the farm in 1955.[177] The Betts, who "loved" the farm, reinstated the name Bronte. In 1961 the Betts sold 25 acres of wetland at the corner of Crowley Lane and Castlereagh Road.[178] The present owner of "beautiful" Bronte is their daughter, Margaret Betts, an accredited cattle producer with the European Union who runs about 80 head of beef cattle on the 75 acres. To provide shelter for the animals and habitat for the native birds, she planted thousands of native trees on the river flats and top of the hill. Margaret is restoring Edwin Pitt senior's big old home with its Hawkesbury cedar woodwork and Carrera marble fireplaces.[179] (Figure 36)

Robert Matcham Pitt replaced his father as managing director of Pitt, Son and Badgery. In the firm's building in "leafy" O'Connell Street he created a "home from home" for clients. Robert was a big man with a "booming laugh", "exuberant voice" and a whistle "like a bird". He often attended the opera, Nellie Melba his "friend and idol". At one of Melba's farewell concerts, Robert gave her thousands of daffodils which she sold the next day in Martin Place in aid of the Sydney Hospital.[180] On his death in 1935, the *Sydney Morning Herald* described Robert, "Doyen of the Wool Trade of New South Wales". Aged almost 86, Robert credited his long and healthy life to his childhood on Bronte, "No one had any money in those days. We were all poor, and lived on what we grew on the home farm".[181] None of Robert's eight children followed their father into the company. On 21st June 1972, Philip Macquarie Pty. Ltd. took control of Pitt, Son and Badgery.[182]

Figure 36. Bronte House, 2008

10 The Great-Grandchildren Take Over

After a long illness, Sarah Pitt, formerly John, wife of Robert Pitt, died of "senile decay" and "cardiac syncope" at Trafalgar on 21st August 1897. Seventy-six-year-old Sarah was "one of Kurrajong's oldest and most respected citizens". Her funeral at St Peters on 22nd was "very largely attended".[183] Two years later to the day, 21st August 1899, Robert Pitt, second son of Elizabeth and Thomas Matcham Pitt, died at Trafalgar of "bronchitis" and "senility". The Richmond Bridge submerged, the funeral director sent Robert's hearse round by Windsor on the 22nd. "A large number of persons followed the cortege as far as the river", with Reverend Howell Price conducting the funeral service in heavy rain on 23rd.

Robert ran his citrus orchard until "several years" before his death at almost 82.[184] Robert posssessed "many good qualities". He was an "affectionate and faithfull" husband, a "devoted and tender" father, and a "kind and hospitable" neighbour. Thus, "In every respect", his "long life was exemplary".[185] Sarah and Robert left four daughters and four sons. Unhappily, fifth son, drover William Pitt, took his life near Peachy Eachy in the Menindee district in February 1871. Henry and Clara were to manage Robert's estate of £2003. Robert, George and Henry each received 100 acres of Trafalgar, while daughters Emma and Clara inherited the other 100 acres and home.[186]

Five children of Sarah and Robert Pitt had married. Anne Pitt wed William Want in Richmond in 1862 and after William died in 1882, Herbert Baldwin in Windsor in 1884. Henry Pitt married Elizabeth Stewart in Sydney in February 1881. Henry was "a good and genuine man", "a man of more than ordinary ability and intelligence", who "took more than a passing interst in the social and political problems of the day". These qualities justify Henry's election as a local councillor for about five years before his death in Kurrajong in 1918.[187] By the way, nine aldermen and six mayors, grandsons and great-grandsons of Mary Pitt, served on Municipal Councils. Thomas Matcham Pitt married Elizabeth Russell at the

Church of St Bartholomew in Pyrmont, on the same day brother Henry wed, 1ˢᵗ February 1881. Thomas left for Queensland about 1873 to farm at Surat in the St George district. Later, he moved to the village of Pittsworth, near Toowoomba, on the Darling Downs.[188] George Wilshire Pitt married Fanny Thompson at the Garrison Church, Miller's Point, in 1885. George also went to Queensland where he managed Gowrie Station in the Charlesville District for over 22 years. He also managed or owned a station on the Langlo River near Adavale.[189] Last married was Sarah Pitt to Henry Timmins, in Narrabri in 1893. Bachelor Robert Essington Pitt had "considerable droving experience, was a splendid horseman, and a remarkably good judge of cattle". Eventually Robert settled on Trafalgar and Emma and Clara lived with him. Bob "was one of those bluff, out-spoken, but broad-minded men... (with) large human sympathies".[190]

On 28ᵗʰ September 1899, Esther Whittell, 82, third daughter of Esther and James Wilshire, died at home of "asthenia" and "senile debility". On 30ᵗʰ the Reverend F. Firth buried her in the Waverley Cemetery. After the Sydney Burial Ground closed, son Henry, a "prolific inventor of agricultural and military machinery", erected a new grave for Henry and Esther at Waverley Cemetery.[191] The last of Esther's children married, Emily Whittell to Thomas Charlton in 1898, and Matilda Hannah Whittell to Arthur Ridley in 1909. Surry Hills has streets called Esther, Whittell and Wilshire.

The last grandchild of Mary Pitt, 85-year-old Elizabeth Mary Wilshire, second daughter of Esther and James Wilshire, died on 5ᵗʰ November 1900. Elizabeth died of "bronchitis" and "senile decay" at 171 Albion Street, Surry Hills, her home since the death of brother William.[192] She was buried near sister Esther in Waverley Cemetery on 6ᵗʰ. Elizabeth made her will in 1894, naming nephews James Thompson Wilshire of North Sydney and Edwin James Wilshire of Summer Hill executors and trustees of her estate. At her death, the estate was £8,349. She asked the trustees to sell

10 The Great-Grandchildren Take Over

her "real and personal property" to provide Esther with an annual income of £200. However, she recommended the trustees keep her properties in George Street and Sussex Street as an investment, "but this recommendation shall not be taken to interfere with the discretionary trust for sale hereinbefore reposed in my trustees". (Elizabeth had sold her property in Esther Street, Surry Hills, for £700 in 1875.[193]) Once Esther died, nieces Beatrice Wilshire and Laura Barton each received £100, while nieces Matilda Whittell, Emily Whittell, Esther de Meyrick, Elizabeth Haigh, Maria Bibb and Alice Elliot shared the rest of the money. Elizabeth gave her household effects to niece Matilda Whittell.[194] Five months after Elizabeth's death, on 5th April 1901, the remains and monument of her parents, Esther and James Wilshire, and her brother and sister-in-law, James Robert and Elizabeth Wilshire, were removed from Sydney Burial Ground to Gore Hill Cemetery.[195]

Anne Wilshire, née Osborne, wife of Joseph Wood Wilshire, died of "cerebral softening, glycosuria, atheroma of cerebral vessels" in Pitt Street, Redfern, on 14th March 1901. The Reverend Albery conducted her funeral on 15th March. Joseph's plot at Rookwood holds the remains of Anne as well as those of son Harold, who died in 1890 and daughter Beatrice, who died in 1938.[196] Seven of Anne and Joseph's nine children married, Osborne and Mary Louisa Howe in 1884, Thomas Herbert and Lucy McDougall in 1887, Edith Annie and Robert McLaurin in 1889, Ernest Henry and Nina Church in 1899, Laura Maude and George Burnett Barton in 1900, and John Matcham and Mary Josephine Roycraft in 1906. Youngest child, Granville Wood Wilshire married Mary Normande Agnes Stirton in 1895, and when Mary died, Clara Douglas Ritchie in 1901, and after Clara died, Ruby Ash in 1918.

Life continued to challenge Sarah Wilshire, second wife of James Robert Wilshire. She lost Esther Phoebe Wilshire in January 1895 and Sarah Jane McLean in May 1897, son Alfred Theodore Wilshire in December 1899, and stepson James Thompson Wilshire in April 1909. Sarah Jane McLean left her share of Wilshire Place to her husband Walter, who sold it to Sarah and Emily Rebekah for £918 15s.[197] Despite Sarah's troubles she supported the Benevolent Asylum, Female Refuge, Infirmary for the Aged, City Mission and funeral reform. As well, the Congregational Church profited from her "unceasing labours".[198] On 29th July 1912, Sarah Wilshire, formerly Thompson, 87, died of "myocarditis", "pneumonia", and "syncope" at Moutrion, The Boulevarde, Strathfield. Minister George Littlemore buried her with daughters Sarah Jane McLeod and Esther Phoebe in the Independent Cemetery at Rookwood on 2nd September.[199] Daughter Emily Rebekah Wilshire inherited Sarah's estate of £2,374 which included Sarah's share of Wilshire Place, mortgaged once again.[200] Emily was buried with her mother and sisters in February 1927. The death of Sarah Wilshire, the last member of the grandchildren's generation, marks the end of *The Family of Mary Pitt* except for a brief review of the fortunes of the Pitt Family.

Seeking a more prosperous life, Mary Pitt and her children, Susannah, Lucy, Thomas, Jemima and Hesther, left their home in Dorset for the penal colony of New South Wales. After arriving at Sydney Cove in the *Canada* in December 1801, the Pitts spent a short period at Parramatta before settling in the Hawkesbury district. Primitive conditions prevailed, but grants of land and cheap convict labour made life easier. The children married, forming the Faithfull, Wood, Pitt, Forrest/Jenkins, and Wilshire families. They raised and schooled the grandchildren, worked hard, helped one another and contributed generously to their communities. By any standard of the time, this generation was most successful, despite early deaths. How well did Mary's grandchildren and their spouses fare? They also married, reared and educated the great-grandchildren, worked hard, helped each other and supported their communities. The grandchildren, apart from one grand-daughter, inherited land. Even so, a small number in this generation experienced financial hardship. That problem aside, the grandchildren's generation displayed many

10 The Great-Grandchildren Take Over

talents as farmers, tanners, stock and station agent, artist, inventor, politicians, wardens, mayors, aldermen, magistrates and justices of the peace. The great-grandchildren appeared equally capable but World War I blighted their lives and especially those of their children.[201] We salute Mary Pitt's foresight and courage.

1	SMH 22 February 1860, p3b; GG 1861, Vol 2, p2453, 15 November
2	GG 1861, Vol 2, p1422, 5 July; GG 1861, Vol 2, p1443, 5 June; GG 1861, Vol 2, pl 443, 5 July; GG 1863, Vol 2, p2304, 23 October
3	*Illawarra Mercury* 1 0 June 1884, p2f
4	*Goulburn Evening Penny Post*, 25 April 1896, p2e
5	SMH 31 August 1860, p5d; *Empire* 31 August 1860, p8d; *Empire* 4 September 1860, pla
6	*Empire* 15 September 1860, p4d
7	Sydney University Archives, *Handbooks 1858-1863*. JTW attended from 1858-1863.
8	Registers of Copies of Will 1800-1901, SAG Will 1/4876
9	Bk 231, No 670, DL
10	Bk 70, No 60, DL
11	Bk 72, No 604, DL
12	Bk 78, No 431, DL; Bk 186, No 490, DL; Bk 72, No 547, DL; Bk 81, No 818, DL; Bk 83, No 924, DL
13	GG 1860, Vol 1, p766, 18 April
14	LA, V&P, 1865, 2, fr 829
15	Bk 121, No 199, DL; Bk 80, No 255, DL
16	Bk 92, Pg 151, DL; Bk 92, Pg 152, DL
17	Bk 76, No 919, DL
18	Insolvency, SRNSW 2/9059, No 5914; GG 1862, Vol 1, p787, 30 Mar; GG 1862,Vol 2 p1485, 11 Aug; GG 1862, Vol 2, p1898, 1 Oct; GG 1862, Vol 2, p2112, 8 Nov; GG 1863, Vol 2, pp1596-7, 11 Jul
19	Bk 188, No 341, DL
20	Land Purchases Bk 168, Nos 2002-2014, DL; Land Purchases Bk 183, No 336-340, DL; County Hunter, Parish Gullongulong, 5th ed. 1964, DL; County Hunter, Parish Tollagong, 3rd ed. 1915, DL
21	Yeend, Peter, ed., *The King's School Parramatta, Register 1831-1999*, 3rd ed., The Council of The King's School Parramatta, 1999, pl53
22	SMH 10 February 1865, p5c,d; MacAlister, Charles, *Old Pioneering Days in the Sunny South*, Chas. MacAlister Book Publication Committee, 1907, pp281-3
23	Griffiths, Glynde, N., *Some Southern Homes of New South Wales*, Shepherd Press, National Trust of Australia, 1976, p61

24 *Goulburn Herald* 22 March 1876, p2e; http://www.nla.gov.au/ enter "Faithfull Medal"
25 Gammage, Bill, *Narrandera Shire*, Gammage, 1986, ch 6, pp62-4; ch 7, pp82-3
26 SMH 9 February 1865, p4e
27 Registers of Copies of Wills 1800-1901, SAG Will 1/6362
28 Bk 63, No 779, DL; Bk 67, No 198, DL; Bk 74, No 716, DL; Bk 75, Nos 797, 798, DL
29 Bk 94, No 896, DL; Bk 95, No 227, DL; Bk 95, No 876, DL; Bk 99, No 159, DL; Bk 105, No 238, DL; Bk 107, No 670, DL
30 Bk 98, No 151, DL; Register 159, No 720, DL
31 Bk 108, No 10, DL
32 Index to Outward Passengers to Interstate, UK, NZ, and Foreign Ports, 1852-1886, Film for Jan 1856, Page 001, Public Record Office of Victoria; Index to Unassisted Inward Passenger Lists for British, Foreign and New Zealand Ports 1852-1923, Fiche 205, p015, Public Record Office of Victoria
33 De Castella, *Australian Squatters*, Translation and Notes by C.B. Thornton-Smith, Melbourne University Press, Carlton, Victoria, 1987, Introduction, ch xxv; ADB 3, Castella De
34 De Castella, Victoria, 1987, p169 (Note 48); De Castella Vic BDM Indexes
35 *Index to Unassisted Inward Passenger Lists for British Foreign and New Zealand Ports 1852-1923*, Fiche 229, pg 001, Public Record Office of Victoria
36 *The Hawkesbury Herald*, 27 May 1904, p16c
37 GG 1858, Vol 2, p1738, 4 Oct; GG 1863, Vol 1, p896, 15 Apr; GG 1863, Vol 1, 1317, 9 Jun
38 Bertie, Charles, *The Story of the Royal Hotel*, Simmons Ltd., 1927, ch 2, p27
39 *Sunday News* 14 November 1926, p7d
40 GG 1862, Vol 1, p473, 1 Mar
41 GG 1855, Vol 2, p2561, 24 Sept
42 Bk 73, No 433, DL
43 SMH 29 July 1861, pp7,8; Sands, John, *Sydney and New South Wales Directory 1863*, Fiche 9, p231; SMH 9 November 1863, p7b
44 LA, V&P 1865-6, 3, fr 276; Bowd, 1982, p135
45 Sands, 1865, Fiche 20, p283; Sands 1867, Fiche 32, p350
46 SMH 1 October 1935, p12d
47 SMH 2 January 1872, p7c; SMH 25 Jan 1873, p9a; Bk 90, No 416, DL
48 SMH 15 September 1869, p8f
49 *Hawkesbury Herald*, 4 December 1903, p16c
50 Aurousseau, George H., *Reminiscences of Old Manly 1868-1880*, 1952, p7
51 SMH 19 November 1870, p4e

10 The Great-Grandchildren Take Over

52   GG 1871, Vol 1, p349, 14 Feb; SMH 10 October 1871, p4f; SMH 25 January 1872, p2f; SMH 30 September 1873, plc
53   Bk 87, No 61, DL; Bk 113, No 715, DL; Sands, 1868, Sydney, Fiche 38, p366
54   Bk 111, No 497, DL
55   LA, V&P 1865, 2, frs 829-45; Parkes Correspondence, Vol 60, p786, ML CY A930
56   Bk 121, No 582, DL
57   Bk 159, No 915, DL; Bk 124, No 248 DL
58   GG 1871, Vol 2, p1466, 29 Jun
59   SMH 9 January 1930, pp12-13
60   GG 1861, Vol 2, p2351, 2 Nov; Bk 272, No 659, DL; Bk, 273, No 160, DL; Bk 273, No 339, DL; Bk 282, No 338, DL; Bk 312, No 845, DL; Bk 84, No 284, DL
61   Gormly Notes 1825-1958, ML MSS 672/ 2, Pt 1, pp57,64
62   http://www.usyd.edu/arms/archives/ (Hit "Information about former students", then "Alumni Sidneienses"
63   Registers of Copies of Wills 1800-1901, SAG Will 4/11198
64   Gibbney H.J. and Smith Ann G., *A Biographical Register 1788-1939*, Vol 11, ANU, Canberra, 1987, pp216-7
65   *Goulburn Evening Penny Post* 25 April 1896, p2e; Gammage, 1986, p53
66   GG 1863, Vol 1, p125 1 Jan; GG 1863, Vol 2, p1662, 1 Jul; Bk 108, No 214 DL
67   *Australian Town and Country Journal* 24 January 1874, p140
68   NSW Academy of Art, *Catalogue of Colonial Works of Art, Exhibited at the Chamber of Commerce March 1872*, Cunninghame and Co., Sydney
69   Parkes Correspondence, Vol 43, pp75, 214, ML CY A913
70   Bk 173, No 764, DL; Bk 196, No 159, DL
71   GG 1872 Vol 1, p619, 8 Mar; GG 1872, Vol 1 p696, 15 Mar; GG 1872, Vol 1, p1156, 29 Apr; GG 1872, Vol 1, p1074, 18 Apr
72   GG 1872, Vol 1, p1074, 19 Apr; GG Vol 1, p1294, 16 May; GG Vol 1, p11641, 3 May
73   GG 1874, Vol 1, p426, 6 May; *Illawarra Mercury* 6 February 1874, p2c
74   *Illawarra Mercury* 3 February 1865, p2b; *Illawarra Mercury* 10 February 1865, p2c; GG 1866, Vol 1, p213, cJan 1866; GG 1867, Vol 1 p278, about Jan 1867
75   Bk 103, No 252, DL, Bk 132, No 683, DL; Bk 110, No 503, DL; Bk 139, No 41 DL
76   The great-grandchildren numbered about 157, more than 40 dying before 30. Again these numbers depend on the accuracy of the birth, death and marriage records.
77   SMH 23 March 1874, p4f
78   Aurousseau, George H., *Reminiscences of Old Manly 1868-1880*, 1952, p7
79   Bk 141, No 716, DL

80	Bk 145, No 561 DL; Bk 156, No 359, DL; Sands 1875, Fiche 69, p419; Sands, 1876, Fiche 77, p443
81	SMH 17 March 1875, p7a
82	SMH 29 February 1876, p5
83	Bk 159, No 730, DL
84	Keavey, Kay, " 'The Boudoir' Had a Grand Piano", *The Australian Womens Weekly*, Keavey, 25 March 1970, p13
85	Bk 172, No 617, DL; SMH 28 April 1877, p9d; Bk 172, 618, DL; Bk 177, No 390 DL. See Vendor Indexes 1876 to 1903 for Pitt
86	Bk 243, No 315, DL
87	Registers of Copies of Wills 1800-1901, SAG Will 3/10490
88	*Illawarra Mercury* 30 May 1876, p2e
89	*Illawarra Mercury* 3 June 1884, p2b,c,d
90	Laycock, K. G., Laycock, *A Pioneer Australian Family*, 2000, p31
91	GG 1878, Vol 1, p645, 9 Feb; GG 1879, Vol 1, p780, 6 Feb; GG 1880, Vol 1, p865, 10 Feb; GG 1881, Vol 1, p886, 9 Feb; GG 1882, Vol 1, p1024, 16 Feb; GG 1883, Vol 1, p965, cFeb; GG 1877, Vol 1, p119, 10 Jan; SMH 12 February 1878, p7b; GG 1881, Vol 1, p843, 5 Feb; GG 1884, Vol 1, p1121, 8 Feb; GG 1888, Vol 1, p1328, 11 Feb
92	*Australian Town and Country Journal* 17 October 1896, p15d
93	Watson, James H., Newspaper Cuttings, Australian Pioneers, North Sydney, pp25-6 ML
94	SMH 17 January 1877, p7b; SMH 22 August 1877, p1d; SMH 18 February 1878, p1d; *Echo* 28 March 1879, p3b; SMH 27 November 1879, 6e
95	SMH 1 October 1935, p12d
96	*Evening News*, 11 March 1879, pp4,5; *Echo* 22 May 1879, p2d
97	*Australian Town and Country Journal* 11 October 1879, p676c
98	LA, V&P, 1877-78, 2, pp849-852
99	Keavey, 1970, p12
100	Maxwell, Charles, F., *Australian Men of Mark*, Vol 2 , Version 1, Melbourne, 1889, Appendix, p9
101	SMH 26 February 1930, p16d
102	Bk 144, No 521, DL; Bk 148, No 65, DL
103	Smith, Alfred, *Some Ups and Downs of an Old Richmondite*, Nepean Family History Society, Emu Plains, 1991, pp88-89
104	Laycock , 2000, p31; Registers of Copies of Wills 1800-1901, SAG Will 2/340; Bk 188, No 341, DL
105	Smith, Alfred, 1991, p130
106	County Hunter, Parish Gullongulong, 5th ed. 1964, DL; County Hunter, Parish Tollagong, 3rd ed., 1915, DL
107	Bk 233, No 379, DL
108	Bk 234, No 482, DL
109	Bk 234, No 985, DL
110	Bk 233, No 872, DL

10 The Great-Grandchildren Take Over

111 Bk 137, No 233, DL; Bk 171, No 15, DL; Bk 233, No 314, DL
112 Registers of Copies of Will 1800-1901, SAG Will 3/3121; Sands, 1879, Fiche 92, p618
113 Butler, B. N., *St Mark the Evangelist Anglican Church Appin, 150 years of Ministry 1838-1988*, p40
114 Registers of Copies of Will 1800-1901, SAG Will 3/8823
115 *Illawarra Mercury* 30 January 1883, p2d,f
116 *Illawarra Mercury* 23 November 1901, p2
117 *Illawarra Mercury* 10 June 1884, p2f; *Illawarra Mercury* 3 June 1884, p2c,d
118 *Australian Town and Country Journal* 6 September 1879, p464
119 Registers of Copies of Will 1800-1901, SAG Will 3/10450; Barwick, Kathleen H., *History of Berkeley New South Wales*, Illawarra Historical Society, 1963, p5
120 See Vendor's Index, IJK, 1889-92 DL
121 Vol 1527, Fols 237-40, DL
122 Bk 1041, No 882, DL
123 See re Nudja: www.wollongong.nsw.gov.au/library/localinfo/unanderra/history.html
124 GG 1885 Vol 1, p1131, 9 Feb GG 1886 Vol 1, p1518, 24 Feb
125 *Australian Town and Country Journal* 23 November 1889, p5
126 Maxwell, Charles, F., *Australian Men of Mark*, Vol 2, Version 1, Melbourne, 1889, pp226-230
127 SMH 22 April 1878, p8g, SMH 8 Jan 1879, pp10,11; Bk 404, No 498, DL
128 Coorah is pictured at: http://www.rootsweb.com/-nswbmfhs/pics/coorah.jpg
129 Bk 298, No 417, DL
130 *Goulburn Herald* 28 January 1888, p5a; SMH 26 July 1935, pp9-10; County Bland, Parish Caragabal, 3rd ed., 1926, Map 19, DL
131 Registers of Copies of Wills 1800-1901, SAG Will 3/16060
132 *Goulburn Post* 9 October 1945, p2a
133 Bk 1030, No 248, DL
134 Cadastral Record Viewer, Parish Ham Common, Portions 168-171, DP752032
135 Bk 489, No 246, DL
136 Bk 389, No 247, DL
137 Bk 247, No 873, DL; Sands, 1883, Fiche 116, p525
138 Sands, 1886, Fiche 143, p813; 1887, Fiche 155, p936; 1888, Fiche 167, p829
139 GG 1885, p 1022, 3 Feb; GG 1886, p1059, 9 Feb
140 https://www.parliament.nsw.gov.au/members/formermembers/Pages/former-members.aspx
141 *The Home* 1 April 1933, pp40,46,56
142 SMH 26 January 1886, p6e; Scarlett, Errol-Lea, *Roots and Branches*,

Collins, Sydney, 1979, ch 7, p119
143   Registers of Copies of Wills 1800-1901, SAG Will 4/18870
144   Parkes Correspondence, Vol 60, pp320, 826 ML CY A930; Vol 42, pp383-4; ML CY A912
145   SMH 4 November 2008, pp1g,3d-h
146   Registers of Copies of Wills 1800-1901, SAG Will 3/18455; Bk 395, No 480, DL; Bk 374, No 478, DL; Bk 374, No 479, DL
147   *Goulburn Evening Penny Post*, 12 December 1889, p4a
148   Sands 1877, Fiche 84, p509; Sands 1883, Fiche 116, p528; Sands 1890, Fiche 188, p963; Bk 111, No 28 DL; Bk 131, No 685, DL; Bk 166, No 891, DL
149   Registers of Copies of Wills 1800-1901, SAG Will 4/5984
150   *Windsor and Richmond Gazette*, 26 August 1893, p4c; Bk 103, No 622, DL
151   Bk 129, No 732 DL; Bk, 303, No 911, DL
152   Research of Janelle Cust
153   Supreme Court of NSW, Probate Division, Will 5567
154   Bk 1156, No 456, DL
155   Cadastral Records Viewer Print, Lot 10, DP 703300, Grose Wold, Kurrajong, Cook County
156   *Hawkesbury Herald* 8 January 1904, p16b
157   *Goulburn Evening Penny Post*, 25 April 1896, p2e
158   Registers of Copies of Wills 1800-1901, SAG Will 4/11198; Bk 506, No 792 DL
159   *Springfield*, Meares and Associates, Sydney, 2000, p13; Information from Jim Maple-Brown, 30 June 2008; For Springfield collection see http://www.nma.gov.au Search "Springfield"
160   SMH 13 October 1896, p1a,8a; SMH 14 October 1896, p7b; *Windsor and Richmond Gazette*, 17 Oct, 1896, p8c, p12b
161   *Australian Town and Counhy Journal* 17 October 1896, p15d; Watson, James H., North Sydney, Newspaper Cuttings, pp25-6; *Hawkesbwy Herald* 4 December 1903, p16b,c
162   Bk 665, No 277, DL
163   Registers of Copies of Wills 1800-1901, SAG Will 4/12756
164   Bowd, D.G., *Origins of Names of Streets, Parks and Features: Windsor Municipality*, Windsor Municipal Council, New South Wales, 1973
165   Bk 817, No 431, DL; Information re will of Julia Pitt from Margaret Betts, 27 March 2006
166   Bk 1173, No 579, DL
167   Bk 1486, No 983, DL; Bk 2163, No 691, DL
168   Bk 1557, No 316, DL
169   Bk 1664, No 574, DL
170   Bk 1752, No 912, DL; Bk 1785, No 531, DL; Bk 1811, No 710, DL; Bk 2081, No 879, DL; Bk 2168, No 592, DL
171   Bk 2236, No 707, DL; Bk 2246, No 524, DL

10 The Great-Grandchildren Take Over

172 Bk 2627, No 650, DL
173 Bk 2301 No 253, DL; Bk 2482 No 41, DL
174 Bk 2638, No 406, DL
175 Cadastral Record Viewer, Parish Ham Common, Locality Agnes Banks, DP162177 (portion 47), DP752032 (portion 46) DL
176 Email 31 March 2006 (10.57 am), Margaret Betts to Janelle Cust
177 Bk 2005, No 344, DL; Bk 2147, No 397, DL; Bk 2270, No 5, DL; Bk 2325, No 816, DL; Bk 2363, No 51, DL
178 Bk 2568 No 942, DL
179 Emails 25,27,31 (10.07 am) March 2006, Margaret Betts to Janelle Cust
180 Keavey, 1970, pp 12-13
181 SMH 1 October 1935, p12d
182 Guide to Australian Business Records http://www.gabr.net.au/biogs/ABE0304b.htm
183 *Windsor and Richmond Gazette* 28 August 1897, pp4a,8a
184 *Windsor and Richmond Gazette* 26 August 1899, p4c
185 Watson, James, H., Newspaper Cuttings, Australian Pioneers, North Sydney, p42
186 Registers of Copies of Wills 1800-1901, SAG Will 4/19505
187 *Windsor and Richmond Gazette* 13 September 1918, p9b
188 *Brisbane Courier* 4 January 1924, p4h
189 S. R. Sellin, *The Fitzwaters*, S.R., Sellin, p257
190 *Windsor and Richmond Gazette* 18 June 1920, p2b
191 Whittell Papers ML A2783
192 Sands 1890, Fiche 188, p9631; Sands 1899, Fiche 289, p1017
193 Bk 159, No 720, DL
194 Registers of Copies of Wills 1800-1901, SAG Will 4/22072
195 Vine Hall, Nick, *Gore Hill Cemetery Transcripts*, Vol 2, Royal Australian History Society and Society of Australian Genealogists, Sydney, 1976
196 Rookwood Cemetery Transcriptions, 2002, SAG, Nearby Graves Report, p3
197 Bk 598, No 993, DL
198 SMH 10 August 1912, p13
199 Rookwood Cemetery Transcriptions, 2002, SAG, Nearby Graves Report, p2
200 Probate Package, No 4/57559; Bk 323, No 98, DL; Bk 458, No 891, DL; Bk 534, No 319, DL; Bk 598, No 994, DL
201 *Sydney Mail* 28 November 1917, p17

BIRTH, MARRIAGE AND DEATH CHARTS

Mary Matcham and Robert Pitt **309**
Susannah Pitt and William Faithfull **311**
William Pitt Faithfull and Mary Deane 313
Alice Faithfull and Andrew Gibson 315
Lucy Pitt and John Wood **317**
George Pitt Wood and Elizabeth Markwell 318
Sophia Wood and Samuel Pinder Henry 322
Thomas Matcham Pitt and Elizabeth Laycock **325**
George Matcham Pitt and Julia Johnson 327
Mary Matcham Pitt and
  Thomas William Eber Bunker Laycock 330
Robert Pitt and Sarah John 333
Jemima Pitt and Austin Forrest and Robert Jenkins **335**
Robert Pitt Jenkins and Maria Louisa Adelaide Plunkett 336
William Warren Jenkins and Matilda Pitt Wilshire 338
Hester Pitt and James Wilshire **341**
Louisa Wilshire and Philip Elliot 343
William Pitt Wilshire and Catherine Maria Robertson 344
William Pitt Wilshire and Margaret Hornery 346
James Robert Wilshire and Elizabeth Thompson 347
James Robert Wilshire and Sarah Thompson 349
Austin Forrest Wilshire and Frances ? and Eliza Pitt 351
Esther Wilshire and Henry Rawes Whitten 354
Thomas Matcham Pitt Wilshire and Helen Eliza Faithfull 356
Joseph Wood Wilshire and Anne Osborne 357

Abbreviations in Family Charts

ADB	*Australian Dictionary of Biography 1788-1850*, vols 1-2, Melbourne University Press, Carlton, Victoria 1966-7; 1851-1890, vols 3-6, Melbourne University Press, Carlton, Victoria, 1976 Australian Dictionary of Biography
IGI	International Genealogical Index
MI	Mutch Indexes of Births Deaths and Marriages 1787-1814; 1815-c1957
PI NSW	New South Wales Probate Index
PI Vic	Victorian Probate Index
SAG	Society of Australian Genealogists
SG	Sydney Gazette
SMH	Sydney Morning Herald
?	Unconfirmed or unknown

Mary Matcham and Robert Pitt

Mary Matcham
b c1748 Ireland? ?F- Thomas Matcham ch 1704
GF- Thomas Matcham (1674-1720); GM- Mary Ford (d 1748)
d 7 November 1815 Sydney, NSW
m **Robert Pitt** 27 December 1770 Child Okeford, Dorset, England ch 9 October 1734 Dorset, England. F- William Pitt (1708-1749); M- Rose Belbin (1701-1782)
bur 6 April 1787 Dorset, England

1 George Matcham Pitt
ch 29 Jan 1772 Sturminster Newton, Dorset, England
d USA

2 Susannah Pitt
ch 1 April 1774 Sturminster Newton, Dorset, England
d 4 September 1820 Richmond, NSW. SG 9 September 1820, p3c
m William Faithfull

3 Lucy Pitt
ch 5 August 1776 Child Okeford, Dorset, England
bur 8 August 1776 Child Okeford, Dorset, England

4 Lucy Pitt
ch 9 November 1777 Child Okeford, Dorset, England
m **John Wood**
d 26 November 1852 Richmond, NSW. NSW V1852 944 38B

5 Thomas Pitt
ch 30 January 1779 Child Okeford, Dorset, England
bur 8 May 1779 Dorset, England

6 William Pitt
ch 30 January 1779 Child Okeford, Dorset, England
d USA

7 Thomas Matcham Pitt
ch 2 May 1781 Sturminster Newton, Dorset, England
m **Elizabeth Laycock**
d 28 January 1821 Richmond, NSW. MI

8 Jemima Pitt
ch 10 June 1783 Sturminster Newton, Dorset, England
m 1 **Austin Alexander Forrest**
m 2 **Robert Jenkins**
d 4 May 1842 Campbelltown, NSW NSW Vl 842 204 26B

9 Hesther Pitt
ch 9 July 1786 Sturminster Newton, Dorset, England
m **James Wilshire**
d 9 May 1836 Sydney, NSW NSW V1836 352 20

Lamble, Barbara, *The Pitts of Dorset and Richmond, NSW*; an account of research in Dorset, London, Bristol and Sydney, 1990. See Lamble for events not otherwise referenced.

Susannah Pitt and William Faithfull

Susannah Pitt
ch 1 April 1774 Sturminster Newton, Dorset, England. F- Robert Pitt; M- Mary Matcham
d 3 September 1820 Richmond, NSW. SG 9 September 1820, p3c
m 1 **William Faithfull** 21 November 1804 Parramatta, NSW. MI ch 14 December 1774 Winchester, Hampshire, England. F- William; M- Ann Dibsdale? IGI
d 16 April 184 7 Richmond, NSW. MI

1 William Pitt Faithfull
b 11 October 1806 Richmond, NSW. MI
d 24 April 1896 Springfield, Goulburn, NSW. NSW 5764
m **MaryDeane**

2 Robert Faithfull
b 2 July 1808 Richmond, NSW. MI
d 26 August 1812 Richmond, NSW. MI

3 Alice Faithfull
b 8 January 1811 Richmond, NSW. MI
d 27 January 1888 Tirranna, Goulburn, NSW. *Goulburn Herald* 28th January 1888, p5a
m **Andrew Gibson**

4 George Faithfull
b 5 January 1814 Sydney, NSW. MI
d 22 October 1855 Wangaratta, Vic. PI Vic 1/844

William Faithfull married a second and third time

m 2 **Margaret Thompson** 29 Nov 1821 Liverpool, NSW. MI
d 28 July 1842 Richmond NSW. MI

1 Helen Eliza Faithfull
b 19 March 1824 Richmond NSW. MI
m **Thomas Matcham Pitt Wilshire** 25 March 1843 Sydney, NSW. MI
d 24 April 1847 SydneyNSW. NSW V1847 334 32B

2 James Robert
b 25 August 1825 Richmond, NSW. MI
d 6 August 1827 Richmond, NSW. MI

m 3 **Maria Bell** 13 June 1843 Richmond, NSW. MI
b 10 April 1795 Cheshunt, Hertford, England. F- Archibald Bell; M- Maria Kitching. IGI
d 29 May 1859 Richmond, NSW. PI NSW 1/4394

William Pitt Faithfull and Mary Deane

William Pitt Faithfull

b 11 October 1806 Richmond, NSW. F- William Faithfull; M- Susannah Pitt

d 24 April 1896 Springfield Goulburn NSW. NSW 5674

m **Mary Deane** 20 January 1844 Sydney, NSW. NSW V1844 5 29

b c1813 Devonshire, England. F- Thomas Deane; M- Ann Pidsley

d 10 December 1889 Springfield, Goulburn, NSW. NSW 6627

1 William Percy Faithfull

b 24 October 1844 Springfield, Goulburn, NSW. NSW V1844 2057 28

d 2 November 1924 Neutral Bay, NSW

m 1 **Emma Louise Geary** 1 May 1878 Sydney, NSW

F- William Henry Geary; M- Susan Geary

d 9 February 1893 Randwick, NSW

m 2 **Kate Montague Geary** 27 April 1909 Adelaide, SA

F- Harry Vincent Geary; M- Jane Geary

d 4 May 1940 North Sydney, NSW

2 George Ernest Faithfull

b 13 April 1846 Goulburn, NSW. NSW Vl 846 1783 3 lA

d 9 September 1910 Inveralochy, Goulburn, NSW

3 Henry Montague Faithfull

b 16 June 1847 Goulburn, NSW. NSW V1847 1624 32A

d 22 October 1908 Elizabeth Bay, NSW

m **Emily Rose Buckland** 28 March 1874 Surry Hills, NSW

b 1850 Sydney. F- Thomas Buckland; M- Mary Buckland

d 4 April 1897 Burradoo, NSW

4 Reginald Faithfull

b 4 January 1850 Goulburn, NSW. NSW V1850 1592 35

d 4 June 1882 Brewarrena Station, near Narrandera, NSW. PI NSW 3/7172

5 Florence Faithfull

b 14 November 1851 Springfield, Goulburn, NSW. NSW Vl851 2482 38A

d 13 September 1949 Springfield, Goulburn, NSW

6 Robert Lionel Faithfull

b 27 July 1853 Goulburn, NSW

d 8 June 1930 Moss Vale, NSW

m **Jessie Alice Gibson** (cousin) 25 April 1888 Tirranna, Goulburn, NSW

d 2 March 1947 Moss Vale, NSW

7 Augustus Lucian Faithful

b 17 April 1855 Springfield, Goulburn, NSW. NSW Vl855 646 42A

d 29 November 1942 Springfield, Goulburn, NSW

m **Ethel Joplin** 17 April 1895 Goulburn, NSW

F- Robert Croudace Joplin; M- Emma Maria Thompson

d 5 May 1959 Goulburn, NSW

8 Constance Mary Faithfull

b 1 July 1857 Springfield, Goulburn, NSW. NSW 6793

d 20 July 1938 England

9 Frances Lilian Faithfull

b 28 June 1859 Springfield, Goulburn, NSW. NSW 7528

d 19 June 1948 Camden, NSW

m **William Hugh Anderson** 16 February 1898 Goulburn, NSW

F- Alexander Anderson

d 16 May 1912 Camden, NSW

Mowle, L. M., *Pioneer Families of Australia*, 5th ed., Rigby, 1978. See for events not otherwise referenced.

Alice Faithfull and Andrew Gibson

Alice Faithfull

b 8 January 1811 Richmond, NSW. F- William Faithfull; M- Susannah Pitt

d 27 January 1888 Tirranna, Goulburn, NSW. *Goulburn Herald* 28th January 1888, p5a

m **Andrew Gibson** 24 February 1827 Sydney, NSW. MI

b 1 August 1796 United Kingdom

d 22 September 1840 Tirranna, Goulburn, NSW

1 Alice Jemima Gibson

b 13 December 1827 Sydney, NSW. NSW V1811 8516 IC

d 27 May 1907 Goulburn, NSW. PI NSW 4/40317

m 1 **James Donaldson** 5 July 1851 Sydney, NSW. NSW V1851 96 37B

F- Stuart Donaldson, of London

d 30 April 1856 Sydney, NSW

m 2 **Andrew Gibson Finlay** 11 October 1862, Tirranna, Goulburn, NSW. Records of St Saviours, Goulburn

b Scotland. F- Robert Brown Finlay; M- Marion Gibson

d 15 September 1907 Goulburn, NSW. PI NSW 4/41311

2 Thomas Jamieson Faithfull Gibson

b 7 December 1830 Tirranna, Goulburn, NSW. NSW V1830 10224 1C

d 30 May 1916 Albury, NSW. PI NSW 4/76662

m **Josephine Lett** 17 February 1859 Goulburn, NSW. F- John Lett

d 16 July 1923 Albury, NSW

3 Andrew Faithfull Gibson

b 18 March 1833 Tirranna, Goulburn, NSW. NSW V1833 733 17

d 6 May 1910 Sydney, NSW

m **Annie Campbell** 10 April 1862 Bombala, NSW. F- Ronald Campbell; M- Ann Campbell

d 15 May 1928 Sydney NSW. PI NSW 4/152529

4 Susannah Jane Gibson

b 31 March 1835 Tirranna, Goulburn, NSW. NSW V1835 851 19

d 8 March 1915 Potts Point, NSW

m **Richard Henry Blomfield** 20 February 1855 Goulburn, NSW

b 12 February 1823 Liverpool, NSW. F- Thomas V. Blomfield; M- Christiana Brooks

d 11 November 1896 Darlinghurst, NSW

5 Frederick Faithfull Gibson

b 15 January 1837 Tirranna, Goulburn, NSW. NSW V1837 1108 21

d 9 April 1913 Tirranna, Goulburn, NSW. PI NSW 4/60612

m **Mary Cunningham** 23 October 1873 Queanbeyan NSW

b 1848 Queanbeyan NSW. F- Andrew Cunningham; M- Mary Cunningham

d 29 August 1923 Sydney, NSW. PI NSW 123537

6 William Faithfull Gibson

b 23 December 1838 Tirrranna, Goulburn, NSW. NSW V1838 1203 23A

d 30 May 1874 Caragabal, Grenfell, NSW

7 Septimus Faithfull Gibson

b 17 October 1840 Tirranna, Goulburn, NSW. NSW V1840 1352 24A

d 2 July 1879 Goulburn, NSW

m **Annie Maria Chisholm** 20 April 1865 Goulburn, NSW

b 13 August 1846 Goulburn, NSW. F- John W. Chisholm; M- Rebecca Stuckey

d 15 September 1888 Woollahra, NSW

Mowle, L. M., *Pioneer Families of Australia*, 5th ed, Rigby, Sydney, 1978. See for events not otherwise referenced.

Lucy Pitt and John Wood

Lucy Pitt
ch 9 November 1777 Child Okeford, Dorset, England
F- Robert Pitt; M- Mary Matcham
d 26 November 1852 Richmond, NSW. NSW V1852 944 38B
m **John Wood** 11 January 1802 Parramatta, NSW. NSW V1802 514 3
b c1775 Deptford, England
d c April 1812 at sea, near Campbell Island, New Zealand? NSW V1812 80 7

1 George Pitt Wood
b 1802 Pacific Ocean or Tahiti, Society Islands. F- John Wood; M- Lucy Pitt
d 24 September 1853 Richmond NSW. NSW V1853 1641 39B
m **Elizabeth Markwell**

2 Sophia Wood
b 11 May 1804 Richmond, NSW. NSW V1804 1477 1A
d 3 September 1851 Tahiti, Society Islands. SMH 3 Dec 1851, p3g
m **Samuel Pinder Henry**

George Pitt Wood and Elizabeth Markwell

George Pitt Wood
b 1802 Pacific Ocean or Tahiti, Society Islands. F- John Wood; M- Lucy Pitt
d 24 September 1853 Richmond, NSW. NSW Vl 853 1641 39B
m **Elizabeth Markwell** 9 September 1826 Richmond, NSW. NSW V1826 535 44
ch 22 April 1810 Richmond, NSW. F- Thomas Markwell; M- Maria Cheshire. NSW V1810 1 2101
d 25 June 1853 Nth Richmond, NSW. NSW V1853 1634 39B

Lucy Sophia Wood
d 8 December 1827 Nth Richmond, NSW, 2 mths. Markwell Grave, St Peters Cemetery, Richmond, NSW

2 John Thomas Wood
bap 21 September 1828 Nth Richmond, NSW. Records of St Peters, Richmond
bur 17 December 1828 Nth Richmond, NSW. Records of St Peters, Richmond

3 William Henry Wood
b 8 November 1829 Nth Richmond, NSW. Records of St Peters, Richmond
d 7 August 1879 Emu Plains, NSW. MI
m **Ann Crowley** 12 August 1847 Richmond, NSW. Records of St Peters, Richmond
b 16 January 1828 Richmond NSW. F- John Crowley Snr.; M- Jane Charlotte Bryant
d 30 August 1893 Emu Plains, NSW. MI

4 George Wood
b 2 July 1831 Nth Richmond NSW. Records of St Peters, Richmond
d 4 December 1894 Taree, NSW. MI
m 1 **Caroline Aston** 8 June 1853 Richmond, NSW. Records of St Peters, Richmond
b 6 December 1834 Nth Richmond NSW. F- William Aston; M- Jane Charlotte Bryant. MI

d 15 August 1860 Nth Richmond, NSW. Records of St Peters, Richmond
m 2 **Mary Collins** 29 August 1861 Richmond, NSW. MI - see Alice Wood
d 5 December 1906 Taree. NSW 14459

5 John Thomas Wood

b 23 November 1832 Nth Richmond, NSW. Records of St Peters, Richmond
d 18 August 1893 Nth Richmond, NSW. NSW 12995
m **Mary Ann Aston** 28 May 1856 Richmond, NSW. NSW 2098
b 30 October 1839 Nth Richmond, NSW. F- William Aston; M- Jane Charlotte Bryant. MI
d 19 August 1914 Naremburn, NSW. NSW 11815

6 Sophia Wood

b 25 June 1834 Nth Richmond, NSW. Records of St Peters, Richmond
d 27 May 1904 Marrickville, NSW. NSW 6033
m **Robert Lamrock** 15 March 1860 Sydney, NSW. NSW 00212
b 1826 Faughanville, Limavady, Ireland. F- James Lamrock; M- Jane Cuthbertson [1]
d 21 May 1906 Marrickville, NSW. NSW 5703

7 LucyWood

b 16 March 1836 Nth Richmond, NSW. Records of St Peters, Richmond
d 7 August 1907 Brushgrove, Maclean, NSW. PI NSW 4/40978
m **William Robert Farlow** 5 April 1854 Richmond, NSW. Records of St Peters Richmond
b 18 October 1830 Richmond, NSW. F- William Farlow; M -Mary Ann Howell. MI
d 13 October 1904 Brushgrove, Maclean, NSW. PI NSW 4/32877

8 Robert Markwell Wood

b 9 November 1837 Nth Richmond, NSW. Records of St Peters, Richmond
d 21 August 1885 Reedy Creek, Singleton, NSW. Arch Gray Index, SAG
m **Louisa Baines** 1 November 1858 Richmond, NSW. NSW 02631 F- John Baines; M- Sarah Baines
d 7 June 1917 Singleton NSW. NSW 06748

9 Alfred Sherwin Wood

b 9 April 1839 Nth Richmond, NSW. Records of St Peters, Richmond

d 19 June 1915 Burwood, NSW [2]

m **Catherine Mary Ferguson** 16 April 1862 Commercial Hotel, West Maitland, NSW. NSW 02214

b 23 May 1840 Dunmore House, near Morpeth NSW. F- Dr John Ferguson; M- Sarah Ferguson [3]

d 27 July 1901 Singleton, NSW [2]

10 Ellen Maria Wood

b 27 October 1840 Nth Richmond, NSW. Records of St Peters, Richmond

d 20 April 1874 Balmain, NSW. Balmain Cemetery Records

11 Mary Ann Wood

b 4 July 1842 Nth Richmond, NSW. NSW V1842 484 54

d 23 February 1910 Gladesville, NSW. NSW 3128

m **James Grant** 20 September 1864 Residence Rev. Thos. Gordon, Balmain, NSW. NSW 01115

d 14 April 1896 Balmain South NSW. NSW 05484

12 Thomas George Wood

b 5 November 1843 Nth Richmond, NSW. Records of St Peters, Richmond

d 21 July 1918 Wellington, NSW. PI NSW 4/1193

m **Jane Matilda Howell** 16 December 1874 Residence Thos Howell, Frederick Town, Orange, NSW. NSW 03491

b 17 April 1845 Richmond, NSW. F- Thomas Howell; M- Elizabeth Crowley. NSW V1845 1314 30A

d 24 May 1882 Dubbo, NSW. PI NSW 4/53089

13 Alice Elizabeth Wood

b 29 June 1845 Nth Richmond, NSW. Records of St Peters, Richmond

d 12 October 1910 St Marys, NSW. Records of St Marys General Cemetery

m **James Hope** 19 January 1871 South Creek, NSW. NSW 03273

b 28 November 1849 Penrith, NSW. F- George Hope, M- Alice Hope NSW

V1849 1652 34A

d 16 December 1912 St Marys, NSW. Records of St Marys General Cemetery

14 Susanna Wood

b 4 March 1847 Nth Richmond, NSW. Records of St Peters, Richmond

d 1 February 1921 Inverell, NSW. Inverell Cemetery Records

m **Thomas Hawkins** 4 November 1869, Yarramundi, Richmond, NSW. NSW 03375

d 4 March 1911 Inverell, NSW. Inverell Cemetery Records

15 Henry Austin Wood

b 26 March 1849 Nth Richmond, NSW. Records of St Peters, Richmond

d 22 April 1849 Richmond, NSW. Records of St Peters, Richmond

16 Henry Austin Wood

b 9 April 1850 Nth Richmond, NSW. NSW V1850 1514 35

d 26 September 1918 Camperdown, NSW. NSW 9231

m 1 **Catherine Isabella Gillett** 8 January 1870 Sydney, NSW. NSW 00025

?d 18 March 1896 Balmain South, NSW. NSW 830

m 2 **Elizabeth Lamrock** 3 October 1906 Sydney, NSW. NSW 8872

Elizabeth (Simpson)

d 1954 Balmain, NSW 26950

17 James Edward Wood

b 7 November 1852 Nth Richmond, NSW. NSW V1852 895 56

d 29 November 1852 Nth Richmond, NSW. NSW V1852 945 38B

---

[1] *Australian Biographical and Genealogical Record, 1842-1899*, Vol 3, Society of Genealogists, North Sydney, 1988, p152 (Lamrock parents)

[2] Dunlop, G. S., of Morpeth, to Janelle Cust, Letter of October 2004, re deaths of Alfred & Catherine Wood

[3] Dunlop, Anne M., of Morpeth, to Geoff Wood, Letter of 27 January 1981, re birth of Catherine Ferguson

Sophia Wood and Samuel Pinder Henry

Sophia Wood
b 11 May 1804 Richmond, NSW. F- John Wood; M- Lucy Pitt. NSW V1804 1477 1A
d 3 September 1851 Tahiti, Society Islands. SMH 3 Dec 1851, p2g
m **Samuel Pinder Henry** 28 June 1821 Parramatta, NSW. MI
b 3 February 1800 Tahiti, Society Islands. F- William Henry; M- Sarah Maben
d 9 June 1852 Tahiti, Society Islands. SMH 31 August 1852, p3d

1 William John Wood Henry
b 17 June 1822 Tahiti, Society Islands?
d 3 November 1842 Isle of Pines, New Caledonia

2 Samuel Pinder Henry II
b 25 September 1823 Tahiti, Society Islands?
d 1865 Tahiti, Society Islands
m 1846 **Isabella Brine Orsmond**, Tahiti, Society Islands?
d 1896 Tahiti, Society Islands?

3 Lucy Ann Henry
b 25 September 1827 Tahiti, Society Islands?
d by 1840?

4 Alfred Henry
b 26 June 1828 Tahiti, Society Islands?
Died early

5 Sophia Henry
b 1 September 1830 Tahiti, Society Islands?
d 16 December 1906 Darling Point, NSW. SMH 17 December 1906 10a
m **James Greer** 27 February 1849 Glebe, NSW. SMH 28 February 1849 p3g
d 22 January 1904 Darling Point; NSW. NSW 03819

6 Alice Henry

b 12 November 1833 Tahiti, Society Islands?

d?

7 Lucy Sarah Henry

b 4 April 1840 Tahiti, Society Islands?

d 8 July 1921 North Sydney, NSW. NSW 14274

m **Joseph Love** c1864 Hong Kong, NSW 14274

d 6 June 1923 North Sydney, NSW. NSW 06957

8 Sarah Roseanna Henry

b 16 April 1843 Tahiti, Society Islands?

d 31 May 1911 Gladesville, NSW. NSW 07438

m **John Henry Bruyeres** 27 February 1862 Darlinghurst, Sydney, NSW. NSW 00170

d before May 1911?

9 Joseph Henry

b 8 July 1844? Tahiti, Society Islands?

m?

d?

10 Caroline Henry

b 4 May 1846 Tahiti, Society Islands?

d 27 October 1906 Potts Point, NSW. NSW 11283

m **William Ebenezer Henry III**, (cousin) 21 November 1868 Ryde, NSW. NSW 3319

b 1845. F- Isaac Shepherd Henry; M- Eliza Charlotte Orsmond

d 29 November 1904 Greenwich, NSW. NSW 14766

11 Henry Henry

died at birth?

Crocombe, R.G. and Marjorie, *The Works of Ta'Unga, Records of a Polynesian Traveller in the South Seas, 1833-1896*, Australian National University Press, Canberra 1968, ch 4. Death of William John Wood Henry

Reeves Family File, Sophia and Samuel Henry, SAG. Gives names and birthdates of children

Neil Gunson, The Deviations of a Missionary Family, The Henrys of Tahiti, in Davidson, J.W. and Scarr, Derrick, eds, *Pacific Island Portraits*, Australian National University Press, Canberra, 1970, ch 2, pp50, 51. Provides spouses of children and years of some events in Tahiti.

Thomas Matcham Pitt and Elizabeth Laycock

Thomas Matcham Pitt
ch 2 May 1781 Sturminster, Newton Dorset, England. F- Robert Pitt: M- Mary Matcham
d 28 January 1821 Richmond, NSW. MI
m **Elizabeth Laycock** 15 February 1813 Parramatta, NSW. MI
b 29 June 1796 Sydney, NSW. F- Thomas Laycock; M- Hannah Pearson [1]
d 1 January 1835 Richmond, NSW. NSW V1835 2493 19

1 George Matcham Pitt
b 16 February 1814 Richmond, NSW. MI
d 12 October 1896 North Sydney, NSW. MI
m **Julia Johnson**

2 Mary Matcham Pitt
b 7 November 1815 Richmond, NSW. MI
d 15 July 1878 Putty, NSW. NSW 10427
m **Thomas William Eber Bunker Laycock** (cousin)

3 Robert Pitt
b 7 September 1817 Richmond, NSW. MI
d 21 August 1899 Kurrajong, NSW [2]
m **Sarah John**

4 William Henry Pitt
b 26 February 1819 Richmond, NSW. MI
d 27 June 1834 Richmond, NSW. NSW V1834 2301 18

5 Eliza Pitt
b 1 November 1820 Richmond, NSW. MI
d 5 February 1861 Paddington, NSW. NSW 1602
m **Austin Forrest Wilshire** (cousin)

[1] Laycock, K. G., Laycock, *A Pioneer Family*, 2000, p10
[2] *Richmond and Windsor Gazette*, 24 August 1899, p1a

George Matcham Pitt and Julia Johnson

George Matcham Pitt
b 16 February 1814 Richmond, NSW. F- Thomas Matcham Pitt; M- Elizabeth Laycock. MI
d 12 October 1896 North Sydney, NSW. MI
m **Julia Johnson** 22 September 1835 Windsor, NSW. NSW V1835 1433 19
b 14 January 1815 Sydney. F- John Johnson; M- Mary Moore. MI
d 2 August 1886 North Sydney, NSW. NSW 6171

1 Thomas Matcham Pitt
b 22 July 1836 Richmond, NSW. NSW V1836 837 20
d 19 Oct 1836 Richmond, NSW. NSW V1836 1102 20

2 George Matcham Pitt
b 28 October 1837 Richmond, NSW. NSW V1837 855 21
d 19 March 1912 Richmond, NSW. MI
m **Elizabeth Town** 19 January 1860 Richmond, NSW. Records of St Peters, Richmond
b 27 July 1833 Richmond, NSW. F- John Gordon Town; M- Elizabeth Onus. MI
d 18 October 1908 Richmond, NSW. MI

3 Jessie Pitt
b 22 January 1839 Richmond, NSW. NSW V1840 913 24A
d 13 October 1887 Collingwood district, Vic. Records of Salli Chmura
m **William Mylan Nicholas Garling** 16 May 1868 Richmond, NSW. Records of St Peters, Richmond
b 1841 Sydney, NSW. F- Frederick Garling; M- Elizabeth Ward. MI
d 30 March 1929 Hunters Hill, NSW. Records of Salli Chmura

4 Julia Eliza Pitt
b 29 November 1841 Richmond, NSW. NSW V1841 944 26A
d 30 July 1894 Manly, NSW. Records of St Peters, Richmond
m **Henry Septimus Badgery** 13 November 1869 Richmond, NSW. MI

b 9 December 1840 Exeter, NSW. F- Henry Badgery; M- Mary Ann Reilly. MI
d 23 August 1917 Exeter NSW. MI

5 Edwin Pitt
b 23 February 1844 Richmond, NSW. NSWV1844 1436 28
d 12 Nov 1918 Artarmon, NSW [1]
m **Julia Johnson** 16 February 1881 Windsor, NSW. Records of St Matthews C of E, Windsor
b 14 January 1849 Windsor, NSW. F- John Johnson; M- Mary Ann Hewitt. MI
d 15 August 1884 Richmond, NSW. Records of St Peters, Richmond

6 Stewart Pitt
b 6April 1846 Richmond, NSW. NSW V1846 1308 31A
d 21 November 1846 Richmond, NSW V1846 684 31B

7 Harry Austin Pitt
b 25 October 1847 Richmond, NSW. NSW V1847 1279 32A
d 27 December 1925 North Sydney, NSW. NSW 16898

8 Robert Matcham Pitt
b 13 December 1849 Richmond, NSW. NSW V1849 1495 35
d 30 September 1935 Sydney, NSW. SMH 1 Oct 1935, p12d
m **Marie Emilie Eugenie Blanchard** 15 August 1874 Sydney, NSW. Records of St Peters, East Sydney
d 9 November 1943 Orange, NSW. SMH 10 Nov 1943, p12b

9 Colin Pitt
b 2 October 1851 Richmond, NSW. NSW V1851 1466 37
d 25 February 1930 Mosman, NSW. SMH 26 February 1930, p14a
m **Louisa Madeline Dowdell** 5 August 1879 Hobart, Tas. Tas 37/1879/486
d 17 June 1925 Mosman, NSW. NSW 01224

10 Charles Bryan Pitt
b 21 March 1854 Richmond, NSW. NSW V1854 1373 40
d 30 May 1926 Gordon, NSW. SMH 31 May 1826, p10a
m 1 **Ada Perry** 8 October 1878 St Leonards, NSW. Records of Salli Chmura

d 15 April 1901 North Sydney, NSW. SMH 16 April 1901, p1a
m 2 **Alice Mary Semmens** 31 May 1906 Balaclava, Vic. Vic 2401
b 12 March 1878 Rushworth, Victoria. F- Thomas Semmens; M- Catherine Conrick. Vic 11334
d July 1949 Dunblane, Scotland. Records of Salli Chmura

11 Frederick Septimus Pitt
b 23 March 1856 Richmond, NSW. Records of St Peters, Richmond
d 10 April 1856 Richmond, NSW. Records of St Peters, Richmond

12 Eva Laura Pitt
b 5 May 1857 Richmond, NSW. MI
d 1 June 1918 Randwick, NSW. NSW 06737
m **Angelo Korff Tornaghi** 27 June 1888 St Leonards, NSW. Records of Christ Church, St Leonards
b 1859 Sydney. F- Angelo Tornaghi; M- Ellen Tornaghi
d 26 April 1937 North Sydney, NSW. NSW 08997

---

[1] Vine Hall, N. J., *Gore Hill Cemetery Transcripts,* Royal Australian Historical Society and Society of Genealogists, Sydney, 1976, Vol 2, p233

Mary Matcham Pitt and Thomas William Eber Bunker Laycock

Mary Matcham Pitt

b 7 November 1815 Richmond, NSW. F- Thomas Matcham Pitt; M- Elizabeth Laycock. NSW V1815 3745 1B

d 15 July 1878 Putty NSW. NSW 10427

m **Thomas William Eber Bunker Laycock** (cousin), 31 August 1835 Windsor, NSW. MI

b 19 January 1815 Halifax, Nova Scotia. F- Thomas Laycock; M- Isabella Bunker

d 14 April 1881 Putty, NSW. NSW 11157

1 Thomas Laycock

b 22 July 1836 Richmond, NSW. NSW V1836 836 20

d 12 July 1897 Putty, NSW

2 Elizabeth Laycock

b 7 October 1838 Richmond, NSW. NSW V1838 842 22

d 16 July 1915 Sydney, NSW. Rookwood Cem. Transcrip. SAG 2002

m **James Farlow** 28 April 1859 Richmond, NSW. Records of St Peters, Richmond

d 10 March 1900 Dubbo NSW

3 Robert Laycock

b 11 July 1840 Putty, NSW. NSW V1840 937 24A

d 1 Jan 1866 Wollombi, NSW. MI

4 Henry Laycock

b 9 July 1843 Putty, NSW. NSW V1843 1362 3A

d 9 July 1904 Putty, NSW

5 Andrew Laycock

b 7 July 1845 Putty, NSW. NSW V1845 1363 3A

d 13 August 1908 Putty, NSW. PI NSW 4/45791

m **Mary Jane Thorley** 1 October 1884 Mt Thorley, Singleton, NSW. Singleton

Parish Records
b 1856 Patricks Plains NSW. F- James Thorley; M- Jane Forbes Thorley, née Galvin
d 8 September 1909 Putty, NSW. PI NSW 4/47279

6 Isabella Eliza Laycock
b 10 March 1847 Putty, NSW. NSW V1847 1558 35
d 1 December 1907 Windsor, NSW. Windsor Catholic Cemetery
m **James Gillespie** 16 February 1872 Windsor, NSW. Records of St Matthews C of E, Windsor
d 26 October 1908, Windsor, NSW. Windsor Catholic Cemetery

7 Emily Jane Laycock
b 19 March 1849 Putty, NSW. NSW V1849 1559 35
d 22 August 1925 Putty NSW
m **Oliver Cobcroft** 3 August 1876 Pitt Town, NSW. MI
b 1850 Tamworth district, NSW. F- William John Cobcroft; M- Elizabeth Rose
d 14 August 1929 Putty NSW. NSW 13136

8 Child
d 1851-3?

9 Mary Matcham Laycock
b 24 April 1855 Putty, NSW. NSW V1855 3537 42 B
d 26 June 1944 Chatswood, NSW
m 1 **James R. Timmins** 21 September 1875 Wollombi, NSW. Wollombi Parish Records
b 15 September 1850 Windsor, NSW. F- John Timmins; M- Elizabeth Scott
d after 1876
m 2 **William Frederick Thirgood** c1879
d 1900?

10 George Laycock
b 3 November 1858 Putty, NSW
d 29 July 1948 Sydney, NSW

m **Ada Emily Cobcroft** 21 February 1882 Wollombi, NSW. Records of St John's, Wollombi
b 1857 Menedebri Station, near Somerton, NSW. F- William John Cobcroft; M- Elizabeth Rose
d 11 October 1916 Singleton, NSW

Laycock, K.G. Laycock, *A Pioneer Australian Family,* 2000, p59. See for events not otherwise referenced.

Robert Pitt and Sarah John

Robert Pitt
b 7 September 1817 Richmond, NSW. F- Thomas Matcham Pitt; M- Elizabeth Laycock. NSW V1817 4266 1B
d 21 August 1899 Kurrajong, NSW. MI
m **Sarah John** 6 September 1843 Richmond, NSW. NSW V1843 274 27C
b 25 January 1820 Richmond, NSW. F- William John; M- Sarah Harvey. MI
d 21 August 1897 Kurrajong, NSW. NSW 09573

1 Anne Pitt
b 24 May 1844 Richmond, NSW. NSW V1844 1453 28
d 1 July 1918 Richmond, NSW. Records of St Peters, Richmond
m 1 **William Want** 15 January 1867 Richmond, NSW. Records of St Phillips, North Richmond
b Norfolk, England. F- William Want; M- Mary Harris
d 26 April 1882 North Richmond, NSW. PI NSW 3/7011
m 2 **Herbert Ernest Baldwin** 23 July 1884 Windsor, NSW. NSW05250
d?

2 Sarah Pitt
b 5 June 1845 Richmond, NSW. NSW V1845 1340 30A
d 9 December 1900 Collarenabri, NSW. NSW 12250
m **Henry Timmins** 14 September 1893 Narrabri, NSW. Records of St Matthews, Narrabri
b 19 January 1853 Richmond NSW. F- John Timmins; M- Elizabeth Scott
d 24 February 1927 Collarenabri, NSW. PI NSW 4/144940

3 William Pitt
b 6 June 1847 Kurrajong, NSW. NSW V1847 1238 32A
d 9 February 1871, near Menindee, NSW. NSW 04339

4 EmmaPitt
b 22 July 1849 Kurrajong, NSW. NSW V1849 1780 34A
d 22 June 1925 Richmond, NSW. PI NSW 4/133745

5 Henry Pitt
b 22 September 1851 Kurrajong, NSW. NSW V1851 1458 37
d 4 September 1918 Kurrajong, NSW. PI NSW 170860
m **Elizabeth Catharine Stewart** 1 February 1881 St Paul's, Sydney, NSW
d 29 August 1934 Narrandera, NSW. PI NSW 4/202006

6 Thomas Matcham Pitt
b 23 September 1853 Kurrajong, NSW. NSW V1853 2658 39A
d 30 December 1923 Toowoomba, Qld. *The Brisbane Courier* 4 January 1924, p4h
m **Elizabeth Russell** 1 February 1881 Pyrmont, Sydney, NSW. NSW 00104
b 1852 Darling Downs, Qld. F- John Russell; M- Nancy Hanna NSW V1852 3458 38A
d 19 July 1936 Qld. Qld 1936/003446

7 Robert Essington Pitt
b 15 December 1855 Kurrajong, NSW. NSW V1855 3572 42B
d 31 May 1920 Kurrajong, NSW. PI NSW 4/106536

8 George Wilshire Pitt
b 1 April 1858 Kurrajong, NSW. NSW 11868
d 11 September 1941, Beerwah, Qld. Qld bdm 1941/00264. Sam Sellin, Waverton
m **Fanny Eleanor Thompson** 11 February 1885 Sydney, NSW
F- James Thompson; M- Anna Avery. Records of Holy Trinity, Millers Point
(Fanny E. Pitt married John McLaren in Sydney in 1898)

9 Clara Elizabeth Pitt
b 12 July 1860 Richmond, NSW. Records of St Peters, Richmond
d 27 August 1940 Kurrajong, NSW. PI NSW 4/257042

10 Ada Mary Pitt
b 19 July 1864 Richmond, NSW. Records of St Peters, Richmond
d 20 September 1865 Richmond, NSW. Records of St Peters, Richmond

Jemima Pitt and Austin Forrest and Robert Jenkins

Jemima Pitt
ch 10 June 1783 Sturminster Newton, Dorset, England. F- Robert Pitt; M- Mary Matcham
d 22 March 1842 Campbelltown, NSW. NSW V1842 204 26B
m 1 **Austin Alexander Forrest** 18 April 1810 Richmond, NSW. MI
d 24 December 1811 Richmond, NSW. MI
m 2 **Robert Jenkins** 22 March 1813 Parramatta, NSW. MI
b 1777. F- Robert Jenkins; M- Mary Warren [1]
d 4 May 1822 Sydney, NSW. MI

1 Eliza Forrest
b 14 April 1811 Richmond, NSW. MI
d 14 May 1811 Richmond, NSW. MI

2 Robert Pitt Jenkins
b 26 January 1814 Sydney, NSW. MI
d 26 October 1859 Anglesey, Wales. PI NSW 1/4673
m **Maria Louisa Adelaide Plunkett**

3 William Warren Jenkins

b 11 July 1816 Sydney, NSW. MI
d 6 May 1884 Berkeley, NSW. NSW 10235
m **Matilda Pitt Wilshire** (cousin)

---

[1] Mowle, L.M. *Pioneer Families of Australia*, 5th ed., Rigby, Sydney, 1978

Robert Pitt Jenkins and Maria Louisa Adelaide Plunkett

Robert Pitt Jenkins
b 26 January 1814 Sydney, NSW. F- Robert Jenkins; M- Jemima Pitt. MI
d 25 October 1859 Anglesey, Wales. PI NSW 1/4673
m **Maria Louisa Adelaide Plunkett** 10 November 1843 Wollongong, NSW.
NSW V1843 346 27C; NSW V1843 2003 93
ch 1 April 1817 Killucan, Roscommon, Ireland. F- Patrick Plunkett; M- Francis Brown
d 26 October 1859 Anglesey, Wales

1 Alice Frances Jemima Jenkins
b 14 April 1845 Surry Hills, NSW. Records of St Marys, Sydney
d 24 September 1925 Vic. [1]
m **Charles Hubert de Castella** 9 September 1865 Sydney, NSW. NSW 00768
b 27 March 1825 Neuchatel, Switzerland [2]
F- Dr Jean-Francois Paul de Castella; M- Eleonore Camille de Riaz
d 30 October 1907 Ivanhoe, Melbourne, Vic. PI Vic 105

2 Robert Augustus Jenkins
b 23 December 1846 Burdekin Terrace, Sydney, NSW
d 26 October 1859 Anglesey, Wales

3 Herbert Frederick William Edmond Jenkins
b 2 July 1849 Bangus, NSW. NSW V1849 1754 66
d 26 October 1859 Anglesey, Wales

4 Ernest George Jenkins
b 23 October 1850 Bangus, NSW. NSW V1850 1939 67
d 26 October 1859 Anglesey, Wales

5 Alfred Frederick Jenkins
b 26 April 1853 Bomballa, NSW. NSW V1853 1682 70
d 25 October 1859 Anglesey, Wales

6 Augustus Patrick Jenkins

b 10 September 1855 Bomballa, NSW. NSW V1855 2189 72

d 25 October 1859 Anglesey, Wales

7 Warren William Jenkins

b 27 October 1857 Bomballa, NSW [1]

d 1 August 1859 Bomballa, NSW [1]

---

[1] Mowle, L.M., *Pioneer Families of Australia*, 5th ed., Rigby, Adelaide 1978

[2] ADB 3, de Castella

William Warren Jenkins and Matilda Pitt Wilshire

William Warren Jenkins
b 11 July 1816 Sydney, NSW. F- Robert Jenkins; M- Jemima Pitt. MI
d 6 May 1884 Berkeley, NSW. NSW 10235
m **Matilda Pitt Wilshire** (cousin) 11 July 1838 St James, Sydney, NSW. NSW V1838, 1713 22B
b 10 December 1818 Sydney, NSW. F- James Wilshire; M- Esther Pitt. MI
d 27 May 1876 Berkeley, NSW. MI

1 William James Robert Jenkins
b 19 April 1839 Campbelltown? NSW. NSW 1008 23A
d 6 August 1908 Chatswood, NSW. SMH 7 August 1908, p6a
m **Susan Letitia Bowen** 14 October 1869 Kurrajong, NSW. Records of St Stephen the Martyr, Kurrajong
b 9 December 1837 Windsor, NSW. F- George Meares Bowen; M- Charlotte Freer. MI
d 21 May 1903 Chatswood, NSW. MI

2 Robert Thomas Jenkins
b 27 September 1840 Berkeley, NSW. NSW V1840 383 25A
d 8 December 1913 Berkeley, NSW
m **Agnes Elizabeth Ewing** 20 January 1885 Wollongong, NSW
b 1853 Pitt Town. F- Reverend Thomas Campbell Ewing; M- Elizabeth Ewing
d 20 March 1925 Cessnock, NSW. NSW 03925

3 Matilda Jemima Jenkins
b 21 March 1842 Berkeley, NSW
d 16 April 1942 North Sydney NSW. NSW 11663

4 Louisa Helen Jenkins
b 10 August 1843 Illawarra, NSW
d 10 November 1926 Neutral Bay, NSW. SMH 11 Nov 1926, p8a,d
m **Johnson George King** 17 October 1871 Wollongong, NSW
d 25 January 1883 Cooma, NSW. PI NSW 3/8577

5 Ellinor Maria Jenkins

b 28 April 1845 Berkeley, NSW. NSW V1845 1816 30A

d 23 January 1933 Vaucluse, NSW. SMH 24 January 1933, p9a

6 Emily Annie Jenkins

b 2 February 1847 Berkeley, NSW

d 17 April 1935 North Sydney, NSW. NSW 08119

m **Anthony Conysby Denny** 4 December 1890 Manly, NSW

d 25 November 1897 Fernmount, Bellingen, NSW

7 Frederick Jenkins

b 15 February 1848 Berkeley, NSW

d 30 April 1897 Waterloo, NSW. *Illawarra Mercury* 4 May 1897, p2f

m **Minnie F.E. Atkinson** 26 October 1874 Sydney, NSW

d?

8 Alice Elizabeth Jenkins

b 20 March 1849 Berkeley, NSW

d 19 August 1932 Wollongong, NSW. SMH 20 August 1932, p12b

m **Walter Graham Robertson** 26 February 1874 Wollongong, NSW

b 1843 Raymond Terrace, NSW. F- James B.R. Robertson; M- Ann

d 8 June 1928 Wollongong, NSW. PI NSW 4/154284

9 Charles Matcham Jenkins

b 25 November 1850 Berkeley, NSW. NSW V1850 1846 37A

d 4 January 1852 Berkeley, NSW. NSW V1852 1170 38B

10 Esther Ada Jenkins

b 12 January 1853 Berkeley, NSW. NSW V1853 1164 39A

d 4 May 1853 Berkeley, NSW

11 Alfred Matcham Jenkins

b 24 September 1857 Berkeley, NSW. NSW 12341

d 23 July 1909 Rose Bay, NSW. SMH 27 July 1909, p6a

m **Bessie Emeline Waldron** 22 January 1885 Glebe, NSW (dissolved)

b 1864 Wollongong, NSW. F- Alfred A. Waldron; M- Lucy Sarah Lovett

(Bessie married William L. Lister in 1899 in the Woollahra district and died in 1935 in North Sydney. 1899/4676; 1935/14660)

Mowle, L. M., *Pioneer Families of Australia,* 5th ed., Rigby, Sydney, 1978. See for events not otherwise referenced.

Hester Pitt and James Wilshire

Hester Pitt
ch 9 July 1786 Sturminster Newton, Dorset, England. F- Robert Pitt; M- Mary Matcham
d 13 May 1836 Sydney, NSW. SG 12 May 1836, p3f
m **James Wilshire** 12 February 1805 Sydney, NSW. MI
ch 9 August 1771 Aylesbury, Buckinghamshire, England.
F- William Wilshire; M- Martha Thompson. IGI
d 9 September 1840 Sydney, NSW. NSW V1840 481 24A

1 Louisa Wilshire
b 13 March 1806 Sydney, NSW. MI
d 9 July 1883 Appin, NSW. NSW 06322
m **Philip Elliot**

2 William Pitt Wilshire
b 15 October 1807 Sydney, NSW. MI
d 12 March 1889 Surry Hills, NSW. NSW 00462
m **Catherine Maria Robertson**

3 James Robert Wilshire
b 29 July 1809 Sydney, NSW. MI
d 30 August 1860 Potts Point, NSW. NSW 01399
m 1 **Elizabeth Thompson**
m 2 **Sarah Thompson**

4 Austin Forrest Wilshire
b 15 September 1811 Sydney, NSW. MI
d 28 May 1889 Glebe, NSW. NSW 03755
m **Eliza Pitt** (cousin)

5 Elizabeth Mary Wilshire
b 27 February 1815 Sydney, NSW. MI
d 5 November 1900 Sydney, NSW. NSW 11275

6 Esther Wilshire
b 19 February 1817 Sydney, NSW. MI
d 26 January 1899 Petersham, NSW. NSW 09940
m **Henry Rawes Whitten**

7 Matilda Pitt Wilshire
b 10 December 1818 Sydney, NSW. MI
d 27 May 1876 Berkeley, NSW. MI
m **William Warren Jenkins** (cousin)

8 Thomas Matcham Pitt Wilshire
b 22 February 1821 Sydney, NSW. MI
d 5 March 1852 Louisa Creek, Mudgee, NSW. SMH 1 April 1852, p3c
m **Helen Eliza Faithfull**

9 John Jackson Wilshire
d 19 December 1822 Sydney, NSW, aged 5 weeks. MI

10 Amelia Jemima Wilshire
d 18 May 1824 Sydney, NSW, aged 3 weeks. MI

11 Joseph Wood Wilshire
b 1 February 1826 Sydney, NSW. MI
d 8 August 1893 Redfern, NSW. NSW 12806
m **Anne Osborne**

Louisa Wilshire and Philip Elliot

Louisa Wilshire
b 13 March 1806 Sydney, NSW. F- James Wilshire; M- Esther Pitt. MI
d 9 July 1883 Appin, NSW. NSW 06322
m **Philip Elliot** 17 May 1831 Sydney, NSW. Records of St James, Sydney
b 1 May 1805 Trentham, Stafford, England. F- Thomas Elliot; M- Jane Liddle.
IGI
d 18 August 1879 Appin, NSW. NSW 04884

1 Thomas Wilshire Elliot
b 19 April 1832 Sydney, NSW. Records of St James, Sydney
d 29 January 1913 Blayney, NSW. NSW 00981
m **Mary Ann Sampson** July 1854 [1] Sydney, NSW.
NSW V1854 1013 41
d 4 October 1871 Mudgee, NSW. NSW 04532

2 Son
b/d 10 May 1833 NSW. Bk 108, No 214, Dept. of Lands

3 Elizabeth Ella Louisa Elliot
b 13 February 1845 Berkeley, NSW. SMH 17 Feb 1845 p2e
d 12 May 1871 Stanhope, Appin, NSW. NSW 03224

---

[1] Day of wedding obscured in Records of St James Anglican Church, Sydney.

William Pitt Wilshire and Catherine Maria Robertson

William Pitt Wilshire
b 15 October 1807 Sydney, NSW. F- James Wilshire; M- Esther Pitt. MI
d 12 March 1889 Surry Hills, NSW. NSW 00462
m **Catherine Maria Robertson** 21 February 1829 Sydney, NSW. NSW V1829 761 13
ch 26 July 1812 Lambeth, Surrey, England. F- James Robertson; M- Anna Maria Ripley. IGI
d 12 October 1848 Sydney, NSW. NSW V1848 302 33B

1 William James Wilshire
b 28 January 1830 Sydney, NSW. NSW V1830 339 14
d 12 November 1830 Sydney, NSW. NSW V1830 9311 2C

2 William James Wilshire
b 23 February 1832 Sydney, NSW. NSW V1832 417 16
d 20 September 1911 Cronulla district, NSW. Woronora Cemetery Records
m **Rosalie Ada Pettingell** 25 July 1855 Sydney, NSW. NSWV1855 1047 43B
b 1838 Sydney, NSW. F- Joseph Pettingell; M- Mary A
d 21 May 1925 Cronulla district, NSW. Woronora Cemetery Records

3 Maria Wilshire
d 4 June 1834 Sydney, NSW, aged 8 weeks. NSW V1834 1965 18

4 Frederick Robertson Wilshire
b 13 March 1837 Sydney, NSW. NSW V1837 370 21
d 7 July 1919 Watson's Bay, Vaucluse, NSW. NSW 15631
m **Lavalette Mary Maria Robertson** 25 March 1863 "Clovelly", Watson's Bay, NSW [1]
F- John Robertson; M- Margaret Emma Davies
d 19 February 1920 Watson's Bay, Vaucluse, NSW. NSW 01214

5 Maria Janet Wilshire
b 20 October 1839 North Richmond, NSW. NSW V1839 507 23A
d 25 June 1923 Cremorne, NSW. SMH 26 June 1923, p8a

m **John Bibb** 23 November 1867 Sydney, NSW. Records of St Pauls, Cleveland St., Sydney
b 1841 Sydney. F- John Bibb; M- Sarah McIntosh
d 21 June 1904 Ashfield, NSW. SMH 22 June 1904, p8a

---

[1] Dick, George Turnbull, *Birth, Death and Marriage Announcements, Sydney Mail 1862-1863*, Adam Press, Glenbrook, 1991, p208; ADB 6, Robertson, re "Clovelly" at Watson's Bay.

William Pitt Wilshire and Margaret Hornery

William Pitt Wilshire
b 15 October 1807 Sydney, NSW. F- James Wilshire; M- Esther Pitt. MI
d 12 March 1889 Surry Hills, NSW. NSW 00462

partnered **Margaret Hornery** (Hordinary) c1862 Kurrajong
b 3 June 1844 Kurrajong, NSW. NSW V1844 80 56
d 13 December 1934 East Kurrajong, NSW. NSW 19188
(Margaret married Albert Packer in 1877. NSW 04242)

1 Elvina Hornery
b 7 May 1863 North Richmond, NSW. NSW 13081
d 11 Nov 1955 Balmain, NSW. NSW 29997
m **John McCabe** 14 September 1881 Richmond, NSW. NSW 04331
d 11 June 1939 Hawkesbury District Hospital, Windsor NSW. NSW 09831

2 William Matcham Hornery (Ornery)
b 25 April 1870 Kurrajong NSW. NSW 16406
d 1 November 1962 Royal North Shore Hospital, St Leonards, NSW. NSW 32501
m **Charlotte Isobel Clarke** 6 August 1898 Windsor NSW. Records of St Matthews C of E. Windsor
d 9 May 1953 Windsor NSW 10022

3 James Albert Hornery
b 22 October 1872 Kurrajong NSW. Records of St Matthews R C Windsor
d?

4 Catherine Maria Hornery
b 25 October 1875 Kurrajong NSW. St Matthews RC Windsor
d 17 September 1947 East Kurrajong, NSW. NSW 18159
m **Herbert James Case** 22 July 1896 Hawkesbury District Hospital, Windsor, NSW. St Matthews C of E Windsor
d 22 December 1952 Hawkesbury District Hospital, Windsor, NSW. NSW 32973

James Robert Wilshire and Elizabeth Thompson

James Robert Wilshire
b 29 July 1809 Sydney, NSW. F- James Wilshire; M- Esther Pitt. MI
d 30 August 1860 Potts Point, NSW. NSW 1399
m 1 **Elizabeth Thompson** 13 August 1836 Sydney, NSW. NSW V1839 123 20
b c1812 England. F- Joseph Thompson; M- Mary Brown. NSW 9771
d 13 August 1846 Darlinghurst, NSW. NSW V1846 518 31B

1 James Thompson Wilshire
b 20 April 1837 Sydney, NSW. NSW V1837 383 21
d 28 April 1909 Neutral Bay, NSW. SMH 29 Apr 1909, p6a
m **Alice Beatrice Quodling** 7 November 1893 Enmore, NSW.
(On the internet access "Former Members of NSW Parliament")
d 13 June 1920 Neutral Bay, NSW. SMH 14 June 1920, p1a

2 Emily Elizabeth Wilshire
b 21 December 1838 Sydney, NSW. NSW V1838 312 23A
d 19 December 1839 Sydney, NSW. NSW V1839 688 23A

3 Mimosa Sarah Wilshire
b 31 March 1840 Sydney, NSW. NSW V1840 544 26A
d 15 March 1924 Strathfield, NSW. NSW 01097
m? **Henry Walter Campion** 24 February 1877 St John the Evangelist's Penge, Surrey, England [1]
d 15 August 1896 Strathfield, NSW. NSW 09469

4 Clara Sophia Wilshire
b 28 June 1841 Sydney, NSW. NSWV1841 545 26A
d 8 August 1925 Strathfield, NSW. SMH 10 Aug 1925, p10a
m **William Henry Quodling** 19 June 1868 Sydney, NSW. NSW00571
d 1 November 1894 Royal Prince Alfred Hospital, Camperdown, NSW. SMH 2 Nov 1894, p1a

5 Matilda Elizabeth Wilshire

b 28August 1842 Sydney, NSW. NSW V1842 546 26A

d 26 January 1879 Woolloomooloo, NSW. PI NSW 3/3121

6 Mayor Joseph Wilshire

b 6 February 1844 Sydney, NSW. SMH 7 February 1844, p3b

d 13 January 1927 Toowoomba Qld. Qld bdm 001093

m **Catherine Mary Anastasia (Annie) Bowes** c1875 Levuka, Ovalau, Fiji [1]

F- John Bowes, M- Mary Farrell

d 15 April 1939 Toowoomba Qld. Qld 002573

7 Alderman Robert Wilshire

b 2 September 1845 Sydney, NSW. SMH 3 September 1845, p3g

d 17 October 1846 Darlinghurst, Sydney, NSW. NSW 536 31B

---

[1] Information from Ted Baker

James Robert Wilshire and Sarah Thompson

James Robert Wilshire
b 29 July 1809 Sydney, NSW. F- James Wilshire; M- Esther Pitt. MI
d 30 August 1860 Potts Point, NSW. NSW 01399
m 2 **Sarah Thompson** 29 May 184 7 Sydney, NSW. NSW V1847 775 47
b c1825 Shadwell, Middlesex, England; F- Joseph Thompson; M- Mary Brown
d 29 July 1912 Strathfield, NSW. NSW 09771

1 Alfred Theodore Wilshire
b 7 September 1849 Sydney, NSW. NSW V1849 346 58
d 7 December 1899, Kiama, NSW. NSW 13652
m **Marianne Lomas Smith** 28 March 1877 Woollahra, NSW. NSW 01647
d 8 July 1947 Manly, NSW. SMH 9 July 1947, p26c

2 Emily Rebecca Wilshire
b 31 March 1851 Sydney, NSW. NSW V1851 706 58
d 24 February 1927 Croydon, NSW. SMH 26 Feb 1927, 14b

3 Sarah Jane Wilshire
b 28 February 1852 Sydney, NSW. NSW V1852 707 58
d 5 September 1896 Burwood, NSW. SMH 7 Sept 1896, p1a
m **Walter James McLean** 26 March 1891 Burwood, NSW. Bk 598, No 993, Dept. of Lands
d?

4 Daughter
b 23 February 1853 Sydney, NSW. SMH 2 March 1853, p3b
d 18 April 1853 Sydney, NSW. SMH 19 April 1853, p3a?

5 Louisa Alma Wilshire
b 6 February 1855 Sydney, NSW. NSW V1855 750 58
d 25 May 1916 Croydon, NSW. SMH 26 May 1916, p6a
m **Samuel George Barff** 16 March 1882 Sydney, NSW. NSW 00386
d 2 August 1917 Summer Hill, NSW. NSW 10200

6 Robert Pitt Wilshire

b 8 February 1857 Sydney, NSW. NSW 00572

d 17 December 1938 Toowoomba, Qld. Qld 05094

7 Esther Phoebe Wilshire

b 4 January 1859 Potts Point, NSW. NSW 00412

d 26 January 1895 Burwood, NSW. SMH 28 Jan 1895, p1a

8 Austin Henry Wilshire

b 8 September 1860 Potts Point, NSW. *Sydney Mail* 15 September 1860, p5b

d 6 August 1923 Neutral Bay, NSW. SMH 7 August 1923, p8a

m **Hephzibah Maude Stewart** 4 April 1888 Woollahra, NSW. NSW 93106

d 10 June 1948 Cremome, NSW. NSW 10766

Austin Forrest Wilshire and Frances ? and Eliza Pitt

Austin Forrest Wilshire
b 15 September 1811 Sydney, NSW. F- James Wilshire; M- Esther Pitt. MI
d 28 May 1889 Glebe, NSW. NSW 03755
partnered **Frances**?

1 Austin Forrest Wilshire
b 2 August 1837 Sydney NSW V1837 227 21
d 5 December 1838 Berrima NSW V1838 3236 22
m **Eliza Pitt** (cousin) 14 February 1839 Campbelltown, NSW. NSW V1839 329 23B
b 1 November 1820 Richmond, NSW. MI
d 5 February 1861 Paddington, NSW. NSW 01602

2 Austin Thomas Wilshire
b 2? October 1841 Sydney, NSW. NSW V1841 271 26A
d 14 March 1899 Yass, NSW. SMH 16 Mar 1899, p1a
m **Frances Josephine Broughton** 23 September 1865 Paddington, NSW.
Records of St Matthias, Paddington, NSW
d 26 September 1912 Sydney, NSW. SMH 27 Sept 1912, p8a
PI NSW 4/61025; Rookwood Cemetery Transcriptions, SAG 2002

3 Edwin James Wilshire
b 21 June 1843 Sydney, NSW. NSW V1843 2402 27A
d 14 June 1924 Mosman, NSW. SMH 16 June 1924, p8a
m **Ada Australia Pracy Hosking** 26 August 1869 Paddington, NSW. NSW 01452
d 27 August 1925 Mosman, NSW. SMH 28 Aug 1925, p10a

4 Thomas Matcham Pitt Wilshire
b 11 February 1844 Chippendale, NSW.
SMH 13 Feb 1844, p3
d by 1861

5 Emily Eliza Wilshire

b 14 February 1845 Chippendale, NSW. SMH 17 February 1845, 2e

d 11 January 1846 Chippendale, NSW. SMH 13 January 1846, p3b

6 Isabel Eliza Wilshire

b 16 September 1846 Chippendale, NSW. SMH 17 September 1846, p3g

d 25 July 1935 Mosman, NSW. SMH 26 July 1935, p10a

m **Edward Southwell Gowrie Ruthven** 31 March 1874 Mulgoa NSW. NSW 03616

d 5 May 1881 Glebe, NSW. NSW 03009

7 Alice Emily Wilshire

b 12 August 1848 Redfern, NSW. NSW V1848 534 33A

d 10 August 1928 North Sydney, NSW. SMH 11 Aug 1928, p14b

m **Francis Lord Jnr.** 8 August 1871 Mulgoa NSW. NSW 03291

d 19 September 1936 Artarmon, NSW. NSW 13416

8 George Pitt Wilshire

b 10 September 1850 Redfern, NSW. SMH 11 September 1850, 3g

d 8 December 1851 Redfern, NSW. SMH 9 December 1851, 3e

9 Percy Wilshire

b 15 February 1852 Redfern, NSW. SMH 19 February 1852, p3e

d 17 March 1903 Sydney Hospital, NSW. SMH 18 March 1903, p63a

10 Emma Mary Wilshire

b 16 August 1853 Redfern, NSW. NSW V1853 3167 39A

d 2 June 1919 Camden, NSW. SMH 3 June 1919, p6a

m **Edward Charles Lawry Hughes** 28 July 1885 Glebe, NSW. Records of St Johns, Glebe

b 1857 F- Samuel T. Hughes; M- Ellen Rosetta Hughes

d 14 August 1902 Moreton Park, NSW. SMH 15 Aug 1902, p1a

11 Marian Elizabeth Wilshire

b 13 July 1855 Redfern, NSW. NSW V1853 4780 42B

d 20 November 1855 Sydney, NSW. NSW V1855 2212 43A

12 Lucy Pitt Wilshire
b 4 March 1857 Sydney, NSW. NSW 00582
d 9 August 1943 Roseville NSW. NSW 17692

13 Arthur Wilshire
b 25 May 1858 Potts Point, NSW. SMH 26 May 1858, p1a
d 7 August 1945 Bellevue Hill, NSW. SMH 8 Aug 1845, p16c
m **Annie Isabel Rutledge** 28 April 1887 Grafton, NSW [1]
b 22 April 1855 Belfast, Ireland. F- Lloyd Rutledge; M- Isabella Bennett
d 8 August 1941 Bellevue Hill, NSW

14 Daughter
b/d 5 February 1861 Sydney, NSW. NSW 01602

---

[1] Cable, Kenneth J. and Jane C. Marchant, *Australian Biographical and Genealogical Record 1842-1899,* Series 2, vol 1, A.B.G.R. and Society of Australian Genealogists, 1985, pp 228

Esther Wilshire and Henry Rawes Whitten

Esther Wilshire
b 19 February 1817 Sydney, NSW. F- Jarnes Wilshire; M- Esther Pitt. MI
d 28 September 1899 Petersham, NSW. NSW 09940
rn **Henry Rawes Whittell** 11 November 1839 Sydney, NSW. NSW V1839 125 23B
b 18 November 1805 Chester, England. F- Charles Whittell; M-Hannah Rawes [1]
d 21 February 1865 Surry Hills, NSW. NSW 00203

1 Matilda Hannah Whittell
b 6 October 1842 Sydney, NSW. SMH 10 October 1842, p3b
d 1 July 1925 Petersham, NSW. SMH 2 July 1925, p8a
rn **Arthur Herbert Ridley** 25 October 1909 Petersham NSW. NSW 11670
d 30 January 1920 Petersham, NSW. SMH 31 January 1920, p12b

2 Charles Whittell
b 2 October 1844 Sydney, NSW. NSW V1844 309 58
d 3 January 1919 Royal Prince Alfred Hospital, Camperdown, NSW. SMH 4 January 1919, p12b
rn **Ellen/Helen Elizabeth Turner** 11 December 1868 Sydney, NSW. NSW 1123
d 16 July 1935 Concord, NSW. NSW 18530

3 Thomas Alfred Whittell
b 24 September 1847 Sydney, NSW. NSW V1847 310 58
d 25 April 1929 Waterloo, NSW. SMH 26 April 1929, p10a
m 1 **Elizabeth Watson** 12 April 1873 Sydney, NSW. NSW 00350
d 25 November 1881 Sydney NSW. NSW 02096
rn 2 **Clara Amelia Keating** 30 May 1883 West Maitland, NSW. NSW 05572
d 23 March 1940 Sydney, NSW. SMH 26 March 1940, p8a.

4 Esther Whittell
b 24 August 1849 Sydney, NSW. NSW V1849 311 58
d 6 October 1944 Bundanoon, NSW. NSW 25907

m **Frank M. de Meyrick** 5 July 1881 Sydney, NSW. Records of St Peters, East Sydney

d 6 August 1895 Penrith, NSW. Records of St Stephen the Martyr, Penrith

5 Alfred Whittell

b 7 June 1851 Sydney, NSW. NSW V1851 442 58

d 12 June 1853 Sydney, NSW. NSW V1853 285 112

6 Elizabeth Whitten

b 23 October 1853 Sydney, NSW. NSW V1853 738 58

d 26 July 1930 Gordon, NSW. SMH 28 July 1930, p8a

m **Bartin Haigh** 5 June 1877 Sydney, NSW [1]

d 19 March 1928 Gordon, NSW. SMH 20 March 1928, p10a

7 Louisa Whittell

b 8 September 1855 Sydney, NSW. NSW V1855 909 58

d 30 June 1875 Surry Hills, NSW. SMH 1 July 1875, p1a; NSW 01479

8 Henry Rawes Whittell

b 9 June 1857 Sydney, NSW. SMH 10 June 1857, p1a

d 16 June 1936 Pennant Hills, NSW. NSW 07861

m **Amelia Annie Menzies** 11 October 1884 Parramatta, NSW [1]

d 31 July 1842 Neutral Bay, NSW. NSW 20707

9 Emily Whittell

b 11 November 1861 Surry Hills, NSW. NSW 02297

d 23 Nov 1946 Mosman, NSW. SMH 24 Nov 1946, p14a

m **Thomas Johnstone Charlton** 7 December 1898, Sydney, NSW. Records of St Philips, Sydney

d 24 June 1949 Mosman, NSW. SMH 27 June 1949, p12a

---

[1] Henry R Whittell, *Family of Whittell 1925*, MI Z D 80, Item 10A

Thomas Matcham Pitt Wilshire and Helen Eliza Faithfull

Thomas Matcham Pitt Wilshire
b 22 February 1821 Sydney, NSW. F- James Wilshire; M- Esther Pitt. MI
d 5 March 1852 Louisa Creek, Mudgee, NSW. SMH 1 April 1852, p3c
m **Helen Eliza Faithfull** 25 March 1843 Richmond, NSW. NSW V1843 265 27c
b 19 March 1824 Richmond, NSW. MI
d 24April 1847 Sydney, NSW. NSW V1847 334 32B; SMH 27 April 1847, p3e

1 Thomas William Faithfull Wilshire
b 12 February 1844 Sydney, NSW. NSW V1844 326 28
d 11 September 1877 Waverley, NSW. SMH 12 Sept 1877, p1a
m 1 **Jane Brabazon Ruthven** 7 March 1867 Paddington, NSW. Records of St Matthias, Paddington
b Downpatrick, Ireland. F- Charles William Ruthven; M- Jane Lawry
(**Jane Brabazon Wilshire** married **Randolph Charles Want** on 10 October 1878 Waverley, NSW. NSW 01859)
d 24 January 1900 France. PI NSW 4/20347?

Joseph Wood Wilshire and Anne Osborne

Joseph Wood Wilshire
b 1 February 1826 Sydney, NSW. F- James Wilshire; M- Esther Pitt. MI
d 8 August 1893 Redfern, NSW. NSW 2806
m **Anne Osborne** 26 February 1847 Wollongong, NSW. Records of St Michaels, Wollongong
b c1826, Strabane, Tyrone, Ireland. F- Dr John Osborne; M- Mary Clarke [1]
d 14 March 1901 Redfern, NSW. NSW 02942

1 Daughter
b/d 19 February 1848 Wollongong, NSW. SMH 1 March 1848, p4b

2 Osborne Wilshire
b 13 May 1849 Wollongong, NSW. NSW V1849 1228 34A
d 25 April 1912 Deniliquin, NSW. NSW 05566
m **Mary Louisa Howe** 23 April 1884 St Kilda, Vic. Vic 2853
d 10 August 1904 Deniliquin, NSW. PI NSW 4/341751

3 Thomas Herbert Wilshire
b 20 June 1851 Berkeley NSW. NSW V1851 1845 37A
d 5 January 1933 Sydney, NSW. SMH 6 Jan 1933, p8a
m **Lucy Minnie McDougall** 8 June 1887 Grafton, NSW. NSW 04942
d 22 July 1948 Strathfield NSW. NSW 21563

4 Henry Clarke Pitt Jenkins Wilshire
b 30 April 1853 Berkeley, NSW. NSW V1853 1768 39A
d 31 August 1853 Berkeley, NSW. NSW V1853 1171 39B

5 Beatrice Louisa Wilshire
b 1 May 1854 Berkeley, NSW. NSW V1854 1054 40
d 17 May 1938 Bondi, NSW. SMH 18 May 1938, p16a

6 Edith Annie Wilshire
b 4 August 1856 Wollongong, NSW. Records of St Michaels, Wollongong
d?
m **Robert William McLaurin** 27 June 1889 Sydney, NSW. St Pauls, Cleveland St, Sydney
d 23 October 1941 Deniliquin NSW. NSW 24152

7 Ernest Henry Wilshire
b 6 February 1858 Wollongong NSW. Records of St Michaels, Wollongong
d 20 October 1935, South Yarra, Vic. Vic 9386
m **Nina Edith Church** 12 April 1899 Sydney, NSW. NSW 02481
d 8 October 1949 Camberwell, Vic. Vic 11356

8 John Matcham Wilshire
b 5 June 1859 Wollongong NSW. Records of St Michaels, Wollongong
d 3 December 1930 Cremorne, NSW. SMH 4 December 1930, p8a
m **Mary Josephine Roycraft** 17 October 1906 Sydney, NSW [2]
d 19 June 1960 Mosman, NSW. NSW 13747

9 Reginald Clarke Wilshire
b 2 October 1861 Wollongong, NSW. Records of St Michaels, Wollongong
d 1 July 1936 North Sydney, NSW. SMH 2 July 1936, p10a

10 Laura Maude Wilshire
b 5 October 1863 Wollongong, NSW. Records of St Michaels, Wollongong
d after 1938?
m **George Burnett Barton** 27 July 1900 Bondi, NSW. NSW 07318
b 9 December 1836 Sydney, NSW. F- William Barton; M- Mary Louisa Whydah
d 12 September 1901 Goulburn, NSW. ADB 2, Barton

11 Granville Wood Wilshire
b 13 November 1866 Wollongong, NSW. Records of St Michaels, Wollongong
d 5 September 1929 North Sydney, NSW. SMH 6 Sept 1929, p12a
m 1 **Mary Normande Agnes Stirton** 6 June 1895 Inverell, NSW NSW 03244
d 19 January 1899 Inverell, NSW. PI NSW 4/19103

m 2 **Clara Douglas Ritchie** 4 July 1901 Auburn, NSW. NSW 06684
d 27 July 1904 Homebush, NSW. SMH 28 July 1904 , p6a
m 3 **Ruby Beatrice Olivette Ash** 4 May 1918 Sydney, NSW. NSW 03504
d 7 June 1969 Mosman, NSW. NSW 18865

12 Harold Burnell Pitt Wilshire
b 8 July 1870 Wollongong, NSW. Records of St Michaels, Wollongong
d 13 July 1890 Redfern, NSW. Rookwood Cemetery Transcriptions, SAG 2002

---

[1] Mowle, L. M., *Pioneer Families of Australia*, 5th ed., Rigby, Australia, 1978
[2] Wilshire H.A., *Genealogical Tree of the Wilshire Family of New South Wales*, 1927 . 8ZD80 , Item 11a

NAME INDEX

A

Abbott, Thomas 66
a'Beckett, Thomas 174
Adams, Philip Francis (Surveyor-General) 292
Addy, William 60
Airey, Christopher 63
Albery, Reverend 297
Allan, Joseph 75
Allwood, Reverend Robert 188
Allwright, George 50
Anderson, William Hugh 290, 314
Antill, Henry Colden 142
Armitage, Elijah 146
Arndell, Dr Thomas 34
Ash, Ruby Beatrice Olivette 359
Aston, Caroline 234, 318
Aston, Mary Ann 234, 289, 319
Aston, William 318, 319
Atkinson, Minnie F.E. 278, 339
Aull, Mrs Robert 178
Aull, Robert 147, 178

B

Bader (Captain) 45
Badgery, Henry 328
Badgery, Henry Septimus 272, 279, 327
Badgery, James 32, 34
Badgery, Julia Eliza (née Pitt) 201, 272, 279, 327
Badgery, Mary Ann (née Reilly) 328
Badgery, Mr and Mrs 37
Bagley, William 62
Baines, John 319
Baines, Louisa 234, 319
Baker, James 26
Baker, Ted iii, 348
Baker, William 26
Balcombe, William (Colonial Treasurer) 113
Baldwin, Herbert Ernest 333
Balmain, William (Surgeon) 25, 65
Bannister, Thomas 228
Barff, Samuel George 349

361

Barns, William 70
Barton, George Burnett 23, 297, 358
Barton, Laura (née Wilshire) 297
Barton, Mary Louisa (née Whydah) 358
Barton, William 358
Bass, John 158
Bathurst, Sir Henry 81
Beal, John 83
Beard, William 73
Beattie, John 75
Beechey, Frederick William (Captain) 147
Belbin, Rose xvi, 309
Bell, Archibald 86, 182, 312
Bell, David 118
Bell, James 191
Bell, Maria 182, 312
Bell, Matilda 202
Bell, William Sims 108
Bennett, Frederick (Medical Practitioner) 150
Bennett, George (Medical Practitioner) 126
Bennett, William 73
Bentley, Thomas 157, 158
Berry, Alexander 106
Betts, Margaret iii, x, 38, 40, 216, 293, 304, 305
Betts, William and Mary 293
Bibb, John 271, 275, 345
Bibb, Maria (née Wilshire) 156, 297, 344
Bibb, Sarah (née McIntosh) 345
Bicknell, George 100, 101
Bifield, Mark 110
Bigge, John Thomas (Commissioner) 85, 88
Biggers, Thomas 33

Bingham, Henry 162
Black, A. 147
Blanchard, Marie Emilie Eugenie 277, 328
Bland, Dr William 208, 210
Blaxcell, Garnham 34
Blaxland, Gregory 51
Bligh, Mrs 65
Bligh, William (Governor) 31, 33, 41, 161
Blomfield, Christiana (née Brooks) 316
Blomfield, Richard Henry 316
Blomfield, Susannah (née Gibson) 188, 283
Blomfield, Thomas V. 316
Bloodworth, James 50, 51
Bodie, Alexander 66
Bogue, Adam 210
Boston, John 25
Boughton, Sam 182
Bourke, John 158
Bourke, Richard (Governor) 142, 143, 144, 151, 152, 153, 155
Bowen, Charlotte (née Freer) 338
Bowen, George Meares 338
Bowen, Susan Letitia 338
Bowes, Catherine Mary Anastasia (Annie) 280, 348
Bowes, John 348
Bowes, Mary (née Farrell) 348
Bradburn, Eliza 269
Bradley, William 155, 199
Braithwaite, Robert (Lieutenant) 3
Brett, Levi 188, 192
Bridge, Elizabeth 112
Brisbane, Thomas (Governor) 99, 103, 109, 113, 115, 126
Brooks, Richard (Captain/Merchant) 80, 84, 86

Name Index

Broughton, Bishop William 177
Broughton, Frances Josephine 351
Browne, John 120
Brown, Henry (Headmaster) 239
Bruyeres, John Henry 323
Bryant, Martin 49
Buckland, Emily Rose 313
Buckland, Mary 313
Buckland, Thomas 313
Bull, George 156
Bunker, Eber (Captain) 65
Burgess, John 114
Burgess, William 63
Burke, John 187
Burn, Bernard 73
Burns, Robert (Poet) 272
Buttsworth, Henry 79
Buyers, John (Captain) 9, 15
Byrne, Hugh 151
Byron, Lord George Gordon (Poet) 272

C

Cameron, Hugh John (Captain) 70
Campbell, Ann 315
Campbell, Annie 274, 315
Campbell Jnr., Robert 75
Campbell, John Thomas 77, 82
Campbell, Robert 26, 38, 45, 46, 51, 61, 63, 65, 66, 75, 81, 89, 101, 103, 106, 240
Campbell, Ronald 315
Campion, Henry Walter 280, 347
Cape, William 113
Cartwright, Reverend Robert 60
Carver, William 192
Case, Herbert James 346
Cassatt, Mary (Artist) 274
Catchpole, Elizabeth 23

Catchpole, Margaret vii, 23, 24, 32, 38, 41
Chapman, William 32
Charlton, Thomas Johnstone 355
Cheshire, Thomas and Ann (née Teasdale) 115
Chisholm, Annie Maria 316
Chisholm, John W. 316
Chisholm, Mrs Caroline 185
Chisholm, Rebecca (née Stuckey) 316
Chisholms of Kippilaw 224
Chmura, Salli iii, 327, 328, 329
Church, Nina Edith 358
Clarke, Charlotte Isobel 285, 346
Clark, John 158
Clarkson, Thomas 75, 103
Clay, John 158
Cleary (servant of Andrew Gibson) 145
Clementson, Isaac 65
Cobbold children 23
Cobbold, John 23
Cobcroft, Ada Emily 332
Cobcroft, Elizabeth (née Rose) 331, 332
Cobcroft, Oliver 278, 331
Cobcroft, William John 331, 332
Collicott, Mary (Matron) 82, 83, 95
Collins, David 25
Collins, Mary 319
Cook, James (Captain) 5
Cooper, Daniel 119, 120, 241, 243
Cooper, Robert 110, 174
Cosby, Henry 162, 164
Cosgrove, Thomas 60
Coughlan, William 156
Cowper, Charles 240, 266
Cowper, Reverend William 64

Cox, Eliza 182
Cox, Mrs Rebecca 62
Cox, Norman 284
Cox, Rebecca 62
Cox, William (Magistrate) 62
Cribb, George 104, 111
Croaker, John 104
Crossley, George (Overseer) 157, 158
Crossley, George (Solicitor) 26, 34, 52
Cross, Reverend John 115
Crowley, Ann 234, 318
Crowley, Jane Charlotte (née Bryant) 318, 319
Crowley, John 178, 318
Crowley Snr., John 318
Cullen, Elizabeth 111
Cunningham, Andrew 316
Cunningham, Mary 274, 316
Cunningham, Peter (Surgeon-Superintendent) 112

D

Dalley, William Bede 244
Dargan, John 111
Dargin, William 175
Darling, Ralph (Governor) 117, 138, 139
Darwin, Charles 147
Davies (Schoolmaster) 100
Deane, Ann 188
Deane, Ann (née Pidsley) 188, 313
Deane, Edgar 188
Deane, Mary iii, iv, ix, 188, 313
Deane, Robert 188
Deane, Thomas 188, 313
de Castella, Alice Frances Jemima (née Jenkins) 196, 336
de Castella, Charles Hubert 269, 336
de Castella, Eleanore Camille (née de Riaz) 270
de Castella, Jean-Francois Paul 270, 336
de Castella, Paul 270, 336
de Castella, Robert 270
de Meyrick, Esther (née Whittell) 203, 284, 296, 297, 354
de Meyrick, Frank M. 284, 355
Denay, Dennis 164
Deniehy, Daniel Henry 242, 261
Denison, Sir William 238, 241
Denny, Anthony Conysby 339
Derbyshire, James 73
Dickson, David Peter 283
Dight, John 86
Dight, Samuel 268
Dillon, Peter 126
Dodds, Alex James 283
Doling, John 103
Donaldson, Alice Jemima 274
Donaldson, George Gibson 283
Donaldson, James 224, 246, 315
Donaldson, Stuart 283, 315
Donaldson, Stuart Alexander 176, 199, 224, 244
Donaldson, Stuart (of London) 315
Donovan, Matthew 164
Dowdell, Louisa Madeline 279, 328
Dowle, Harold and Henry 292
Dowle, Henry 292
Dowle, Richard 292
Dunn, Johnnie 268

E

Eagar, Edward 101
Ebrill, Thomas 107, 145, 181

Egan, Daniel 229
Elder, Dr 16
Elliot, Alice 297
Elliot, Elizabeth Ella Louisa 196, 343
Elliot, Jane (née Liddle) 140, 343
Elliot, Louisa (née Wilshire) iv, 33, 99, 117, 140, 196, 231, 235, 274, 280, 289, 341, 343, 357
Elliot, Philip iv, 140, 141, 153, 166, 168, 196, 341, 343
Elliot, Thomas 140, 175, 343
Elliot, Thomas Wilshire 142, 231, 281, 343
Evans, George 62
Evans, Jennett 62
Ewing, Agnes Elizabeth 338
Ewing, Elizabeth 338
Ewing, Thomas Campbell (Reverend) 277, 338
Eyre, Alfred 175, 238, 267
Eyre, John 63, 99
Eyre, Susannah (née Wilshire) 99

F

Faithfull, Alice iv, 72, 117, 128, 311, 315
Faithfull, Ann (née Dibsdale) 25, 38, 311
Faithfull, Augustus Lucian 243, 290
Faithfull, Constance Mary 245, 314
Faithfull, Florence 242, 314
Faithfull, Frances Lilian 245, 314
Faithfull, George iv, 72, 92, 108, 157, 158, 159, 161, 162, 165, 176, 188, 198, 206, 233, 239, 257, 283, 311
Faithfull, George Ernest 199, 268, 290, 313
Faithfull, Helen Eliza iv, 114, 182, 312, 342, 356
Faithfull, Henry Montague 199, 268, 288, 290, 313
Faithfull, James Robert 115
Faithfull, Margaret (née Thompson) 88, 121, 179, 182, 312
Faithfull, Maria (née Bell) 182, 188, 237, 283, 312
Faithfull, Mary (née Deane) iii, iv, ix, 188, 245, 288, 313, 314
Faithfull, Reginald 242, 268, 289, 313
Faithfull, Robert iv, 37, 41, 72, 115, 311
Faithfull, Robert Lionel 289, 314
Faithfull, Susannah (née Pitt) iv, 24, 72, 85, 88, 106, 283, 290, 309, 311, 313, 315
Faithfull, William iv, ix, 24, 25, 26, 27, 31, 32, 36, 37, 38, 60, 62, 64, 71, 79, 85, 87, 107, 114, 117, 121, 130, 133, 155, 162, 177, 179, 182, 201, 202, 228, 238, 239, 259, 276, 283, 309, 311, 312, 313, 315, 316, 356
Faithfull, William Percy 188, 199, 202, 268, 288, 313
Faithfull, William Pitt iv, ix, 32, 108, 109, 118, 122, 123, 124, 138, 141, 142, 143, 151, 154, 155, 158, 159, 160, 162, 173, 176, 179, 184, 188, 199, 202, 208, 209, 223, 225, 228, 230, 232, 237, 239, 240, 241, 242, 243, 245, 249, 257, 266, 268, 274, 290, 311, 313
Fanning, John 158
Farlow, James 278, 330

Farlow, Mary Ann (née Howell) 319
Farlow, William 234, 319
Farlow, William Robert 319
Farr, Elizabeth 50
Fenton, Thomas 118
Fenton, William 75
Ferguson, Catherine Mary 234, 320
Ferguson, Dr John 320
Ferguson, Sarah 320
Finlay, Alice Jemima (née Gibson) 118, 123, 162, 224, 315
Finlay, Andrew Gibson 315
Finlay, Lily 283
Finlay, Marion (née Gibson) 315
Finlay, Minnie 283
Finlay, Robert Brown 315
Firth, Reverend F. 296
FitzRoy, Charles (Governor) 223, 224, 228
FitzRoy, Robert (Captain) 147
Flinders, Matthew 78
Folger, Thomas 70
Forbes, Francis (Chief Justice) 115
Forbes, Francis Ewin 110
Ford, Mary 309
Forrest, Austin Alexander 60, 310, 335
Forrest, Eliza iv, 335
Forrest, Jemima (née Pitt) iv, 31, 36, 60, 62, 65, 310, 335, 336, 338
Foster, Henry 197
Foster, William 73
Foveaux (Lieutenant Governor) 15
Franklin, John (Governor) 161
Franklin, Lady Jane 159, 161
Franks, Edward 110

Fraser, Charles 71
Frazier, Andrew 105, 111
Fry, Oliver 164
Fullager (Owner of saleyards) 247, 271
Fulton, Henry (Reverend) 23, 65, 84, 86, 87

G

Gainsborough, Thomas 243
Gambier, Samuel 2, 7
Garling, Darcy and Ida 292
Garling, Elizabeth (née Ward) 327
Garling, Frederick 83, 327
Garling, Frederick (Solicitor) 83
Garling, Jessie 292
Garling, William Mylan Nicholas 272, 327
Gaudry, William 66, 70
Geary, Daniel 143
Geary, Emma Louise 313
Geary, Harry Vincent 313
Geary, Jane 313
Geary, Kate Montague 313
Geary, Susan 313
Geary, William Henry 313
Georges (Commissioner) 2
Gibson, Alice Jemima 118, 123, 162, 224, 315
Gibson, Alice (née Faithfull) iv, 72, 117, 128, 179, 198, 208, 224, 230, 239, 246, 273, 283, 289, 311, 314, 315
Gibson, Andrew iv, viii, 117, 118, 128, 138, 143, 144, 154, 158, 159, 161, 162, 167, 175, 244, 311, 315
Gibson, Andrew Campbell 283
Gibson, Andrew Faithfull 143, 224, 266, 274, 283, 284, 315

Gibson, Frederick Faithfull 155, 274, 283, 316
Gibson, George Faithfull 283
Gibson, Jessie Alice 289, 314
Gibson, Norman 283, 284
Gibson, Septimus Faithfull 176, 274, 283, 316
Gibson, Susannah Jane 155, 246, 316
Gibson, Thomas Jamieson Faithfull 143, 246, 283, 315
Gibson, William Faithfull 155, 283, 316
Gilberthorpe, Thomas 75, 110
Gilbert, John 268
Gilders, James 29
Gillespie, James 278, 331
Gillett, Catherine Isabella 321
Gipps, Lady 194
Gipps, Sir George (Governor) 158, 159
Goodenough, Phillip 48
Gordon, James (Captain) 51, 52
Gore (Captain) 199
Gore, William 33, 70
Gore, William (Provost Marshall) 70
Graham, George 159
Grant, James 234, 320
Gray, Elizabeth 75
Greenway, Francis 108, 130
Greer, James 226, 230, 322
Grimes, Charles 65
Grose, Major Francis 24, 25
Gunson, Neil 324

H

Hagerstein (Peter the Swede) 15
Haigh, Bartin 284, 355
Haigh, Elizabeth (née Whittell) 231, 297
Hal, Frans 243
Hall, Ben 268
Halloran, Laurence 113
Hankinson, James 114
Hardy, Richard 159
Hargreave, John 158
Harman, James 75
Harrigan, Jeremiah 51
Harris, John 75, 77, 84
Harroll, Mary 141
Hascroft, John 104
Hassall, Mr 111, 160
Hassall, Rowland (Reverend) 79
Hassall, Thomas (Reverend) 100
Hasselburg, Frederick 47
Hatcher, James 192
Hawkesbury, Lord 24
Hawkins, Thomas 234, 321
Hawkins, Thomas F. 120
Hayes, Michael 66
Hayes, Sir Henry Browne 30
Henry, Alfred 322
Henry, Alice 323
Henry, Caroline 182, 323
Henry, Eliza Charlotte (née Orsmond) 323
Henry, Henry 182, 323
Henry, Isaac Shepherd 323
Henry, Joseph 182, 323
Henry, Lucy Ann 182, 322
Henry, Lucy Sarah 182, 323
Henry, Reverend William 99
Henry, Samuel Pinder iv, 99, 100, 104, 111, 126, 139, 145, 147, 150, 181, 182, 226, 230, 317, 322
Henry, Sarah (née Maben) 99, 182, 322, 323
Henry, Sarah Roseanna 182, 323

Henry, Sophia 104, 105, 177, 192, 226, 230, 322
Henry, Sophia (née Wood) iv, 24, 30, 40, 99, 104, 105, 106, 128, 161, 177, 192, 226, 230, 234, 317, 318, 319, 322
Henry, William Ebenezer 323
Henry, William John Wood 107, 322, 324
Heselton (Captain) 276, 277
Hewitt, Sophia and Henry 115
Hibbart, William 66
Higgins (Mate) 24
Hill, Dr Patrick 243
Hill, George 225
Hill, Joshua 145
Hill, Reverend Richard 117, 125, 151
Hobby, Thomas 34
Hodges, John 70
Holding, Miles 48, 51, 52
Holt, General Joseph 67
Holt, Joshua 75
Hook, Charles 46, 50
Hope, Alice 320
Hope, George 320
Hope, James 234, 320
Hornery, Catherine Maria 275, 346
Hornery, Elvina 275, 346
Hornery, James Albert 275, 346
Hornery, Margaret 275, 285, 346
Hornery, Tom 236
Hornery, William Matcham 275, 346
Hosking, Ada Australia Pracy 351
Hosking, John 185
Hoskinson, Mr 268
House (Captain) 12
Howe, John 75

Howell, Elizabeth (née Crowley) 320
Howell, George 161
Howell, Jane Matilda 234, 320
Howell Price (Reverend) 295
Howell, Thomas 320
Howe, Mary Louisa 297, 357
Howe, William 197
Hughes, Edward Charles Lawry 352
Hughes, Ellen Rosetta 352
Hughes, Samuel T. 352
Humm, Daniel 75
Hunter, John (Governor) 26, 61

I

Inall, Edward and Margaret 146
Irving, Clark 241, 242

J

Jackson, Richard 50
Jacob, Vickers 110
James, David 209
James, Mr B. 244
James, Thomas Horton 120
Jamison, Sir John 114
Jefferson, John (Reverend) 16
Jenkins, Alfred Frederick 229, 336
Jenkins, Alfred Matcham 256, 281, 339
Jenkins, Alice Elizabeth 209, 278, 339
Jenkins, Alice Frances Jemima 196, 336
Jenkins, Augustus Patrick 243, 337
Jenkins, Charles Matcham 235, 339
Jenkins, Ellinor Maria 209, 339
Jenkins, Emily Annie 209, 339

Name Index

Jenkins, Ernest George 209, 336
Jenkins, Esther Ada 235, 339
Jenkins, Frederick 209, 229, 278, 336, 339
Jenkins, Herbert Frederick William Edmond 209, 336
Jenkins, Jemima 72, 105, 108, 110, 113, 120, 122, 123, 151, 178, 196, 209, 281, 336, 338
Jenkins, Louisa Helen 209, 278, 338
Jenkins, Louisa (née Plunkett) iv, 187, 196, 257, 269
Jenkins, Mary (née Warren) 65, 91, 335
Jenkins, Matilda Jemima 209, 338
Jenkins, Matilda Pitt (née Wilshire) iv, x, 81, 160, 194, 196, 231, 235, 256, 277, 335, 338, 342
Jenkins, Robert iv, viii, 65, 66, 67, 68, 70, 71, 72, 74, 75, 76, 77, 78, 79, 80, 81, 83, 84, 85, 88, 91, 103, 104, 105, 106, 110, 128, 160, 187, 253, 310, 335, 336, 338
Jenkins, Robert Augustus 208, 336
Jenkins, Robert Pitt iv, 72, 113, 151, 161, 184, 187, 208, 225, 236, 240, 241, 243, 249, 257, 335, 336
Jenkins, Robert Thomas 209, 281, 282, 338
Jenkins, Susannah and Elizabeth 106
Jenkins, William 70, 243, 249, 337
Jenkins, William James Robert 160, 253, 338
Jenkins, William Warren iv, x, 75, 113, 160, 174, 184, 187, 195, 209, 225, 240, 243, 248, 249, 257, 266, 281, 335, 338, 342
John, Ann 186
John, John William 186
John, Sarah (née Harvey) iv, 186, 325, 333
Johnson, Emily 292
Johnson, John (Builder) 236
Johnson, John (Potter) 147
Johnson, Julia iv, viii, 147, 279, 325, 327, 328
Johnson, Mary 147, 178
Johnson, Richard 29
Johnston, Esther 125
Johnston, Lieutenant Colonel George 33
Johnston, Robert 125
Johnston, William 104, 133
Joplin, Emma Maria (née Thompson) 314
Joplin, Ethel 290, 314
Joplin, Robert Croudace 314

K

Kable, Henry 66, 70
Kable, Lord 68
Keams, Antony 52
Keating, Clara Amelia 284, 354
Kelly, William 66
Kemp, A.F. 34
Kennedy, Catherine 174
King, Johnson George 338
King, Louisa Helen 282
King, Philip Gidley (Governor) xvi, 2, 3, 5, 9, 11, 21, 24, 30, 31, 36, 61, 65, 74
Kinsela, Mary 104
Kitchen, Henry (Architect) 79, 107
Klensendorlffe, William 119

Knox, E. 241

L

Lack, R. 73
Lahiff, Alderman 275
Lamb, Edward 75, 110
Lamble, Barbara xv
Lamrock, Elizabeth 321
Lamrock, James 319
Lamrock, Jane (née Cuthbertson) 319
Lamrock, Robert 234, 319
Lane, Thomas 235
Lang, John Dunmore (Reverend) 222, 226
La Trobe, Charles (Governor) 233
Laud, William 23
Lawson, William 34
Laycock, Andrew 201, 330
Laycock, Edward 158
Laycock, Elizabeth iv, 64, 147, 310, 325, 327, 330, 333
Laycock, Emily Jane 201, 331
Laycock, George 248, 280, 331
Laycock, Hannah (née Pearson) 64, 90, 121, 146, 147, 177, 179, 325
Laycock, Henry 201, 330
Laycock, Isabella Eliza 201, 331
Laycock, Isabella (née Bunker) 146, 330
Laycock, K.G. 90, 280, 332
Laycock, Mary Matcham (née Pitt) iv, 74, 146, 177, 248, 278, 325, 330, 331
Laycock, Rebecca 64
Laycock, Robert 201, 330
Laycock, Samuel 112
Laycock, Thomas 25, 64, 90, 146, 147, 325, 330
Laycock, Thomas William Eber Bunker 146, 267, 280, 325, 330
Laycock, William 122, 177
Legg, Thomas 70
Leighton, John 78
Lennox, Charles (Duke of Richmond) 5
Lett, John 315
Lett, Josephine 246, 315
Levitt, John 236
Levy, Solomon 111, 112, 120
Lewin, John William vii
Lhotsky, John 143
Littlemore, George (Minister) 298
Longford (Parramatta) 73
Lord, Edward 229
Lord, Francis 288, 352
Lord, Simeon 40, 52, 54, 70, 84, 86
Love, Joseph 323
Loveridge, Bertha 104, 108
Lowe, Robert 209, 222, 237
Lucas, Nathaniel 79
Lynch, Dennis 125
Lyon, Thomas 124

M

Macarthur, Hannibal Hawkins 199
Macarthur, James 197
Macarthur, John 199
Macarthur, William 160
Macleay, Alexander 199
Macquarie, Elizabeth 61, 62, 82
Macquarie, Lachlan (Governor) 57, 65, 70, 90, 101, 102, 103, 115, 285
Magrath, Ansley 60, 63
Major Joseph 15
Mannix, William 71

Name Index

Mansel, William 108
Maple-Brown iii, ix, 291, 304
Marchment, Robert 87
Markwell, Elizabeth 115, 317, 318
Markwell, John 234
Markwell, Maria (née Cheshire) 318
Markwell, Thomas 60, 115, 178, 318
Marsden, Samuel (Reverend) 24, 27, 30, 62, 64, 66, 99, 101
Martens, Conrad 188, 214, 236
Martin, James (Premier) 273
Mason, William 37
Masterson, John 110
Matcham, George iv, vii, viii, xv, xvi, 1, 2, 3, 4, 6, 7, 72, 93, 108, 147, 156, 157, 162, 177, 178, 200, 201, 208, 236, 237, 247, 265, 268, 271, 272, 276, 278, 279, 282, 285, 291, 309, 325, 327
Matcham, Hester xvi
Matcham, Mary iv, xv, xvi, 74, 146, 177, 248, 278, 285, 309, 311, 317, 325, 330, 331, 335, 341
Matcham, Mary (née Matcham) iv, xv, xvi, 74, 146, 177, 248, 278, 285, 309, 311, 317, 325, 330, 331, 335, 341
Matcham, Thomas iii, iv, xv, 6, 31, 32, 33, 36, 45, 61, 62, 64, 68, 71, 74, 76, 81, 85, 86, 88, 138, 147, 182, 186, 200, 202, 228, 239, 248, 257, 267, 291, 295, 309, 310, 312, 325, 327, 330, 333, 334, 342, 351, 356
Matthews (Richmond) 333
Maunsell, Robert (Reverend) 146

May, Laurence 73
McAlister (Constable) 197
McAlister (Lieutenant) 139
McAlister, Mr 144
McCabe, John 285, 346
McCann, James 158
McDougall, Lucy Minnie 357
McEnroe, J. (Reverend) 269
Mcfarlane, James 154
McGowen, Catherine 191, 192
McIntosh, Charles 70
McIntyre, John 120
McKay, David 73
McLaurin, Robert William 358
McLean, Sarah (née Wilshire) 186, 280, 284, 297, 298, 347
McLean, Walter James 349
McMahon, Mary 75
McPhail, John 209
Meares, Matthew (Reverend) 187, 200
Meehan, James (Surveyor) 62, 111
Melba, Nellie 293
Menzies, Amelia Annie 284, 355
Minchin, Lieutenant William 65
Mitchell, Sir Thomas Livingstone 140
Moran, Dr Francis 112, 119
Moran, Patrick 119
Moreton, Sarah 144, 145
Morris, James 27
Mortimer, Ben 236
Mossman, Samuel 228
Murray, Robert 50, 51, 54
Murrell, Joseph (Captain) 53

N

Neale, Henry 53, 54, 62
Nelson, Catherine xv
Nelson, Edmund (Reverend) 1

371

Nelson, Lord Horatio xv, 2
Nepean, Evan 24
Newsham, Thomas Piers 63
Nicholls, Isaac 77
Nobbs, George 145
Noble, Richard 243
Norman, John 75
North, Samuel (Magistrate) 156

O

Oakes, Francis 83
O'Brien, John 198
Oliver, Mr 174
Orsmond, Isabella Brine 226, 322
Osborne, Alick 235
Osborne, Anne iv, 200, 342, 357
Osborne, Henry 200, 225
Osborne, J. 200
Osborne, John 200, 357
Osborne, Mary (née Clarke) 200, 357
Osburn, James William 108
Owen, Henry D. 120

P

Packer, Albert 275, 346
Page, William 29
Palmer, John 23, 29, 34, 35
Parker, William 70
Parkes, Henry (Politician) 209, 210, 222, 225, 238, 240, 273, 274, 285
Parsons, T. 188
Paterson, William (Lieutenant Colonel) 36
Patton (Captain) 2
Perry, Ada 279, 328
Pettingell, Rosalie Ada 271, 344
Phillip, Arthur (Governor) 5, 24

Piddington, William 225
Pike, John (Captain) 70
Piper, John 84
Pitt, Ada Mary 248, 334
Pitt, Anne 201, 295, 333
Pitt, Charles Bryan 247, 328
Pitt, Clara Elizabeth 248, 334
Pitt, Colin 247, 279, 328
Pitt, Edwin 201, 247, 292, 293, 328
Pitt, Eliza iv, ix, 160, 161, 201, 272, 279, 325, 327, 341, 351
Pitt, Elizabeth (née Laycock) iv, 64, 65, 71, 79, 87, 88, 107, 121, 146, 147, 160, 248, 267, 278, 291, 310, 325, 327, 330, 333, 334
Pitt, Emma 201
Pitt, Esther (see also Pitt, Hester) iv, 338, 343, 344, 346, 347, 349, 351, 354, 356, 357
Pitt, Eva Laura 247, 282, 329
Pitt, Frederick Septimus 247, 329
Pitt, George Matcham iv, viii, xvi, 72, 108, 147, 156, 157, 162, 177, 178, 200, 201, 208, 236, 237, 247, 265, 268, 271, 272, 276, 278, 279, 282, 291, 309, 325, 327
Pitt, George Wilshire 248, 296, 334
Pitt, Harry Austin 201, 328
Pitt, Henry iv, 146, 248, 295, 325, 334
Pitt, Hester (see also Pitt, Esther) 341
Pitt, Irene Emilie 292
Pitt, Jemima iv, 31, 36, 60, 310, 335, 336, 338
Pitt, Jessie 157, 272, 327
Pitt, Julia Eliza 201, 272, 279, 327

Pitt, Julia Eva 292
Pitt, Julia (née Johnson) iv, viii, 147, 201, 272, 279, 292, 304, 325, 327, 328
Pitt, Lucy iv, 5, 267, 309, 317, 318, 322, 353
Pitt, Marie Emilie Eugenie (née Blanchard) 277, 292, 328
Pitt, Mary Matcham iv, 74, 146, 325, 330
Pitt, Mary (née Matcham) iii, iv, xv, xvi, 1, 5, 6, 7, 21, 24, 27, 62, 64, 71, 74, 88, 99, 146, 177, 210, 221, 248, 278, 285, 289, 295, 296, 298, 299, 309, 311, 317, 325, 330, 331, 334, 335, 341
Pitt, Robert iv, vii, xv, xvi, 3, 72, 113, 151, 161, 184, 186, 187, 208, 225, 236, 240, 241, 243, 245, 248, 249, 257, 265, 295, 309, 311, 317, 325, 333, 335, 336, 341, 350
Pitt, Robert Essington 248, 296, 334
Pitt, Robert Matcham 201, 272, 277, 278, 291, 293, 328
Pitt, Sarah 201, 247, 248, 295, 296, 333
Pitt, Sarah (née John) iv, 186, 201, 247, 248, 295, 296, 325, 333
Pitt, Stewart 201, 328
Pitt, Susannah iv, 24, 309, 311, 313, 315
Pitt, Thomas 32, 34, 60, 79, 146, 177, 309
Pitt, Thomas Matcham iii, iv, 6, 31, 32, 33, 36, 45, 61, 62, 64, 68, 71, 74, 76, 81, 85, 86, 88, 138, 147, 182, 186, 200, 202, 228, 239, 248, 257, 295, 310, 312, 325, 327, 330, 333, 334, 342, 351, 356
Pitt, William iv, vii, ix, x, xvi, 3, 6, 24, 32, 35, 108, 109, 113, 118, 122, 123, 124, 125, 128, 138, 141, 142, 143, 151, 154, 155, 156, 158, 159, 160, 162, 173, 176, 177, 179, 181, 182, 184, 188, 199, 201, 202, 203, 208, 209, 222, 223, 224, 225, 228, 230, 232, 235, 237, 239, 240, 241, 242, 243, 245, 249, 253, 257, 266, 268, 270, 271, 274, 275, 285, 290, 295, 309, 311, 313, 333, 341, 344, 346
Pitt, William Henry iv, 146, 325
Pitt, William (Prime Minister) 6
Plunkett, Captain Patrick 187
Plunkett, Francis Louisa (née Brown) 187
Plunkett, John Hubert 187, 240
Plunkett, Julianne 187
Plunkett, Maria Louisa Adelaide 187, 335, 336
Plunkett, P. 187
Plunkett, William Edmond 249, 269
Polack, Hannah 147
Pomare I 12, 17, 100, 101, 103, 104, 111, 226
Pomare II 12, 100, 101, 103, 104, 111, 226
Pomare III 111
Potts, Emma and Joseph 199
Powell, Edward 37
Pritchett, Richard Charles 120
Puddicombe, Alfred (Reverend) 288
Pulpit (an Englishman) 13

Purcell (Captain) 50

Q

Quodling, Alice Beatrice 347
Quodling, William Henry 280, 347

R

Raine, John 119
Read, Will 158
"Red Bill" (William Faithfull's servant) 184
Reddall, Thomas (Clergyman) 122
Redfern, William 77
Redmond, John 60
Reiby, Mary 74, 75
Reiby, Miss 82
Rickerby, Thomas 31
Ridley, Arthur Herbert 354
Rigney, John (Reverend) 187
Riley, Alexander 52, 77
Riley, Thomas 202
Riley, William Edward 139, 166
Ritchie, Clara Douglas 297, 359
Roberts, David 236
Roberts, Mary 108
Robertson, Anna Maria (née Ripley) 126, 344
Robertson, Catherine Maria 125, 341, 344
Robertson, James 126, 344
Robertson, James B.R. 339
Robertson, John 126, 344
Robertson, Lavalette Mary Maria 344
Robertson, Leighton 164
Robertson, Margaret Emma (née Davies) 344
Robertson, Walter Graham 339

Roberts, W.A. 271
Roberts, William 154
Robey, Ralph 241, 242
Rochester, James 268, 280
Rodd, Brent Clements 138
Rodgers, Joseph 252
Rogers, Jeremiah 245
Rose, Mary (née Topp) 3
Rose, Thomas 3, 7
Ross (Reverend) 202
Rouse, George 37
Rouse, Richard 37
Rowe, Mr (auctioneer) 84
Rowley, George 269
Roycraft, Mary Josephine 297, 358
Rubenstein, William D. 106
Rusden, Francis Townsend 247
Rusden, G.W. 159
Rushton, Thomas 36
Rushworth, Robert 31
Russell, Elizabeth 295, 334
Russell, John 334
Russell, Nancy (née Hanna) 334
Ruthven, Charles William 356
Ruthven, Edward Southwell Gowrie 352
Ruthven, Jane Brabazon 276, 356
Ruthven, Jane (née Lawry) 356
Rutledge, Annie Isabel 353
Rutledge, Isabel (née Bennett) 353
Rutledge, Lloyd 353
Ryan, Darby 81
Ryan, John 32

S

Salter, Joseph 75
Sampson, Mary Ann 281, 343
Sanders, Thomas 66
Sandilands, Alexander (Captain) 139

Savigny, W.H. (Reverend) 246
Scott, Augusta 121
Scott (Captain) 12
Scott, Elizabeth 121, 331, 333
Scott, Frances 121
Scott, James 82
Scott, John 121
Scott, Margaret 121
Scott, Thomas 101
Scott, William 121, 156, 157
Selkirk, John 191
Sellin, Sam iii, 334
Semmens, Alice Mary 329
Semmens, Catherine (née Conrick) 329
Semmens, Thomas 329
Shakespeare, William (Playwright) 272
Sharply, Daniel (Constable) 174
Shaw, George 78
Sherwin, William 75, 167
Sherwood, John 84
Shutt, Walter 75
Simmons, James 124
Simms, Alfred 112
Slater, Thomas 140
Smith, Alfred 154, 182, 184, 237
Smith, Charles 145, 177
Smith, Charles (servant) 145
Smith, Charles Throsby 78
Smith, Henry Gilbert 235, 272
Smith, James (builder) 79, 84
Smith, James (Parramatta) 109, 112
Smith, James (superintendent) 164
Smith, Joseph 99, 142, 145, 158, 170
Smith, Marianne Lomas 349
Smith, Mary 202

Smyth, G.B. (Lieutenant) 158
Snedon, Ms 292
Somersby, William 175
Spark, Alexander 120
Spencer, Thomas 27, 32
Stack (Reverend) 281
Starsmord, William 142
Steel, Peter 186
Steel (Reverend) 160
Stephen, Sir Alfred 241
Steven, Margaret 89, 106
Stevens, John (Judge) 154
Stewart, Elizabeth Catharine 334
Stewart, George (Police Magistrate) 159
Stewart, Hephzibah Maude 284, 350
Stewart, James (Captain) 29
Stewart, Robert 240
Stewart, William (Captain) 53, 62
Stewart, William (Doctor) 191
Stiles, Henry (Reverend) 147, 179
Stirton, Mary Normande Agnes 297, 358
Stone, Edward 108
Stone, J. (Reverend) 277
Sullivan, Thomas 247, 271

T

Ta'Unga 181, 212, 324
Taylor, Richard (Reverend) 161
Taylor, Thomas (Captain) 249
Taylor, William 281
Terry, Samuel 110, 119
Therry, Roger (Justice) 242
Thirgood, William Frederick 331
Thompson, Andrew 33
Thompson, Ann 138
Thompson, Anna (née Avery) 334
Thompson, Anne 152

Thompson, Elizabeth iv, 152, 341, 347
Thompson, Fanny Eleanor 334
Thompson, James 152, 186, 193, 266, 275, 284, 296, 297, 334, 347
Thompson, Joseph 152, 347, 349
Thompson, Joseph, Susannah and Anne 152
Thompson, Margaret 88, 179, 312
Thompson, Mary (née Brown) 152, 347, 349
Thompson, Samuel 266
Thompson, Sarah iv, 202, 341, 349
Thomson, Edward Deas 199
Thorley, James 331
Thorley, Jane Forbes (née Galvin) 331
Thorley, Mary Jane 280, 330
Thornton, George 226
Thurlow, William 225, 229, 237
Timmins, Elizabeth (née Scott) 121, 331, 333
Timmins, Henry 296, 333
Timmins, James R. 331
Timmins, John 331, 333
Tofield, James 113
Tornaghi, Angelo 282, 329
Tornaghi, Angelo Korff 329
Tornaghi, Ellen 329
Tornaghi, Eva Laura (née Pitt) 247, 282, 329
Town, Elizabeth 247, 272, 327
Town, Elizabeth (née Onus) 247, 272, 327
Town, John Gordon 327
Tristram, William 81
Turnbull, John 9, 11, 18
Turner, Ellen Elizabeth (see also Turner, Helen Elizabeth) 284
Turner, George Cooper 179
Turner, Thomas 104

U

Underwood, James 52, 68
Unwin, T.W. (Reverend) 285

V

Vandercom, James 104
Vincent, John (Reverend) 140

W

Waddy (Lieutenant) 159
Waldron, Alfred A. 339
Waldron, Bessie Emeline 339
Waldron, Lucy Sarah (née Lovett) 339
Wallis, Arthur (Reverend) 182
Walpole (Captain) 139
Walpole, Joseph Kidd (Reverend) 182
Walsh, W.H. (Reverend) 202
Walton, Eliza 144
Walton, Robert 75
Want, Mary (née Harris) 333
Want, Randolph Charles 356
Want, William 295, 333
Waple, Mrs 115
Watson, Elizabeth 284, 354
Weaver, Charles 110
Weiss, Elizabeth 175
Wentworth, D'Arcy 77, 84
Wentworth, William Charles 120, 195, 232
Weston, Jesse 191
Weston, John 81
Whalan, Patrick 156
Wharmby, Christopher 144

Wheeler, Thomas 70, 71
Whitaker, Lewis Duncan 247
White, Henry 191
White, John 66
White (Lieutenant Colonel) 158
Whittaker, Abraham 75
Whittaker (servant) 145
Whittell, Alfred 203, 231, 354, 355
Whittell, Charles 165, 215, 354
Whittell, Elizabeth 231
Whittell, Emily 296, 297, 355
Whittell, Esther 203, 284, 296, 354
Whittell, Esther (née Wilshire) iv, 72, 81, 140, 151, 161, 164, 203, 280, 284, 285, 296, 342, 354
Whittell, Hannah (née Rawes) 165, 296, 354
Whittell, Henry Rawes 164, 203, 231, 269, 284, 354, 355
Whittell, Louisa 231, 355
Whittell, Matilda Hannah 296, 354
Whittell, Thomas Alfred 203, 354
Wild, Mrs 141
Wilkinson, E.S. (Reverend) 289
Wilkinson, William (Captain) 4
Williams, John 66
Williams, Joseph (Constable) 191
Williamson, James (Acting Commissary) 35
Williams (Reverend) 105
Williams, Thomas 60
Wills, Sarah 53
Wilshire, Alderman Robert 200, 348
Wilshire, Alfred Theodore 203, 297, 349
Wilshire, Amelia Jemima 108, 342
Wilshire, Anne (née Osborne) iv, 200, 297, 342, 357
Wilshire, Arthur 267, 288, 353
Wilshire, Austin Forrest iv, ix, 64, 113, 152, 160, 177, 179, 185, 186, 188, 224, 237, 243, 245, 267, 273, 276, 285, 288, 325, 341, 351
Wilshire, Austin Henry 266, 280, 284, 350
Wilshire, Austin Thomas 186, 288, 351
Wilshire, Beatrice Louisa 235, 289, 357
Wilshire, Clara Sophia 186, 347
Wilshire, Edith Annie 249, 358
Wilshire, Edwin James 186, 273, 288, 296, 351
Wilshire, Elizabeth Mary 73, 182, 200, 231, 269, 273, 288, 296, 341
Wilshire, Elizabeth (née Thompson) iv, 125, 152, 185, 186, 267, 280, 284, 297, 341, 347, 348, 352
Wilshire, Eliza (née Pitt) iv, ix, 160, 161, 201, 202, 203, 239, 267, 272, 279, 288, 325, 327, 341, 351, 352
Wilshire, Emily Eliza 203, 352
Wilshire, Emily Elizabeth 152, 347
Wilshire, Emily Rebekah 230, 298
Wilshire, Emma Mary 231, 288, 352
Wilshire, Ernest Henry 249, 358
Wilshire, Esther iv, 72, 81, 140, 151, 161, 164, 280, 285, 342, 354
Wilshire, Esther Phoebe 245, 297, 350
Wilshire, Esther (see also Wilshire,

Hester) iv, 72, 81, 140, 151, 161, 164, 280, 285, 342, 354
Wilshire, Frederick Robertson 156, 271, 344
Wilshire, George Pitt 230, 231, 352
Wilshire, Granville Wood 276, 297, 358
Wilshire, Harold Burnell Pitt 276, 359
Wilshire, Helen Eliza (née Faithfull) iv, 114, 182, 202, 239, 312, 342, 356
Wilshire, Henry Clarke Pitt Jenkins 235, 357
Wilshire, Hester (see also Wilshire, Esther) 285
Wilshire, Isabel Eliza 203, 288, 352
Wilshire, James iv, vii, viii, 23, 27, 29, 30, 31, 33, 34, 35, 36, 40, 45, 60, 61, 62, 64, 66, 72, 73, 74, 75, 76, 77, 79, 80, 81, 83, 85, 86, 88, 94, 103, 107, 108, 112, 113, 117, 119, 124, 125, 137, 138, 152, 156, 160, 164, 174, 175, 182, 186, 200, 235, 266, 271, 273, 277, 285, 288, 296, 297, 310, 338, 341, 343, 344, 346, 347, 349, 351, 356, 357
Wilshire, James Robert iv, ix, 35, 113, 152, 177, 180, 181, 184, 185, 186, 192, 193, 194, 199, 202, 203, 209, 210, 222, 223, 224, 225, 229, 232, 237, 238, 239, 241, 243, 244, 245, 257, 265, 266, 267, 280, 288, 297, 341, 347, 349
Wilshire, James Thompson 152, 186, 193, 266, 275, 284, 296, 297, 347
Wilshire, Jane Brabazon (née Ruthven) 276, 356
Wilshire, John Jackson 108, 342
Wilshire, John Matcham 249, 358
Wilshire, Joseph (Mayor) 186, 192, 193, 195, 275, 348
Wilshire, Joseph Wood iv, 124, 200, 209, 231, 235, 243, 248, 257, 266, 273, 275, 289, 297, 342, 357
Wilshire, Laura Maude 358
Wilshire, Louisa iv, 33, 99, 117, 140, 235, 289, 341, 343, 357
Wilshire, Louisa Alma 238, 284, 349
Wilshire, Lucy Pitt 267, 353
Wilshire, Maria Janet 156, 271, 344
Wilshire, Maria (née Robertson) iv, 125, 126, 156, 271, 341, 344
Wilshire, Marian Elizabeth 267, 352
Wilshire, Martha (née Thompson) 27, 341
Wilshire, Matilda Elizabeth 186, 280, 348
Wilshire, Matilda Pitt iv, x, 81, 160, 335, 338, 342
Wilshire, Mimosa Sarah 186, 347
Wilshire, Osborne 200, 357
Wilshire, Percy 230, 352
Wilshire, Reginald Clarke 276, 358
Wilshire, Robert Pitt 245, 350
Wilshire, Sarah Jane 230, 284, 349
Wilshire, Sarah (née Thompson) iv, 186, 202, 280, 284, 297,

298, 341, 347, 349
Wilshire, Thomas Herbert 235, 357
Wilshire, Thomas Matcham Pitt 86, 138, 182, 186, 200, 202, 228, 239, 257, 312, 342, 351, 356
Wilshire, Thomas William Faithfull 182, 202, 228, 238, 239, 259, 276, 356
Wilshire, William 27, 341
Wilshire, William James 156, 175, 235, 271, 344
Wilshire, William Pitt iv, vii, x, 35, 113, 125, 128, 138, 156, 181, 182, 184, 203, 222, 224, 228, 235, 240, 243, 253, 270, 271, 274, 275, 285, 341, 344, 346
Wilson, Charles 100
Wilson, William 65, 66
Wollstonecraft, Edward 106
Wood, Alfred Sherwin 161, 234, 320
Wood, Alice Elizabeth 233, 234, 320
Wood, Arthur Sherwin 289
Wood, Charlotte Elizabeth 289
Wood, Clara Caroline 289
Woodd, George N. (Reverend) 165
Wood, Edith May 289
Wood, Elizabeth (née Markwell) 115, 233, 234, 257, 289, 317, 318, 320
Wood, Ellen Maria 320
Wood, Eva Laura 289
Wood, Frank George 289
Wood, Frederick William 289
Wood, Fred Hamilton 289
Wood, George 161, 188, 234, 289, 318, 320
Wood, George Pitt iv, 12, 26, 79, 82, 84, 87, 88, 104, 109, 115, 118, 121, 128, 178, 188, 230, 233, 234, 289, 317, 318
Wood, Henry Aston 289
Wood, Henry Austin 233, 234, 289, 321
Wood, James Edward 234, 321
Wood, John iv, viii, 5, 6, 9, 14, 15, 24, 32, 37, 45, 46, 48, 49, 50, 51, 52, 53, 54, 55, 84, 106, 107, 110, 115, 117, 121, 124, 233, 234, 289, 309, 317, 318, 322, 324
Wood, John (of Chipping) 106, 110
Wood, John Rowland 289
Wood, John Thomas 161, 234, 289, 318, 319
Woodley, Robert 79
Wood, Lucy 11, 15, 45, 62, 65, 71, 79, 82, 84, 86, 87, 88, 99, 105, 108, 111, 115, 122, 161, 177, 226, 230, 234, 257
Wood, Lucy Sophia 318
Wood, Mary Ann 211, 234, 320
Wood, Robert Markwell 161, 234, 319
Wood, Sophia iv, 24, 30, 40, 99, 106, 128, 161, 234, 317, 318, 319, 322
Wood, Susanna 233, 234, 321
Wood, Thomas George 188, 234, 320
Wood, William Henry 121, 234, 289, 318
Wright, S. (Captain) 117
Wychellow, William 144
Wylde, Thomas 77

Y

Yates, William (Minister) 152
Young, James 112

Z

Zucarelli (Artist) 243

www.ingramcontent.com/pod-product-compliance
Lightning Source LLC
Chambersburg PA
CBHW071852290426
44110CB00013B/1112